T0367065

CATO

II

LCL 552

CATO

ORATIONS

OTHER FRAGMENTS

EDITED AND TRANSLATED BY

GESINE MANUWALD

HARVARD UNIVERSITY PRESS

CAMBRIDGE, MASSACHUSETTS

LONDON, ENGLAND

2023

LOEB CLASSICAL LIBRARY® is a registered trademark
of the President and Fellows of Harvard College

Library of Congress Control Number 2022060465
CIP data available from the Library of Congress

ISBN 978-0-674-99755-4

*Composed in ZephGreek and ZephText by
Technologies 'N Typography, Merrimac, Massachusetts.
Printed on acid-free paper and bound by
Maple Press, York, Pennsylvania*

CONTENTS

CONTENTS

M. PORCIUS CATO

ORATIONES (F 17–254A)

Cato occupies an important position in the history of Roman oratory, as he is regarded as marking the start of true Roman oratory. For in Cicero's Brutus, *which has significantly shaped later conceptions of the development of Roman oratory, Cato is identified as the earliest Roman orator by whom written utterances worth reading were available to later generations (T 13); while Cicero acknowledges the existence of earlier speeches and a few earlier orators, he does not regard these as worthy of attention (Suerbaum 1996/1997). Cicero does not deny that Cato is ancient and that his oratory therefore does not meet the standards of Cicero's time; yet he recognizes that Cato's speeches already include the main characteristics of oratory (T 13). Even though this assessment might be exaggerated (influenced by Cicero's high regard for Cato as a person and by debates about the oratorical styles of Atticism and Asianism), this account indicates that in Cicero's time more information was available about Cato's speeches than about those of earlier orators and that his speeches had certain discernible stylistic traits valued by at least some later authors.*

By the time Cicero was working on the Brutus, *he had identified more than 150 speeches by Cato (T 13). The fact that Cicero says that he had found and read that number*

2

ORATIONS (F 17–254A)

of speeches and his comment that hardly any of the orators of his time were interested in Cato suggest that no collected edition of Cato's speeches was readily available at that point. In the dialogue Cato *Cicero has "Cato" say that he is writing up his famous defense speeches (T 22): it is uncertain to what extent this claim has a historical basis or could be taken to point to a (planned) edition of defense speeches. A fragment in which Cato refers to a written version of one of his earlier speeches adduced in preparing another (Orat. F 173) shows at least that the practice of writing up speeches and using writing in their composition was sufficiently widely known as to be something that could be cited in argument; this text also demonstrates that Cato kept written copies of at least some speeches, though these might have been mainly notes rather than fully polished versions (see Carawan 1990). Later sources imply that some of Cato's orations circulated in written form (T 14, 32b, 34; Orat. F 67, 95, 157), and some were (also) included in the* Origines *(Orig. F 87–93, 104–7). Ancient authors active after Cicero's time, such as Quintilian, Gellius, and the grammarians and lexicographers of late antiquity, must have had access to texts of the speeches: they discuss them and quote from them to illustrate argumentative and stylistic features or the use of particular*

3

CATO

words. In this period Cato's orations had become a model
for some subsequent orators, while others regarded them
as old-fashioned. The greater interest shown by these later
writers, taken together with Cicero's comments about his
own efforts in "finding" them and the far greater number
and greater precision of references to Cato's speeches in
Cicero's later works, suggests that Cato's speeches were
rediscovered only shortly before Cicero embarked on the
Brutus and were then made available, so that his contemporaries, the archaists, and the grammarians of late antiquity had access to these orations (Baumgart 1905, 20–34).

Today about 80 titles of speeches by Cato and about 250
fragments (not all assigned to specific speeches) are known
(assumptions about exact numbers and dates vary between
editions). Further speeches attributed to Cato are indicated in historiographical works by other authors: as with
any speeches in works of ancient historiography, their authenticity is doubtful (see esp. F 18A–H).

Cato is said to have started appearing as a public
speaker from his youth (T 26; no records about particular
early speeches survive; it is unclear to what extent some
might have been delivered in small towns around Rome:
T 55) and to have continued until the year of his death
(T 14, 37, 60, 82). The earliest attested speeches (some
most likely inauthentic, though the occasions are plausible) date from 195 BC, the year of Cato's consulship (Orat.
F 17A, 17–18, 18A–H); the surviving fragments extend
until the year of Cato's death (Orat. F 196–99A). Most of
the evidence relates to speeches clearly or probably given
in the year of Cato's censorship (184 BC; cf. Scullard 1973,
152–65; Astin 1978, 324–28); Livy states that Cato delivered a number of harsh speeches against those whom, as

4

censor, he removed from the Senate, in which he seems to have explained the reasons for his actions (Orat. F 69).

Cato's interventions consist of political speeches, concerning foreign policy; reports on activities abroad; domestic, legal, and administrative matters; as well as forensic speeches, both for the prosecution and for the defense (T 22, 32b, 37, 59, 60, 64, 81, 82). The attribution to a particular category is not always straightforward, as many forensic speeches have a political dimension, and some political speeches also display criticism of individuals. Most of the political speeches relate to discussions in the Senate (dealing with foreign and domestic policy, including lawmaking and appropriate behavior); few are attested as addressed to the People. The known forensic speeches comprise more prosecution than defense speeches. Among the defense speeches, there are some for Cato himself (from the period between 191/90 and 154 BC): for Cato was often taken to court and had a lot of enemies (T 26, 32b, 60; cf. Cic. Sull. 23). He is reported to have never been convicted (T 42, 64, 82), while defending himself successfully in forty-four cases (T 42, 82) or being a defendant in almost fifty cases (T 60). A few sources refer to a lawsuit in which Cato faced charges in his eighty-sixth year (T 32b, 37, 60), probably reflecting the fact that Cato continued to be taken to court and to defend himself until the very end of his life, but the date is probably not accurate (as other dates in these sources). A small number of items point to oratorical settings outside of Rome, such as fragments from or references to speeches addressed to soldiers (Orat. F 35, 172, 208–9), to equestrians in Numantia (Orat. F 17–18), or to the Athenians (Orat. F 20).

The most extensive fragments form parts of the two

speeches attested as having been inserted into the Origines *(cf. T 34), the speech on behalf of the Rhodians, of 167 BC (Orat. F 163–71; Orig. F 87–93), and the speech against Ser. Galba about the Lusitanians, given in the year of Cato's death, 149 BC (Orat. F 196–99A; Orig. F 104–7). Still, for none of the speeches is the extant information sufficient to reconstruct them or to analyze their oratorical and argumentative structure, beyond the identification of scattered examples of standard oratorical elements (on Cato as orator, see Astin 1978, 131–56).*

Some testimonia mention specific characteristics of Cato's speeches. Since all these testimonia come from later authors, basing themselves on the written versions of the orations and information about Cato's life, there is hardly any information on the delivery and impact of the speeches; comments mostly concern content and stylistic details. (For an overview of stylistic and rhetorical features in Cato's speeches, see Sblendorio Cugusi 1982, 31–44; 1987). Like his other works, the speeches take a factual and down-to-earth approach. They reveal Cato's political views and his opinions on correct moral behavior and appropriate conduct in office, and they are based on his knowledge of the law (T 4, 8, 20b, 22, 26, 32b, 37, 51). Cato's oratory is described, with hindsight, as archaic and rough (T 13, 15, 16, 47, 52), as acute, refined, clever, brief, using shrewd aphorisms, and as being subtle in presentation and proof, employing rhetorical figures (T 13), lean like that of the Attic orators (T 13, 53), short and concise (T 46; cf. T 85), solemn (T 78), stern and sharp (T 31, 32b), aggressive (T 73), and "at the same time graceful and powerful, pleasant and compelling, full of jests and severe, sententious and belligerent" (T 58). The fragments confirm

that Cato's oratorical style could vary according to context. Some sources claim that all of Cato's speeches began with an appeal to the gods (T 91).

The following rhetorical figures are explicitly noted in Cato's speeches by ancient authorities, applying the categories of later periods (for others observed by scholars, see General Introduction: Cato's Language and Style): sententia (T 13; Orat. F 17), partitio (T 86), exouthenismos (Orat. F 20), chreia (Orat. F 133), responsio (Orat. F 169), use of several synonyms (Orat. F 59), paranomasia (Orat. F 151), epagoge (Orat. F 166, 169), paraleipsis / praeteritio (Orat. F 173), concise narrative (Orat. F 214), anakoinosis / communicatio (Orat. F 236–37). Cicero implies that Cato's orations did not display prose rhythm to the extent that speeches in his own day did (T 13; cf. Orat. F 169A); yet Diomedes identifies a particular ancient rhythmical structure in Cato (T 84). Indeed, structured rhythmical sequences, similar to features found in the poets Ennius and Plautus, often used to emphasize parallel sequences or contrasting terms, have been identified (esp. Habinek 1985, 180–94). At any rate, Cicero indicates that Cato did not allow hiatus between words (T 17). While Cato's attitude to Greek literature and culture was ambiguous, ancient authorities detected the influence of Greek writers such as Thucydides and Demosthenes in his oratory (T 56, 57).

For convenience, in this edition the fragments of Cato's orations are presented in the order of ORF⁴ (see General Introduction: Organization of This Edition; cf. also esp. the edition by Sblendorio Cugusi 1982, with additions in Sblendorio Cugusi 1987, esp. 46–61). Since ORF⁴ numbers testimonia and fragments consecutively, the first frag-

*ment (after the testimonia) is F 17. Here the testimonia
in ORF⁴ have been inserted into the Testimonia section
with a different numbering (see Concordances). Following
ORF⁴ for the fragments means that F 1 to 16 do not exist
for the orations. Fragments of the speeches added beyond
those given in ORF⁴ are marked by a capital letter after
their number (e.g., F 17A). ORF⁴ presents the attested
speeches in their assumed chronological order, followed by
speeches that can be identified, but about which there is
too little information on date or context to slot them in*

ON *LEX OPPIA* (F 17A)

*During his consulship (195 BC), Cato opposed the repeal
of* Lex Oppia sumptuaria / de mulieribus *(T 82), a sumptuary law against female luxury introduced in 215 BC
(LPPR, p. 254; Baltrusch 1989, 52–59; Elster 2003, 217–
20; Zanda 2011, 102–4; on female ornaments, see also
Orig. F 109). Despite Cato's opposition and that of two
Tribunes of the People, M. Iunius Brutus and P. Iunius
Brutus, a law proposed by the other Tribunes of the People
of that year, M. Fundanius and L. Valerius, was approved
(*Lex Valeria Fundania de lege Oppia sumptuaria abro-
ganda; *LPPR, pp. 267–68; Elster 2003, 294–96), and* Lex
Oppia *was repealed (Liv. 34.1.1–8.3; Val. Max. 9.1.3; Zo-
nar. 9.17). Cato is likely to have voiced his opposition in
an oration (CCMR, App. A: 142). A speech on that topic
in the context of this discussion is put into Cato's mouth in
Livy; it is probably inauthentic, especially as it seems not*

(F 200–234). Finally, there are fragments transmitted for Cato, but not assigned to a specific work; they are placed here because they are likely to come from oratorical contexts based on their content and/or context (F 235–54). Almost all the pieces in this last group might also belong to works of other literary genres (see Introduction to Incertorum operum reliquiae*). On Cato's speeches, in addition to notes in standard editions and commentaries, see, e.g., Baumgart 1905; Fraccaro [1910a–d; 1911] 1956; Till 1935; Janzer 1937; Marmorale 1949; Brouwers 2001.*

ON *LEX OPPIA* (F 17A)

to show known characteristics of Cato's style and to include anachronistic statements (cf. also T 31). Moreover, elsewhere, when the original is available, Livy refrains from reproducing a Catonian oration (F 67, 171; similarly Sall. Cat. *31.6) or provides a summary (F 69); the text in Livy may, however, reflect Catonian points of view (Tränkle 1971, 10–16; Ruebel 1972, 60–68; Scullard 1973, 257; Sblendorio Cugusi 1982, 511–12; Cugusi 2001, 1:417; Perl and El-Qalqili 2002; for an overview of scholarly views, see Mastrorosa 2006, 591–92n5). In any case, the debate as reported in Livy can be seen as illustrating views on the role and impact of women in society in both Cato's and Livy's times and as an element in shaping the portrayal of Cato's attitude to women (Bond 1979; Desideri 1984; Robert 2003; Mastrorosa 2006).*

CATO

F 17A Liv. 34.1.7–4.19

*In response to requests to abolish the law, Livy has Cato
criticize female madness as well as the women's immodest
and unrestrained behavior, denounce extravagance, argue*

TO EQUESTRIANS IN NUMANTIA
(F 17–18)

*Two sources provide verbatim quotations from a speech
Cato is said to have made to equestrians, one of them
specifying the location as Numantia (F 17). Such a speech
would have been delivered during Cato's consulship (195
BC), when he was fighting in the Iberian peninsula, as
Numantia was a settlement of the Celtiberians (cf. T 82),
and this oration would then be the oldest speech by Cato
attested by fragments. While the literal quotations suggest*

F 17 Gell. *NA* 16.1.1–4

verba Musoni philosophi Graeca digna atque utilia audiri
observarique; eiusdemque utilitatis sententia a M. Catone
multis ante annis Numantiae ad equites dicta.—[1] adulescentuli cum etiamtum in scholis essemus, ἐνθυμημά-
τιον hoc Graecum quod adposui dictum esse a Musonio
philosopho audiebamus, et quoniam vere atque luculente
dictum verbisque est brevibus et rotundis vinctum, per-
quam libenter memineramus: [2] ἄν τι πράξῃς καλὸν
μετὰ πόνου, ὁ μὲν πόνος οἴχεται, τὸ δὲ καλὸν μένει·
ἄν τι ποιήσῃς αἰσχρὸν μετὰ ἡδονῆς, τὸ μὲν ἡδὺ οἴ-

F 17A Livy, *History of Rome*

that such freedom should not be allowed to women, and affirm that laws exist for the benefit of society.

TO EQUESTRIANS IN NUMANTIA
(F 17–18)

authenticity (on the style, see Traglia 1985, 354–55; on the comparison with the Greek version, see Gamberale 1969, 144–46), it has been noted that military speeches, mostly attested in ancient historiography, are typically fictions and that these "fragments" could come from a "speech" originally included in the Origines, *written by Cato for his character in the work, but not necessarily delivered in that form (Suerbaum 1996/1997, 192–93).*

F 17 Gellius, *Attic Nights*

Greek words by Musonius, the philosopher [C. Musonius Rufus, Stoic, 1st cent. AD], of value and worth hearing and bearing in mind; and a remark of equal usefulness made by M. Cato many years earlier to equestrians at Numantia.—[1] When we were still young and at school, we used to hear that this Greek sentiment, which I have appended, was uttered by Musonius, the philosopher, and, since it is truly and brilliantly said, and arranged in a brief and elegant expression, we very willingly committed it to memory [F 51 Hense]: [2] "If you accomplish anything noble with toil, the toil passes, but the noble deed endures; if you do anything shameful with pleasure, the plea-

χεται, τὸ δὲ αἰσχρὸν μένει. [3] postea istam ipsam
sententiam in Catonis oratione quam dixit Numantiae
apud equites positam legimus. quae etsi laxioribus paulo
longioribusque verbis comprehensa est praequam illud
Graecum quod diximus, quoniam tamen prior tempore
antiquiorque est, venerabilior videri debet. [4] verba ex
oratione haec sunt: "cogitate cum animis vestris: si quid
vos per laborem recte feceritis, labor ille a vobis cito
recedet, bene factum a vobis dum vivitis non abscedet;
sed siqua per voluptatem nequiter feceritis, voluptas cito
abibit, nequiter factum illud apud vos semper manebit."

F 18 Fest., p. 220.9–13 L.

OPTIONATUS, ut decurionatus, pontificatus dicitur, ut
Cato in ea, quam habuit apud equites: "maiores seorsum
atque divorsum pretium paravere bonis atque strenuis,
decurionatus, optionatus, hastas donaticas, aliosque ho-
nores."

CONSULAR SPEECHES IN THE
IBERIAN PENINSULA (F 18A–H)

*While Cato was engaged in the Iberian peninsula in his
consular year (195 BC) and into the following one, he must
have given a number of speeches to soldiers (cf. F 17–18)
and in negotiations with local groups and contractors. Examples of utterances on such occasions are put into Cato's
mouth in Livy (F 18A–G), and a speech to soldiers is men-*

sure passes, but the shame endures." [3] Later, we read
that very same sentiment included in a speech by Cato
that he delivered at Numantia to equestrians. Although it
is expressed somewhat more loosely and diffusely in comparison with that Greek [version] that we have mentioned,
yet, since it is prior in time and more ancient, it ought to
be regarded as worthy of greater respect. [4] The words
from the speech are as follows: "Consider this in your
minds: if through toil you have done something well, that
toil will quickly pass from you, the good deed will not leave
you as long as you live; but, if through pleasure you have
done something in any way dishonorable, the pleasure will
quickly pass away, but that dishonorable deed will remain
with you forever."

F 18 Festus

optionatus ["position of an *optio* / junior officer"] is used
just as *decurionatus* ["position of a *decurio*"] and *pontificatus* ["position of a *pontifex*"], as Cato [says] in that
[speech] that he delivered to equestrians: "The ancestors
offered distinct and diverse rewards to good and energetic
individuals, [namely] positions of a *decurio*, positions of a
junior officer, presentation lances, and other honors."

CONSULAR SPEECHES IN THE
IBERIAN PENINSULA (F 18A–H)

*tioned in Appian (F 18 H). While these speeches are gener-
ally regarded as inauthentic, the references provide a
fuller portrayal of Cato's oratory: the contexts of these
speeches are plausible, and they offer testimony on how
Cato was viewed by later ancient authors.*

13

F 18A Liv. 34.9.12

Cf. *Op. cet.* F 54.

F 18B Liv. 34.11.3–4

F 18C Liv. 34.12.5–7

F 18D Liv. 34.13.4–10

F 18E Liv. 34.14.3–4

F 18F Liv. 34.17.7–10

Cf. T 32a.

F 18G Liv. 34.21.3–4

F 18H App. *Hisp.* 40

ON THE TRIUMPH TO THE PEOPLE
(F 19)

Upon his return from the province after his consular year, Cato celebrated a triumph in Rome (194 BC; Liv. 34.46.2–3). He apparently gave a speech to the People about it

F 19 Prisc., *GL* II, p. 87.15–18

. . . ; vetustissimi tamen comparativis etiam huiuscemodi sunt {est quando}[1] usi. Cato [*Orig.* F 152] . . . idem ad populum de triumpho: "asperrimo atque arduissimo aditu." . . . [*Orat.* F 19, 186, 178, 161, 182].

[1] sunt *vel* sunt est quando *vel* est sunt quando *vel* est quando *vel* * * est quando (st?) *codd.*

F 18A Livy, *History of Rome*

Cf. *Op. cet.* F 54.

F 18B Livy, *History of Rome*

F 18C Livy, *History of Rome*

F 18D Livy, *History of Rome*

F 18E Livy, *History of Rome*

F 18F Livy, *History of Rome*

Cf. T 32a.

F 18G Livy, *History of Rome*

F 18H Appian, *Roman History* 6. *The Iberian Book*

ON THE TRIUMPH TO THE PEOPLE
(F 19)

(CCMR, App. A: 143), unless he spoke about someone else's triumph on another occasion.

F 19 Priscian

. . . ; the very early [writers], though, used comparatives of this type too {it is when}. Cato [*Orig.* F 152] . . . The same [Cato said in the speech] to the People about the triumph: "with the roughest and most arduous access." . . . [*Orat.* F 19, 186, 178, 161, 182].

CATO

TO THE ATHENIANS (F 20)

*Cato spent time in Greece as a military tribune (191 BC)
during the war against Antiochus III the Great (192–188
BC), when he also acted as a Roman envoy. In that context
Cato could have spoken to the Athenians about Antiochus.
Plutarch reports that a speech of Cato was said to be extant, which he delivered in Greek in Athens and in which
he mentioned that he admired the virtues of the ancient*

F 20 Iul. Rufin., §6, *RLM*, pp. 39.31–40.9

ἐξουθενισμός. figura haec fit, cum rem aliquam extenua-
mus et contemtam facimus, ut . . . Cato apud Athenienses:
"Antiochus epistulis bellum gerit, calamo et atramento
militat."

Cf. Dem. *Phil.* 1.30: ἃ μὲν ἡμεῖς, ὦ ἄνδρες Ἀθηναῖοι, δεδυνή-
μεθ᾿ εὑρεῖν ταῦτ᾿ ἐστίν. ἐπειδὰν δ᾿ ἐπιχειροτονῆτε τὰς γνώ-
μας, ἂν ὑμῖν ἀρέσκῃ, χειροτονήσετε, ἵνα μὴ μόνον ἐν τοῖς
ψηφίσμασι καὶ ταῖς ἐπιστολαῖς πολεμῆτε Φιλίππῳ, ἀλλὰ
καὶ τοῖς ἔργοις.; Liv. 31.44.9: Athenienses quidem litteris verbisque, quibus solis valent, bellum adversus Philippum gerebant.

TO THE ATHENIANS (F 20)

*Athenians and was delighted to see such a beautiful and
grand city; Plutarch then rejects the story and claims that
Cato spoke to the Athenians through an interpreter, although he could have done so directly (Op. cet. F 67a).
This fragment points to a Latin version of a speech given
in Athens, but this oration need not be the one mentioned
by Plutarch.*

F 20 Iulius Rufinianus

exouthenismos ["scorn, contempt"]. This figure occurs
when we belittle some matter and make it contemptible,
as . . . Cato to the Athenians: "Antiochus wages war by
letters; with pen and ink he does his soldiering."[1]

Cf. Demosthenes: This is the scheme, Athenians, that we have
been able to contrive. When you give your votes, if it seems good
to you, then you will vote for this, so that you may fight Philip
[Philip II, king of Macedonia] not only with decrees and dis-
patches, but also with deeds.; Livy, *History of Rome*: Indeed, the
Athenians were waging war against Philip with letters and words,
the only things by which they were strong.

[1] Some similarity between the statement quoted for Cato and
the passage of Demosthenes has been observed, which is relevant
to the question of the extent to which Cato might have been influenced by Greek oratory and specifically this Greek orator (cf.
T 56, 57; see General Introduction).

OF THE TRIAL ON HIS CONSULSHIP
(F 21–55)

After his consulship (195 BC) and his return from Greece (191 BC; cf. F 49), Cato was taken to court (charge uncertain) and delivered a speech in his defense. It is this speech out of all of Cato's attested orations to which the largest number of surviving fragments can be assigned, if it is assumed, as is usually the case, that slightly different types of references in the sources all denote the same speech. An account of Cato's activities in the Iberian peninsula during his consular year, which was apparently an element of this speech, was presumably also included in the final book of

F 21 Charis., *GL* I, p. 202.23–25 = p. 263.5–8 B.

industrie M. Cato dierum dictarum de consulatu suo: "egoque iam pridem cognovi atque intellexi atque arbitror rem publicam curare industrie summum periculum esse."

F 22 Charis., *GL* I, p. 229.21–29 = p. 297.11–21 B.

atque pro et . . . Cato dierum dictarum de consulatu suo: "atque quamquam multa nova miracula fecere inimici mei, tamen nequeo desinere mirari eorum audaciam atque confidentiam."

F 23 Charis., *GL* I, p. 199.21–29 = p. 259.15–25 B.

falso . . . adverbialiter . . . M. Cato dierum dictarum de consulatu suo: "ei rei dant[1] operam, ut mihi falso maledicatur."

---

[1] dant *Cauchii ex deperdito cod. excerpta, Putschen:* dam *cod.*

OF THE TRIAL ON HIS CONSULSHIP
(F 21–55)

the Origines *and can be found in Livy (Liv. 34.8.4–21.8),*
who, from the detailed nature of his narrative and from
correspondences with the content of some of the surviving
fragments, appears to have been familiar with Cato's re-
port (Tränkle 1971, 16–29; Scullard 1973, 258–59). On the
possible structure of the speech, see Sblendorio Cugusi
1980; 1982, 147–48; on aspects of chronology and geogra-
phy of Cato's activities in the Iberian peninsula, see Knapp
1980.

F 21 Charisius

industrie ["diligently"]: M. Cato [uses it in the speech] of
the trial on his consulship: "And I have long since realized,
and have understood, and believe that looking after the *res
publica* diligently is a most dangerous task."

F 22 Charisius

atque instead of *et* ["and"; cf. T 69]: . . . Cato [says in the
speech] of the trial on his consulship: "And although my
enemies have done many novel and extraordinary things,
still, I cannot stop wondering at their audacity and temer-
ity."

F 23 Charisius

falso ["wrongly, untruthfully"] . . . as an adverb . . . M. Cato
[uses it in the speech] of the trial on his consulship: "they
put effort into that issue, so that I should be wrongly
abused."

F 24 Fest., p. 140.29 L.

MALEDI‹CTORES dicebantur ab antiquis quos›[1] nos ap-
pellamus ‹maledicos›[2] . . . Hispania re . . .[3]

[1] *suppl. ex Epit.*   [2] *suppl. ex Epit.*   [3] ‹Cato cum
proficisceretur in› Hispaniam, re‹movendi maledictores› *Ursi-
nus* | re *aut* nu *cod.*

F 25 Charis., *GL* I, p. 220.19–23 = p. 285.1–6 B.

secus pro aliter . . . Cato de consulatu suo: "secus aetatem
agerem quam illi egissent."

F 26 Charis., *GL* I, p. 216.17–18 = p. 279.28–29 B.

absolute quanto Cato de consulatu suo: "videtote quanto
secus ego fecerim."

F 27 Serv. auct. ad Verg. *Ecl.* 4.5

"ab integro": vel denuo vel ab initio: Cato de suo consulatu: "omnia ab integro paranda erant."

F 28 Charis., *GL* I, p. 205.17–20 = p. 266.24–28 B.

maturrime M. Cato dierum dictarum de consulatu suo:
"laudant me maximis laudibus, tantum navium, tantum
exercitum, tantum ‹com›meatum[1] non opinatum esse

[1] *add. cod. descr.*

F 24 Festus

maledi<ctores ["slanderers"] was the term used by the ancients for those whom > we call *<maledici>*: . . . the Iberian peninsula . . .[1]

[1] The quotation, giving an example of the use of the word *maledictores* by an ancient writer, is mostly lost. Reconstructions have attributed it to Cato, on the basis of an assumed reference to his time in the Iberian peninsula.

F 25 Charisius

secus instead of *aliter* ["differently"] . . . Cato [uses it in the speech] on his consulship: "I would spend my life differently from how they had spent theirs."

F 26 Charisius

Cato [uses] *quanto* ["to what extent," usually "by how much"] in an absolute way [i.e., without a correlative] [in the speech] on his consulship: "see [pl.] to what extent I have acted differently."

F 27 Servius, *Commentary on Virgil*

"anew": either "once again" or "from the beginning": Cato [says in the speech] on his consulship: "everything was to be prepared once again / from the beginning."

F 28 Charisius

maturrime ["very quickly / early"; cf. F 49]: M. Cato [uses it in the speech] of the trial on his consulship: "they praise me with the greatest praises, [saying] that no human being was believed to have been able to raise so many ships, so

quemquam hominem comparare potuisse; id me tam maturrime comparavisse."

F 29 Charis., *GL* I, p. 207.25–29 = p. 269.8–13 B.

nocte M. Cato dierum dictarum de consulatu suo: "deinde postquam Massiliam praeterimus, inde omnem classem ventus auster lenis fert; mare velis florere videres. ultra angulum Gallicum ad Illiberim atque Ruscinonem[1] deferimur: inde nocte aura profecti sumus."

  [1] ad Illiberim atque Ruscinonem *Lindemann*: at illi menim adque rusci nomen *cod.*

F 30 Gell. *NA* 4.17.15

id ipsum autem verbum M. Cato sub alia praepositione dicit in oratione quam de consulatu suo habuit: "ita nos"[1] inquit "fert ventus ad primorem[2] Pyrenaeum, qua[3] proicit in altum."

  [1] nos *codd. rec.*: hos *codd.*   [2] primorem *Mommsen*: priorem *codd.*   [3] qua *Holford-Strevens*: quo *codd.*

F 31 Charis., *GL* I, p. 209.6–9 = p. 271.1–6 B.

obviam pro obvius . . . M. Cato dierum dictarum de consulatu suo: "mihi atque classi obviam fiunt" . . .

many troops, so many supplies,[1] and that I raised that so very quickly."

[1] For this translation, *opinatum esse* has been assumed to have a passive sense (as it sometimes has in Latin of this period), and *quemquam hominem* has been taken together.

F 29 Charisius

nocte ["at night"]: M. Cato [uses it in the speech] of the trial on his consulship: "Then, after we passed Massilia [mod. Marseille], from then on a gentle south wind carries the entire fleet onward; you could see the sea blossoming with sails. We are carried beyond the Gallic bay [mod. Gulf of Lion] to Illiberis and Ruscino [rivers and places in present-day southwestern France (cf. Strab. 4.1.6; Polyb. ap. Ath. 8.4, p. 332A)]: from there we set out at night with a breeze."

F 30 Gellius, *Attic Nights*

But M. Cato uses that very verb [-*icere*] with another prefix in the speech that he delivered on his consulship: "So," he says, "the wind carries us to the promontory of the Pyrenees [mod. Cap de Creus], where it extends [*proicit*] into the deep [sea] [cf. Liv 26.19.11]."

F 31 Charisius

obviam instead of *obvius* ["in the path"]: . . . M. Cato [uses it in the speech] of the trial on his consulship: "they appear in the path of me and of the fleet" . . .

CATO

F 32 Charis., *GL* I, pp. 222.31–23.2 = p. 287.13–19 B.

usquequaque, quasi diceret longe lateque, M. Cato dierum dictarum de consulatu suo: "omnia tumultus plena,
simul hostium copiae magnae contra me sedebant; usquequaque lacessebamur." quod manifestius idem ita disserit
[F 34]: "interea ad socios nostros sedulo dispertieram, alio
frumentum, alio legatos, alio litteras, alio praesidium usquequaque."

F 33 Charis., *GL* I, p. 208.23–26 = p. 270.16–19 B.

necessum M. Cato dierum dictarum de consulatu suo:
"eas res non posse sustineri, nisi eo praesidia magna frumentumque *1 nam ita dicunt palam necesse esse obcura-
tam" *2 positio sermonis.

1 frumentumque ‹mitterentur› *H. Meyer*
2 obscuratum *Cauchii ex deperdito cod. excerpta: lac. indica-
vit ed. princ. qua, ut Keil monet, quaedam exhausta esse videntur,
quibus* necessum *a positione* necessus *duci dictum fuit*: necessario necessus necessum occulto *excerpta cod. Bernensis*

F 34 Charis., *GL* I, pp. 222.31–23.2 = p. 287.13–19 B.

Cf. F 32.

24

F 32 Charisius

usquequaque ["everywhere, on every side, in every possible respect"], as if he were to say "far and wide," [was used by] M. Cato [in the speech] of the trial on his consulship: "Everything was full of disorder; simultaneously large troops of the enemy were encamped against me; we were challenged on every side." The same [Cato] sets this out more clearly as follows [F 34]: "Meanwhile I had made distributions among our allies diligently, to one of them grain, to another legates, to yet another letters and to yet another protection on every side."[1]

[1] Context and content suggest that the second quotation comes from the same speech although the source does not say so explicitly. On Cato's military letters, see Introduction to *Epistula(e)*.

F 33 Charisius

necessum ["indispensable, inevitable"]: M. Cato [uses it in the speech] of the trial on his consulship:[1] "that those matters cannot be maintained unless great defenses and grain [are sent?] there; for they say so openly that it is necessary [*necesse*] for it to have been taken care of [?]" . . . the original form of the word [?].

[1] The corrupt and possibly lacunose quotation does not include the exact form of the word prompting the reference; yet the concept of necessity is expressed with a variant of the lemma.

F 34 Charisius

Cf. F 32.

F 35 Fronto, *Ad Verum imp.* 2.20 (pp. 128.20–29.6 van den Hout)

[FRONTO:] ipsum hoc tuum a te diu⟨ti⟩na[1] prudentia consultum, quod non ante signis conlatis manum cum hostibus conseruisti quam levibus proeliis et minutis victoriis militem imbueres, nonne Cato docuit, orator idem et imperator summus? ipsa subieci verba, in quibus consiliorum tuorum expressa vestigia cerneres:[2] "interea unamquamque turmam, manipulum, cohortem temptabam, quid facere possent. proeliis levibus[3] spectabam, cuiusmodi quisque esset. si quis strenue fecerat, donabam honeste, ut alii idem vellent facere, atque in contione verbis multis laudabam. interea aliquot ⟨p⟩au⟨ca⟩ castra[4] feci, sed ubi anni tempus venit, castra hiberna . . ."[5]

[1] diutina *lac. suppl. Mai*: *nihil distinxit ita cod. auctore Haulero*: divina *Cornelissen*   [2] cerneris *Mai*: cernes *Meyer*
[3] levibus *Mai*: lenibus *cod.*   [4] ⟨p⟩au⟨ca⟩ castra *Mai*: aucastra *cod.*   [5] hiberna ⟨apud Emporias posui⟩ *Jordan*: hiberna ⟨constitui⟩ *Haines*

F 36–37 Charis., *GL* I, p. 214.28–31 = p. 277.24–27 B.

pone versus M. Cato dierum dictarum de consulato suo: "nostros pone versus hosteis esse ab dextera parte," item idem: "postquam auspicavi atque exercitum adduxi pone versus[1] castra hostium."

[1] versus *Putschen*: versum *add. Cauchii ex deperdito cod. excerpta*

F 35 Fronto, *Correspondence*

[FRONTO:] This very plan of yours that you adopted on the basis of your well-tried sagacity, that you did not enter into combat with the enemy in a pitched battle before you could give the soldier experience with light skirmishes and small victories, did not Cato, the greatest orator and equally the greatest general, show it? I have appended the very words, in which you might see traces of your plans expressed: "Meanwhile I would put to the test each squadron, maniple, and cohort, [to see] what they could do. In light skirmishes I would observe what the quality of each one was. If anyone had done something with energy, I would reward them fairly, so that others would want to do the same, and I would praise them in the assembly with many words. Meanwhile I set up several small camps, but when the time of year came, winter camps . . ."

F 36–37 Charisius

pone versus ["to the rear of"]: M. Cato [uses it in the speech] of the trial on his consulship: "that our men are to the rear of our enemy from the right-hand side"; likewise the same [Cato]: "after I had taken the auspices and led the army to the rear of the camp of the enemy."[1]

[1] On the basis of context and content, it is assumed that the second quotation comes from the same speech, although the source does not say so explicitly (cf. Liv. 34.14.1–3).

F 38 Charis., *GL* I, pp. 217.25–18.2 = pp. 281.18–82.2 B.

satis diverse accipitur: . . . item satis pro intente Cato
dierum dictarum de consulatu suo: "iam apud vallum nostri satis agebant."

F 41, 40, 39 Charis., *GL* I, p. 213.3–8 = p. 275.18–26 B.

porro M. Cato dierum dictarum de consulatu suo: "inde
pergo porro ire in Turtam,"[1] idem supra: "itaque porro in
Turtam proficiscor servatum illlos"; . . . porro pro in futurum M. Cato in eodem: "me sollicitum atque exercitum[2]
habitum esse atque porro fore" . . .

[1] Turtam *vel* turtum *codd. et ex deperdito cod. excerpta*
[2] exercitum *vel* excitum *codd. et ex deperdito cod. excerpta*

F 42 Charis., *GL* I, p. 221.11–15 = pp. 285.27–86.2 B.

temere pro facile . . . Cato de consulatu suo: "si cuperent
hostes fieri, temere fieri nunc possent."[1]

[1] non possent *Putschen*: non possint *Cauchii ex deperdito cod.
excerpta*

F 38 Charisius

satis ["sufficiently"] is understood in different ways: . . .
likewise, Cato [uses] *satis* instead of *intente* ["intently"] [in
the speech] of the trial on his consulship: "our men were
already intently busy by the rampart."

F 41, 40, 39 Charisius

porro ["hereafter, further"]: M. Cato [uses it in the speech]
of the trial of his consulship: "from there I proceed to
advance further toward Turta";[1] the same [Cato] earlier
[in the speech]: "therefore I set off further toward Turta
to save those"; . . . *porro* instead of *in futurum* ["in future"]: M. Cato [uses it] in the same [text; cf. F 86]: "that
I was kept disturbed and troubled and will be hereafter"[2] . . .

[1] Apparently, a place in the Iberian peninsula, probably in the
area of the Turdetani (Liv. 34.17.1–2, 34.19.1–7) and perhaps
identical with the town of Turda (Liv. 33.44.4; cf. Knapp 1980,
51). García (1952–1953) suggests that it may be a corruption of
Turia (a river in the Iberian peninsula), understood as the name
of a town, and that the text should be amended accordingly.

[2] The sequence of the first and the second excerpt in the
original speech is indicated by the quoting author; for the third
excerpt it is said only that it comes from the same text, but the
relative position is not specified.

F 42 Charisius

temere ["heedlessly"] instead of *facile* ["easily"] . . . Cato
[says in the speech] on his consulship: "if they desired to
become enemies, they could now become such easily."

F 43 Fest., p. 142.17–20 L.

MEDIOCRICULO usus est in ea quam dixit Cato in consulatu: "ridibundum magistratum gerere,[1] pauculos homines, mediocriculum exercitum obvium duci."

> [1] gerere *Ursinus*: genere *cod.*: *del. Scaliger (cf. Epit.)*

Cf. Paul. *Fest.*, p. 143.7–9 L.; Osbern, *Derivationes* M 37.6 (p. 419 Bertini); M 188 (p. 435 Bertini).

F 44 Charis., *GL* I, p. 222.14–15 = p. 286.23–25 B.

tertium M. Cato de consulatu suo: "id ego primo minus animadverti; veniunt iterum atque tertium tumultuosius."

F 45 Charis., *GL* I, p. 214.8–11 = p. 277.1–5 B.

pedetemptim . . . , Cato dierum dictarum de consulatu suo: "eam ego viam pedetemptim temptabam."

F 46 Charis., *GL* I, p. 224.5–6 = p. 288.29–30 B.

vicissim Cato de consulatu suo: "qui maximis[1] vicibus"[2] inquit "ac vicissim," . . .

> [1] maximis *Fabricius*: maxim (*h. e.* maximus) *cod.*
> [2] vocibus *Cauchii ex deperdito cod. excerpta, Putschen*

F 47 Fest., p. 364.1–2 L.

"RECTO FRONTE ceteros sequi si norit": Cato in dissertatione consulatus.

F 43 Festus

Cato used *mediocriculus* ["rather mediocre"] in that [speech] that he delivered in his consulship:[1] "to carry out an office in a laughable way; very few people, a rather mediocre army to be led forward in the path."

[1] It is assumed that this description refers to the speech that Cato delivered about his consulship rather than one given during his consulship.

F 44 Charisius

tertium ["for a third time"]: M. Cato [uses it in the speech] on his consulship: "at first I noticed this less; they come a second and a third time with more uproar."

F 45 Charisius

pedetemptim ["step by step, cautiously"] . . . , Cato [uses it in the speech] of the trial on his consulship: "I was testing that path step by step / cautiously."

F 46 Charisius

vicissem ["in turn"]: Cato [used it in the speech] on his consulship: "they who with the greatest reversals," he says, "and in turn," . . .

F 47 Festus

"if he should know that others follow in a straight line" [cf. *Orig.* F 95; *Op. cet.* F 24]: Cato in the disquisition on his consulship.

F 48 Charis., *GL* I, p. 218.15–16 = p. 282.14–16 B.

sempiterno Cato dierum dictarum de consulatu suo: "ego mihi haec monimenta[1] sempiterno posui quae cepi."

[1] mi haec monimenta *cod.*: mihi monumenta haec *Putschen*

F 49 Charis., *GL* I, p. 205.12–14 = p. 266.16–19 B.

maturissime M. Cato dierum dictarum de consulatu suo: "item ubi ab Thermopulis[1] atque ex Asia maximos tumultus maturissime disieci atque consedavi."

[1] item u(b)ti a(bt)thermopolieis *cod.*: ita moti ad Thermopylas *Cauchii ex deperdito cod. excerpta*

F 50 Charis., *GL* I, p. 222.14–18 = p. 286.23–28 B.

tertium M. Cato de consulatu suo: . . . [F 44] . . . timidius idem in eadem Cato: "censores qui posthac fiunt, formidulosius atque segnius atque timidius pro re publica nitentur."

F 51 Apul. *Apol.* 17.9–10

M. autem Cato nihil oppertus, ut alii de se praedicarent, ipse in o{pe}ratione[1] sua scriptum reliquit, cum in Hispa-

[1] operatione *codd. (in mg. m. recentiss.* c oratione)

F 48 Charisius

sempiterno ["forever"]: Cato [uses it in the speech] of the trial on his consulship: "I have set up for myself forever these monuments that I have captured."

F 49 Charisius

maturissime ["very quickly / early"; cf. F 28]: M. Cato [uses it in the speech] of the trial on his consulship: "likewise, when I had very quickly cast out and settled the very large tumults from Thermopylae [in Greece] and out of Asia [cf. Plut. *Cat. Mai.* 13–14]."

F 50 Charisius

tertium ["for a third time"]: M. Cato [uses it in the speech] on his consulship: . . . [F 44] . . . *timidius* ["more diffidently"]: the same Cato [uses it] in the same [speech]: "those who become censors hereafter will exert themselves for the public benefit more fearfully, and more slothfully, and more diffidently."

F 51 Apuleius, *Apologia*

And M. Cato did not wait for others to praise him, but left a written record himself in a speech[1] of his that, when he

---

[1] The Latin word "speech" can be restored fairly confidently. The speech referred to must date to the time after Cato's consulship, and it is plausible that such a statement would have been made in a speech in which Cato explains his conduct. Thus, the attribution of the fragment to this speech is plausible even though the source does not indicate its context and occasion.

niam[2] consul proficisceretur, tris servos solos ex urbe duxisse; [10] quoniam ad villam publicam venerat, parum visum qui uteretur, iussisse duos pueros in foro de mensa emi, eos quinque in Hispaniam duxisse.

  [2] hispania *(non vid. addit. fuisse compend.) cod.*: hispaniã *cod. descr.*

F 52 Fest., p. 170.22–27 L.

NAVI>TAS secundum incorr . . . tos quos nunc n<autas> . . . Cato[1] in ea, quam scr<ipsit cum in Hispaniam profisce>retur, cum ait: "navitae . . . vinum atque oleum, ver . . ."

  [1] <navi>tas secundum incorr<uptam consuetudinem dic>tos quos nunc n<autas dicimus, testis est> Cato *Ursinus (fere)*

F 53 Plin. *HN* 14.91

idem Cato cum in Hispaniam navigasset,[1] unde cum triumpho rediit: "non aliud vinum," inquit, "bibi[2] quam remiges,"[3] in tantum dissimilis istis qui etiam convivis alia quam sibimet ipsis ministrant aut procedente mensa subiciunt.

  [1] navigasset *Mayhoff*: navigaret *codd.*   [2] bibi *edd.*: bibit *codd.*   [3] remiges *edd.*: remeans *codd.*

Cf. F 175; Frontin. *Str.* 4.3.1; Val. Max. 4.3.11.

set off for the Iberian peninsula as consul, he had taken just three slaves from the city [of Rome]; [10] that, when he had come to the Villa Publica [office for senior magistrates in the Campus Martius, meeting place for troops], this had seemed too little for his needs, and he had ordered two slaves to be bought off the stand in the Forum, and he had taken those five to the Iberian peninsula [cf. F 55; *Op. cet.* F 58.27].

F 52 Festus

navi ⟩*tae* [archaic and poetic form] according to . . . [?] whom [they] now [call] *n* ⟨*autae* ⟩ ["seamen, sailors"] . . . Cato in that [speech] that he wro⟨te when he set off for the Iberian peninsula⟩, when he says: "seamen . . . wine and oil . . . [?]"[1]

---

[1] What can be inferred for the content of the corrupt quotation agrees with an assumed element of this speech about Cato's consulship. Festus, though, says that the speech was delivered when Cato set off for the Iberian peninsula; yet, there may be some confusion.

F 53 Pliny the Elder, *Natural History*

The same Cato, when he had sailed to the Iberian peninsula, whence he returned with a triumph [194 BC], said:[1] "no other wine did I drink than the oarsmen [drank]"; to such an extent was he different from those who serve even to their guests different [wines] from the ones that [they] serve] to themselves or who substitute [inferior ones] as the meal progresses.

---

[1] The statement must come from a speech delivered after Cato's return from the Iberian peninsula, but it does not have to be the one delivered at this trial.

CATO

F 54 Plut. *Cat. Mai.* 5.7

ὁ δὲ Κάτων, ὥσπερ νεανιευόμενος ἐπὶ τούτοις, καὶ τὸν
ἵππον ᾧ παρὰ τὰς στρατείας ὑπατεύων ἐχρῆτο φησὶν
ἐν Ἰβηρίᾳ καταλιπεῖν, ἵνα μὴ τῇ πόλει λογίσηται τὸ
ναῦλον αὐτοῦ.

F 55 Plut. *Cat. Mai.* 10.1–6

ὕπατος δὲ μετὰ Φλάκκου Οὐαλερίου τοῦ φίλου καὶ
συνήθους ἀποδειχθείς, ἔλαχε τῶν ἐπαρχιῶν ἣν Ἐντὸς
Ἰσπανίαν Ῥωμαῖοι καλοῦσιν. ἐνταῦθα δ' αὐτῷ τὰ μὲν
καταστρεφομένῳ τῶν ἐθνῶν, τὰ δ' οἰκειουμένῳ διὰ
λόγων, πολλὴ στρατιὰ τῶν βαρβάρων ἐπέπεσε, καὶ
κίνδυνος ἦν αἰσχρῶς ἐκβιασθῆναι· διὸ τῶν ἐγγὺς
Κελτιβήρων ἐπεκαλεῖτο συμμαχίαν. [2] αἰτούντων δ'
ἐκείνων τῆς βοηθείας διακόσια τάλαντα μισθόν, οἱ
μὲν ἄλλοι πάντες οὐκ ἀνασχετὸν ἐποιοῦντο Ῥωμαίους
βαρβάροις ἐπικουρίας ὁμολογῆσαι μισθόν, ὁ δὲ
Κάτων οὐδὲν ἔφη δεινὸν εἶναι· νικῶντας μὲν γὰρ ἀποδώσειν παρὰ τῶν πολεμίων, οὐ παρ' αὐτῶν, ἡττωμένων δὲ μήτε τοὺς ἀπαιτουμένους ἔσεσθαι μήτε τοὺς
ἀπαιτοῦντας. [3] ταύτην δὲ τὴν μάχην κατὰ κράτος
ἐνίκησε, καὶ τὰ ἄλλα προὐχώρει λαμπρῶς. Πολύβιος

ORATIONS

F 54 Plutarch, *Life of Cato the Elder*

But Cato, acting like an insolent youthful in such matters
[i.e., getting rid of beings no longer needed], says that he
left behind in the Iberian peninsula even the horse that he
used for the military campaigns as consul [195 BC], so that
he might not charge the state for its transportation.[1]

[1] Such a comment must have been made after Cato's return
from the Iberian peninsula, but it does not have to come from the
speech delivered at this trial.

F 55 Plutarch, *Life of Cato the Elder*

Having been elected consul [for 195 BC] with Valerius
Flaccus [L. Valerius Flaccus], his close friend, he [Cato]
received the province that the Romans call Hither Iberia.
Here, while he was subduing some of the peoples and
winning over others by negotiation, a large army of "barbarians" fell upon him, and there was a risk of being forced
out disgracefully. Therefore, he called for an alliance with
the neighboring Celtiberians [peoples in the Iberian pen-
insula]. [2] When they demanded two hundred talents as
a reward for such assistance, all others thought it intoler-
able that Romans should agree with "barbarians" a reward
for assistance. But Cato said that it was not terrible; for, if
they were victorious, they could pay with assets of the
enemy, not of their own, whereas, should they be vanquished, neither those making the demand nor those of
whom it was made would be left [*Op. cet.* F 58.24]. [3] In
that battle [at Emporiae] he was victorious in accordance
with all his might, and the rest proceeded brilliantly. Indeed, Polybius [Polyb. 19.1; cf. Liv. 34.17.11] says that in

37

CATO

μέν γέ φησι τῶν ἐντὸς Βαίτιος¹ ποταμοῦ πόλεων
ἡμέρᾳ μιᾷ τὰ τείχη κελεύσαντος αὐτοῦ περιαιρεθῆ-
ναι—πάμπολλαι δ᾽ ἦσαν αὗται καὶ γέμουσαι μαχί-
μων ἀνδρῶν· αὐτὸς δέ φησιν ὁ Κάτων πλείονας εἰλη-
φέναι πόλεις ὧν διήγαγεν ἡμερῶν ἐν Ἰβηρίᾳ, καὶ
τοῦτο κόμπος οὐκ ἔστιν, εἴπερ ὡς ἀληθῶς τετρακόσιαι
τὸ πλῆθος ἦσαν. [4] τοῖς μὲν οὖν στρατιώταις πολλὰ
παρὰ τὴν στρατείαν ὠφεληθεῖσιν ἔτι καὶ λίτραν ἀρ-
γυρίου κατ᾽ ἄνδρα προσδιένειμεν, εἰπὼν ὡς κρεῖττον
εἴη πολλοὺς Ῥωμαίων ἀργύριον ἢ χρυσίον ὀλίγους
ἔχοντας ἐπανελθεῖν· εἰς δ᾽ αὐτὸν ἐκ τῶν ἁλισκομένων
οὐδὲν ἐλθεῖν λέγει πλὴν ὅσα πέπωκεν ἢ βέβρωκε. [5]
"καὶ οὐκ αἰτιῶμαι," φησί, "τοὺς ὠφελεῖσθαι ζητοῦν-
τας ἐκ τούτων, ἀλλὰ βούλομαι μᾶλλον περὶ ἀρετῆς
τοῖς ἀρίστοις ἢ περὶ χρημάτων τοῖς πλουσιωτάτοις
ἁμιλλᾶσθαι καὶ τοῖς φιλαργυρωτάτοις περὶ φιλαργυ-
ρίας." [6] οὐ μόνον δ᾽ αὑτόν, ἀλλὰ καὶ τοὺς περὶ αὐτὸν
ἐφύλαττε καθαροὺς παντὸς λήμματος. ἦσαν δὲ πέντε
θεράποντες ἐπὶ στρατείας σὺν αὐτῷ. τούτων εἷς ὄνομα
Πάκκιος ἠγόρασε τρία τῶν αἰχμαλώτων παιδάρια·
τοῦ δὲ Κάτωνος αἰσθομένου, πρὶν εἰς ὄψιν ἐλθεῖν,
ἀπήγξατο. τοὺς δὲ παῖδας ὁ Κάτων ἀποδόμενος εἰς τὸ
δημόσιον ἀνήνεγκε τὴν τιμήν.

¹ Βαίτιος Stephanus: βαιτίου vel βέλτιος codd.

Cf. Frontin. Str. 4.7.35.

38

a single day the walls of all the cities on this side of the river Baetis [mod. Guadalquivir]—and they were very many and full of warlike men—were torn down at his command. And Cato himself says [*Orig.* F 135; *Op. cet.* 58.25, 65] that he captured more cities than he spent days in the Iberian peninsula; and this is not a mere boast, as, in fact, there were four hundred in number. [4] To the soldiers, who reaped huge benefits from the campaign, he gave a pound of silver per man besides, saying that it was better to have many Romans return with silver than a few with gold [*Op. cet.* F 58.26]. But as regards himself, he says that no part of the booty went to him, except what he ate and drank [*Op. cet.* F 58.25]. [5] "And I do not find fault," he says, "with those seeking to profit from such situations, but I wish rather to compete in bravery with the bravest than in wealth with the richest and in greed for money with the greediest." [6] And he strove to keep not only himself, but also those around him free from all unjust gain. He had five attendants with him on the campaign [cf. F 51]. One of these, whose name was Paccius, bought three boys from among the public prisoners; but when Cato had noticed it, before he had come into his presence, he hanged himself [*Op. cet.* F 58.27]. Cato sold the boys and restored the price to the public treasury.[1]

---

[1] Cato's comments on his behavior in the province (or some of them) could come from the speech given at this trial.

ABOUT *LEX IUNIA DE FENERATIONE*
(F 56–57)

Cato is attested to have given a speech in connection with a Lex Iunia dealing with usury (F 56). Since the two fragments are likely to belong to the same speech, although the lex is not named in the second passage (F 57), Cato apparently argued against the bill (dissuasio). When exactly and by which member of the gens Iunia the bill was proposed is uncertain (LPPR, p. 273; Elster 2003, 313–15); it is often placed in the late 190s BC. Since the proposal is not men-

F 56 Fest., p. 268.7–13 L.

PRORSUS porro vorsus, nisi forte ex Graeco πρό. Cato de feneratione legis Iuniae:[1] "Camer<i>ni[2] cives nostri oppidum pulchrum habuere, agrum optimum atque pulcherrimum, rem fortunatissimam. cum Romam veniebant, prorsus devertebantur pro hospitibus ad amicos suos."

[1] de feneratione <in dissuasione> legis Iuniae *Mueller*
[2] Camer<i>ni *Ursinus*: camerni *cod.*

ABOUT *LEX IUNIA DE FENERATIONE*
(F 56–57)

*tioned elsewhere, some scholars assume that the law was
not approved; yet the fact that the sources refer to the
measure as a* lex *might suggest that it came into effect.
For various theories on the dating and motivation of this
initiative as well as the difficulties connected with the interpretation, see Scullard 1973, 257; Astin 1978, 319–23;
Sblendorio Cugusi 1982, 188–89; on Cato's opposition to
usury, see* Op. cet. *F 52;* Agr. praef.; *Liv. 32.27.3–4.*

F 56 Festus

prorsus ["forward, straight on"], "turned forward," unless
[it is derived] from the Greek *pro* ["before, in front"]. Cato
[says in the speech] on usury concerning *Lex Iunia*: "The
inhabitants of Camerinum, our citizens,[1] had a beautiful
town, the best and most beautiful farmland, most fortunate political circumstances. When they came to Rome,
they straightaway turned off the road for lodging toward
their friends as their hosts."

[1] Camerinum (mod. Camerino, in central-eastern Italy) was
allied with Rome since just before 300 BC and later had a *foedus
aequum* with Rome. Therefore, to indicate a close relationship,
the inhabitants may be called "our citizens," although it is uncertain whether this is technically correct. For clarity, the Latin text
should perhaps be emended to *Camer‹ti›ni*, since *Camerini*
typically refers to the inhabitants of the town of Cameria (in
Latium), which had disappeared by Cato's time.

F 57 Non., p. 64.18–22 M. = 89 L.

PEDATO positum pro repetitu vel accessu, quasi per pedem, sicuti nunc vulgo dicitur, tertio pedato.[1] Cato Originum lib. I [*Orig.* F 20]: "igitur tertio pedato bellum nobis
facere."—idem in dissuasione de feneratione: "tertio autem pedato item ex fenore discordia excrescebat."

[1] tertio pedato *del. Mueller, "fort. recte" Lindsay*

AGAINST Q. MINUCIUS THERMUS ON
FALSE BATTLES (F 58)

*Q. Minucius Thermus (trib. mil. 202, trib. pl. 201, aed. cur.
198, praet. 196, cos. 193 BC), when praetor, carried out
successful military activities in Hither Iberia (Liv. 33.26.1–
4, 33.43.8, 33.44.4–5). Later, in his consulship and the
following years, he fought against the Ligurians (in north-
western Italy), but he was denied a triumph upon his return to Rome in 190 BC (Liv. 37.46.1–2). In the following year, Thermus was one of ten legates sent to Asia to
implement the treaty to end the war against Antiochus III
the Great (192–188 BC) (MRR 1:363; Liv. 38.39.1; Polyb.
21.46); Thermus died on the return journey in 188 BC in
fights with the Thracians (Liv. 38.41.3, 38.46.7, 38.49.8).*

*Cato is said to have delivered two speeches criticizing
Thermus' activities, quoted with different titles (cf. F 59–
63, 64–65), though it has been suggested that all surviving*

F 57 Nonius Marcellus

pedato ["at the stage / assault"; cf. *Orig.* F 143] is used
instead of "at renewal" or "on approach," as if by means of
the foot [*per pedem*], as one now says commonly, "at the
third stage" [*tertio pedato*]. Cato [says] in the first book of
the *Origines* [*Orig.* F 20]: "thus on the third assault to
make war against us."—The same [Cato] in the speech
advising rejection concerning usury: "but likewise at the
third stage discord was growing out of usury [cf. M. Porcius Cato (*ORF*[4] 41 F 2)]."

AGAINST Q. MINUCIUS THERMUS ON FALSE BATTLES (F 58)

*fragments might come from a single speech (e.g., Scullard
1973, 133–34, 258). Whether the oration "on false battles"
belongs to the context of the denied triumph has to remain
uncertain. The description "false battles," appearing in the
identification of the piece, though not in the fragment
(OLD s.v. falsus 6), might mean that Cato alleges that
battles Thermus claims to have conducted never happened
and thus perhaps that the conditions for a triumph were
not fulfilled. The* decemviri *mentioned in the fragment are
probably the local officials in an allied community, but the
geographical location of the incident and the reference
point remain open. On the fragment, its style, and its comparison with other oratorical texts, see Sblendorio Cugusi
1982, 195–205; Goldberg 1983, 203; Coletti 1990; Courtney 1999, 85–87.*

F 58 Gell. *NA* 10.3.15–19

sed siquis est tam agresti aure ac tam hispida quem lux ista
et amoenitas orationis verborumque modificatio parum
delectet, amet[1] autem priora idcirco quod incompta et
brevia et non operosa, sed nativa quadam suavitate sunt,
quodque in his umbra et color[2] quasi opacae[3] vetustatis
est, is, siquid iudicii habet, consideret in causa pari M.
Catonis, antiquioris hominis, orationem, ad cuius vim et
copiam Gracchus nec adspiravit. [16] intelleget, opinor,
Catonem contentum eloquentia aetatis suae non fuisse et
id iam tum facere voluisse, quod Cicero postea perfecit.
[17] in eo namque libro, qui de falsis pugnis inscriptus est,
ita de Q. Thermo conquestus est: "dixit a decemviris parum bene sibi cibaria curata esse. iussit vestimenta detrahi
atque flagro caedi. decemviros Bruttiani verberavere, videre multi mortales. quis hanc contumeliam, quis hoc
imperium, quis hanc servitutem ferre potest? nemo hoc
rex ausus est facere; eane fieri bonis, bono genere gnatis,
boni consultis![4] ubi societas? ubi fides maiorum? insignitas
iniurias plagas, verbera, vibices, eos[5] dolores atque car-
nificinas per dedecus atque maximam contumeliam in-
spectantibus popularibus suis atque multis mortalibus te
facere ausum esse! set quantum luctum, quantum gemi-
tum, quid lacrimarum, quantum fletum factum audivi!

1 delectet, amet *Holford-Strevens*: delectat, amat *codd.*
2 color *codd. rel.*: calor *unus cod.*: squalor *Bentley*
3 opacae *codd.*: opicae *Markland*
4 consultis *codd.*: consulitis *codd. rec.*: consuetis *Mommsen*
5 eos *codd.*: eis *codd. Non.*: vis *Perottus*

F 58 Gellius, *Attic Nights*

But if there is anyone with such a rustic and such a dull
ear so that the brilliance and loveliness of the speech and
the measured arrangement of the words [in Cic. *Verr.*
2.5.161–63] bring them little delight, while they like earlier material for the reason that it is unadorned, concise,
and unstudied, yet has a certain natural charm, and that
in it there is a shade and color of almost misty antiquity,
let such a person, if they have any judgment at all, examine
a speech in a similar case, of M. Cato, a man of a still
earlier time, to whose vigor and copiousness of language
Gracchus [C. Sempronius Gracchus (*ORF*⁴ 48 F 48–49)]
did not come close. [16] They will realize, I think, that
Cato was not content with the eloquence of his time and
wished to do even then what Cicero later accomplished
with perfection. [17] For in that volume that is entitled "on
false battles" he complained about Q. Thermus as follows:
"He said that provisions for him had not been satisfactorily
attended to by the *decemviri*. He ordered them to be
stripped naked and scourged with a lash. The Bruttiani
[public servants] flogged the *decemviri*, many people saw
it. Who could endure such an insult, who such tyrannical
behavior, who such servitude? No king has ever dared to
do this; that such [treatment] happens to good men, born
of a good family, and experienced in what is good! Where
is the alliance? Where is the good faith of the forefathers?
That you have dared to inflict signal wrongs, blows, lashes,
stripes, those pains and tortures, accompanied by disgrace
and extreme ignominy, while their fellow citizens and
many other people looked on! But what great grief, what
great groaning, what tears, what great lamentation have I

servi iniurias nimis aegre ferunt: quid illos, bono genere
gnatos, magna virtute praeditos, opinamini animi habuisse
atque habituros dum vivent?" [18] quod Cato dixit "Bruttiani verberavere," nequi fortasse de "Bruttianis" requirat,
id significat: [19] cum Hannibal Poenus cum exercitu in
Italia esset et aliquot pugnas populus Romanus adversas
pugnavisset, primi totius Italiae Bruttii ad Hannibalem
desciverunt. id Romani aegre passi, postquam Hannibal
Italia decessit superatique Poeni sunt, Bruttios ignomi-
niae causa non milites scribebant nec pro sociis habebant,
sed magistratibus in provincias euntibus parere et praemi-
nistrare servorum vicem iusserunt. itaque hi sequebantur
magistratus, tamquam in scaenicis fabulis qui dicebantur
"lorarii," et quos erant iussi, vinciebant aut verberabant;
quod autem ex Bruttiis erant, appellati sunt "Bruttiani."

Cf. Non., p. 187.24–27 M. = 276 L.

AGAINST Q. MINUCIUS THERMUS ON
THE TEN MEN (F 59–63)

*This further speech against Q. Minucius Thermus (cf.
F 58) focuses on the charge that he killed ten free men; they
are a group of people different from the* decemviri men-

F 59 Gell. *NA* 13.25.12–14

[FAVORINUS:] hoc ornatus genus in crimine uno vocibus
multis atque saevis exstruendo ille iam tunc M. Cato anti-

heard to have occurred! Slaves bitterly resent injustice: what feelings do you think that such men, born of a good family, endowed with high character, had and will have so long as they live?" [18] When Cato said "the Bruttiani flogged," lest anyone should inquire about *Bruttiani* by any chance, it means this: [19] when Hannibal the Carthaginian was in Italy with his army, and the Roman People had fought several battles that went against them, the Bruttii [an ancient Italic people] were the first of all Italy to defect to Hannibal. The Romans were angered at that and, after Hannibal had left Italy and the Carthaginians had been defeated, for the sake of ignominy, they did not enroll the Bruttii as soldiers or treat them as allies, but commanded them to serve the magistrates when they went to their provinces and to perform the duties of slaves [cf. App. *Hann.* 61.252–53]. Accordingly, they accompanied the magistrates, like those who were called "floggers" in plays on stage, and they bound or flogged those whom they had been ordered; and because they were from the Bruttii, they were called *Bruttiani*.

AGAINST Q. MINUCIUS THERMUS ON THE TEN MEN (F 59–63)

tioned in F 58 (see, e.g., Kienast 1979, 51–52; on F 59 see Courtney 1999, 87–88).

F 59 Gellius, *Attic Nights*

[FAVORINUS:] This kind of oratorical adornment, consisting in building up a single charge by a great number of

47

quissimus in orationibus suis celebravit, sicut in illa quae
inscripta est de decem hominibus, cum Thermum accusavit quod decem liberos homines eodem tempore interfe-
cisset, hisce verbis eandem omnibus rem significantibus
usus est, quae quoniam sunt eloquentiae Latinae tunc
primum exorientis lumina quaedam sublustria, libitum est
ea mihi ἀπομνημονεύειν: "tuum nefarium facinus peiore
facinore operire postulas, succidias humanas facis, tantam
trucidationem facis, decem funera facis, decem capita
libera interficis, decem hominibus vitam eripis indicta
causa, iniudicatis, incondemnatis." [13] item M. Cato in
orationis principio, quam dixit in senatu pro Rhodiensi-
bus, cum vellet res nimis prosperas dicere, tribus vocabulis idem sentientibus dixit. [14] verba eius haec sunt
[F 163]: "scio solere plerisque hominibus in rebus secundis atque prolixis atque prosperis animum excellere atque
superbiam atque ferociam augescere ⟨atque crescere⟩."[1]

[1] add. Hertz

F 60 Fest., p. 208.29–35 L.

OBSTINATO, obfirmato, perseveranti, ut tenere possit, . . .
Cato in Q. Thermum de X. hominibus: "rumorem famam
flocci fecit, ⟨inter⟩cutibus[1] stupris obstinatus, insignibus
flagitiis."[2]

[1] cutibus *vel* cupitus *vel* captus *codd.*: cupitus *ed. princ.*: capi-
tas *ed. Aldina*   [2] flagitiis *vel* flagris *codd.*

Cf. Prisc., *GL* II, p. 271.1–7: praeterea invenitur apud vetustissimos "intercus intercutis," et proprie "intercus aqua" dicitur, quam

severe terms, was frequently used even then by the famous M. Cato, a man from the distant past, in his speeches; for example in that one that is entitled "on the ten men," when he prosecuted Thermus because he had put to death ten freeborn men at the same time, he used the following words, all expressing the same thing, which, as they are some faint flashes of Latin eloquence, which was then dawning for the first time, it has pleased me to call to mind: "You seek to cover up your abominable crime with a worse crime, you slaughter men like swine, you create such a massacre, you cause ten deaths, you slay ten free men, you take life from ten humans, untried, unjudged, uncondemned." [13] Likewise, M. Cato, at the beginning of the speech that he delivered in the Senate on behalf of the Rhodians, when he wished to describe excessive prosperity, used three words meaning the same. [14] These are his words [F 163]: "I know that it is common for very many people in favorable, benign, and prosperous circumstances to be puffed up in spirit and to increase ⟨and grow⟩ in arrogance and insolence." [cf. F 196].

F 60 Festus

obstinatus ["stubborn, hardened"], obdurate, persisting, so that he could maintain, . . . Cato [says in the speech] against Q. Thermus on the ten men: "he regarded rumor and reputation as irrelevant, hardened in private illicit sexual intercourse and conspicuous disgraceful offenses."

Cf. Priscian: Moreover, among the very early [writers] *intercus, intercutis* ["subcutaneous"] is found, and properly one says *intercus aqua* ["dropsy"], which the Greeks call "dropsy." . . . But Cato used that [word] like an adjective, saying "hardened in private

49

CATO

Graeci ὕδρωπα nominant. . . . Cato autem quasi adiectivo eo est usus, dicens "intercutibus stupris obstinatus" pro "intestinis," ut sit secundum eum "hic" et "haec" et "hoc intercus," id est "qui" vel "quae" vel "quod intra cutem est."

F 61 Fest., p. 140.17–21 L.

M‹UL›TIFA‹CERE antiqui dicebant sicut› magniface‹re, item et› pa‹rvifacere›[1] . . . ‹Cato› in ea quam ‹scripsit contra Q. Minucium Thermum de›X hominibus: "‹neque fidem neque iusiurandum› neque pud‹icitiam multifacit"›[2] . . .

  [1] *suppl. Epit.*   [2] *suppl. Epit.*

Cf. Paul. *Fest.*, p. 141.2–5 L.: multifacere dicitur sicut magnifacere et parvifacere. Cato: "neque fidem neque iusiurandum neque pudicitiam multifacit." quod merito ab usu recessit, quia quantitas numero non aestimatur, nec desiderat multitudinem.

F 62 Fest., p. 466.2–9 L.

SACRAMENTO dicitur quod ‹iuris iurandi sacratio›ne interposita actum ‹est. unde quis sacra›mento dicitur interrogari,[1] quia . . . ‹Cato› in Q. Thermum de X. ‹hominibus›: ". . . erant, ne mala . . . t; scelera nefaria fie . . . ‹sacrame›nto traderetur lege est . . ."

  [1] *suppl. Epit.*

[*intercutibus*] illicit sexual intercourse," instead of *intestinis* ["internal"], so that, according to him, it is *intercus* for all three genders, that is, "who or what is under the skin."

F 61 Festus

‹The ancients used *multifacere* ["to value greatly"] like› *magniface‹re* ["to value much"], likewise also› *pa‹rvifacere›* ["to value little"] . . . ‹Cato› [says] in that [speech] that ‹he wrote against Q. Minucius Thermus on› the ten men: "‹neither loyalty, nor an oath,› nor chas‹tity does he value much› . . ."

Cf. Paul the Deacon, *Epitome of Festus*: *multifacere* ["to value greatly"] is used like *magnifacere* ["to value much"] and *parvifacere* ["to value little"]. Cato [says]: "neither loyalty, nor an oath, nor chastity does he value much." Here he turned away from common usage with justification because degree is not measured by number and does not need a large quantity.

F 62 Festus

sacramento ["by a confirming oath, under oath"] is called what ‹is› done when ‹the confirmation of an oath› has been pledged. ‹Hence someone› is said to be questioned under oath, because . . . ‹Cato› [says in the speech] against Q. Thermus about the ten ‹men›: ". . . they were, so that not bad . . . ; outrageous crimes . . . ‹under o›ath to be transmitted, by law it is . . ."[1]

[1] The text of the fragment is too corrupt to enable a reconstruction of the sentence structure.

CATO

F 63 Fest., p. 466.14–19 L.

SPICIUNT antiquos di‹xisse sine praepos›itione, testis est
Cato in ea, quam ‹habuit in Q. Thermum› de decem[1]
hominibus: "ut solent, . . . ‹son›ivios,[2] nisi qui sempiterni
sunt, quos . . . rant, ne‹c›[3] spiciunt neque ratos . . ."

[1] septem *cod.*   [2] ‹son›ivios *Augustinus*
[3] ne‹c› *Dacier*

FROM EITHER SPEECH AGAINST
Q. MINUCIUS THERMUS (F 64–65)

F 64 Fest., p. 364.17–21 L.

RATISSIMA quoque ab his quae rata dicimus; unde etiam
rationes dictae. Cato in Q. Thermum: "erga rempublicam
multa beneficii ratissima atque gratissima."

F 65 Prisc., *GL* II, p. 377.10–12

"fitur" etiam pro "fit" dicebant. M. Cato censorius in Quin-
tum Thermum: "postquam diutius fitur." idem . . . [F 77]

F 63 Festus

That the ancients used *spiciunt* ["they observe"] ‹without a pre›fix [i.e., used the verb as simplex], Cato is a witness in that [speech] that ‹he delivered against Q. Thermus› on the ten men: "as they are accustomed to, . . . those that make a rattling sound, except those who are eternal, whom . . . , neither do they observe nor do they . . . approved . . ."[1]

1 The text of the fragment is again very corrupt.

FROM EITHER SPEECH AGAINST Q. MINUCIUS THERMUS (F 64–65)

For these fragments it is unclear to which speech against Q. Minucius Thermus they might belong (cf. F 58, 59–63).

F 64 Festus

ratissima ["most approved"; neut. pl.] too [is derived] from what we call *rata* ["approved"]; hence also *rationes* ["accounts, principle"] is said. Cato [says in the speech] against Q. Thermus: "toward the *res publica* many most approved and most welcome forms of benefit."

F 65 Priscian

They also used *fitur* instead of *fit* ["it occurs"; passive instead of active form]. M. Cato, the ex-censor, [uses it in the speech] against Quintus Thermus: "after it occurs for longer." The same . . . [F 77]

AGAINST M'. ACILIUS GLABRIO
(F 66–66A)

*M'. Acilius Glabrio was one of the men who in 190 BC
stood for the censorship of the following year (like Cato
himself). The Tribunes of the People P. Sempronius Gracchus and C. Sempronius Rutilus took him to court, claim-
ing that some of the booty from the war against Antiochus
III the Great (192–188 BC) had neither been displayed
in the triumph nor handed over to the treasury; Cato
provided testimony in the trial. Glabrio then withdrew
his candidacy, and after several hearings the case was
dropped. In the historical account of the case, Livy (F 66A)
provides a summary of what Cato said as a witness*

F 66 Fest., p. 268.22–25 L.

PENATORES qui penus gestant. Cato adversus M'.[1] Acilium
quarta: "postquam na{ti}vitas[2] ex navibus eduxi, non
ex militibus atque nautis piscatores penatores feci,[3] sed
† arum †[4] dedi."

[1] m. *cod.*   [2] na{ti}vitas *Augustinus*: nativitas *cod.*
[3] feci *Ursinus*: fici *cod.*
[4] aurum *Dacier*: arma *Mommsen (ap. Jordan)*

F 66A Liv. 37.57.9–58.2

eodem anno censuram multi et clari viri petierunt. quae
res, tamquam in se parum magni certaminis causam haberet, aliam contentionem multo maiorem excitavit. [10]

ORATIONS

AGAINST M'. ACILIUS GLABRIO
(F 66–66A)

(CCMR, App. A: 148); this might be based on a speech of Cato's but is not an authentic record. Festus' text as transmitted (F 66) implies that Cato delivered four speeches against Glabrio, though the numeral might have entered the text as a misreading of the transmission (Sblendorio Cugusi 1982, 214). It is also uncertain whether Festus' reference to a speech "against" M'. Acilius Glabrio refers to the occasion described by Livy or to attack(s) by Cato separate from the witness statement (on the context, see Scullard 1973, 137, 259; Barzanò 1996).

F 66 Festus

penatores ["people who obtain or supply provisions"], those who carry provisions. Cato [says] against M'. Acilius in the fourth [speech]: "After I had led the seamen [cf. F 52] forth from the ships, I did not turn soldiers and seamen into fishermen [and] people who obtain provisions, but gave them gold [?]."[1]

[1] The translation tentatively adopts Dacier's emendation (argued for by Churchill 2000b; see also Alfonsi 1975, 40).

F 66A Livy, *History of Rome*

In the same year [190 BC] many distinguished men sought the censorship. This situation, although of itself it provided insufficient reason for a great quarrel, provoked another, much greater conflict. [10] The candidates were:

petebant T. Quinctius Flamininus, P. Cornelius Cn. f. Scipio, L. Valerius Flaccus, M. Porcius Cato, M. Claudius Marcellus, M'. Acilius Glabrio, qui Antiochum ad Thermopylas Aetolosque devicerat. [11] in hunc maxime, quod multa congiaria[1] † habuerat †[2] quibus magnam partem hominum obligarat, favor populi se inclinabat. [12] id cum aegre paterentur tot nobiles, novum sibi hominem tantum praeferri, P. Sempronius Gracchus et C. Sempronius Rutilus, ⟨tribuni plebis,⟩[3] ei diem dixerunt, quod pecuniae regiae praedaeque aliquantum captae in Antiochi castris neque in triumpho tulisset neque in aerarium rettulisset. [13] varia testimonia legatorum tribunorumque militum erant. M. Cato ante alios testes conspiciebatur; cuius auctoritatem perpetuo tenore vitae partam toga candida elevabat. [14] is testis quae vasa aurea atque argentea castris captis inter aliam praedam regiam vidisset, ea se in triumpho negabat vidisse. [15] postremo in huius maxime invidiam desistere se petitione Glabrio dixit, quando quod taciti indignarentur nobiles homines, id aeque novus competitor intestabili periurio incesseret. [58.1] centum milium multa inrogata erat; bis de ea certatum est; tertio, cum de petitione destitisset reus, nec populus de multa suffragium ferre voluit, et tribuni eo negotio destiterunt. [2] censores T. Quinctius Flamininus M. Claudius Marcellus creati.

---

[1] congiaria vel concilia *codd.*: ⟨e⟩ copia r⟨e⟨ ⟩gia (habuerat) *Madvig*   [2] † habuerat † *codd.* ⟨ex⟩hibuerat *Ursinus*: ⟨dist⟩ribuerat *Wesenberg*: dederat *Zingerle, "fort. recte" Briscoe*: ⟨pr⟩aebuerat *Nitsche*: ⟨t⟩ribuerat *Engel*   [3] ⟨tr. pl.⟩ *ed. Rom.*: *om. codd.*: *fort. ante nomina scribendum putat Briscoe*

T. Quinctius Flamininus, P. Cornelius Scipio, Gnaeus' son, L. Valerius Flaccus, M. Porcius Cato, M. Claudius Marcellus, and M'. Acilius Glabrio, who had defeated Antiochus and the Aetolians at Thermopylae [191 BC, as consul]. [11] The support of the People was inclining most toward him because he had made [?] many distributions by which he had secured the endorsement of a large number of individuals. [12] When many nobles took it ill that a new man was so significantly preferred to them, P. Sempronius Gracchus and C. Sempronius Rutilus, ‹Tribunes of the People,› summoned him to court because he had neither carried in the triumph nor deposited in the treasury a certain quantity of the king's money and the booty that had been taken in Antiochus' camp. [13] The testimony of the legates and military tribunes was conflicting. M. Cato was taken account of before other witnesses, even though his white toga [i.e., his being a candidate] diminished the authority acquired by an unbroken consistency of life. [14] As a witness, he stated that he had not seen in the triumph the gold and silver vessels that he had seen with the rest of the royal plunder when the camp had been taken. [15] Eventually, mainly for the purpose of generating ill will against him [Cato], Glabrio declared that he was withdrawing his candidacy since, seeing that a situation that the nobility accepted with silent resentment was challenged by a rival candidate, likewise a new man, with shameful perjury. [58.1] A fine of a hundred thousand sesterces had been proposed; the issue was fought over in court twice; on the third occasion, because the defendant had withdrawn his candidacy, the People were unwilling to vote on the fine, and the Tribunes abandoned that business. [2] T. Quinctius Flamininus and M. Claudius Marcellus were elected censors.

CATO

ON THE MONEY OF KING
ANTIOCHUS (F 67)

*In 187 BC the Tribunes of the People Q. Petillius and Q.
Petillius (Spurinus) (MRR 1:369) put forward a bill to set
up an investigation into money exacted from king Antiochus III the Great and not delivered to the treasury, including scrutiny of the behavior of P. Cornelius Scipio
Africanus maior (cos. 205, 194, censor 199 BC [ORF⁴ 4])*

F 67 Liv. 38.54.1–12

morte Africani crevere inimicorum animi, quorum princeps fuit M. Porcius Cato, qui vivo quoque eo adlatrare
magnitudinem eius solitus erat. [2] hoc auctore existiman-
tur Petillii et vivo Africano rem ingressi et mortuo rogationem promulgasse. [3] fuit autem rogatio talis: "velitis
iubeatis, Quirites,¹ quae pecunia capta ablata coacta ab
rege Antiocho est quique sub imperio eius fuerunt, [4]
quod eius in publicum relatum non est, uti de ea re Ser.
Sulpicius praetor urb⟨an⟩us² ad senatum referat, quem
eam rem velit senatus quaerere de iis qui praetores nunc
sunt." [5] huic rogationi primo Q. et L. Mummii interce-
debant: . . . [6] Petillii nobilitatem et regnum in senatu

---

¹ Quirites *Brisson*: queratur *codd.*
² urb⟨an⟩us *ed. Rom.*: urbis *codd.*

ORATIONS

ON THE MONEY OF KING
ANTIOCHUS (F 67)

*and his brother L. Cornelius Scipio Asiaticus (cos. 190
BC)* (Rogatio Petillia de pecunia regis Antiochi: LPPR,
*pp. 275, 506; Elster 2003, 329–32). Cato spoke in favor of
the bill and thus contributed to bringing opposition to it
to an end.*

F 67 Livy, *History of Rome*

With the death of Africanus [P. Cornelius Scipio Africanus
maior] the courage of his opponents increased; chief
among them was M. Porcius Cato, who, even during the
former's lifetime, had made a habit of railing at his emi-
nence. [2] It is thought that at his [Cato's] instigation the
Petillii commenced their suit against Africanus while he
was alive and put forward a bill after his death [cf. Gell.
NA 4.18.7]. [3] The bill was worded like this: "May it
please you to commend, Romans, that, with regard to the
money appropriated, removed, and exacted from king Antiochus and those who were under his command, [4] and
to such part as was not delivered to the public purse, Ser.
Sulpicius, the urban praetor [Ser. Sulpicius Galba, praet.
urb. 187 BC], should, in relation to that matter, put to the
Senate the question of which of those who are now praetors the Senate wishes to investigate the matter." [5] At
first Q. and L. Mummius [trib. pl. 187 BC] tried to veto
this bill: . . . [6] The Petillii continued to attack the nobility and the regal comportment of the Scipios in the Sen-

Scipionum accusabant. . . . [11] M. Cato suasit rogationem—exstat³ oratio eius de pecunia regis Antiochi—et
Mummios tribunos auctoritate deterruit ne adversarentur
rogationi. [12] remittentibus ergo iis intercessionem, omnes tribus uti rogasse‹n›t⁴ iusserunt.

³ extat *ed. Frobeniana 1535*: esse *vel* est et *vel* exstat et *codd.*
⁴ rogasse‹n›t *Vossius*: rogasset *vel* rogas *codd.*

ON THE CONSPIRACY (F 68)

*This might be a speech on the Bacchanalian affair in 186
BC (Liv. 39.8–19), as Livy describes aspects of it as a
"conspiracy" (Liv. 39.8.1–2), but the term could also refer*

F 68 Fest., p. 280.24–25 L.

PR{A}ECEM singulariter idem in ea, quae est de coniura-
tione.

AGAINST L. QUINCTIUS FLAMININUS
(F 69–71)

*In the year of his censorship (184 BC) Cato, along with
his colleague L. Valerius Flaccus, expelled L. Quinctius
Flamininus (cos. 192 BC) from the Senate and delivered a
speech charging him with unacceptable behavior. Ancient
authors provide slightly different narratives of the incident, and it is uncertain how each of them relates to Cato's*

ate. . . . [11] M. Cato spoke in favor of the bill—his speech on the money of king Antiochus is extant –, and with his influence he deterred the Mummii, the Tribunes, from opposing the bill. [12] Accordingly, when these withdrew their veto, all the tribes voted for acceptance of the bill as proposed.

ON THE CONSPIRACY (F 68)

to other events that might be defined as such; the single source on this speech does not reveal any details.

F 68 Festus

prex ["entreaty, prayer"; usually pl.]: the same [Cato] [uses it] in the singular in that [speech] that there is on the conspiracy.

AGAINST L. QUINCTIUS FLAMININUS (F 69–71)

original speech (Cic. Sen. 42; Val. Max. 2.9.3, 4.5.1; Plut. Cat. Mai. 17.1–6 [Op. cet. F 70]; Flamin. 18–19; [Aurel. Vict.] Vir. ill. 47.4 [T 82]; cf. Sen. Contr. 9.2). On the sources for and the different versions of the incident in the various accounts, see Carawan 1990; Suerbaum 1993; see also Scullard 1973, 157–58, 261; Astin 1978, 79–80.

CATO

F 69 Liv. 39.42.5–43.1

censores M. Porcius et L. Valerius metu mixta exspectatione senatum legerunt; septem moverunt senatu, ex quibus unum insignem et nobilitate et honoribus, L. Quinctium Flamininum consularem. [6] . . . Catonis et aliae
quidem acerbae orationes exstant in eos quos aut senato-
rio loco movit aut quibus equos ademit, [7] longe gravis-
sima in L. Quinctium oratio, qua si accusator ante notam,
non censor post notam usus esset, retinere L. Quinctium
in senatu ne frater quidem T. Quinctius, si tum censor
esset, potuisset. [8] inter cetera obiecit ei Philippum Poe-
num, carum ac nobile scortum, ab Roma in Galliam provinciam spe ingentium donorum perductum. [9] eum
puerum, per lasciviam cum cavillaretur, exprobrare consuli saepe¹ solitum, quod sub ipsum spectaculum gladiatorium abductus ab Roma esset, ut obsequium amatori
venditaret. [10] forte epulantibus iis, cum iam vino inca-
luissent, nuntiatum in convivio esse nobilem Boium cum
liberis transfugam venisse; convenire consulem velle, ut
ab eo fidem praesens acciperet. [11] introductum in taber-

¹ per lasciviam . . . saepe *Heraeus*: lasciviam . . . persaepe
codd.: ⟨per⟩ lasciviam persaepe *Badius Ascensius 1513*

F 69 Livy, *History of Rome*

The censors M. Porcius [Cato] and L. Valerius [L. Valerius
Flaccus, cos. 195 BC] revised the membership of the Senate amid suspense mixed with apprehension [184 BC].
They removed seven men from the Senate, including one
man well-known both because of his noble birth and the
offices he had held, L. Quinctius Flamininus, an ex-consul
[cos. 192 BC]. [6] . . . While there are extant also other
harsh speeches by Cato against those whom he either removed from the senatorial rank or deprived of their horses
[i.e., equestrian status], [7] by far the most scathing is the
speech against L. Quinctius; and if he had delivered it as
a prosecutor before putting down the mark of censure, not
as a censor after putting down the mark, not even his
brother, T. Quinctius [T. Quinctius Flamininus, cos. 198
BC], could have kept L. Quinctius in the Senate if he had
then been censor. [8] Among other things he [Cato]
charged him [L. Quinctius] with having induced the Carthaginian Philippus, a highly valued and well-known male
prostitute, to come from Rome to the province of Gaul by
holding out the hope of substantial gifts. [9] That boy,
when bantering in playfulness, would often scold the consul on the grounds that he had been taken away from
Rome right before a gladiatorial show, so that he could
provide his lover with his paid services. [10] When they
happened to be having dinner and were already flushed
with wine, word had been brought to them at table that a
Boian nobleman had come as a deserter with his children
[Boii: a people in mod. France]; that he wished to meet
the consul to receive in person a guarantee of protection
from him. [11] He [the Boian] had been shown into the

naculum per interpretem adloqui consulem coepisse.
inter cuius sermonem Quinctius scorto "vis tu," inquit
"quoniam gladiatorium spectaculum reliquisti, iam hunc
Gallum morientem videre?" [12] et cum is vixdum serio
adnuisset, ad nutum scorti consulem stricto gladio, qui
super caput pendebat, loquenti Gallo caput primum per-
cussisse, deinde, fugienti fidemque populi Romani atque
eorum qui aderant imploranti latus transfodisse. [43.1]
Valerius Antias, ut qui nec orationem Catonis legisset et
fabulae tantum sine auctore editae credidisset, aliud argu-
mentum, simile tamen et libidine et crudelitate peragit.

F 70 Liv. 39.43.5

in extrema oratione Catonis condicio Quinctio fertur, ut si
id factum negaret ceteraque quae obiecisset, sponsione
defenderet sese: sin fateretur, ignominiane sua quemquam doliturum censeret, cum ipse vino et venere amens
sanguine hominis in convivio lusisset?

F 71 Isid. *Diff.* 1.113(5)

inter amorem et cupidinem. "aliud est," inquit Cato, "Phi-
lippe, amor, longe aliudque[1] cupido. accessit ilico alter ubi

---

[1] aliudque *vel* aliud quia *vel* aliusque *vel* aliumque *vel* alidque
vel aliud *codd.*

tent and begun to address the consul by means of an interpreter. As the man was speaking, Quinctius said to the prostitute: "Since you missed the gladiatorial show, would you now like to see this Gaul dying?" [12] And when he had nodded, only half-seriously, at the nod of a prostitute, the consul had unsheathed his sword, which was hanging above his head, and first landed a blow on the head of the Gaul while he was speaking, then, as he fled, begging for the protection of the Roman People and of those present, he had run it through his side. [43.1] Valerius Antias [*FRHist* 25 F 55a], as he had not read Cato's speech and had merely believed a story published without any confirmed source, presents another version, though similar in lust and brutality.

F 70 Livy, *History of Rome*

At the end of Cato's speech a proposal is made to Quinctius: if he denied that incident and the other matters he had reproached him with, he should defend himself by a judicial wager; but if he admitted [the charges], would he think anyone would feel grief at his disgrace when he, while out of his mind with wine and venery, had played with a person's lifeblood at dinner?

F 71 Isidore, *On Differences between Words*

[The difference] between *amor* ["love"] and *cupido* ["desire, lust"]. *"amor,"* Cato says, "Philippus, is one thing, and *cupido* is a significantly different thing. One advanced at

alter recessit; alter bonus, alter malus." alii verius amorem
et bonum dixerunt et malum, cupidinem semper malum.

AGAINST L. VETURIUS (F 72–82)

*This is probably another speech from Cato's censorship
(184 BC), referring to the removal of an individual's equestrian status (cf. T 33), apparently connected with irregu-*

F 72 Fest., p. 466.22–26 L.

STATA SACRIFICIA sunt, quae certis diebus fieri debent.
Cato in ea, quam scribsit de L. Veturio, de sacrificio commisso, cum ei equum ademit: "quod tu, quod in te fuit,
sacra stata, sollempnia, capite sancta deseruisti."

F 73 Fest., p. 268.13–22 L.

PROHIBERE COMITIA, dicitur vitiare diem morbo, qui
vulgo quidem maior, ceterum ob id ipsum comitialis ap-
pellatur. Cato in ea oratione, quam scribsit de sacrificio[1]

---

[1] sacrificio *edd.*: sacrilegio *cod.*

once where the other withdrew; one is good, the other is bad."[1] Others have said more correctly that *amor* is both good and bad and that *cupido* is always bad.

[1] The fragment can be attributed to this speech if the Philippus addressed is identified with the male prostitute (F 69) and an argument is assumed in which Cato ostensibly addresses him or quotes an address to him (which might suit versions giving the lover a more active role better than others). For the same distinction between *amor* and *cupido*, see Afranius, *Tog.* 23–24 R.³; for another distinction between words of similar meaning, see F 131.

AGAINST L. VETURIUS (F 72–82)

larities in sacrificial matters and lack of physical fitness. Further details about this L. Veturius cannot be ascertained (Scullard 1973, 261; Astin 1978, 82).

F 72 Festus

stata sacrificia ["sacrifices occurring at fixed times"] are those that have to happen on certain days. Cato [says] in that [speech] that he wrote about L. Veturius, on the faulty sacrifice, when he deprived him of his horse [i.e., equestrian status]: "since, so far as it was down to you, you have abandoned the rites occurring at fixed times, ceremonial ones, sacred by the threat of capital punishment."

F 73 Festus

prohibere comitia ["to prevent *comitia*"] means to vitiate a day by an illness that is commonly called "greater," otherwise for that very reason "comitial." Cato [says] in that speech that he wrote on the faulty sacrifice: "When we

67

CATO

commisso: "domi cum auspicamus, honorem me deum[2] immortalium velim habuisse. servi,[3] ancillae, si quis eorum sub centone crepuit, quod ego non sensi, nullum mihi vitium facit. si cui ibidem servo aut ancillae dormienti evenit, quod comitia prohibere solet, ne id[4] quidem mihi vitium facit."

2 me deum *Augustinus*: medium *cod.*   3 *post* servi, *non post* habuisse *distinctio in cod.*   4 id *Dacier*: is *cod.*

F 74 Prisc., *GL* II, p. 208.1–4

"Anio" etiam "Anienis"—quod antiqui secundum analogiam "Anien" nominativum proferebant. Cato contra Veturium: "aquam Anienam[1] in sacrarium inferre oportebat. non minus XV milia Anien abest."

1 Anienam *Lipsius*: anienen *vel* anienem *codd.*

F 75 Gell. *NA* 17.2.19–20

"tanta" inquit "sanctitudo fani est ut numquam quisquam violare sit ausus." "sanctitas" quoque et "sanctimonia" non minus Latine dicuntur, sed nescioqui[1] maioris dignitatis est verbum "sanctitudo," [20] sicuti M. Cato in L. Veturium "duritudinem" quam "duritiam" dicere gravius putavit: "qui illius" inquit "impudentiam norat et duritudinem."

1 nescioqui *Madvig*: nescioquid *codd., quo servato* verbo *Hertz*

Cf. Non., p. 100.17–18 M. = 143 L.

take auspices at home, I would wish to have paid honor to the immortal gods. As regards slaves, maids, if any of them has made a noise under a blanket, which I have not noticed, that does not give rise to a fault for me. If anything happens there to any sleeping slave or maid that usually prevents *comitia*, not even that gives rise to a fault for me."

F 74 Priscian

Anio [river in Italy, tributary of the Tiber], also *Anienis* [gen.]—since the ancients used *Anien* as the nominative by way of analogy. Cato [says in the speech] against Veturius: "It was necessary to bring water from the Anio into the sanctuary. The Anio [*Anien*] is not fewer than 15 miles [ca. 22.5 km] away."

F 75 Gellius, *Attic Nights*

"So great is the sanctity [*sanctitudo*] of the shrine," he [Q. Claudius Quadrigarius] says [*FRHist* 24 F 28], "that no one has ever dared to violate it." And *sanctitas* and *sanctimonia* are equally good Latin, but the word *sanctitudo* somehow has greater dignity, [20] just as M. Cato, [in the speech] against L. Veturius, thought it weightier to say *duritudo* than *duritia* ["hardness, insensibility"]: "who knew," he says, "that man's impudence and insensibility."[1]

---

[1] Solodow (1977) suggests that *duritudo* might have been chosen for rhythmical reasons, combined with a sophisticated word order, as *duritia* appears elsewhere (F 128).

F 76 Prisc., *GL* II, p. 230.15–20

excipitur "imber imbris" et ab eo composita, ut "September Septembris," "October Octobris," quod similis est numerus syllabarum tam in nominativo quam in genetivo. vetustissimi tamen genetivo quoque similem nominativum eorum proferebant. Cato de sacrificio commisso: "mense Octobri fecimus, Novembris reliquus erat."

F 77 Prisc., *GL* II, p. 377.10–13

"fitur" etiam pro "fit" dicebant. M. Cato . . . [F 65] . . . idem de Lucio Veturio: "Graeco ritu fiebantur[1] Saturnalia."

  [1] fiebantur *cod. corr.*: fiebant *codd.*

F 78 Gell. *NA* 6.22.1–4

nimis pingui homini et corpulento censores ‹constat›[1] equum adimere solitos, scilicet minus idoneum ratos esse cum tanti corporis pondere ad faciendum equitis munus. [2] non enim poena id fuit, ut quidam existimant, sed munus sine ignominia remittebatur. [3] ‹M.›[2] tamen Cato in oratione quam de sacrificio commisso scripsit obicit

  [1] *add. Holford-Strevens*   [2] *add. Holford-Strevens*

F 76 Priscian

An exception is *imber*, *imbris* ["rain"; nom., gen.], and
compounds derived from it, like *September*, *Septembris*
["September"; nom., gen.], *October*, *Octobris* ["October";
nom., gen.], since the number of syllables is the same in
the nominative as in the genitive. The very early [writers],
though, also used a nominative of those [words] like the
genitive. Cato [says in the speech] on the faulty sacrifice:
"we did it in the month of October, November [*Novembris*; nom.] was remaining."

F 77 Priscian

They also used *fitur* instead of *fit* ["it occurs, takes place";
passive instead of active form]. M. Cato . . . [F 65] . . . The
same [Cato in the speech] about Lucius Veturius: "The
Saturnalia took place [imperfect passive form] according
to Greek practice."[1]

1 The Saturnalia mirrored the Greek festival of Kronia, in
honor of Cronus, the equivalent of the Roman god Saturn (cf.
Macrob. *Sat.* 1.7.36).

F 78 Gellius, *Attic Nights*

That the censors were accustomed to take the horse [i.e.,
equestrian status] away from too fat and corpulent a person ‹is well known›, evidently, because they thought that
someone with the weight of such a huge body was less
suited to performing the duties of an equestrian. [2] For
that was not a punishment, as some think, but it was a
relief of duty without disgrace. [3] Yet ‹M.› Cato, in the
speech that he wrote on the faulty sacrifice, brings this

CATO

hanc rem criminosius, uti magis videri possit cum ignominia fuisse. [4] quod si ita accipias, id profecto existimandum est, non omnino inculpatum neque indesidem visum esse cuius corpus in tam inmodicum modum luxuriasset exuberassetque.

F 79 Plut. *Cat. Mai.* 9.6

τὸν δὲ ὑπέρπαχυν κακίζων "ποῦ δ᾽ ἄν" ἔφη "τῇ πόλει σῶμα τοιοῦτον γένοιτο χρήσιμον, οὗ τὸ μεταξὺ λαιμοῦ καὶ βουβώνων ἅπαν ὑπὸ τῆς γαστρὸς κατέχεται;"

F 80 Serv. auct. ad Verg. *Aen.* 4.121

quidam "trepidant" ab equis, qui hodieque trepidare dicuntur, appellari putant. Cato: "sedere non potest in equo trepidante."

F 81 Prisc., *GL* II, p. 509.22–24

"ico" paenultima brevi profertur in praesenti teste Capro, sed producit eam in praeterito perfecto et mutat o finalem in i: "ico ici," unde "ictus." Cato censorius de Veturio: "hostem num[1] icit?"

1 num *vel* numum *vel* numim *vel* nummi *vel* mum *vel* numun *vel* nummi *vel* numium *vel* nimium *vel* non *vel* numiicit *vel* *icit(n) *codd.*: unum (*vel* nullum) *suppl. Mommsen*

matter forward more in the style of an accusation, so that it could appear more to have been associated with disgrace. [4] If you understand it like this, one must certainly assume that a person was not looked upon as wholly free from guilt and slothfulness, if their body had spread and grown to such excessive dimensions.

F 79 Plutarch, *Life of Cato the Elder*

Railing at the very fat man, he [Cato] said: "Where can such a body be of service to the state, when every part of it between gullet and groins is in the power of the belly?"[1]

[1] If it is assumed that the fat man criticized is the individual who has the horse taken away (cf. F 78), the fragment can be attributed to this speech (cf. *Op. cet.* F 64).

F 80 Servius Danielis, *Commentary on Virgil*

Some believe that *trepidant* ["they tremble"] is derived from horses that even today are said to tremble. Cato [says]: "he cannot sit on a trembling horse."[1]

[1] As the fragment mentions a horse, it might belong to this speech about the individual deprived of equestrian status.

F 81 Priscian

ico ["I strike"] is pronounced with a short penultimate syllable in the present [tense] according to Caper [Flavius Caper, 2nd cent. AD], but it lengthens it in the perfect and changes the final *o* to *i*: *ico*, *ici*, whence *ictus* [past participle]. Cato, the ex-censor, [says in the speech] about Veturius: "Surely, he hasn't struck an enemy?"

F 82 Non., p. 149.2–3 M. = 217 L.

PLEBITATEM, ignobilitatem. Cato[1] pro Veturio:[2] "propter tenuitatem et plebitatem."

[1] C. Cotta *Meyer*   [2] pro L. Turio *Popma*

ON THE CHARACTER OF
CLAUDIUS NERO (F 83–84)

The context of the speech about Claudius Nero is uncertain; as it deals with the man's character, it is usually assumed to be linked to Cato's censorship (184 BC). The identity of this Claudius Nero is unknown; Ti. Claudius

F 83 Prisc., *GL* II, p. 228.3–5

"illi" pro "illius" Cato in Marcum Cae{ci}lium[1] [F 118]: "ecquis[2] illi modi esse vult?" idem de moribus Claudii Neronis[3] "isti" pro "istius": "pecunia mea rei publicae profuit quam isti modi uti tu es."

[1] Cae{ci}lium *Meyer*: caecilium *codd.*   [2] ecquis *vel* haec quis *vel* et quis *codd.*   [3] *eronis *vel* heronis *codd.*

F 82 Nonius Marcellus

plebitas ["plebeian status"], humble origin. Cato [says in the speech] on behalf of Veturius:[1] "because of poverty and plebeian status."

[1] The other testimonia mentioning a speech of Cato's concerning a person with that name define the speech as "about" (F 72, 77, 81) or "against" Veturius (F 74, 75). The critical nature of these fragments confirms such a characterization. The description "on behalf" then must be an error (adopting a common version of titles of Roman judicial speeches), or indicate another speech by Cato concerning a Veturius not otherwise attested (F 205 Cugusi: *Pro Veturio*), or be the result of a confusion of names in the transmission.

ON THE CHARACTER OF
CLAUDIUS NERO (F 83–84)

Nero (leg. 185, praet. 181 BC) or Ap. Claudius Nero (trib. mil., leg. 198, praet. 195, leg. 189 BC) have been suggested as potential candidates (e.g., Scullard 1973, 158–59n3, 261; Astin 1978, 81; Sblendorio Cugusi 1982, 229–30).

F 83 Priscian

illi [unusual form of gen. of pronoun *ille*, "that"] instead of *illius* [is used by] Cato [in the speech] against Marcus Caelius [F 118]: "does anyone want to be [a person] of that kind?" The same [Cato] [in the speech] on the character of Claudius Nero [uses] *isti* instead of *istius* [same declension of another demonstrative pronoun]: "my money has benefited the *res publica*, [more] than [have individuals] of that kind that you are."

F 84 Non., p. 64.19–21 M. = 88 L.

FULGURATORES. ut extispices et aruspices, ita hi fulgurum inspectores. Cato de moribus Claudi Neronis: "haruspicem, fulguratorem si quis adducat."

ON THE ALLOWANCES FOR
PURCHASING A HORSE (F 85–86)

In this speech in the Senate, Cato promoted the proposal to make more money available for public horses, presumably to increase the number of people with a public horse (on the term aes equestre, *see Gai. Inst. 4.27; Paul. Fest., p. 71.18 L.). This discussion is often referred to Cato's censorship (184 BC), because a review of the equestrian*

F 85–86 Prisc., *GL* II, pp. 318.20–19.4

in "-aes" Latinum unum masculinum "hic praes huius praedis" et unum neutrum "hoc aes huius aeris," cuius plurales obliqui in raro sunt usu, "aera aerum aeribus." Cato in oratione, qua in senatu suasit, ut plura aera eques-

F 84 Nonius Marcellus

fulguratores ["interpreters of lightnings"]. Like observers of entrails and observers of prodigies, so these are inspectors of lightnings. Cato [says in the speech] on the character of Claudius Nero: "if anyone should adduce an observer of prodigies, an interpreter of lightnings."

ON THE ALLOWANCES FOR PURCHASING A HORSE (F 85–86)

property qualification is part of the censors' duties (cf. T 33; F 69, 72–82; e.g., Scullard 1973, 160, 262; Astin 1978, 82). Priscian's description, however, if taken literally, points to a speech in support of someone else's proposal; such a speech is unlikely to date to Cato's censorship (Kienast 1979, 75–76).

F 85–86 Priscian

For words ending in *-aes* there is in Latin one masculine form (*hic*) *praes*, (*huius*) *praedis* ["this guarantor"; nom., gen. sg.] and one neuter form (*hoc*) *aes*, (*huius*) *aeris* ["this bronze / money"; nom., gen. sg.], of which the oblique cases in the plural are used rarely, *aera, aerum, aeribus* [acc., gen., dat. / abl. pl.]. Cato [says] in the speech by which he advised in the Senate that there should be more allowances for purchasing horses: "Now I believe that there should be arranged the provision of no fewer than two thousand and two hundred allowances for purchasing

tria fierent: "nunc ergo arbitror oportere institui,[1] quin minus[2] duobus milibus ducentis[3] sit aerum equestrium." in eodem:[4] "de aeribus equestribus de duobus milibus actum."[5]

[1] institui *Lipsius*: restitui *codd.*   [2] quin minus *Hertz*: qui minus *vel* quo minus *codd.*: ne quo minus *Lipsius*: quo ne minus *Zumpt*   [3] duobus milibus ducentis *vel* milibus actum ducenti *codd.*   [4] Cato in eodem (*sc. libro*) *Meyer*   eadem *Krehl*   'pertinet fortasse de aeribus equestribus *ad titulum orationis' Krehl*   [5] actum *vel* auctum *codd.*

Cf. Charis., *GL* I, pp. 120.33–21.5 = pp. 154.28–55.3 B.: aeribus Lucretius II [2.637], "pulsabant aeribus aera," cum in his nominibus hoc quoque nomen esse videatur, quae singulari quidem numero per omnes casus eunt, plurali non nisi per nominativum et accusativum et vocativum tantum, ut iura maria rura aera: Cato, ut plura aera equestria fia<n >t,[1] "aeribus equestribus de duobus milibus a CC";[2] Paul. *Fest.*, p. 25.11 L.: AERIBUS pluraliter ab aere, id est aeramento, Cato dixit.

[1] fia<n >t *ed. princ.*: fiat *cod.*   [2] milibus ac ducentis *Lindemann*

ON THE BUILDING OF A BASILICA
(F 87)

When censor (184 BC), Cato had a basilica, named after him (Basilica Porcia), built, the first structure of this kind, in Rome (Liv. 39.44.7 [T 33]; [Aurel. Vict.] Vir. ill. 47.5

horses." In the same [text]:[1] "as for the allowances for purchasing horses arrangements having been made concerning two thousand."

[1] The Latin word refers back to an implied *liber* ("work, book"; masc.) although the text has been designated as an *oratio* ("speech"; fem.) in what immediately precedes (cf. F 39).

Cf. Charisius: *aeribus* [abl. pl.] [is used by] Lucretius in [Book] 2 [2.637], "they struck bronze with bronzes," though this noun too seems to be among those nouns that in the singular at any rate go through all cases, in the plural only through the nominative, accusative, and vocative, like *iura* ["laws"], *maria* ["seas"], *rura* ["lands"], *aera* ["bronzes / monies"]: Cato [says, advising] that there should be more allowances for purchasing a horse: "as for the allowances for purchasing a horse, concerning two thousand and 200 [?]"; Paul the Deacon, *Epitome of Festus*: *aeribus* [abl. pl.] in the plural from *aere* [abl. sg.], that is a strip of bronze, was said by Cato.

ON THE BUILDING OF A BASILICA
(F 87)

[T 82]; Plut. Cat. Mai. 19.3; Cat. Min. 5.1). He seems to have presented this building project in a speech, perhaps against opposition (Astin 1978, 84).

CATO

F 87 Prisc., *GL* II, p. 433.1–4

a vilico etiam "vilico" et "vilicor" dicebant antiqui. Cato in oratione, quae inscribitur uti basilica aedificetur: "antequam is vilicare coepit."

ON THE INDIGETES (F 88)

The indication of the topic of this speech provided by the text of the single source is usually interpreted as di indigetes *("native gods"). On that basis, since, at least later in the Roman Republic, the censors also looked after temples, it is often assumed that Cato may have given a speech on the shrines of the* di indigetes *during his censorship (184 BC). Scholz (1989) points out that the description of the topic could then only be a shorthand and suggests instead*

F 88 Fest., p. 456.18–25 L.

‹SEQUESTER› is dicitur, qui inter aliquos c . . . inter eos convenerit . . . quid, ut ei reddat, qui id . . . stiterit.[1] Cato in ea ora‹tione quam habuit› . . . de Indigitibus: "sinunt . . . ut bona rapiant aut . . . sequestro dent."[2]

[1] ‹qui certant, medius, ut› inter eos convenerit ‹ita tenet depositum ali›quid ut ei reddat cui id ‹deberi iure sibi con›stiterit *Ursinus (fere)*   [2] sequestro dent *Augustinus*: seques prodent *cod.*

F 87 Priscian

Derived from *vilicus* ["overseer"] the ancients also used *vilico* and *vilicor* ["to act as an overseer"; active and deponent form of verb]. Cato [says] in the speech that is entitled "that a basilica should be built": "before that man began to act as an overseer."

ON THE INDIGETES (F 88)

that the description (de Indigitibus) *refers to a people in the Iberian peninsula called Indigetes, whom Cato confronted when he was assigned the province of Hither Iberia (195 BC): this interpretation would give a* terminus post quem *for the speech, but a precise date and context cannot be determined. As the single remaining fragment is lacunose, its meaning is uncertain; therefore, it does not provide evidence for establishing further details.*

F 88 Festus

‹*sequester*› ["depositary, trustee, intermediary"] is a term for a person who between some . . . between them something should be agreed . . . so that he gives it back to him, who has . . . that. Cato in that spee‹ch that he delivered› . . . on the Indigetes: "they allow . . . that they snatch away the property or . . . they give to a trustee."

CATO

ON FEEDING A YOUNG EWE LAMB
(F 89–92)

The date and the context of this speech are uncertain. Since
the censors were in charge of agricultural matters and the

F 89 Prisc., *GL* II, p. 257.17–18

Cato Censorius de agna musta pascenda: musta agna pro
"nova" dixit.

Cf. Non., p. 136.4–5 M. = 197 L.

F 90 Prisc., *GL* II, p. 85.4–5

"citra citerior"—vetustissimi tamen "citer" protulisse in-
veniuntur. Cato de agna pascenda: "citer ager alligatus ad
sacra erit."

Cf. Prisc., *GL* III, p. 40.29–31.

F 91 Fest., p. 280.13–14 L.

PASTALES⟩ . . . ⟨in⟩scienter Cato dixit in ea ⟨quam scrib-
sit⟩ . . . ⟨pa⟩scalis[1] ovis vetuit. . . .

    [1] ⟨pascuales oves pastales in⟩scienter Cato dixit in ea ⟨quam
scribsit de musta agna: "ali pa⟩scalis" *Mueller*   scalis (c *in-
cert.*) *cod. teste Loewio*: pastales *Epit.*

Cf. Paul. *Fest.*, p. 281.3 L.: PASTALES oves Cato posuit pro pascuales.

ON FEEDING A YOUNG EWE LAMB
(F 89–92)

care of temples, it has been suggested that the intervention might belong to Cato's censorship (184 BC).

F 89 Priscian

Cato, the ex-censor,[1] [in the speech] on feeding a young ewe lamb: he said *musta agna* ["young ewe lamb"] instead of "new."

> [1] Since Cato is frequently called "ex-censor" (*Censorius*) for identification, this description does not provide any information on the potential date of this speech (i.e., that it should be dated to the period after Cato's censorship).

F 90 Priscian

citra, citerior ["on the near side"; adv. positive, adj. comparative]—yet the very early [writers] are found to have used *citer* ["on the near side"; adj. positive]. Cato [says in the speech] on feeding a ewe lamb: "the land on the near side will have been dedicated for religious use."

F 91 Festus

pastales > ["pasturing"; pl.] . . . out of <ig>norance Cato said in that [speech] <that he wrote> . . . he forbade <pa>sturing [<pa>*scalis*] sheep.[1] . . .

> [1] Since the extract from Cato refers to sheep, it has conjecturally been attributed to this speech, although the identification of the work from which it comes has been lost.

Cf. Paul the Deacon, *Epitome of Festus*: Cato put *pastales oves* ["pasturing sheep"] instead of *pascuales*.

F 92 Fest., p. 142.4–8 L.

MAGNI‹FICIUS pro magnificentius usurp›avit[1] Cato in ea,
quam ‹scribsit de pascenda musta a›gna:[2] "quis homo . . .
l pulchrius purgat ‹aut magnificius." . . .›[3]

[1] *suppl. Ursinus (ex Epit.)*
[2] *suppl. Mueller*   [3] *suppl. Ursinus (ex Epit.)*

Cf. Paul. *Fest.*, p. 143.2–3 L.

ON CLOTHING AND VEHICLES (F 93)

*This speech relates to Cato's activities as censor (184 BC),
when he had the value of items such as clothing and vehicles set at several times their worth and thus increased
the tax due on them (cf. Liv. 39.44.2–3 [T 33]; Plut. Cat.
mai. 18.2–3; Nep. Cat. 2.3 [T 26]). Because of the frag-*

F 93 Prisc., *GL* II, p. 226.14–23

sed Plautus in Vidularia: "neutri reddibo" dixit dativum,
cuius genetivus "neutrius" sine dubio est, quamvis vetustissimi soleant omnium in -ius terminantium genetivum et
in -i dativum etiam in -i genetivum et in -o dativum in
genere masculino et neutro, in feminino vero secundum
primam declinationem in -ae diphthongum proferre. M.
Cato in censura de vestitu et vehiculis: "nam periniurium
siet, cum mihi ob eos mores, quos prius habui, honos de-

F 92 Festus

magni‹ficius ["more magnificently"; alternative form of comparative adv.; cf. F 180, 242] was used instead of *magnificentius›* by Cato in that [speech] that ‹he wrote on feeding a young ewe l›amb:[1] "which person . . . purifies more beautifully ‹or more magnificently" . . .›

[1] The attribution of this passage to this speech rests on the conjectural restoration of the lacunose source text identifying the work of Cato referred to.

ON CLOTHING AND VEHICLES (F 93)

ment's content, it has been assumed that it might be one of the first speeches Cato delivered after assuming the office of censor (e.g., Scullard 1973, 260; Sblendorio Cugusi 1982, 218–19).

F 93 Priscian

But Plautus, in *Vidularia* [Plaut. *Vid.* F V(I).2 Lindsay = V.2 Monda]: "I will return this to neither of them [*neutri*]," used *neutri* as a dative, whose genitive doubtless is *neutrius*, even though the very early [writers] are accustomed, for all words ending in *-ius* in the genitive and in *-i* in the dative, also to put forth a genitive ending in *-i* and a dative ending in *-o* in the masculine and neuter gender, but in the feminine, according to the first declension, a diphthong in *-ae*. M. Cato, during his censorship, [said in the speech] on clothing and vehicles: "For it would be a great injustice when an honor should be given to me on account

tur, ubi datus est, tum uti eos mutem atque alii modi sim,"
pro "alius modi."

Cf. Prisc., *GL* II, p. 266.16–23; *GL* III, p. 8.1–8.

ON STATUES (F 94–95)

*These two passages point to further speeches against too
much luxury and display (potentially unjustified), though
it is uncertain whether these pieces refer to the same oration, as the focus is described differently in the source texts*

F 94 Fest., p. 364.10–14 L.

REDEMPTITAVERE item, ut clamitavere, Cato idem in ea,
qua egit de signis et tabulis: "honorem † temptitavere †,"[1]
ait, "libere facta[2] benefactis non redemptitavere."

   [1] emptitavere *Ursinus*: redemptitavere *alii*
   [2] l. efacta *cod.*: male facta *Ursinus*: bene facta *alii*

F 95 Plin. *HN* 34.31

exstant Catonis in censura vociferationes mulieribus statuas Romanis[1] in provinciis poni; nec tamen potuit inhi-
bere, quo minus Romae quoque ponerentur, sicuti Corne-
liae Gracchorum matri, quae fuit Africani prioris filia.

   [1] statuas romanis *vel* romanis statuas *codd.*

of those character traits that I possessed previously, so that, once it has been given, I should then change those and adopt another [*alii*] way of life," instead of "another [*alius*] way of life" [different forms of gen. of *alius*; for the concept, see Sall. *Iug.* 85.1–2, 85.8–9].

ON STATUES (F 94–95)

(Scullard 1973, 260; Astin 1978, 83). The second item (F 95) assumes several interventions and situates them in Cato's censorship (184 BC).

F 94 Festus

redemptitavere ["they made up for repeatedly"] likewise, just as *clamitavere* ["they shouted repeatedly"; frequentative forms]. The same Cato says in that [speech] in which he argued about statues and paintings: "They made up for / bought [?] honor repeatedly; they did not make up repeatedly for bad deeds by good deeds."

F 95 Pliny the Elder, *Natural History*

There are extant tirades made by Cato during his censorship, against erecting statues to women in Roman provinces. Yet all the same he could not prevent that at Rome too some were erected, for instance, for Cornelia, the mother of the Gracchi [Ti. Sempronius Gracchus (*ORF*[4] 34) + C. Sempronius Gracchus (*ORF*[4] 48)], who was the daughter of Africanus the elder [P. Cornelius Scipio Africanus maior (*ORF*[4] 4)].

AGAINST LEPIDUS (F 96)

Context and content of this speech are uncertain (Scullard 1973, 260–61). The Lepidus against whom this speech is directed could perhaps be M. Aemilius Lepidus (cos. 187,

F 96 Fronto, *De feriis Alsiensibus* 2 (pp. 226.20–27.1 van den Hout)

[FRONTO:] Catonem quoque in oratione adversus Lepidum verbum[1] cantari solitum commemorasse, cum ait: "statuas positas Ochae atque Dionysodoro[2] effeminatis, qui[3] magiras[4] facerent."

    [1] <id> verbum *Mommsen*   [2] Dionysidoro *Mai*
    [3] qui *cod. secundum ed. Maii*: ut *incertum cod. auctore* Haulero   [4] magirias *Ellis*

ON SPOILS (F 97)

Cato seems to have argued against the increasing practice of individuals to claim spoils from the enemy and display them in their homes (for this practice, see Liv. 10.7.9,

F 97 Serv. auct. ad Verg. *Aen.* 4.244

"lumina morte resignat": . . . . alii tradunt resignare vetuste ita dictum, ut nos adsignare dicimus pro damno, ut est apud Catonem in Lucium Furium de aqua [F 103]: "quod attinet ad salinatores aerarios cui cura vectigalium resignat,"[1] et idem in oratione ne spolia figantur[2] nisi de

    [1] resignat *vel* resignantur *vel* resignatur *codd.*
    [2] figantur *Thilo*: vigantur *vel* figerent *codd.*: figerentur *Festus*

AGAINST LEPIDUS (F 96)

175, censor 179 BC) or his son M. Aemilius Lepidus (trib. mil. 190 BC).

F 96 Fronto, *Correspondence*

[FRONTO:] that Cato too recalled in the speech against Lepidus a phrase that was commonly repeated, when he says: "that statues were put up for the effeminate Ochas and Dionysodorus, who played the role of kitchen maids."[1]

[1] For a discussion of the meaning of the fragment, see van den Hout 1988, *ad loc.*

ON SPOILS (F 97)

23.23.6; Plin. HN 35.7; for Cato's comments on booty see also F 98, 224–26).

F 97 Servius Danielis, *Commentary on Virgil*

"he [Mercury] unseals [*resignat*] the eyes from death": . . . Others transmit that "to unseal" [*resignare*] is used in ancient style so, as we say "to reckon" [*adsignare*] as a loss, as is found in Cato [in the speech] against Lucius Furius on water [F 103]: "as regards the operators of salt works for the treasury, he who is in charge of taxes enters [money] as a debt," and the same [Cato] [says] in the speech argu-

hoste capta: "sed tum ubi † ludi misi[3] sunt revertantur[4] resignatis vectigalibus."

[3] ludi misi *vel* indiuisi *codd.*: ii dimissi *ed. Petri Danielis*: ludos dimissi *F. Schoellius*   [4] revertentur *Jordan*

Cf. Fest., p. 352.4–8 L.: RESIGNARE antiqui pro rescribere ponebant, ut adhuc subsignare dicimus pro subscribere. Cato de spoliis, ne figerentur, nisi quae de ho<ste capta essent: "sed tum ubi ii demissi sunt,> rev<ertantur resignatis vectigalibus.">[1]

[1] *suppl. Scaliger*

ON BOOTY (F 98)

Cato apparently delivered another speech on military booty, arguing that any booty captured should be given over to public use and not be displayed at home (Astin

F 98 Prisc., *GL* II, pp. 367.14–68.3

genetivus fit addita ablativo singulari "rum": ab hac re harum rerum, a die dierum; qui tamen in aliis fere omnibus usu apud plerosque deficit. . . . Cato Censorius in oratione, quam scripsit, uti praeda in publicum referatur: "miror audere atque religione[1] non tenere<i>[2] statuas deo-

[1] religione *vel* religionem *vel* relegionem *codd.*
[2] tenere<i> *Hertz*: tenere *codd.*

ing that spoils should not be put up unless taken from
the enemy: "but then, when the games [?] have been adjourned [?],[1] let them return with taxes entered as a debt."[2]

[1] It is uncertain how the corrupt transmission of this clause
(different in the Festus passage) should be restored.

[2] The explanation for this expression is slightly different in the
adduced Festus passage; in any case it seems to refer to the need
to make some sort of official payment (see also Sblendorio Cugusi
1982, 247–48).

Cf. Festus: The ancients put *resignare* ["to enter money as a debt,
debit against one's account in favor of someone else"] instead of
rescribere ["to pay back money in writing, by transferring it to the
creditor's account"], as we still say *subsignare* ["to write below"]
instead of *subscribere*. Cato [says in the speech] on spoils, arguing
that they should not be put up unless any had been taken from
the enemy: "but then, when these have been sent down, let them
return with taxes entered as a debt."

ON BOOTY (F 98)

*1978, 86; for Cato's comments on booty, see also F 97,
224–26).*

F 98 Priscian

The genitive is created by adding *-rum* to the ablative
singular: from *hac re* ["this thing"; abl.] *harum rerum* [gen.
pl.], from *die* ["day"; abl.] *dierum* [gen. pl.]; that, however,
in almost all other [words] has died out in usage among
most people. . . . Cato, the ex-censor, [says] in the speech
that he wrote, arguing that booty should be given over to
public use: "I am amazed that they dare—and are not
constrained by religious scruples—to set up at home stat-

rum, exempla earum facierum, signa domi pro supellectile statuere."

AGAINST L. FURIUS ON WATER
(F 99–105)

The identity of this L. Furius is uncertain (sometimes identified with L. Furius Purpurio, cos. 196 BC). Cato seems to have charged Furius because he had diverted public water for private use (F 103, 104); responsibility for water supply rested with the censors (for rules on the use of public water see Frontin. Aq. 94). Cato appears to have raised charges or taken action against others for similar reasons (Liv. 39.44.4 [T 33]; Plut. Cat. Mai. 19.1). Chari-

F 99 Charis., *GL* I, p. 126.22–24 = p. 160.30–33 B.

domi suae Varro de sermone Latino libro V. nec enim potest adverbium dici cui suae pronomen adest. Cato de multa contra L. Furium: "domi meae saepe fuit," et est genetivus.

F 100 Charis., *GL* I, p. 208.19–20 = p. 270.11–12 B.

necessario M. Cato in L. Furium de multa: "necessario faciendum fuit" . . .

ues of the gods, representations of their looks [*facie-rum*], and images in place of household furniture."

AGAINST L. FURIUS ON WATER
(F 99–105)

sius gives the topic of a speech against L. Furius as "penalty" (F 99, 100, 101, 102) and identifies the reason as expensive purchases (F 102); since the fragment quoted in this context refers to water, all these pieces might come from the same speech and indicate that a penalty was imposed for illegal use of water (Scullard 1973, 161, 262; Astin 1978, 84).

F 99 Charisius

domi suae [is used] by Varro [in his work] on Latin speech in Book 5 [F 62 Goetz / Schoell]. Nor in truth can [a word] be called an adverb [*domi*: "at home / in one's house"] to which the pronoun *suae* ["his / her / their"] is attached. Cato [says in the speech] on the penalty against L. Furius: "he was often in my house," and it [i.e., *meae*] is a genitive.

F 100 Charisius

necessario ["necessarily"]: M. Cato [uses it in the speech] against L. Furius on the penalty: "necessarily it had to be done" . . .

CATO

F 101 Charis., *GL* I, pp. 211.32–12.2 = p. 274.12–16 B.

prorsum . . . , M. Cato in L. Furium de multa: "prorsum quodcumque iubebat fecisse neque quemquam observavisse."

F 102 Charis., *GL* I, p. 216.10–12 = p. 279.20–23 B.

quanti, cum interrogamus nec emimus; quanto,[1] cum emptam rem quaerimus. atqui Cato in L. {in}[2] Furium de multa de caro emptis: "o quanti ille agros" inquit "emit, qua aquam duceret" . . .

[1] quanti interrogamus. neque minus quanto *Cauchii ex deperdito cod. excerpta*
[2] in L. *Cauchii ex deperdito cod. excerpta*: in I in *cod.*

F 103 Serv. auct. ad Verg. *Aen.* 4.244

Cf. F 97.

F 104 Fest., p. 516.24–29 L.

VINDICIAE appellantur res eae, de quibus controversia est: quod potius dicitur ius quia fit inter eos qui contendunt. {M.}[1] Cato in ea quam scribsit[2] L. Furio de aqua:[3] ". . . s praetores secundum populum vindicias dicunt."

[1] M. *habent vel om. codd.*   [2] scribsit *vel* scribit *vel* scripsit *codd.*   [3] L. Furio de aqua *vel* de aqua L. Furio *codd.*: in L. Furium de aqua *Mueller*

F 101 Charisius

prorsum ["straight ahead, directly, absolutely"] . . . , M. Cato [uses it in the speech] against L. Furius on the penalty: "that they had done directly whatever he ordered and that nobody had observed it."

F 102 Charisius

quanti ["how much"], when we ask and do not buy [gen. of price]; *quanto* ["how much"], when we ask about an item that was bought [abl. of price]. And yet Cato says [in the speech] against L. {against} Furius on the penalty for items bought at a high price: "oh, for how much [gen.] has that man bought the fields, from where to draw water" . . .

F 103 Servius Danielis, *Commentary on Virgil*

Cf. F 97.

F 104 Festus

vindiciae ["interim possession of disputed property granted by the praetor" or "items in dispute"] is the term for those things about which there is controversy: that is rather called *ius* ["legal procedure"] because it occurs among those who contend in a lawsuit. {M.} Cato in that [speech] that he wrote against L. Furius on water: ". . . [?] the praetors assign interim possession in accordance with the People."

F 105 Gell. *NA* 10.24.10

sed ut plerique "diepristini," ita M. Cato in oratione contra
Furium "dieproximi" dixit; . . .

Cf. Non., p. 153.9–10 = 224 L.: PROXUMI, id est proxumo. Cato
contra Furium "die proxumi hoc" dicit; . . .

AGAINST OPPIUS (F 106)

*The identity of this Oppius is uncertain. He seems to be
criticized for not fulfilling obligations, i.e., for not supply-
ing as much wine (perhaps for public sacrifices) as he was
required to according to the contract entered. Since over-*

F 106 Fest., p. 312.14–21 L.

QUADRANTA⟨L⟩[1] vocabant antiqui, quam ex Graeco am-
phoram dicunt,[2] quod vas pedis quadrati octo et XL capit
sextarios. . . . et Cato contra Oppium: "vinum redemisti,
praedia pro vini quadrantalibus sexaginta in † pulli †[3] dedisti, vinum non dedisti."

[1] quadranta *cod., Epit.*   [2] dicunt *edd.*: dicant *cod.*
[3] publicum *Ursinus*

F 105 Gellius, *Attic Nights*

But just as very many people [said] *diepristini* ["on the previous day"; instead of *die pristino*, see Gell. *NA* 10.24.8], so M. Cato, in the oration against Furius, said *dieproximi* ["on the following day"; instead of *die proximo*] . . .

Cf. Nonius Marcellus: *proxumi*, that is *proxumo*. Cato says [in the speech] against Furius "on this following day"; . . .

AGAINST OPPIUS (F 106)

sight of such matters was among the duties of censors, this could be one of Cato's censorial speeches (Scullard 1973, 162, 263; Astin 1978, 85).

F 106 Festus

The ancients called *quadranta⟨l⟩* [unit of liquid measure, volume of a cubic Roman foot, ca. 26 liters] what they refer to as *amphora* [equal to 2 *ternae* or 48 *sextarii*] [taken] from the Greek, since the container of a cubic foot holds 48 *sextarii*. . . . And Cato [says in the speech] against Oppius: "You have contracted for wine, you have given pledges for sixty *quadrantal* of wine to the public [?], you have not given wine."

ON THE OLIVE GROVE (F 107–7A)

F 107 Fest., p. 280.26–27 L.

"PULCHRALIBUS atque † cupidus †"[1] idem in ea, quae est
de fundo oleario.

  [1] cupidiis *Ursinus*: cupediis *Dacier*

F 107A Fest., p. 280.15–18 L.

. . . s appellat in ea ora‹tione, quae est de fundo olea›rio:[1]
"Tarenti, plus C. . . . uam ignaro[2] Tarentino . . .

  [1] *suppl. Lindsay*　　　[2] in agro *Scaliger*

ON THE OLIVE GROVE (F 107–7A)

If in this speech Cato again referred to luxury items, it might also date to his censorship, but other contexts are equally possible.

F 107 Festus

"for / with dainties and delicacies [?]" [*pulchralibus atque † cupidus †*][1] the same [Cato said] in that [speech] that there is on the olive grove.

[1] The use of the dative / ablative for the lemma and its combination with another word suggest that this expression is a quotation and the nouns were used in this case by Cato. The form and the meaning of the second noun can only be conjectured (cf. Paul. *Fest.*, p. 42.9–10 L.).

F 107A Festus

. . . he calls in that spee⟨ch that there is on the olive gro⟩ve:[1] "of / at Tarentum [mod. Taranto], more . . . to an ignorant Tarentian . . .

[1] If the title of the speech indicating the origin of the fragment is restored correctly, this fragment might come from Cato's speech on the olive grove (doubts in Sblendorio Cugusi 1982, 506–7). His authorship is not directly attested in the lacunose text, but, beyond a short gap on either side, this quotation is preceded and followed by several quotations from other Catonian speeches. Because of the lacuna, just before the identification of the source of the quotation it is unclear which lemma it is meant to illustrate.

ON LETORIUS (?) (F 108)

The name of the person who is the object of this speech as well as the oration's content and context are uncertain. A possible connection with the plebeian aedile of 202 BC, L.

F 108 Non., p. 137.21–23 M. = 200 L.

MUSIMONES, asini, muli aut equi breves. . . . Cato de † Letorio:[1] "asinum aut musimonem aut arietem."

[1] L. Vetorio *Jordan*: L. Turio *Maiansius*

AGAINST ANNIUS (F 109)

The identity of Annius and the precise meaning of the single fragment are uncertain (for suggestions, see, e.g., Scullard 1973, 264–65). The speech is usually assigned to Cato's censorship (184 BC); Astin (1978, 82n17) tenta-

F 109 Fest., p. 394.11–24 L.

sed per se super significat quidem supra, ut cum dicimus: super illum cedit. verum ponitur etiam pro de, Graeca consuetudine, ut illi dicunt ὑπέρ. . . . Cato contra Annium: "nemo antea fecit super tali re cum hoc magistratu utique rem."[1]

[1] utique rem *cod.*: ut quaererem *Mommsen*

ON LETORIUS (?) (F 108)

Laetorius (MRR 1:316; cf. F 217–18), is sometimes considered (Scullard 1973, 257; Kienast 1979, 41).

F 108 Nonius Marcellus

musimones ["mouflons" (cf. Plin. *HN* 8.199; Strab. 5.2.7)], asses, mules, or short horses. . . . Cato [says in the speech] on Letorius [?]: "an ass, or a mouflon, or a ram [acc.]."

AGAINST ANNIUS (F 109)

tively considers that the speech could be directed against the consul of 153 BC (T. Annius Luscus) and be connected with M. Claudius Marcellus' election to a third consulship for 152 BC (cf. F 185–86).

F 109 Festus

But on its own *super* means in fact *supra* ["on top of, above"], as when we say: "in a position above him he withdraws." But it is also used instead of *de* ["about"], according to Greek custom, as they say *hyper*. . . . Cato [says in the speech] against Annius: "nobody previously has done anything about [*super*] such a matter with this magistrate, so that I inquired [?]."[1]

[1] The final part of the translation of the fragment is tentatively based on a conjecture by Mommsen.

AGAINST Q. SULPICIUS (F 110)

This could be another of Cato's censorial speeches (184 BC), connected with the opponent's removal from their order; yet such a comment could also be made in a non-censorial speech in a political or judicial confrontation.

F 110 Fest., p. 168.15–23 L.

NASSITERNA est genus vasi aquari ansati et patentis, quale est quo equi perfundi solent. . . . et Cato in ea oratione, quam composuit in Q. Sulpicium: "quotiens vidi trulleos,[1] nassiternas pertusos,[2] aqualis matellas sine ansis."

[1] trulleos (*vel* truleos *vel* trulios) *Scaliger*: truilos *cod.*
[2] pertusos *Augustinus*: perfusos *cod.*

ON THE TRIBUNE OF THE PEOPLE
M. CAELIUS (F 111–20)

The context of this speech is a conflict with a Tribune of the People called M. Caelius, whom Cato presents as an idler and empty talker. The interpretation of the description of the situation is uncertain, and the wording of the title as given in the sources is unusual (Gellius: F 111; Festus: F 113, 119), so that various contexts and changes to the text have been suggested (e.g., Fraccaro [1910c] 1956, 237–47; Janzer 1937, 45–46; Till 1937, 36–40; Scullard 1973, 161, 262–63; Astin 1978, 86; Kienast 1979, 79;

AGAINST Q. SULPICIUS (F 110)

The fragment suggests criticism of someone's luxury by comparison with a frugal life or of someone's slovenliness (for the terms see Cato, Agr. 10.2, 11.3). The identity of Q. Sulpicius is uncertain (Scullard 1973, 265; Astin 1978, 82).

F 110 Festus

nassiterna ["pot"] is a kind of container for water with handles and large, such as that with which horses are usually washed down. . . . And Cato [says] in that speech that he composed against Q. Sulpicius: "whenever I saw washbasins, perforated pots, vessels for water without handles."

ON THE TRIBUNE OF THE PEOPLE
M. CAELIUS (F 111–20)

Sblendorio Cugusi 1982, 259). If the transmitted versions are kept, one has to assume that the Tribune intended to intervene against Cato, apparently by requesting an account of his activities, and that these plans were answered by Cato with a counterattack, in which he criticized and ridiculed the opponent and might have mentioned his own public service (Till 1953, 440–43). If the speech belongs to Cato's censorship, as has been suggested, M. Caelius would have been a Tribune of the People in 184 BC (MRR 1:375).

F 111 Gell. *NA* 1.15.8–9

cumprimis autem M. Cato atrocissimus huiusce vitii in-
sectator est. [9] namque in oratione quae inscripta est si
se Caelius[1] tribunus plebis appellasset: "numquam" inquit
"tacet, quem morbus tenet loquendi tamquam veterno-
sum bibendi[2] atque dormiendi. quod si non conveniatis
cum convocari iubet, ita cupidus orationis conducat qui
auscultet.[3] itaque auditis, non auscultatis, tamquam phar-
macopolam.[4] nam eius verba audiuntur, verum se[5] nemo
committit si aeger est."

[1] si se Caelius *vel* si se caelus *vel* sic selius *vel* si Secelium
codd.: si quis Caelius *Janzer (1937, 46)*   [2] bibendi *codd. rec*:
vivendi *codd.*   [3] auscultet *codd.*: auscultent *Lambecius*
      [4] pharmacopolam *codd. rec.*: armacopolam *vel* arma copulam
vel armacapolam *codd.*   [5] se *codd.*: se ‹ei› *Hertz*

F 112 Gell. *NA* 1.15.10

idem Cato in eadem oratione, eidem M. Caelio tribuno
plebi vilitatem obprobrans non loquendi tantum verum
etiam tacendi: "frusto" inquit "panis conduci potest vel uti
taceat vel uti loquatur."

F 111 Gellius, *Attic Nights*

But M. Cato in particular is an extremely fierce persecutor of this fault [i.e., empty loquacity]. [9] For in the speech that is entitled "if Caelius, Tribune of the People, should have challenged him" he says: "That person is never silent who is afflicted by the disease of talking, as someone suffering from drowsiness by that of drinking and sleeping. For if you [pl.]¹ should not come together when he orders [you] to be assembled, he, so eager for a speech, may hire someone who listens. And so you hear him, but you do not listen, just as if he were a seller of drugs.² For that man's words are heard, but no one entrusts themselves [to him] if they are sick."

¹ Probably Roman citizens, whom a Tribune of the People could call to a meeting.   ² The choice of a Greek word for a kind of apothecary (*pharmacopola*) might be linked to Cato's mistrust of Greek doctors, as expressed elsewhere (esp. *Op. cet.* F 5; for the term's negative connotations, see Hor. *Sat.* 1.2.1–3).

F 112 Gellius, *Attic Nights*

The same Cato, in the same speech [cf. F 111], upbraiding the same M. Caelius, a Tribune of the People, for the cheapness not only of his speech but also of his silence, says: "For a crust of bread he can be hired, either to be silent or to speak."

F 113 Fest., p. 466.19–22 L.

‹SPA›TIATOREM, erratorem Cato in M.[1] Caelium si se appellavisset: "in coloniam, me‹he›rcules, scribere nolim, si trium virum sim, spatiatorem atque fescenninum."

[1] M. *Augustinus*: an *cod.*

Cf. Paul. *Fest.*, p. 467.7 L.: SPATIATOREM pro erratorem Cato posuit.

F 114–15 Macrob. *Sat.* 3.14.9–10

sic nimirum M. Cato senatorem non ignobilem Cae{ci}-lium[1] spatiatorem et Fescenninum vocat eumque staticulos dare his verbis ait: "descendit de cantherio, inde staticulos dare, ridicularia fundere." et alibi in eundem: "praeterea cantat ubi collibuit, interdum Graecos versus agit, iocos dicit, voces demutat, staticulos dat." [10] haec Cato, cui, ut videtis, etiam cantare non serii hominis videtur: . . .

[1] Cae{ci}lium *Eyssenhardt*: caecilium *codd.*

Cf. Ioannes Saresberiensis, *Policraticus* 8.12.18 (*PL* 199, col. 758C): Catoni quoque visum est bene cantare non serii hominis esse. unde nimirum Marcum senatorem non ignobilem Cecilium spaciatorem et Fescenninum vocat, eumque staticulos dare his verbis ait: "descendit de canterio; inde staticulos dare, ridicularia fundere"; et alibi: "praeterea cantat ubi collibuit, interdum Grecos versus agit, iocos dicit, voces demictat, staticulos dat."

F 113 Festus

⟨*spa*⟩*tiator* ["an idle walker"], a wanderer: Cato [uses it in the speech] against M. Caelius, if he should have challenged him: "I would not want to enroll for a colony, by ⟨He⟩rcules, if I should be one of the triumvirs, an idle walker and lampooner" [cf. F 114–15].

F 114–15 Macrobius, *Saturnalia*

So, without doubt, M. Cato calls the not ignoble senator[1] Cae{ci}lius an idle walker and lampooner [cf. F 113], and he says, with these words, that he strikes poses: "He dismounts from his nag, then strikes poses, spouts jokes." And elsewhere [he says] against the same individual: "Furthermore, he sings when it strikes his fancy, sometimes declaims Greek verses, tells jokes, talks in different voices, strikes poses." [10] Thus Cato, to whom, as you can see, even singing does not seem to be an activity of a serious person: . . .

Cf. John of Salisbury: It seemed also to Cato that singing well was not appropriate for a serious person. For that reason, without doubt, he calls the not ignoble senator Marcus Caecilius an idle walker and lampooner, and he says, with these words, that he strikes poses: "He dismounts from his nag, then strikes poses, spouts jokes." And elsewhere [he says]: "Furthermore, he sings when it strikes his fancy, sometimes declaims Greek verses, tells jokes, talks in different voices, strikes poses."

1 Probably not meant literally and rather a designation of M. Caelius' official position as a Tribune of the People.

F 116 Paul. *Fest.*, p. 52.17–21 L.

CITERIA appellabatur effigies quaedam arguta et loquax ridiculi gratia, quae in pompa vehi solita sit. Cato in Marcum Cae{ci}lium:[1] "quid ego cum illo dissertem amplius, quem ego denique credo in pompa vectitatum iri[2] ludis pro citeria atque cum spectatoribus sermocinaturum?"

[1] Cae{ci}lium *edd.*: caecilium *codd.*   [2] iri *Scaliger*: ire *codd.*

F 117 Fest., pp. 266.29–68.1 L.

PRO SCAPULIS cum dicit Cato, significat pro iniuria verberum. nam conplures leges erant in cives rogatae, quibus sanciebatur poena verberum. his significat prohibuisse[1] multos suos civis in ea oratione, quae est contra M. Caelium: "si em[2] percussi, saepe incolumis abii; praeterea pro republica,[3] pro scapulis atque aerario multum rei publicae profui{t}."[4]

[1] prohibuisse *Ursinus*: prohibus se *cod.*
[2] <host>em *Scaliger*
[3] pro republica *del. Jordan*
[4] profui{t} *Augustinus*: profuit *cod.*

F 116 Paul the Deacon, *Epitome of Festus*

citeria ["clown"] was the word used for some talkative and loquacious likeness (for fun), which was customarily carried in a procession. Cato [says in the speech] against Marcus Cae{ci}lius: "Why should I debate further with that man, whom, in the end, I believe will be borne habitually in the procession at the games in place of a clown and will chat to the spectators?"

F 117 Festus

When Cato says *pro scapulis* ["in respect of the shoulder blades"], he means "in respect of the injustice of flogging." For many laws had been presented to the citizens by which the penalty of flogging was forbidden under pain of punishment. By these [words] he [Cato] indicates that he had protected many of his fellow citizens, in that speech that there is against M. Caelius: "If I struck him down, I have often walked away unharmed;[1] moreover, in respect of the *res publica*, of the shoulder blades,[2] and the treasury I have been of great benefit to the *res publica*."

[1] Lindsay (1913, 116) interprets the first sentence of the fragment as words of a *carnifex* and therefore sees "often" as belonging to the introductory subordinate clause. Such a reading can only be hypothetical (*contra* Till 1937, 57–58). [2] A reference to laws banning magistrates from scourging Roman citizens outright and ensuring the right of appeal for the affected citizens; the introduction of one of these laws is generally attributed to Cato in scholarship (*Leges Porciae de provocatione / de tergo civium*: *LPPR*, pp. 268–69; Elster 2003, 296–301).

F 118 Prisc., *GL* II, p. 228.3

Cf. F 83.

F 119 Fest., p. 170.27–37 L.

⟨NAEVIAM SILVAM⟩[1] vocitatam extra ⟨urbem⟩[2] . . . rum,
quod Naevi cu⟨iusdam fuerit⟩[3] . . . nemora Naevia ap . . .
ait:[4] quam obprobri loco . . .[5] quod in ea morari adsu⟨es-
sent⟩ . . . ⟨ho⟩mines,[6] testis est M. Ca⟨to in ea oratione
quam scripsit⟩ in Caelium si se appella⟨visset:⟩ ". . . a
porta Naevia atque ex . . ." . . . unt proverbi . . .[7]

  [1] *suppl. Epit.*   [2] *suppl. Epit.*   [3] *suppl. Epit.*
  [4] ⟨quam⟩ nemora Naevia ap⟨pellata etiam fuisse Verrius⟩ ait
Mueller   [5] ⟨obici ab antiquis solere⟩ *Ursinus*
  [6] adsu⟨essent⟩ perditi ac nequam ho⟩mines *Ursinus*
  [7] ⟨unde dic⟩unt proverbi⟨um natum esse⟩ *Ursinus*

F 120 Plut. *Cat. Mai.* 9.11

πρὸς δὲ δήμαρχον ἐν διαβολῇ μὲν φαρμακείας γενόμενον, φαῦλον δὲ νόμον εἰσφέροντα καὶ βιαζόμενον,
"ὦ μειράκιον," εἶπεν, "οὐκ οἶδα, πότερον χεῖρόν ἐστιν
ὃ κίρνης πιεῖν ἢ ὃ γράφεις κυρῶσαι."

110

F 118 Priscian

Cf. F 83.

F 119 Festus

The so-called ⟨Naevian wood⟩ outside the ⟨city⟩ . . . ,
since i⟨t belonged to so⟩me Naevius, . . . Naevian groves
. . . he says: how in place of reproach . . . that ⟨pe⟩ople
were accu⟨stomed⟩ to spend time there . . . a witness is
M. Ca⟨to in that speech that he wrote⟩ against Caelius if
he should ⟨have⟩ challenged him: ". . . from the Naevian
gate [in the Servian Wall at Rome] and from . . ." . . . proverb [Otto 1890, 237, s.v. *Naevius*]

F 120 Plutarch, *Life of Cato the Elder*

To a Tribune of the People, charged with using poison,
then putting forward and trying to force through a bad bill,
he [Cato] said: "Young man, I do not know which is worse,
to drink what you mix or to ratify what you write."[1]

---

1 Since this fragment voices criticism of a Tribune of the
People, it is sometimes thought to belong to this speech (cf. Scullard 1973, 263). As no names are mentioned and a further item
of reproach is introduced, it could also come from another context (cf. *Op. cet.* F 64).

ON CENSORIAL QUARRELS (F 121–22)

This speech must refer to quarrels in which Cato became involved as a result of his activities as a censor in 184 BC

F 121–22 Fest., p. 280.18–23 L.

⟨"PERI⟩CULATUS ⟨SUM"⟩ Cato ait in ea oratione, quam scribsit ad[1] litis censorias. PARSI non peperci, ait Cato in eadem oratione: "scio fortunas secundas neglegentiam prendere solere: qu⟨a⟩e uti prohibitum irem, quod in me esset, meo labori non parsi."

[1] ob *Jordan*

Cf. Paul. *Fest.*, p. 281.7–8 L.

AGAINST C. PISO (F 123)

This speech too might belong to the year of Cato's censorship (184 BC), especially if the opponent is C. Calpurnius Piso, who was praetor in Further Iberia in 186 BC (MRR 1:371) and returned to Rome for a triumph over the Lusitanians and Celtiberians in 184 BC (Liv. 39.42.2–3). Yet the information in the single source is too unspecific to

F 123 Prisc., *GL* II, p. 533.2–11

"curro" etiam repetita priori syllaba "cucurri" facit praeteritum, quod in compositione invenitur apud quosdam auctorum geminationem primae syllabae servans, apud alios autem minime, ut . . . Cato contra G. Pisonem: "video hac tempestate concurrisse omnes adversarios."

ON CENSORIAL QUARRELS (F 121–22)

(Liv. 39.44.9 [T 33]; Plut. Cat. Mai. *19.2). In this context Cato seems to have highlighted his own principles.*

F 121–22 Festus

‹*"peri›culatus ‹sum"*› ["I have risked / put to the proof"] is said by Cato in that speech that he wrote for censorial quarrels. *parsi*, not *peperci* ["I have spared"; different forms of perfect], is said by Cato in the same speech: "I know that negligence usually seizes hold of good fortune [cf. F 163]: to work toward preventing that, so far as I can, I have spared no effort on my part."

AGAINST C. PISO (F 123)

enable a precise identification of individuals and contexts: the fragment could belong to any speech by which Cato prosecuted a C. Piso or in which he defended himself against a C. Piso (Scullard 1973, 151n2, 272; Astin 1978, 82n18).

F 123 Priscian

curro ["I run"] also creates the past *cucurri* with repetition of the first syllable; this is found in the compound forms in some of the authors, preserving the doubling of the first syllable, in others, however, not at all, as . . . Cato [says in the speech] against C. Piso: "I see that at this time / in this disturbance all opponents have come together [*concurrisse*: perfect infinitive without repetition of syllable]."

CATO

FROM CENSORIAL SPEECHES
(F 124–27)

*Since the content and the context of these notices recall
duties of the censors, it has been suggested that they refer
to speeches delivered in the year of Cato's censorship (184*

F 124 Gell. *NA* 4.12.1–3

siquis agrum suum passus fuerat sordescere eumque indi-
ligenter curabat ac neque araverat neque purgaverat, sive
quis arborem suam vineamque habuerat derelictui, non
id sine poena fuit, sed erat opus censorium, censoresque
aerarium faciebant. [2] item quis[1] eques Romanus equum
habere gracilentum aut parum nitidum visus erat inpoli-
tiae notabatur; id verbum significat quasi tu dicas incuriae.
[3] cuius rei utriusque auctoritates[2] sunt, et M. Cato id
saepenumero adtestatus est.

[1] quis *codd.*: siquis *unus cod., de Buxis*: quisquis *C. F. W.
Müller*: qui *Vogel*   [2] auctoritates *vel* auctoritate *codd.*

Cf. Paul. *Fest.*, p. 95.26–27 L.

F 125 Plin. *HN* 8.210

placuere autem et feri sues. iam[1] Catonis censoris orationes aprunum exprobrant callum.

[1] feri sues iam *(Beatus Rhenanus) Gelenius*: feris uesiam *vel*
feri uesicae *codd.*

FROM CENSORIAL SPEECHES
(F 124–27)

BC). Details cannot be determined, and Cato could also have referred to these matters at some other time than during his censorship (or not even in speeches).

F 124 Gellius, *Attic Nights*

If anyone had allowed their land to run to waste and was looking after it carelessly and had neither plowed nor weeded it, or if anyone had given over their orchard or vineyard to neglect, this did not go without punishment, but it was the responsibility of the censors, and the censors would reduce such a person to the lowest class of citizens. [2] Likewise, any Roman equestrian who had been seen to have a skinny or poorly groomed horse, was branded with *inpolitia* ["slovenliness"]; that word means the same thing as if you said *incuria* ["carelessness"]. [3] There are authorities for both these matters, and M. Cato has frequently provided testimony.

F 125 Pliny the Elder, *Natural History*

But wild boar too has been popular. Already the speeches of Cato the censor[1] find fault with [the consumption of] boar's meat.

[1] Cato could be called "censor" for identification rather than for dating the utterances referred to; then there is no explicit indication of the time of these speeches.

F 126 Paul. *Fest.*, p. 52.14 L.

"CLOACALE FLUMEN" dixit Cato pro cloacarum omnium conluvie.[1]

   [1] conluuie *vel* coluene *vel* conluenae *vel* colluenae *codd.*

F 127 Prisc., *GL* II, p. 260.6–7

dicebant tamen et "hoc specum" et "haec speca." Cato: "speca prosita,[1] quo aqua de via abiret."

   [1] pro siti *vel* ppositi *vel* ppsita *vel* propositi *codd.*: apposita *ed. ante Krehlianam*: posita *ex codd. suis Krehl*

ON HIS VIRTUES AGAINST THERMUS
(F 128–35)

Apparently in response to accusations by Thermus, Cato delivered a speech to highlight his own achievements and character (F 128–31); the speech described as delivered against Thermus after Cato's censorship (184 BC) is probably the same (F 133, 134). The opponent cannot be the Q. Minucius Thermus who is the focus of earlier speeches by Cato (F 58–65), since that Q. Minucius Thermus died in 188 BC, and this oration against Thermus (if all the fragments belong to the same speech) is dated to the period after Cato's censorship (F 133). Either he is a different Q. Minucius Thermus not otherwise known to have had dealings with Cato, or, with a different reconstruction of the

F 126 Paul the Deacon, *Epitome of Festus*

"*cloacale flumen*" ["a river of sewage"] was said by Cato for the waste water of all sewers.

F 127 Priscian

Still they used both *hoc specum* and *haec speca* ["cave, channel"; neut. and fem. forms, usually masc. *specus*]. Cato [says] [cf. *Orig.* F 154]: "a channel situated along the way, so that the water might run off the street."

ON HIS VIRTUES AGAINST THERMUS
(F 128–35)

first name in F 134, this Thermus might be L. Minucius Thermus, who was a legate in Hither Iberia (probably) in 182–180 BC, a legate in Istria in 178 BC, and one of the legates sent in 154 BC to negotiate in conflicts between the Ptolemaic kings (MRR 1:383, 385, 389, 451; RE Minucius 15, 63; cf. F 177–81). Fragments transmitted under slightly different titles, also referring to Cato's character and consulship, respectively (F 132, 135; cf. F 234A–B), might belong to this speech or could point to separate speeches (Scullard 1973, 164, 264; Astin 1978, 105–7 with n. 5; Sblendorio Cugusi 1982, 277–78; Linderski 1996, 377–78).

F 128 Fest., p. 350.26–36 L.

REPASTINARI ager is dicitur, ut Verrius existimat, cuius natura[1] mutatur fodiendo, cum aut silvester excodicatur[2] aut lapis mollitur frangendo, ut fiat † pascui †,[3] vel pecoribus herba vel hominibus satione. Cato in ea, quam scribsit de suis virtutibus contra Thermum: "ego iam a principio in parsimonia atque in duritia, atque industria omnem adulescentiam meam abstinui[4] agro colendo, saxis Sabinis, silicibus repastinandis atque conserendis."

[1] natura *Ursinus (cf. Epit.)*: natum *cod.*   [2] excodicatur *edd.*: ex quo dicatur *cod.*   [3] pascuus *Scaliger*   [4] obstinui *Ursinus*

F 129 Fest., p. 198.9–17 L.

ORDINARIUM hominem Oppius[1] ait dici solitum scurram et improbum, qui assidue in litibus moraretur: ob eamque causam in ordine staret adeuntium praetorem. . . . ⟨Cato⟩ in ea oratione, quam scribit de suis virtutibus contra Thermum: "quid mihi fieret, si non ego stipendia {in ordine}[2] omnia ordinarius meruissem semper?"[3]

[1] Opilius *alii edd.*
[2] in ordine *supra lineam in cod. uno*: *del. Ursinus (non ed. princ.)*
[3] semper *om. cod. unus (non ed. princ.)*

F 128 Festus

repastinari ["to be turned over again in preparation for planting"] is used, as Verrius [M. Verrius Flaccus] believes, with reference to that land whose nature is changed by digging, when either wood is cleared by rooting it up or rock is softened by crushing it, so that it becomes suitable for pasture [?], whether for animals by grass or for humans by sowing [edible crops]. Cato [says] in that [speech] that he wrote on his own virtues against Thermus: "From the very beginning, in poverty and in austerity, and with assiduity, I spent all my youth abstemiously with tilling fields, turning over Sabine[1] rocks and flint again in preparation for planting and sowing."

[1] Cato had inherited a property in the country of the Sabines (cf. T 26, 55).

F 129 Festus

Oppius says that *ordinarius homo* ["a person in line"] used to be a name for a buffoon and a shameless individual, who constantly wasted time in lawsuits; and for that reason he would stand in the line [*ordo*] of those approaching the praetor. . . . ‹Cato› [says] in that speech that he writes on his own virtues against Thermus: "What would happen to me if I had not always earned all my military stipend {in order} as an ordinary soldier [*ordinarius*]?"

F 130 Fest., p. 196.9–18 L.

⟨ORATORES⟩ ex Graeco quod est ἀρητῆρ⟩ες dictos existimant . . . gentes qui missi[1] . . . ⟨m⟩agistratus populo Romano . . . ⟨solerent⟩[2] ἀρᾶσθαι, ⟨id est testari⟩[3] . . . est ab aequitate; eos nostri alii[4] pro legatis appellant, ut Cato in ea quam scripsit de suis virtutibus contra Thermum: "M. Fulvio consuli legatus sum in Aetoliam, propterea quod ex Aetolia complures venerant: Aetolos[5] pacem velle: de ea re oratores Romam profectos." et . . . [*Orig.* F 15].

[1] *fort.* gentesque missi *Lindsay in app.*   [2] *suppl. Epit.*
[3] *suppl. Epit.*   [4] antiqui *Mueller*   [5] venerant ⟨dicentes⟩ Aetolos *Jordan*

Cf. Paul. *Fest.*, p. 197.1–3 L.

F 131a Gell. *NA* 16.14.1–2

festinare et properare idem significare atque in eandem rem dici videntur. [2] sed M. Cato id differre existimat eaque hoc modo divisa (verba sunt ipsius ex oratione quam de suis virtutibus habuit): "aliud est properare, aliud festinare. qui unum quid mature transigit, is properat; qui multa simul[1] incipit neque perficit, is festinat."

[1] simul *vel* sibi *codd.*

[1] There are further references to this statement (cf. F 131b), which provide basically the same text (though often in shortened form and with more textual difficulties); these are important as they not only identify the quotation as a remark of Cato but also indicate the work it belongs to: "in the speech that is entitled 'on his own virtue against Thermus'" (Scholion), or "in that [speech]

F 130 Festus

They believe that ⟨*oratores*⟩ ["speakers / envoys"] are called thus on the basis of the Greek term that is *arētēr⟩es* ["people who pray"] . . . nations, those who have been sent . . . ⟨m⟩agistrates to the Roman People . . . ⟨were accustomed⟩ to pray [*arasthai*], ⟨that is to invoke⟩ . . . is from equity; others of our people call them thus instead of "envoys" [*legati*], as Cato in that [speech] that he wrote on his own virtues against Thermus: "I was sent as an envoy [*legatus*] for M. Fulvius, the consul [M. Fulvius Nobilior, cos. 189 BC], to Aetolia, for the reason that several had come from Aetolia, [with the message] that the Aetolians wanted peace; that about this matter speakers / envoys [*oratores*] had set out for Rome."[1] And . . . [*Orig.* F 15].

[1] On the meaning of *orator* and *legatus* in this passage, see Neuhauser 1958, 140; on the historical context see Linderski 1996, esp. 388–89.

F 131a Gellius, *Attic Nights*

festinare ["to speed"] and *properare* ["to hasten"] seem to indicate the same and to be used of the same thing. [2] But M. Cato thinks that there is a difference and that they are distinguished in this way (these are his own words from the speech that he delivered on his own virtues): "It is one thing to hasten, another to speed. He, who finishes any one thing in good time, hastens; he, who begins many things at the same time and does not complete them, speeds."[1]

that there is against Thermus on his own virtues" (Festus), or "in the speech that Cato wrote on his own virtues" (Nonius Marcellus).

CATO

F 131b Isid. *Diff.* 1.235(440)

inter properare et festinare. Marcus Cato sic distinguit
dicens: "qui unumquidque[1] mature transigit[2] properat.
qui multa[3] simul incipit neque perficit, is festinat. ego
unumquidque[4] adortus eram transigebam."

[1] unumquidque *vel* unumquicque *vel* unumquemque *vel* nam
quidque *vel* unumquodque *codd.*   [2] is *post* transigit *add.*
Arévalo   [3] unumquodque *post* multa *add. codd.* duo
[4] unumquidque *vel* unumquicque *vel* unumquidquid *vel*
unumquodque *codd.*

Cf. Schol. Bob. ad Cic. *Mil.* 49 (p. 124.2–9 Stangl): verbum hoc
properandi non sum nescius aput quosdam indifferenter accipi
ac solere unum videri festinare et properare. visum est igitur mihi
propter eos quibus aliquod studium proprie loquendi est auctore
ipso M. Catone haec verba distinguere. quippe aliud esse properare, aliud festinare ipse nos, ut dicebam, Cato docuit in oratione
quae inscribitur de virtute sua contra Thermum: "qui unumquodque mature transigit, prope‹rat; qui multa simul incipit neque
perficit, is festinat›"; Fest., p. 268.2–7 L.: ‹. . . PROPERARE et
festinare distinguuntur apud Catonem›[1] in ea, quae est contra
Thermum de suis virtutibus: "aliud est properare, aliud festinare.
qui unum quidquid[2] mature transigit, is[3] properat: qui multa simul incipit neque perficit, is[4] festinat."; Paul. *Fest.*, p. 269.3–5 L.:
PROPERARE aliud est, aliud festinare; qui unum quid mature
transigit, is properat; qui multa simul incipit neque perficit, is
festinat.; Non., p. 441.17–21 M. = 709 L.: FESTINARE et PROPE-
RARE veteres voluerunt habere distantiam. Cato oratione quam
de suis virtutibus scripsit: "aliud est properare, aliud festinare. qui
unum quidquid[5] mature transigit, is properat; qui multa simul
incipit neque perficit, festinat."

[1] *suppl. Epit.*   [2] quidquid *cod.*[1]: quodque *cod.*[2]: quid
Epit.   [3] i *cod.*[1]: is *cod.*[2]   [4] i *cod.*[1]: is *cod.*[2]   [5] quidquid *vel* quid *codd.*

F 131b Isidore, *On Differences between Words*

[The difference] between *properare* ["to hasten"] and *festinare* ["to speed"]. Marcus Cato distinguishes thus, saying: "Who finishes each single thing in good time, hastens. He, who begins many things at the same time and does not complete them, speeds. I have always finished each single thing that I had undertaken."

F 132 Isid. *Orig.* 20.3.8

honorarium vinum, quod regibus et potentibus honoris
gratia offertur. Cato de innocentia sua: "quum essem in
provincia legatus, quamplures ad praetores et consules
vinum honorarium dabant: numquam accepi, ne privatus
quidem."

F 133 Iul. Rufin., §18, *RLM*, p. 43.21–28

διάνοια. haec figura fit proprie, cum proponitur non id
quod fieri oportet, sed quod fit. . . . applicatur huic figurae
etiam χρεία, sententia necessaria, ut Cato in Thermum[1]

[1] Thernum *ed. princeps Basileensis, em. Stephanus*

F 132 Isidore, *Origins*

honorarium vinum ["honorary wine"], because it is offered to kings and powerful people for the sake of honor. Cato [says in the speech] on his innocence:[1] "When I was a legate in the province,[2] very many people gave honorary wine to praetors and consuls: I never accepted it, not even as a private person."

[1] This source does not mention Thermus and identifies the oration's topic as *de innocentia* ("on his innocence"); if this description is regarded as equivalent to *de suis virtutibus* ("on his own virtues") (F 128, 129, 130, 131), the fragment can be seen as belonging to the same oration (for a similar issue, cf. F 135). If a separate speech *de innocentia* is assumed in line with the difference in wording, the fragment should be assigned to that one (cf. F 234A–B). The speech from which this fragment comes obviously postdates Cato's activity as a legate. Since he served in this role on at least three occasions in the late 190s and early 180s BC and could refer back to these legateships at any time afterward, this comment does not identify a specific date for this speech.

[2] None of Cato's legateships involved activity in a "province" in the sense of a territory administered by Rome; since "province" here seems to refer to a location (rather than "a function or task assigned to a magistrate"), it might be used less technically and denote an area outside of Rome in which Roman officials are active.

F 133 Iulius Rufinianus

dianoia ["expression of thought"]. This figure of speech occurs properly when not what should happen, but what happens is put forward. . . . Attached to this figure of speech is also *chreia* ["maxim"], a necessary statement, as Cato [says in the speech] against Thermus after his censor-

post censuram: "qui ventrem suum non pro hoste habet, qui pro re publica, non pro sua obsonat, qui stulte spondet, qui cupide aedificat."

F 134 Fest., pp. 420.26–22.5 L.

SACREM . . . ⟨. . . C⟩ato adver⟨sus Q. Minucium The⟩rmum post ⟨censuram⟩ . . . crem[1] in sin . . . quando pro . . . me sacrem . . . primis fiet . . .

1 ⟨porcum sa⟩crem *Mueller*

F 135 *Incerti gratiarum actio Constantino Augusto* 13.3 (*Pan. Lat.* V)

praeclara fertur Catonis oratio de lustri sui felicitate. iam tunc enim in illa vetere re publica ad censorum laudem pertinebat, si lustrum felix condidisse⟨n⟩t,[1] si horrea messis implesset, si vindemia redundasset, si oliveta larga fluxissent.

1 condidisse⟨n⟩t *Livineius*: condidisset *codd.*

ship: "someone who regards their belly not as an enemy,
who feasts in proportion with public funds, not their own,
who stupidly gives pledges, who eagerly builds."

F 134 Festus

sacrem ["sacred"; unusual form of acc. sg. masc.] . . .
‹. . . C›ato ag‹ainst Q. Minucius The›rmus after ‹his
censorship› . . . when for . . . me sacred . . . especially it
will happen . . . [?][1]

[1] The words of the quoted excerpt have been transmitted in
such an incomplete state that it is impossible to construct a proper
clause and provide a coherent translation.

F 135 Unknown author, *Speech of Thanks to Constantine
the Great*

Cato's speech on the good fortune of his *lustrum* [term as
censor] is celebrated as famous. For then already, in that
ancient *res publica*, it was relevant to the esteem of censors whether they had concluded a fortunate *lustrum*,
whether the harvest had filled the barns, whether the vin-
tage had been in copious supply, whether the olive yards
had given a great yield.[1]

[1] The sketched content of the speech alluded to, if seen as a
description of Cato's achievements, may suggest that the passage
refers to this oration on his virtues (for another question of attribution, cf. F 132). Stark (1953) highlights the problematic nature of the testimonium and concludes that it should be approached cautiously or even disregarded (questioned by Astin
1978, 106n5). If what is said is to be taken literally and based on
good evidence, the speech from which this extract comes would
have to be dated to the time of a *lustrum* (five-year period) after
the year in which Cato became censor (184 BC).

ON ELECTIONEERING (F 136)

This speech might be connected with Lex Cornelia Baebia
de ambitu *of 181 BC (LPPR, p. 277; Elster 2003, 339–40):
discussions about this law or the underlying issues could
have prompted a speech about* ambitus. *If this is the context, it is uncertain whether this* Lex Baebia *is the same as
the one mentioned in F 137–38. Since matters concerning*

F 136 Prisc., *GL* II, p. 182.1–7

vetustissimi tamen et "altera utra" et "alterum utrum" et
"alterius utrius" solebant proferre et . . . Cato de ambitu:
"sed sunt partim, qui duarum rerum alterius utrius causa
magistratum petunt."

AGAINST MODIFICATION OF
LEX BAEBIA (F 137–38)

*In this speech, Cato argued against a proposed modifica-
tion of a* Lex Baebia. *The intervention is usually referred
to a law of 181 BC limiting the number of praetors in office
each year (Lex Baebia de praetoribus: LPPR, pp. 277–78;
Elster 2003, 340–42; cf. Liv. 40.44.2; no longer in force
from 179 BC: see Liv. 40.59.5, 41.8.1). If this is the same
law as* Lex Baebia de ambitu *(cf. F 136), Cato's speech
would deal with the removal of an element of the law. If it
is a separate law, the speech would concern aspects of the*

ON ELECTIONEERING (F 136)

ambitus *were taken up at other times too (cf.* Lex [Corne-lia Fulvia] de ambitu*: LPPR, p. 288; Elster 2003, 400–401 [159 BC]), Cato's speech could also relate to another occasion (on the potential contexts, evidence, and arguments, see Fraccaro [1910c] 1956, 227–32; Scullard 1973, 172–73, 266; Astin 1978, 329–31; Kienast 1979, 92–93).*

F 136 Priscian

Yet the very early [writers] were accustomed to use *altera utra* and *alterum utrum* and *alterius utrius* ["either / one of two"; nom. sg. fem., nom. sg. neut., gen. sg.] and . . . Cato [says in the speech] on electioneering: "but there are some people who, for the sake of one out of two matters [*alterius utrius*], seek a magistracy."

AGAINST MODIFICATION OF
LEX BAEBIA (F 137–38)

regulations. According to the wording in the main source (F 137: derogare, *not* abrogare*), the issue under discussion was not the complete abolishment of the law* (Lex de lege Baebia deroganda*: LPPR, p. 279; Elster 2003, 349–50; tentatively dated to ca. 179 BC) and rather a repeal or modification of parts. Due to the lack of evidence, other potential contexts for this speech cannot be ruled out (see Astin 1978, 329–31).*

F 137 Fest., p. 356.27–32 L.

ROGAT est consulit populum, vel petit ab eo, ut id sciscat, quod ferat. unde nos quoque in consuetudine habemus pro petere et orare. Cato in dissuasione, ne lex Baebia derogaretur, ait: "hoc potius agam, quod hic rogat."

F 138 Non., p. 470.29–33 M. = 755 L.

LARGI, pro largire. . . . Cato lege Baebia: "pecuniam inlargibo[1] tibi."

[1] inlargiuo *cod.*

AGAINST MODIFICATION OF
LEX ORCHIA (F 139–46)

In 182 BC, C. Orchius, a Tribune of the People (MRR *1:382), put forward a bill, by decree of the Senate, intended to limit the number of guests at dinner parties and thus to curb the growing luxury* (Lex Orchia de coenis: LPPR, *p. 276; Elster 2003, 337–39). Later, there were apparently movements to abolish or modify that law. Cato seems to have argued against such attempts, criticizing extravagance. If the plural in Macrobius is not merely rhetorical, Cato may have mentioned* Lex Orchia *in more than one speech (F 142). Festus seems to refer to a single speech on this law, though with different descriptions, for which the text is not entirely certain (F 139, 140). If the choice of*

F 137 Festus

rogat is "consults the People" or "asks them that they approve what he proposes." Hence we too have it in use for "to ask" and "to beseech." Cato says in the speech arguing that *Lex Baebia* should not be modified: "I will rather do what this man asks."

F 138 Nonius Marcellus

largi, instead of *largire* ["give generously"; active instead of deponent form]. . . . Cato [says in the speech on] *Lex Baebia*:[1] "I will give money generously to you [active future form]."

[1] If Cato's speech on electioneering (F 136) relates to a *Lex Baebia*, this fragment could also belong to that speech, since the content of the *Lex Baebia* referred to here is not identified and cannot be inferred from the contents of the fragment.

AGAINST MODIFICATION OF
LEX ORCHIA (F 139–46)

words in one of these references is exact and meaningful (F 139: derogare*), the matter at issue concerned changes to the law (cf. F 137–38). It is not entirely clear when Cato's speech was delivered and what the initiative's relation to another sumptuary law,* Lex Fannia cibaria *of 161 BC (LPPR, pp. 287–88; Elster 2003, 396–400; Zanda 2011, 107–8), which presumably replaced* Lex Orchia de coenis, *might be (F 142), and thus what kind of regulations Cato argued for. For discussion and different views, see, e.g., Fraccaro (1910c) 1956, 233–37; Scullard 1973, 172, 265–66; Astin 1978, 91; Stok 1985; Baltrusch 1989, 77–85; Zanda 2011, 106–7.*

F 139 Fest., p. 220.15–17 L.

OBSONITAVERE saepe obsonavere. Cato in suasione[1] ⟨ne⟩[2] de lege Orchia[3] derogaretur: "qui[4] antea obsonitavere, postea centenis[5] obsonitavere."[6]

[1] suasione *vel* suasoria *codd.*: suasione *ed. princ.*   [2] *add. Augustinus*   [3] de lege orcia *vel* de lege oricia *codd.*: ne legi Orchiae *Augustinus*   [4] *fort.* VI (*i.e.* senis) *vel* qui VI *Lindsay in app.*   [5] centenis *codd. pler.*: cantenis *cod. unus ante corr.*: centeni *Scaliger*   [6] *post* obsonitavere *add.* significat autem convivari *ed. princ.* (*ex Epit.*)

F 140 Fest., pp. 280.30–82.1 L.

PERCUNCTATUM PATRIS FAMILIAE NOMEN ne quis servum mitteret, lege sanctum[1] fuisse ait Cato in ea, qua legem Orchiam {dis}suadet.[2]

[1] lege sanctum *Ellendt*: lege anotum *cod.*   [2] qua legem Orchiam {dis}suadet *edd.*: quam legem orciam dissuadet *cod.*

F 141 Schol. Bob. ad Cic. *Sest.* 138 (p. 141.15–18 Stangl)

. . . implet exhortationem bonae sectae ad conservationem rei p. pertinentis. non aliter et M. Cato in legem Orchiam, conferens ea quae virtus . . .[1] ut summae gloriae sint a virtute proficiscentia, dedecoris vero praecipui existimentur quae voluptas suadeat non sine labe vitiorum.

[1] *lac indic. Mai*: ⟨et quae voluptas hominibus comparet ita⟩ *Hildebrandt*

F 139 Festus

obsonitavere ["they feasted frequently"], they often feasted. Cato in the speech advising that no modifications should be made to *Lex Orchia* [said]: "those who previously feasted frequently, later feasted frequently for one hundred each [unit of money to be supplied; cf. F 142]."[1]

[1] An expression strengthening and specifying the contrast might be missing in the first half of the fragment (see Sblendorio Cugusi 1982, 349–50).

F 140 Festus

That it had been made a punishable offense by law for anyone to send a slave to inquire after the name of the head of the household [*percunctatum patris familiae nomen*] is what Cato says in that [speech] by which he supports *Lex Orchia*.[1]

[1] These slaves were tasked with finding out details about important individuals, convey these to their masters, and then potentially invite some of these to dinner parties. When the number of guests was limited, this activity became less necessary, or it could be banned as part of the measures against sumptuous feasts.

F 141 Scholia Bobiensia to Cicero, *Pro Sestio*

. . . he [Cicero] performs an exhortation to good principles pertaining to the preservation of the *res publica*. Likewise, M. Cato too, with respect to *Lex Orchia*, comparing those things that virtue . . . , so that what proceeds from virtue entails the greatest glory, but what lust advises, not without the stain of vices, is regarded as entailing the greatest shame.

CATO

F 142 Macrob. *Sat.* 3.17.2–5

prima autem omnium de cenis lex ad populum Orchia
pervenit, quam tulit C. Orchius tribunus plebi de senatus
sententia tertio anno quam Cato censor fuerat. cuius verba
quia sunt prolixa praetereo, summa autem eius praescri-
bebat numerum convivarum. [3] et haec est lex Orchia de
qua Cato mox orationibus suis vociferabatur, quod plures
quam praescripto eius cavebatur ad cenam vocarentur.
cumque auctoritatem novae legis aucta necessitas implo-
raret, post annum vicesimum secundum legis Orchiae
Fannia lex data est, anno post Romam conditam secundum Gellii opinionem quingentesimo octogesimo octavo.
[4] ... [5] ... Fanniae autem legis severitas in eo supera-
bat Orchiam legem quod in superiore numerus tantum
modo cenantium cohibebatur licebatque secundum eam
uni cuique bona sua inter paucos consumere, Fannia autem etiam sumptibus modum fecit assibus centum, unde
a Lucilio poeta festivitatis suae more "centussis" vocatur.

F 142 Macrobius, *Saturnalia*

And the first law of all those on dining to come before the People was *Lex Orchia*, which C. Orchius, a Tribune of the People, put forward in accordance with a Senate's decree in the third year [182 BC] after Cato had been censor [184 BC]. I pass over its text as it is long; but, in short, it prescribed the number of guests. [3] And this is the *Lex Orchia* about which Cato was soon shouting in his speeches, because, he claimed, more people were being invited to dinner than was provided for by its regulation. And when increased need was crying out for the authority of a new law, in the twenty-second year after *Lex Orchia*, *Lex Fannia* was passed [*Lex Fannia cibaria*, 161 BC (*LPPR*, pp. 287–88; Elster 2003, 396–400)], in the five-hundred and eighty-eighth year after the founding of Rome [here dated to 749/8 BC], according to Gellius' opinion [Cn. Gellius (*FRHist* 14 F 29)]. [4] . . . [5] . . . And the severity of *Lex Fannia* surpassed *Lex Orchia* in that by the earlier [law] only the number of diners was limited and, according to it, it was permitted to every individual to use up their assets among a few people, but *Lex Fannia* also set a limit to expenditures of one hundred asses, whence it is called by the poet Lucilius [F 1172 M. = 1241 W.], with his customary wit, the "hundred-as [law]" [cf. Gell. *NA* 2.24.3–6].

CATO

F 143 Macrob. *Sat.* 3.17.13

Sulla mortuo Lepidus consul legem tulit et ipse cibariam
(Cato enim sumptuarias leges "cibarias" appellat).

F 144 Serv. ad Verg. *Aen.* 1.726

"atria": ut supra diximus, tangit Romanam historiam; nam,
ut ait Cato, et in atrio et duobus ferculis epulabantur antiqui: . . .

F 145 Plut. *Cat. Mai.* 8.2

κατηγορῶν δὲ τῆς πολυτελείας ἔφη χαλεπὸν εἶναι
σωθῆναι πόλιν ἐν ᾗ πωλεῖται πλείονος ἰχθὺς ἢ βοῦς
[*Op. cet.* F 58.2, 63].

Cf. Plut. *Mor.* 668C (*Quaest. conv.* 4.2); Polyb. 31.25.5a; Diod.
Sic. 31.24, 37.3.6; Ath. 6 (p. 274F).

F 143 Macrobius, *Saturnalia*

After Sulla's death [L. Cornelius Sulla, d. 78 BC] Lepidus as consul moved a law and himself [referred to it as] one on rations (for Cato calls sumptuary laws "those on rations").[1]

[1] This testimonium does not refer Cato's choice of words to a particular speech or mention *Lex Orchia*. A remark on sumptuary laws might belong to this speech, but could also be made in other contexts. The law referred to may be *Lex Aemilia sumptuaria* of 115 BC (*LPPR*, p. 320; Baltrusch 1989, 86–88; Elster 2020, 175–77), here attributed to another representative of the *gens Aemilia* (perhaps M. Aemilius Lepdius [cos. 78 BC] or Mam. Aemilius Lepidus Livianus [cos. 77 BC]), or a separate law.

F 144 Servius, *Commentary on Virgil*

"halls" [*atria*]: As we said above [on Verg. *Aen.* 1.637], he [Virgil] touches upon Roman history; for, as Cato says,[1] the ancients had meals both in the atrium and with two courses: . . .

[1] Cato could have made a comment on the frugality of the ancients in discussions on *Lex Orchia*; yet, other contexts are equally possible. Some editors connect this passage with descriptions of ancient Roman customs in the *Origines* (*Orig.* F 144).

F 145 Plutarch, *Life of Cato the Elder*

Inveighing against the extravagance, he [Cato] said that it was hard for a city to be saved in which a fish sold for more than an ox [*Op. cet.* F 58.2, 63].[1]

[1] Again (cf. F 144) Cato could have commented on great attention to food in discussions on *Lex Orchia*; yet, other contexts or a self-contained aphorism are also possible (cf. *Op. cet.* F 58.2, 63).

F 146 Amm. Marc. 16.5.2

id enim etiam Tusculanus Cato prudenter definiens, cui Censorii cognomentum castior vitae indidit cultus: "magna," inquit, "cura cibi, magna virtutis incuria."

ON MILITARY MATTERS IN ISTRIA
(F 147)

This speech comments on military campaigns in Istria (peninsula in the Adriatic Sea). Since the Romans were fighting in the area on several occasions, the speech cannot be dated precisely: it may be connected with the campaign in 178/77 BC (Liv. 41.1–5), eventually leading to the Roman conquest of the region (thus ORF[4]; Sblendorio Cugusi 1982; Cugusi and Sblendorio Cugusi 2001), or it

F 147 Fest., p. 280.27–28 L.

PUNCTATORIOLAS[1] levis pugnas appellat Cato in ea, quam dixit de re Histriae militari.

[1] punctariolas *Epit.*: pugnariolas *Jordan*

Cf. Paul. *Fest.*, p. 281.13 L.: PUNCTARIOLAS leves pugnas identidem ipse dixit.

F 146 Ammianus Marcellinus

Furthermore, Cato of Tusculum, whose rather austere manner of living conferred upon him the additional name Censorius ["ex-censor"], wisely defining that point, says: "great care for food, great lack of care for virtue."[1]

[1] In this case as well (cf. F 144, 145), Cato could have spoken about too much concern for food in discussions on *Lex Orchia*, while other contexts are also possible (cf. *Op. cet.* F 81).

ON MILITARY MATTERS IN ISTRIA
(F 147)

could be linked with later discussions in the Senate in 171/70 BC, in reaction to complaints about the behavior of the consul of 171 BC in that area (Liv. 43.1.5–12, 43.5.3–6; see Scullard 1973, 267; Chassignet 1987, 287). Agnew (1939) suggests that F 245 might belong to this speech.

F 147 Festus

punctatoriolae ["skirmishes"] is what Cato calls light fights in that [speech] that he delivered about military matters in Istria.

AGAINST M. FULVIUS NOBILIOR
(F 148–51)

These fragments comment on and criticize the behavior of
M. Fulvius Nobilior (cos. 189, censor 179 BC) as general
(F 148–49) and censor (F 150). They might come from a
single speech delivered after M. Fulvius Nobilior's censor-
ship (F 150), attacking the way in which he carried out

F 148 Gell. *NA* 5.6.24–26

Marcus Cato obicit M. Fulvio Nobiliori quod milites per
ambitum coronis de levissimis causis donasset. [25] de qua
re verba ipsa apposui Catonis. "iam[1] principio quis vidit
corona donari[2] quemquam, cum oppidum captum non esset aut castra hostium non incensa essent?" [26] Fulvius
autem, in quem hoc a Catone dictum est, coronis donave-
rat milites quia[3] vallum curaverant aut qui[4] puteum strenue foderant.

    [1] iam *vel* nam *vel* am *(spatio litt. init. rel.) vel* a *codd.*
    [2] corona donari *vel* coronari *codd.*   [3] quia *codd.*: qui{a}
nonnulli codd. rec., Lion   [4] qui *codd., nonnulli codd. rec.*:
quia *plerique codd. rec.*

F 149 Cic. *Tusc.* 1.3

sero igitur a nostris poetae vel cogniti vel recepti. quamquam est in Originibus solitos esse in epulis canere convi-
vas ad tibicinem de clarorum hominum virtutibus [*Orig.*
F 113b]. honorem tamen huic generi non fuisse declarat
oratio Catonis, in qua obiecit ut probrum M. Nobiliori

AGAINST M. FULVIUS NOBILIOR
(F 148–51)

*this office and alluding to earlier actions, or from different
speeches given at different times (Fraccaro [1910c] 1956,
247–53; Scullard 1973, 266–67; Sblendorio Cugusi 1982,
294–96; Linderski 1996, 395–98).*

F 148 Gellius, *Attic Nights*

Marcus Cato charges M. Fulvius Nobilior with having
awarded wreaths to soldiers for the most trifling reasons,
for the sake of popularity. [25] I have appended Cato's own
words on that matter: "Now, to begin with, who ever saw
anyone presented with a wreath when a town had not
been taken[1] or an enemy's camp had not been burned?"
[26] But Fulvius, against whom this was said by Cato, had
awarded wreaths to soldiers because they had watched
over a rampart or who had dug in a well with energy.

[1] This might be an allusion to the controversy over whether
M. Fulvius Nobilior's capture of the town of Ambracia in 189 BC
met the conditions for a triumph (Liv. 38.7.4–13, 38.44.6).

F 149 Cicero, *Tusculan Disputations*

At a late date, then, poets became known or were received
by our people. Yet it is stated in the *Origines* that guests
at dinner parties were in the habit of singing of the glori-
ous deeds of famous individuals to the accompaniment of
a flute player [*Orig.* F 113b]. However, that there was no
appreciation for this class is demonstrated by a speech of
Cato in which he raised it as a matter of disgrace against

quod is in provinciam poetas duxisset; duxerat autem consul ille in Aetoliam, ut scimus, Ennium.

F 150 Fest., p. 356.17–23 L.

RETRICIBUS cum ait Cato in ea, quam scribsit, cum edissertavit Fulvi Nobilioris censuram, significat aquam eo nomine, quae est supra viam Ardeatinam inter lapidem secundum et tertium; qua inrigantur horti infra viam Ardeatinam et Asinariam usque ad Latinam.

F 151 Cic. *De or.* 2.256

[CAESAR STRABO:] alterum genus est, quod habet parvam verbi immutationem,[1] quod in littera positum Graeci vocant παρονομασίαν; ut Nobiliorem "mobiliorem" Cato [*Op. cet.* F 43]; aut, ut idem, cum cuidam dixisset "eamus deambulatum" et ille "quid opus fuit de?" "immo vero" inquit "quid opus fuit te?" aut eiusdem responsio[2] illa: "si tu et adversus et aversus impudicus es."

[1] immutationem *vel* imitationem *codd.*
[2] sponsio *vel* responsio *codd.*

M. Nobilior that he had taken poets to his province; and, as we know, he, when consul [189 BC], had taken Ennius to Aetolia.

F 150 Festus

When Cato says *retricibus* in that [speech] that he wrote when he discussed in detail Fulvius Nobilior's censorship, he means by that term the water supply that runs above the Via Ardeatina [leading from Rome southward to Ardea] between the second and the third [mile]stone; with that [water] the gardens below the Via Ardeatina and Asinaria [starting from the Porta Asinaria in Rome] up until the Latina [starting from the (later) Porta Latina in Rome] are irrigated.

F 151 Cicero, *On the Orator*

[CAESAR STRABO:] There is another category [of pun], which consists in a slight change of a word, which, when it concerns a letter, the Greeks call *paranomasia* ["assonance"]; for example [*Op. cet.* F 43], when Cato [called] someone named "the more Noble" [*Nobilior*] "the more Mobile" [*mobilior*],[1] or when the same [Cato] had said to a certain man, "Let us go for a deambulation," and, on the other asking "What need of *de* [i.e., the prefix]?," he [Cato] said "On the contrary in fact, what need of thee [*te*]?," or that answer of the same man [Cato] "if you are immoral both forward and backward [*et adversus et aversus*]."

---

[1] The first quotation in this passage might come from a speech against M. Fulvius Nobilior (whence it is often attributed to this speech), but could also be a remark about him or another person of that name in another context.

ON MILITARY TRIBUNES (F 152–53)

This speech might belong to 171 BC, when on the Senate's instructions the consuls asked the People to forgo their right to elect military tribunes and instead to let consuls and praetors appoint them (Liv. 42.31.5). Cato could have

F 152 Non., p. 67.18–21 M. = 93 L.

PROLETARI dicti sunt plebei, qui nihil rei publicae exhibeant, sed tantum prolem sufficiant. Cato de tribunis militum: "expedito pauperem plebeium atque proletarium."

F 153 Non., pp. 194.29–95.2 = 286 L.

CLIVUS generis masculini, ut plerumque. neutri aput Memmium invenimus, cuius auctoritas dubia est: . . . Cato de tribunis militum: "loca ardua et cliva depressa."

AGAINST P. FURIUS ON BEHALF OF THE IBERIANS (F 154–55)

In 171 BC the Iberians complained about exploitation by Roman magistrates. The Senate appointed five men, including Cato (on his general support for the Iberians, see Cic. Div. Caec. 66 [T 3]), to look into the matter and also introduced clear rules for determining the price of grain

ON MILITARY TRIBUNES (F 152–53)

commented on this issue; yet statements on military tribunes could also occur in other contexts (Scullard 1973, 268; Astin 1978, 118; Kienast 1979, 90).

F 152 Nonius Marcellus

proletari ["members of the lowest class of citizens"] is a name for plebeians as they produce nothing for the *res publica*, but provide only offspring [*proles*]. Cato [says in the speech] on military tribunes: "he shall free / get ready a poor plebeian and low-class person."

F 153 Nonius Marcellus

clivus ["slope"], of masculine gender, as mostly. We find it of neuter gender in Memmius [trib. pl. 66, praet. 58 BC (F 1 *FPL*[4])], whose authority is doubtful: . . . Cato [says in the speech] on military tribunes: "high places and downward slopes [*cliva*: neut.]."

AGAINST P. FURIUS ON BEHALF OF THE IBERIANS (F 154–55)

to be supplied by the province (Liv. 43.2 = Orat. F 110 Cugusi). P. Furius Philus, praetor in Hither Iberia in 174 BC (MRR 1:404), was then investigated because of his alleged misconduct in the province and went into voluntary exile (Scullard 1973, 201–2, 268).

CATO

F 154 Ps.-Asc. in Cic. *Div. Caec.* 66 (p. 203.24–26 Stangl)

"M. Catonem illum Sapientem" [T 3]: Cato hic accusavit Sergium Galbam pro direptis Lusitanis [F 196–99A] et P. Furium pro iisdem, propter iniquissimam aestimationem frumenti.

F 155 Charis., *GL* I, p. 224.14–16 = p. 289.8–10 B.

utrinde Cato pro Hispanis de frumento: "utrubi bona, utrubi mala gratia capiatur, utrinde iram, utrinde factiones[1] tibi pares."

[1] *ed princ.*: utrinque iram utrinde faction. *cod.*   factionem *Cauchii ex deperdito cod. excerpta*

IN SUPPORT OF *LEX VOCONIA*
(F 156–60)

A law put forward by the Tribune of the People Q. Voconius Saxa stipulated restrictions for the inheritance rights of women (Lex Voconia de mulierum hereditatibus: LPPR, pp. 283–84; Baltrusch 1989, 73–77; Elster 2003, 374–80). In Cicero (F 156) this initiative is dated to 169 BC. Cato

F 154 Ps.-Asconius on Cicero, *Divinatio in Caecilium*

"the famous M. Cato, the 'Wise'" [T 3]: This Cato charged
Sergius Galba [Ser. Sulpicius Galba (F 196–99A)] on behalf of the ravaged Lusitanians [people in the Iberian pen-
insula] and P. Furius on behalf of the same, because of the
very unfair assessment of the value of grain.

F 155 Charisius

utrinde ["from either side"]: Cato [uses it in the speech]
on behalf of the Iberians about grain:[1] "in which of two
places goodwill, in which of two places ill will may be
obtained, from either side anger, from either side dealings
equal in your [sg.] view."[2]

[1] Since P. Furius Philus served as praetor in Hither Iberia and
the price of grain was an issue in the subsequent investigation, it
is likely that this fragment comes from the speech against him,
although the source does not name him.   [2] The second half
of the fragment is an incomplete clause, lacking a verb governing
the nouns.

IN SUPPORT OF *LEX VOCONIA*
(F 156–60)

*spoke in support of this law (Scullard 1973, 205–6, 268–
69; Astin 1978, 113–18; Kienast 1979, 93–96; for an overview of* Lex Voconia *and associated questions see, e.g.,
Weishaupt 1999).*

CATO

F 156 Cic. *Sen.* 14

["CATO":] equi fortis et victoris senectuti comparat suam. quem quidem probe meminisse potestis; anno enim unde-vicesimo post eius mortem hi consules, T. Flamininus et M'. Acilius, facti sunt; ille autem Caepione et Philippo iterum consulibus mortuus est, cum ego quinque et sexa-ginta annos natus legem Voconiam magna voce et bonis lateribus suasi.[1]

[1] suasi. sed . . . *Forchhammer*: suasisset *vel* suassimsem *vel* suasissem *codd.*

F 157 Liv. *Epit.* 41

Q. Voconius[1] Saxa tr. pl. legem tulit, nequis mulierem heredem institueret. suasit legem M. Cato. extat oratio eius.

[1] Voconius *Sigonius*: volonius *vel* velonius *codd.*

F 158 Gell. *NA* 17.6.1–3, 8–10

M. Cato Voconiam legem suadens verbis hisce usus est: "principio vobis mulier magnam dotem adtulit; tum mag-nam pecuniam recipit, quam in viri potestatem non conmittit, eam pecuniam viro mutuam dat; postea, ubi irata[1] facta est, servum recepticium sectari atque flagitare virum iubet." [2] quaerebatur "servus recepticius" quid esset. libri statim quaesiti allatique sunt Verrii Flacci de obscuris Catonis. in libro secundo scriptum inventum est

[1] ubi irata *vel* ubi rapta *vel* nisi rata *codd.*

F 156 Cicero, *On Old Age*

["CATO":] He [Ennius] compares his old age to that of a brave and victorious horse [Enn. T 33 *FRL*]. You can surely remember him well; for in the nineteenth year after his death the present consuls, T. Flamininus and M'. Acilius [T. Quinctius Flamininus and M'. Acilius Balbus, cos. 150 BC] were elected; and he died in the consulship of Caepio and Philippus (for a second time) [Cn. Servilius Caepio and Q. Marcius Philippus, cos. 169 BC], when I, at the age of sixty-five, argued for *Lex Voconia*, with a loud voice and mighty lungs.

F 157 Livy, *Epitome*

Q. Voconius Saxa, a Tribune of the People, put forward a law, that nobody should appoint their wife their heir. M. Cato argued for the law. His speech is extant.

F 158 Gellius, *Attic Nights*

M. Cato, when arguing for *Lex Voconia*, used these words: "To start with, the woman brought a great dowry to you; then she holds back a large sum of money, which she does not entrust to the control of her husband, [and] she lends that money to her husband; later, when she has become angry, she orders a *servus recepticius* to follow the husband constantly and make demands of him." [2] The question was asked what a *servus recepticius* was. At once the books of Verrius Flaccus on the obscurities of Cato were requested and produced. In the second book [M. Verrius Flaccus (F 2 *GRF*)] it was found written that *servus recep-*

149

"recepticium servum" dici nequam et nulli pretii, qui cum venum esset datus redhibitus ob aliquod vitium receptusque sit. [3] "propterea" inquit "servus eiusmodi sectari maritum et flagitare pecuniam iubebatur, ut eo ipso dolor maior et contumelia gravior viro fieret, quod eum servus nihili petendae pecuniae causa conpellaret." [4] . . . [8] ipse etiam Cato mulierem demonstrare locupletem volens "mulier" inquit "et magnam dotem dat et magnam pecuniam recipit," hoc est: et magnam dotem dat et magnam pecuniam retinet. [9] ex ea igitur re familiari quam sibi dote data retinuit pecuniam viro mutuam dat. [10] eam pecuniam cum viro forte irata repetere instituit, adponit ei[2] flagitatorem "servum recepticium," hoc est proprium servum suum, quem cum pecunia reliqua receperat neque dederat doti sed retinuerat; non enim servo mariti imperare hoc mulierem fas erat, sed proprio suo.

[2] ei *Nonius Marcellus*: et *vel om. codd. Gell.*

Cf. Fest., p. 356.23–27 L.; Non., p. 54.6–17 M. = 76 L.

F 159 Serv. auct. ad Verg. *Aen.* 1.573

"urbem quam statuo vestra est": hoc schema de antiquioribus sumptum possumus accipere; ait enim Cato in legem Voconiam: "agrum quem vir habet tollitur" et Terentius "eunuchum quem dedisti nobis, quas turbas dedit."

ticius was the name applied to a slave who was worthless and of no value, who, after having been sold, was returned because of some fault and taken back. [3] "Therefore," he [Verrius Flaccus] says, "a slave of that kind was ordered to hound the husband and demand money, in order that the man's vexation might be greater and the insult put upon him more bitter for the very reason that a worthless slave was soliciting him for the payment of money." [4] . . . [8] Cato himself too, wishing to describe the woman as rich, says: "The woman both brings a great dowry and holds back a large sum of money"; that is, she both gives a great dowry and retains a large sum of money. [9] From that property, then, that she retained for herself after having given the dowry, she lends money to her husband. [10] When she happened to be vexed with her husband and determined to demand that money back, she appoints as someone to demand it from him a *servus recepticius*, that is, a slave of her very own, whom she had held back with the rest of the money and had not given as part of the dowry, but had retained; for it was not right for the woman to give such an order to a slave of her husband, but only to one of her very own.

F 159 Servius Danielis, *Commentary on Virgil*

"the city that I establish is yours": We can accept that this mode of expression [attraction of the case of the noun in the main clause to the case of the relative pronoun] has been taken from the fairly ancient [writers]; for Cato says with respect to *Lex Voconia*: "the land that the husband owns is taken away" and Terence: "the eunuch whom you have given to us, what disturbances has he caused" [Ter. *Eun.* 653].

F 160 Gell. *NA* 6.13.1–3

Quem classicum dicat M. Cato, quem infra classem.—[1] "classici" dicebantur non omnes qui in quinque classibus erant, sed primae tantum classis homines, qui centum et viginti quinque milia aeris ampliusve censi erant. [2] infra classem autem appellabantur secundae classis ceterarumque omnium classium, qui minore summa aeris quam[1] supra dixi, censebantur. [3] hoc eo strictim notavi, quoniam in M. Catonis oratione qua Voconiam legem suasit quaeri solet, quid sit classicus, quid infra classem.

[1] quod *vel* quam *codd.*: quam quod *F. Skutsch*

ON FREEING MACEDONIA (F 161–62)

The war against Perseus, king of Macedonia, begun in 171 BC (Third Macedonian War), was brought to an end with the Battle of Pydna in 168 BC by L. Aemilius Paullus (cos. 182, 168 BC [ORF[4] 12]), after previous unsuccessful attempts by others. Cato presumably spoke in a discussion

F 161 Prisc., *GL* II, pp. 87.15–88.10

. . . ; vetustissimi tamen comparativis etiam huiuscemodi sunt {est quando}[1] usi. . . . [*Orig.* F 152; *Orat.* F 19, 186, 178] . . . idem Cato de Macedonia liberanda: "idque perpetuius atque firmius repsit." . . . [*Orat.* F 182].

[1] sunt est quando *vel* est sunt quando *vel* est quando *vel* est quando (st?) *codd.*

F 160 Gellius, *Attic Nights*

Whom M. Cato calls *classicus* ["someone belonging to the highest class of citizens"] and whom *infra classem* ["below the class"].—[1] Not all those who were enrolled in the five classes were called *classici*, but only the individuals of the first class, who were rated at a hundred and twenty-five thousand asses or more. [2] But those of the second class and of all the other classes, who were rated at a smaller sum of asses than I mentioned above, were called *infra classem*. [3] I have briefly noted this, because in connection with M. Cato's speech, by which he argued for *Lex Voconia*, the question is often raised what is *classicus* and what [is] *infra classem*.

ON FREEING MACEDONIA (F 161–62)

in the Senate on the future arrangements for governing Macedonia, when it was agreed that the Macedonians should be "free" and their land should not be turned into a Roman province (Liv. 45.17–18; see Scullard 1973, 212–13, 269; Kienast 1979, 117–18).

F 161 Priscian

. . . ; the very early [writers], though, used comparatives of this type too {it is when}. . . . [*Orig.* F 152; *Orat.* F 19, 186, 178] . . . The same Cato [says in the speech] on freeing Macedonia: "and this crept forward more continuously and more strongly." . . . [*Orat.* F 182].

F 162 SHA (Ael. Spart.), 1 *Hadr.* 5.3

quare omnia trans Eufraten ac Tigrim reliquit exemplo, ut
dicebat,[1] Catonis, qui Macedonas liberos pronuntiavit,
quia tueri non poterant.[2]

[1] dicebant *vel* dicebat *codd.*   [2] potera{n}t *Baehrens*

ON BEHALF OF THE RHODIANS
(F 163–71)

*In the Third Macedonian War (171–168 BC), the Rhodi-
ans were broadly supportive of the Romans but also
friendly toward Perseus, king of Macedonia; yet they did
not provide active support to him, while they made attempts to initiate negotiations between Perseus and the
Romans. Legates sent to Rome were admitted to the Senate
only after the Roman victory and then congratulated the
Romans. When the Senate had heard and discussed the
case of the Rhodians, it was inclined to confront the Rhodians and punish them for entertaining feelings of disloy-
alty (cf. Rogatio Iuventia de bello Rhodiis indicendo, 167
BC: LPPR, p. 286; Elster 2003, 389–92). Cato then gave a
famous speech in support of the Rhodians, arguing that
there was no reason to punish anyone for what they may
have intended to do, but did not do (Sall. Cat. 51.5 [FRHist
5 T 12c; Orat. F 126b Cugusi]; Liv. 45.3.3–8, 45.20.4–
25.10; Polyb. 30.4–5; App. Pun. 65.291; Diod. Sic. 31.5).*

F 162 *Historia Augusta* (Aelius Spartianus), *Life of Hadrian*

Whereupon he [the emperor Hadrian] relinquished everything beyond the Euphrates and the Tigris [in the war against the Parthians], in line, as he used to say, with the example of Cato, who declared the Macedonians as free, because they could not be watched over.[1]

[1] This passage refers to a statement by Cato on the status of the Macedonians and thus is likely to refer to the situation after the war against them; it is not made explicit whether this comment comes from a speech.

ON BEHALF OF THE RHODIANS
(F 163–71)

Eventually, a formal declaration of war was prevented; but Rhodes lost a large part of its territory on the mainland and became subject to Rome (for brief overviews of the historical context, see, e.g., CAH² VIII 336–38; Schmitt 1957, 143–57).

Cato's speech was later in circulation separately and included in the Origines *(Orig. F 87–93; cf. Orat. F 163, 171). Substantial sections of the speech survive (the most extensive record of any Catonian speech) since Gellius devotes a chapter to reviewing the oration's critique by Cicero's freedman M. Tullius Tiro, who faulted Cato's style and argumentative techniques and quotes extensive sections in the course of this discussion. Thus, this is the only speech by Cato for which argument, structure, and style can nowadays be explored in greater detail.*

On aspects of the format of this speech, its historical context, and its role in the development of Roman politics,

see, e.g., Haffter 1940; Leeman 1963, 44–47 (on style); Fraenkel 1968, 125–28 (on rhythm and style); Scullard 1973, 217, 269; Astin 1978, 123–24, 137–39, 273–82; Calboli 1978/2003; Malcovati 1978; Kienast 1979, 118–24;

F 163 Gell. *NA* 6.3.1–14

quid Tiro Tullius, Ciceronis libertus, reprehenderit in M. Catonis oratione quam pro Rodiensibus in senatu dixit; et quid ad ea, quae reprehenderat, responderimus.—[1] civitas Rodiensis et insulae opportunitate et operum nobilitatibus et navigandi sollertia navalibusque victoriis celebrata est. [2] ea civitas, cum amica atque socia populi Romani foret, Persa tamen, Philippi filio, Macedonum rege, cum quo bellum populo Romano fuit, amico usa est, conixique sunt Rodienses legationibus Romam saepe missis id bellum inter eos componere. [3] sed ubi ista pacificatio perpetrari nequivit, verba a plerisque Rodiensibus in contionibus eorum ad populum facta sunt ut, si pax non fieret, Rodienses regem adversus populum Romanum adiutarent. [4] sed nullum super ea re publicum decretum factum est. [5] at ubi Perses victus captusque est, Rodienses pertimuere ob ea quae conpluriens in coetibus populi acta dictaque erant, legatosque Romam miserunt qui temeritatem quorundam popularium suorum deprecarentur et fidem consiliumque publicum expurgarent. [6] legati postquam Romam venerunt et in senatum intromissi sunt verbisque suppliciter pro causa sua factis e curia[1] excesserunt, sententiae rogari coeptae; [7] cumque

---

[1] factis e curia *Malaspina*: facti securi *vel* factis securi *codd.*

Goldberg 1983, 204, 207; Traglia 1985, 353–54 (on style); Courtney 1999, 78–85; von Albrecht 2012, 20–28 (on style).

F 163 Gellius, *Attic Nights*

What Tullius Tiro, Cicero's freedman, criticized in M. Cato's speech that he delivered on behalf of the Rhodians in the Senate, and what we said in response to what he had criticized.—[1] The community of Rhodes was well known for the favorable location of the island, the excellence of its buildings, its skill in seamanship, and its naval victories. [2] Although it was a friend and ally of the Roman People, that community nevertheless treated as a friend Perseus, Philip's son and king of the Macedonians, with whom the Roman People were at war, and the Rhodians tried to settle that war between those by often sending embassies to Rome. [3] But when that peacemaking could not be brought to a successful conclusion, statements were made by many Rhodians to the People in their public meetings, saying that, if peace was not made, the Rhodians should aid the king against the Roman People. [4] But no official resolution was passed about that matter. [5] But when Perseus was defeated and taken prisoner, the Rhodians were in great fear because of what had been done and said on many occasions in the gatherings of the People; and they sent envoys to Rome, to seek pardon for the hastiness of some of their fellow citizens and clear the community's loyalty and policy from censure. [6] When the envoys had come to Rome and been admitted to the Senate and, after humbly pleading their cause, had left the Senate house, the senators' opinions began to be sought. [7] And when

157

partim senatorum de Rodiensibus quererentur maleque
animatos eos fuisse dicerent bellumque illis faciendum
censerent, tum M. Cato exsurgit et optimos fidissimosque
socios, quorum opibus diripiendis possidendisque non
pauci ex summatibus viris intenti infensique[2] erant, defen-
sum conservatumque pergit orationemque inclutam dicit,
quae et seorsum fertur inscriptaque est pro Rodiensibus,
et in quintae Originis libro scripta est. [8] Tiro autem Tullius, M. Ciceronis libertus, sane quidem fuit ingenio homo
eleganti haudquaquam rerum litterarumque veterum in-
doctus, eoque ab ineunte aetate liberaliter instituto admi-
niculatore et quasi administro in studiis litterarum Cicero
usus est. [9] sed profecto plus ausus est quam ut tolerari
ignoscique possit. [10] namque epistulam conscripsit ad
Q. Axium,[3] familiarem patroni sui, confidenter nimis et
calide,[4] in qua sibimet visus est orationem istam pro Rodiensibus acri[5] subtilique iudicio percensuisse. [11] ex ea
epistula lubitum forte nobis est reprehensiones eius quas-
dam attingere: maiore scilicet venia reprehensuri Ti-
ronem, cum ille reprehenderit Catonem. [12] culpavit
autem primum hoc, quod Cato inerudite et anagogos
[ἀναγώγως], ut ipse ait, principio nimis insolenti nimisque
acri et obiurgatorio usus sit, cum vereri sese ostendit ne
patres gaudio atque laetitia rerum prospere gestarum de
statu mentis suae deturbati non satis consiperent neque
ad recte intellegendum consulendumque essent idonei.
[13] "in principiis autem" inquit "patroni, qui pro reis[6]

---

[2] infensique *vel* infessique *codd.*: incensique *Ciacconius*

[3] Axium *ed. Iunt. 1513*: anxium *codd.*   [4] calide *Carrio*:
callide *codd.*   [5] acri *codd. rec.*: sacri *codd.*   [6] reis *vel*
regis *vel* regibus *codd.*

some of the senators were complaining about the Rhodians, and said that they had been disloyal, and advised that
a war be undertaken against them, then M. Cato arose and
proceeded to defend and preserve the very good and very
loyal allies, to whom not a few of the most distinguished
men were hostile, with the aim to plunder and possess
their wealth; and he delivered a famous speech, which
both is in circulation separately, entitled "on behalf of the
Rhodians," and is written in the fifth book of the *Origines*
[*FRHist* 5 T 12b]. [8] Now Tullius Tiro, M. Cicero's freedman, was unquestionably a person of refined taste, by no
means unacquainted with early history and literature; and
he, liberally educated from his earliest years, was used as
an assistant and in a sense as a manager in his literary activities by Cicero. [9] But surely he [Tiro] showed more
presumption than can be tolerated and excused. [10] For
he wrote a letter to Q. Axius, a friend of his patron, with
excessive assurance and warmth, in which, as it appeared
to him, he criticized that speech on behalf of the Rhodians
with a keen and fine judgment. [11] By chance we felt like
touching upon some of his criticisms from that letter, certainly with the intention of showing greater forbearance
in relation to Tiro, although he criticized Cato. [12] And
he first found fault with this, that Cato "ignorantly and
absurdly," as he himself says, used a preamble that was
excessively arrogant, excessively severe, and faultfinding,
when he [Cato] declared that he feared that the fathers,
deprived of their balance of mind through joy and exultation at the success achieved, might not be sufficiently sane
and not in a fit state to understand and deliberate properly.
[13] "But in openings," he [Tiro] says, "advocates who are

159

dicunt, conciliare sibi et complacare iudices debent, sensusque eorum exspectatione causae suspensos rigentesque honorificis verecundisque sententiis commulcere, non iniuris atque imperiosis minationibus[7] confutare." [14] ipsum deinde principium apposuit, cuius verba haec sunt [*Orig.* F 87]: "scio solere plerisque hominibus rebus[8] secundis atque prolixis atque prosperis animum excellere, atque superbiam atque ferociam augescere atque crescere. quo{d}[9] mihi nunc magnae curae est, quod haec res tam secunde processit, ne quid in consulendo advorsi eveniat, quod nostras secundas res confutet, neve haec laetitia nimis luxuriose eveniat. advorsae res s‹aep›e domant[10] et docent, quid opus siet[11] facto, secundae res laetitia transvorsum trudere solent a recte[12] consulendo atque intellegendo. quo maiore opere dico suadeoque, uti haec res aliquot dies proferatur, dum[13] ex tanto gaudio in potestatem nostram redeamus."

[7] minationibus *vel* munitionibus *codd.*   [8] rebus *codd.*: in rebus *Gell.* NA *13.25.14*   [9] quo{d} *v. d. in ed. Torn. 1592*: quod *codd.*   [10] s‹aep›e domant *Calboli*: se domant *vel* se donant *codd.*: {s}edomant *Pricaeus*   [11] siet *vel* sit vel sit sibi et *codd.*   [12] recte *de Buxis*: recto *codd.*   [13] dum *de Buxis*: cum *codd.*

Cf. F 59, 122; *Inc.* F 50.

F 164 Gell. *NA* 6.3.15–16

"quae deinde Cato iuxta dicit, ea" inquit "confessionem faciunt, non defensionem, neque propulsationem translationemve criminis habent, sed cum pluribus aliis communicationem, quod scilicet nihili ad purgandum[1] est. atque

[1] purgandum *unus cod., de Buxis*: pugnandum *codd.*

pleading on behalf of the accused ought to win over to their side and propitiate the judges, and, while they are tense with anticipation of the case and unbending, to soothe their minds with complimentary and respectful language, not to silence them with insults and arrogant threats." [14] Then he has appended the very beginning, the words of which are as follows [*Orig.* F 87]: "I know that it is common for very many people in favorable, benign, and prosperous circumstances to be puffed up in spirit and to increase ⟨and grow⟩ in arrogance and insolence. Therefore, it is now of great concern for me, since this enterprise has proceeded so successfully, that nothing untoward should emerge in our deliberations to diminish our prosperity, and that this joy should not become too exuberant. Adverse circumstances often subdue and show what ought to be done; a prosperous situation, because of joy, commonly drives us off course away from right deliberation and understanding. Therefore, it is with even greater emphasis that I say and recommend that this matter be deferred for a few days, until we regain our self-control from so great rejoicing."

F 164 Gellius, *Attic Nights*

"Then," he [Tiro] says, "the things that Cato says next amount to a confession, not a defense; for they do not contain a refutation or shifting of the charge, but the sharing of it with many others, which of course amounts to nothing in the way of proof of innocence. Moreover," he

etiam" inquit "insuper profitetur Rodienses, qui accusa-
bantur quod adversus populum Romanum regi magis cu-
pierint faverintque, id eos cupisse atque favisse utilitatis
suae gratia, ne Romani Perse quoque rege victo ad superbiam ferociamque {et}[2] inmodicum ⟨in⟩[3] modum insoles-
cerent." [16] eaque ipsa verba ponit, ita ut infra scriptum
[*Orig.* F 88]: "atque ego quidem arbitror Rodienses noluisse nos ita depugnare uti depugnatum est, neque regem
Persen vinci. sed[4] non Rodienses modo id noluere, sed
multos populos atque multas nationes idem noluisse arbitror. atque haut scio an partim eorum fuerint qui non
nostrae contumeliae causa id noluerint evenire, sed enim
id metuere, ⟨ne⟩[5] si nemo esset homo quem vereremur,
quidquid luberet[6] faceremus, ne sub solo imperio nostro
in servitute nostra essent; libertatis suae causa in ea sententia fuisse arbitror. atque Rodienses tamen Persem publice numquam adiuvere.[7] cogitate,[8] quanto nos inter nos
privatim[9] cautius facimus. nam unusquisque nostrum, si
quis advorsus[10] rem suam quid fieri arbitrantur, summa vi
contra nititur, ne advorsus eam[11] fiat; quod illi tamen per-
pessi."

2 *del. Eussner*   3 *hic add. Holford-Strevens: ante* inmodicum *Eussner*   4 vinci. sed *Madvig:* vicisse *codd.*

5 *add. Schaefer (on the text see also Viré 1979)*   6 luberet
vel liberet *vel* iuberet *codd.*   7 adiuvere *de Buxis:* adiuvare
vel adiuvasse *codd.*   8 cogitate *vel* cogitatos *vel* cogitare *codd.*

9 nos privatim *unus cod., Gronovius* (privatim *iam Lipsius*)*:*
nostrivatim *vel* nostri nativi *codd.*   10 advorsus *Meyer:* adversus *codd.*   11 eam *unus cod.:* ea *codd. rel.*

says, "he also acknowledges that the Rhodians, who were accused of being well disposed and favorably inclined more toward the king against the Roman People, were well disposed and favorably inclined for the sake of their own advantage, in case, with king Perseus also defeated, the Romans might become overbearing {also} in terms of arrogance and aggression <to> an immoderate extent." [16] And he gives the words themselves, as written below [*Orig.* F 88]: "And for my part, I think that the Rhodians did not want us to fight the war to the end in the way in which it was fought to the end, nor [did they want] king Perseus to be defeated. But it was not only the Rhodians who did not want that, but there were many peoples and many nations who did not want that either, I believe. And I am inclined to think that there were some of them of who did not want that to happen, not for the sake of a disgrace for us, but because they feared this, <that>, if there was nobody of whom we were afraid, we would do whatever we pleased, that they might be under our sole dominion, enslaved to us; I believe that it was because of their own freedom that they were of that opinion. And the Rhodians still never officially aided Perseus. Consider how much more cautiously we deal with one another in private. For each one of us, if they think that anything is being done against their interests, strive against it with the greatest force, so that nothing happens against these [interests]; yet they [the Rhodians] have put up with that."

F 165 Gell. *NA* 6.3.26–27

postea verba haec ex eadem oratione ponit [*Orig.* F 89]:
"ea nunc derepente tanta beneficia ultro citroque, tantam
amicitiam relinquemus? quod illos dicimus voluisse facere, id nos priores facere occupabimus?"[1] [27] "hoc" inquit[2] "enthymema nequam et vitiosum est. responderi
enim potuit: 'occupabimus certe; nam si non occupaveri-
mus, opprimemur, incidendumque erit in insidias, a quibus ante non caverimus.' . . ."

[1] occupabimus *vel* occupavimus *codd.*
[2] inquit *vel* inquam *codd.*

F 166 Gell. *NA* 6.3.34–36

post deinde usum esse Catonem dicit in eadem oratione
argumentis parum honestis et nimis audacibus ac non viri
eius qui alioqui[1] fuit, sed vafris ac fallaciosis, et quasi
Graecorum sophistarum sollertiis. [35] "nam cum obice-
retur" inquit "Rodiensibus quod bellum populo Romano
facere voluissent, negavit poena esse dignos,[2] quia id non
fecissent, etsi maxime voluissent," induxisseque eum dicit
quam dialectici epagogen [ἐπαγωγήν] appellant, rem admodum insidiosam et sophisticam neque ad veritates magis quam ad captiones repertam, cum conatus sit exemplis
decipientibus conligere confirmareque, neminem qui
male facere voluit plecti aequum esse, nisi quod factum
voluit etiam fecerit. [36] verba autem ex ea oratione M.
Catonis haec sunt [*Orig.* F 90]: "qui acerrime adversus eos

[1] qui alioqui *Hertz:* qui alio *vel* qualis *codd.*
[2] poena esse dignos *Madvig:* p(a)ene sed ignosci *codd.*

F 165 Gellius, *Attic Nights*

Later he [Tiro] gives the following words from the same speech [*Orig.* F 89]: "Shall we now suddenly abandon these great services given and received and such a great friendship? Shall we be the first to do what we say they wished to do?" [27] "This," he [Tiro] says, "is a worthless and faulty enthymeme ['abbreviated argument']. For it could be replied: 'Certainly we shall anticipate them, for if we do not anticipate them, we shall be overwhelmed, and we will have to fall into the snares against which we failed to guard in advance.' . . ."

F 166 Gellius, *Attic Nights*

Then he [Tiro] says that later in the same speech Cato used arguments that were not sufficiently honest and were excessively audacious, not suited to the kind of man that he was otherwise, but cunning, and deceitful, and like the subtleties of the Greek sophists. [35] "For although," he [Tiro] says, "he charged the Rhodians with having wished to make war on the Roman People, he declared that they did not deserve punishment, because they had not done so, even though they greatly wanted it." And he [Tiro] says that he [Cato] introduced what the logicians call *epagoge* ["argument by induction"], a most treacherous and sophistical device, designed not so much for ascertaining truths as for presenting verbal quibbles, since by deceptive examples he tried to establish and prove that nobody who wished to do wrong deserved to be punished, unless they also did what they wished done [cf. F 197]. [36] Now M. Cato's words from that speech are as follows [*Orig.* F 90]: "He who speaks most strongly against them says this, that

165

dicit ita dicit, hostes voluisse fieri. ecquis[3] est tandem qui vestrorum,[4] quod ad sese attineat, aequum censeat poenas dare ob eam rem, quod arguatur male facere voluisse? nemo, opinor; nam ego, quod ad me attinet, nolim."

[3] ecquis *Gronovius*: et quis *codd.*   [4] qui vestrorum *vel* qui nostrorum *codd.*: vestrorum qui *unus cod., v. d. ap. Ursinum*: nostrorum qui *cod. unus, de Buxis* (vostrorum), *Gronovius*

F 167 Gell. *NA* 6.3.37

deinde paulo infra dicit [*Orig.* F 91]: "quid nunc? ecqua[1] tandem lex est tam acerba, quae dicat 'si quis illud facere voluerit, mille minus dimidium familiae multa esto; si quis plus quingenta iugera habere voluerit, tanta poena esto; si quis maiorem pecuum numerum habere voluerit, tantum damnas[2] esto'? atque nos omnia plura habere volumus, et id nobis impune est."

[1] ecqua *Meyer*: et qua *vel* et qu(a)e *codd.*   [2] damnas *Ciacconius, cod. Ursini*: dam(p)na *vel* damni *vel* damnis *codd.*

they wished to be enemies. Is there then anyone among you who, as far as they are concerned, would think it fair to pay a penalty for the reason that they are accused of having wished to do wrong? Nobody, I think; for as far as I am concerned, I should not."

F 167 Gellius, *Attic Nights*

Then a little further on he [Cato] says [*Orig.* F 91]: "What now? Is there then any law so severe as to say: 'If anyone has wished to do that, the fine shall be a thousand [sesterces] less than half their property; if anyone has wished to have more than five hundred *iugera* [one *iugerum* = ca. two-thirds of an acre], the penalty shall be so much; if anyone has wished to have a greater number of cattle [i.e., than permitted], they shall be obliged to pay that much.'?[1] And we wish to have everything in greater numbers, and this is without punishment for us."

1 An allusion to a law restricting the possession of land on the *ager publicus* to five hundred *iugera* and only allowing the pasturing on it of not more than one hundred bigger and five hundred smaller animals. Most of the sources refer the law to the fourth century (367 BC), but this passage, along with others in Plutarch and Appian (Plut. *Ti. Gracch.* 8.1–2; App. *B Civ.* 1.8.33–34), has given rise to the suggestion that the regulations might have been renewed or revived in the second century, so that Cato would be referring to a recent example (cf. *Lex Licinia Sextia de modo agrorum*: LPPR, pp. 217–18; Flach 1994, 285–94; *Lex de modo agrorum*: Elster 2003, 365–67 [with overviews of the sources and discussion]).

CATO

F 168 Gell. *NA* 6.3.38

postea ita dicit [*Orig.* F 92]: "sed si honorem non aequum
est haberi ob eam rem, quod bene facere voluisse quis
dicit neque fecit tamen, Rodiensibus oberit,[1] quod non
male fecerunt, sed quia[2] voluisse dicuntur facere?"

[1] oberit *unus cod., Gronovius*: taberit *vel* *aberit *vel* non aberit *vel* tale erit *codd.*: obstabit *Heraeus*: calamitate erit *Fraenkel
(1968, 128)*   [2] quia *codd.*: del. *Madvig*

F 169 Gell. *NA* 6.3.43–51

haec Tiro in Catonem non nimis frigide neque sane inani-
ter; [44] sed enim Cato non nudam nec solitariam nec
inprotectam hanc ἐπαγωγήν, sed multis eam modis prae-
fulcit multisque aliis argumentis convelat, et, quia non
Rodiensibus magis quam rei publicae consultabat, nihil
sibi dictu factuque in ea re turpe duxit quin omni sententiarum via servatum ire socios niteretur. [45] ac primum
ea non incallide conquisivit, quae non iure naturae aut
iure gentium fieri prohibentur, sed iure legum rei alicuius
medendae aut temporis causa iussarum; sicut est de numero pecoris et de modo[1] agri praefinito. [46] in quibus
rebus, quod prohibitum est fieri quidem per leges non licet; velle id tamen facere, si liceat, inhonestum non est.
[47] atque eas res contulit sensim miscuitque cum eo,
quod neque facere neque velle per sese honestum est; tum
deinde, ne disparilitas conlationis evidens fieret, pluribus
id propugnaculis defensat neque tenues istas et enucleatas

[1] modo *Carrio:* domo *codd.*

168

F 168 Gellius, *Attic Nights*

Later he [Cato] says as follows [*Orig.* F 92]: "But if it is not right for honor to be conferred for that reason that someone says that they had wished to act rightly, but still did not act so, shall it do harm to the Rhodians, that they did not act badly, but that they are said to have wanted to act so?"

F 169 Gellius, *Attic Nights*

This [is what] Tiro [says] against Cato, not too insipidly and not completely pointlessly. [44] But, in fact, Cato did not [present] this *epagoge* ["argument by induction"] as something bare, isolated, and unsupported, but he propped it up in many ways and wrapped it in many other arguments; and, since he was not taking thought more of the Rhodians than of the *res publica*, he regarded nothing in that matter to be a discreditable thing for him to do or to say, provided that he strove by every line of argument to save the allies. [45] And first of all, he very cleverly sought out what is prohibited to be done, not by the law of nature or by the law of nations, but by the law of statutes passed to remedy some matter or because of a temporary situation; such for example is the one on the number of cattle or on a defined amount of land. [46] In such cases what is forbidden cannot lawfully be done; still, to wish to do it, if it should be allowed, is not dishonorable. [47] And he gradually compared and connected such actions with what in itself it is neither lawful to do nor to wish. Then finally, in order that the dissimilarity of the comparison should not become evident, he defends it by numerous bulwarks

voluntatum in rebus inlicitis reprehensiones, qualia in philosophorum otio disputantur, magni facit, sed id solum ex summa ope nititur, ut causa Rodiensium, quorum amicitiam retineri ex re publica fuit, aut aequa iudicaretur aut quidem certe ignoscenda. atque interim neque fecisse Rodienses bellum neque facere voluisse dicit, interim autem facta sola censenda dicit atque in iudicium vocanda, sed voluntates nudas inanesque neque legibus neque poenis fieri obnoxias; interdum tamen, quasi deliquisse eos concedat, ignosci postulat et ignoscentias utiles esse rebus humanis docet ac, nisi ignoscant, metus in re publica rerum novarum movet; sed enim contra, si ignoscatur, conservatum iri ostendit populi Romani magnitudinem. [48] superbiae quoque crimen, quod tunc praeter cetera in senatu Rodiensibus obiectum erat, mirifica et prope divina responsionis figura elusit et eluit. [49] verba adeo ipsa ponemus Catonis, quoniam Tiro ea[2] praetermisit [*Orig.* F 93]: [50] "Rodiensis superbos esse aiunt id obiectantes, quod mihi et[3] liberis meis minime dici[4] velim. sint sane superbi. quid id ad nos attinet? idne irascimini, si quis superbior est quam vos?"[5] [51] nihil prorsus hac compellatione dici potest neque gravius neque munitius adversus homines superbissimos facta, qui superbiam in sese amarent, in aliis reprehenderent.

[2] ea *vel* eam *codd.*   [3] et *vel* e *codd.*
[4] dici *vel lac. codd.*: deici *Hertz*: obici (*tum* nolim) *Sauppe*
[5] vos *Wagener*: nos *codd.*

and does not put much weight on those trivial and straight-forward censures of desires in unlawful matters, such as are discussed in the leisure moments of philosophers, but strives with his utmost effort for this alone, namely that the cause of the Rhodians, whose friendship it was in the interests of the *res publica* to retain, should be considered either as just or in any event at least as pardonable. Accordingly, at one point he says that the Rhodians did not make war and did not want to do so; but at another he says that only actions should be considered and judged, while mere empty wishes are liable neither to laws nor punishment; sometimes, however, as if admitting that they misbehaved, he demands that they be pardoned and explains that pardon is expedient in human relations, and, if they should not grant pardon, arouses fears of uprisings in the *res publica*; but on the other hand, if pardon should be granted, he shows that the greatness of the Roman People will be maintained. [48] The charge of arrogance too, which above other things was then brought against the Rhodians in the Senate, he disposed of and washed away by an amazing and almost divine mode of reply. [49] We shall give Cato's very words, since Tiro has passed over them [*Orig.* F 93]: [50] "They say that the Rhodians are arrogant, voicing a charge that I should on no account wish to have pronounced against me and my children. Let them be arrogant. How does this affect us? Are you angry about this, if someone is more arrogant than you?" [51] Absolutely nothing could be said with greater weight or better support than this reproof made against extremely proud individuals, who loved pride in themselves and condemned it in others.

CATO

F 169A Gell. *NA* 6.3.52–53

praeterea animadvertere est in tota ista Catonis oratione
omnia disciplinarum rhetoricarum arma atque subsidia
mota esse; sed non proinde ut in decursibus ludicris aut si-
mulacris proeliorum voluptariis fieri videmus. non enim,[1]
inquam, distincte nimis atque compte atque modulate res
acta est, sed quasi in ancipiti certamine, cum sparsa acies
est, multis locis Marte vario pugnatur, sic in ista tum causa
Cato, cum superbia illa Rodiensium famosissima multorum odio atque invidia flagraret, omnibus promisce tuendi
atque propugnandi modis usus est et nunc ut optime
meritos commendat, nunc[2] tamquam si innocentes purgat, ⟨nunc⟩[3] ne bona divitiaeque eorum expetantur obiur-
gat, nunc {et}[4] quasi sit erratum deprecatur, nunc ut ne-
cessarios rei publicae ostentat, nunc clementiae, nunc
mansuetudinis maiorum, nunc utilitatis publicae commo-
nefacit. [53] eaque omnia distinctius numerosiusque for-
tassean dici potuerint, fortius atque vividius potuisse dici
non videntur.

[1] enim *vel om. codd.*   [2] nunc *de Buxis:* tunc *codd.*
[3] *add. Hertz*   [4] *del. Hertz*

F 170 App. *Pun.* 65.289–91

τοιαῦτα μὲν καὶ ὁ Πούπλιος εἶπεν· ἡ δὲ βουλὴ κατὰ
ἄνδρα παρ᾽ ἑκάστου ψῆφον ᾔτει, καὶ ἐς τὴν Σκιπίωνος
γνώμην αἱ πλείους συνέδραμον. ἐγίγνοντο οὖν αἱ
συνθῆκαι, τρίται αἵδε, Ῥωμαίοις καὶ Καρχηδονίοις

F 169A Gellius, *Attic Nights*

Further, it is to be observed that throughout that entire speech of Cato's all the weapons and auxiliary forces of the rhetorical arts have been set in motion; but we do not see this being done as it is in military maneuvers for show or mock battles staged for the sake of entertainment. For the case was not pleaded, I say, with an excess of refinement, elegance, and musicality, but just as in a battle with uncertain outcome, when the troops have been scattered, the contest rages in many parts of the field with varying fortunes, so in that case at that time, when that most notorious arrogance of the Rhodians was intensely subjected to the hatred and hostility of many, Cato used every method of protection and defense without discrimination, and now he commends them as of the highest merit, now he exculpates them as if blameless, ⟨now⟩ he insists with criticism that their property and riches should not be demanded, now he asks for pardon {and} as if there was an error, now he shows them as friends of the *res publica*, now he adduces clemency, now the mildness of the ancestors, now the public interest [*FRHist* 5 T 12e]. [53] All this might perhaps have been said in a more orderly and rhythmical style; it does not seem that it could have been said with greater vigor and vividness.

F 170 Appian, *Roman History* 8.1. *The African Book*

And such things Publius [P. Cornelius Scipio Africanus maior, cos. 205, 194, censor 199 BC (*ORF*⁴ 4)] said; the Senate asked for a vote from each individual, and the majority agreed with Scipio's view. Thus, a treaty was made, the third one, by the Romans and the Carthaginians with

πρὸς ἀλλήλους. [290] καὶ ὁ Σκιπίων ἐς αὐτὰς ἐδόκει
μάλιστα τοὺς Ῥωμαίους ἐναγαγέσθαι, εἴτε τῶν εἰρη-
μένων οὔνεκα λογισμῶν, εἴτε ὡς ἀρκοῦν Ῥωμαίοις ἐς
εὐτυχίαν τὸ μόνην ἀφελέσθαι Καρχηδονίους τὴν ἡγε-
μονίαν· εἰσὶ γὰρ οἳ καὶ τόδε νομίζουσιν, αὐτὸν ἐς
Ῥωμαίων σωφρονισμὸν ἐθελῆσαι γείτονα καὶ ἀντί-
παλον αὐτοῖς φόβον ἐς ἀεὶ καταλιπεῖν, ἵνα μή ποτε
ἐξυβρίσειαν ἐν μεγέθει τύχης καὶ ἀμεριμνίᾳ. [291] καὶ
τόδε οὕτω φρονῆσαι τὸν Σκιπίωνα οὐ πολὺ ὕστερον
ἐξεῖπε τοῖς Ῥωμαίοις Κάτων, ἐπιπλήττων παρωξυμ-
μένοις κατὰ Ῥόδον.

F 171 Liv. 45.25.2–4

tunc sententiae interrogari coeptae. infestissimi Rhodiis
erant qui consules praetoresve aut legati gesserant in
Macedonia bellum. plurimum causam eorum adiuvit M.
Porcius Cato, qui asper ingenio tum lenem mitemque
senatorem egit. [3] non inseram simulacrum viri copiosi,
quae[1] dixerit referendo; ipsius oratio scripta exstat,[2] Originum quinto libro inclusa. [4] Rhodiis responsum ita red-
ditum est ut nec hostes fierent nec socii permanerent.

[1] viri copiosi, quae *ed. Frobeniana 1531*: viri copias idque
cod.: veri copiose quae *Madvig*: viri copiose id quod *Hertz*: <cum>
viri copia sit, quae *Novák*: viri curiose quae *Heraeus*
[2] extat *cod.*

each other.[1] [290] And Scipio in particular seemed to have urged the Romans on to it, either for the reasons mentioned [cf. App. *Pun.* 56.244–45] or because he considered it sufficient for the success of the Romans just to have deprived the Carthaginians of their supremacy. There are some who believe also this, that for the sake of moderation of the Romans he wished to keep a neighbor and rival to them as an object of fear forever, so that they might never become insolent amid the greatness of their prosperity and freedom from care. [291] And that Scipio thought so, Cato, not long after, publicly declared to the Romans when he reproached them for being angry with Rhodes [*FRHist* 5 T 12d].

[1] The three treaties probably refer to a pact between Carthage and Rome in the war against Pyrrhus (279 BC) as well as the peace treaties at the end of the First (264–241 BC) and the Second Punic Wars (218–201 BC).

F 171 Livy, *History of Rome*

Then the senators' opinions began to be sought. The chief enemies of the Rhodians were those who, as consuls, praetors, or legates, had been conducting the war in Macedonia. Their [the Rhodians'] cause was most greatly assisted by M. Porcius Cato, who, though of a harsh temperament, on this occasion played the part of a tolerant and mild senator. [3] I shall not include a pale copy of this eloquent man by reporting what he said; the speech of the man himself is preserved in written form, included in the fifth book of the *Origines* [*FRHist* 5 T 12a]. [4] A reply was made to the Rhodians on terms that they neither became enemies nor continued to be allies.

AGAINST GALBA TO SOLDIERS
(F 172)

*Cato's speech to the soldiers against Galba might belong
to about 167 BC, when L. Aemilius Paullus (cos. 182, 168
BC [ORF⁴ 12]) had brought the Third Macedonian War
(171–168 BC) to an end by defeating king Perseus at the
Battle of Pydna, and then soldiers, spurred on by Ser. Sulpicius Galba (cos. 144 BC [ORF⁴ 19]; cf. F 196–99A), who
had been a military tribune, criticized Paullus' distribution of booty in the context of his triumph (Liv. 45.35–39).
If the speech was indeed given to soldiers, it would have
been directed against Galba, but not have been part of a
formal trial.*

F 172 Gell. *NA* 1.23.1–13

Quis fuerit Papirius Praetextatus, quae⟨que⟩ istius causa
cognomenti sit, historiaque {ista} omnis super eodem Papirio cognitu iucunda.—[1] historia de Papirio Praetextato
dicta scriptaque est a M. Catone in oratione qua usus est
ad milites contra Galbam, cum multa quidem venustate
atque luce atque munditia verborum. [2] ea Catonis verba
huic prorsus commentario indidissem, si libri copia fuisset
id temporis cum haec dictavi. [3] quod si non virtutes
dignitatesque verborum, sed rem ipsam scire quaeris, res
ferme ad hunc modum est. [4] mos antea senatoribus Romae fuit in curiam cum praetextatis filiis introire. [5] tum
cum in senatu res maior quaepiam consultata eaque in

AGAINST GALBA TO SOLDIERS
(F 172)

Aulus Gellius, quoting from memory, reports a story that formed part of Cato's speech but does not reproduce Cato's words. Gellius identifies the protagonist as Papirius Praetextatus: it has been suggested that he might have misremembered the name and that the story may instead refer to a Sulpicius Praetextatus and have been inserted into the speech as Cato compared the behavior of an ancestor of the family with that of Ser. Sulpicius Galba (e.g., Scullard 1973, 218, 269–70).

F 172 Gellius, *Attic Nights*

Who Papirius Praetextatus was, ‹and› what the reason is for that additional name, and the {that} entire story about that same Papirius, pleasant to get to know.—[1] The story of Papirius Praetextatus was told and committed to writing by M. Cato in the speech that he delivered to soldiers against Galba, with great charm, brilliance, and elegance of diction. [2] I would have included those words of Cato in this commentary straightaway, if a copy of the book had been available at the time when I dictated this. [3] But if you are keen to get to know, not the nobility and dignity of the language, but the matter itself, the story is roughly as follows: [4] it was formerly the custom for senators at Rome to enter the Senate house with their sons in *togae pratextae* [i.e., under age]. [5] In those days, when some matter of greater importance had been discussed in the

177

diem posterum prolata est, placuitque, ut eam rem super
qua tractavissent ne quis enuntiaret priusquam decreta
esset, mater Papirii pueri, qui cum parente suo in curia
fuerat, percontata est filium quidnam in senatu patres
egissent. [6] puer respondit tacendum esse neque id dici
licere. [7] mulier fit audiendi cupidior; secretum rei et
silentium pueri animum eius ad inquirendum everberat:
quaerit igitur compressius violentiusque. [8] tum puer
matre urgente lepidi atque festivi mendacii consilium
capit: actum in senatu dixit utrum videretur utilius exque
re publica esse unusne ut duas uxores haberet, an ut una
apud duos nupta esset. [9] hoc illa ubi audivit, animus
compavescit, [10] domo trepidans egreditur; ad ceteras
matronas per⟨git⟩.[1] venit ad senatum postridie matrum
familias caterva lacrimantes atque obsecrantes;[2] orant,
una potius ut duobus nupta fieret quam ut uni duae. [11]
senatores ingredientes in curiam, quae illa mulierum in-
temperies et quid sibi postulatio istaec vellet mirabantur.
[12] puer Papirius in medium curiae progressus, quid
mater audire institisset, quid ipse matri dixisset, rem sicut
fuerat denarrat. [13] senatus fidem atque ingenium pueri
exosculatur, consultum facit uti posthac pueri cum patri-
bus in curiam ne introeant praeter ille unus Papirius,

[1] per⟨git⟩ *Heraeus:* per⟨fert⟩ *Klotz*
[2] *post* obsecrantes *distinxit Holford-Strevens*

Senate and adjourned to the following day, and it was agreed that nobody should mention the matter that they had handled until it was decided, the mother of the boy Papirius, who had been in the Senate house with his father, asked her son what the fathers had dealt with in the Senate. [6] The boy replied that one had to be silent and it was not permitted to mention it. [7] The woman became more eager to hear; the secrecy of the matter and the boy's silence stirred her mind to inquiry: she therefore questioned him more pressingly and urgently. [8] Then the boy, because of his mother's insistence, developed the plan of a witty and amusing falsehood: he said that the question had been dealt with in the Senate whether it seemed more expedient and to the advantage of the *res publica* for one man to have two wives or for one woman to have two husbands. [9] As soon as she has heard that, her mind becomes full of fear; [10] trembling, she rushes from the house; she moves on to other matrons. On the following day a crowd of matrons comes to the Senate, with tears and entreaties; they beg that one woman might be married to two husbands rather than two women to a single man. [11] The senators, as they entered the Senate house, were wondering what this immoderate behavior of the women was and what such a demand was aiming for. [12] The boy Papirius, stepping forward to the middle of the Senate house, told in detail what his mother had insisted on hearing, what he himself had said to his mother, the whole story as it had happened. [13] The Senate greatly admired the boy's loyalty and cleverness and passed a decree that thereafter boys should not enter the Senate house with their fathers with the single exception of that Papirius; and

179

eique[3] puero postea cognomentum honoris gratia inditum Praetextatus ob tacendi loquendique in aetate praetextae prudentiam.

[3] eique *cod. deperd.*, *Macrobius*: atque *vel* estque *vel* hocque *codd.*

Cf. Macrob. *Sat.* 1.6.19–25; Polyb. 3.20.3–4.

ON HIS OWN LUXURY (F 173–75)

After Cato had become well-off by his frugality, he seems to have been accused of private luxury, in response to which he outlined his parsimonious, unassuming, and honest lifestyle (cf. e.g., T 32a, 32b, 39, 56, 57, 63) as well as his meticulousness in relation to the public finances, apparently including references to his activities as praetor and consul (Fraccaro [1910d] 1956; Scullard 1973, 221, 268, 270; Astin 1978, 92–93, 107–8; Stok 1985). Only F 173 mentions a speech; the other two passages (F 174, 175) report statements by Cato on his frugality without clear indication of their provenance. Therefore, it is not certain that all these comments derive from this speech, as they could also belong to other contexts. The remarks in

F 173 Fronto, *Ad M. Antoninum* 1.2.11–12 (pp. 90.11–91.10 van den Hout)

[FRONTO:] quoniam mentio παραλείψεως habita est, non omittam quin te impertiam quod de figura ista studiosius animadverterim, neque Graecorum oratorum neque Romanorum, quos ego legerim, elegantius hac figura usum quemquam quam M. Porcium in ea oratione, quae de

that boy was henceforth given the additional name Praetextatus as an honor, because of his sagacity in keeping
silent and in speaking, while at the age of wearing the *toga
praetexta*.

ON HIS OWN LUXURY (F 173–75)

*F 174 refer to a time when Cato was at least seventy years
of age and might thus be connected with censorial reviews
in 164, 159, or 154 BC or date after* Lex Fannia *of 161 BC
(cf. F 142). F 173 is the longest continuous fragment surviving from any speech of Cato and is quoted for its use of
a rhetorical feature, defined as a particular form of* praeteritio *(though not a typical example of its standard use).
As the piece includes quotations from another of Cato's
orations (F 203), it must be dated after that one and demonstrates that writing was used in preparing speeches and
that written copies were kept of at least some of them (see
Introduction to* Orations*).*

F 173 Fronto, *Correspondence*

[FRONTO:] Since mention of *paraleipsis* ["*praeteritio*"]
has been made, I will not omit to share with you what I
have observed about that figure of speech by rather diligent study, namely that none of either the Greek or the
Roman orators whom I have read have used this figure
more elegantly than M. Porcius [Cato] in that oration that

181

CATO

sumptu suo inscribitur, in qua sic ait: "iussi caudicem pro-
ferri, ubi mea oratio scripta erat de ea re, quod sponsio-
nem feceram cum M. Cornelio. tabulae prolatae; maiorum[1] bene facta perlecta; deinde quae ego pro re p(ublica)
fecissem leguntur. ubi id utrumque perlectum est, deinde
scriptum erat in oratione: 'numquam ego pecuniam neque
meam neque sociorum per ambitionem dilargitus sum.'
attat,[2] noli noli scribere,[3] inquam, istud: nolunt audire.
deinde recitavit: 'numquam ⟨ego⟩[4] praefectos per sociorum vestrorum oppida inposivi, qui eorum bona, liberos[5]
diriperent.' istud[6] quoque dele: nolunt audire. recita
porro. 'numquam ego praedam neque quod de hostibus
captum esset neque manubias inter pauculos amicos meos
divisi, ut illis eriperem qui cepissent.' istuc quoque dele:
nihil ⟨e⟩o minus[7] volunt dici; non opus est recitato. 'numquam ego evectionem datavi, quo amici mei per symbolos
pecunias magnas caperent.' perge istuc quoque uti cum
maxime[8] delere. 'numquam ego argentum pro vino con-
giario inter apparitores atque amicos meos disdidi[9] neque
eos malo publico divites feci.' enimvero usque istuc ad
lignum dele. vide sis,[10] quo loco res[11] p(ublica) siet, uti[12]
quod rei p(ublicae) bene fecissem, unde gratiam capie-

---

[1] maiorum *Mai*: malorum *cod. ut vid.*   [2] at tu *vel* atta-
men *Orth*   [3] peribere *Mommsen*: servare *Novák*: recitare
Haines: *del. Leo*   [4] numquam ⟨ego⟩ *Schaefer*: numquos
cod.: numquam *Mähly*   [5] bona ⟨coniuges⟩ liberos *Meyer,
Schaefer*: bona liberos ⟨servos⟩ *Castiglioni*   [6] istuc *Jordan*
[7] nihil ⟨e⟩o minus *vel* nihilo magis *Allen*: nihilominus *cod.*:
nihil minus *Jordan*   [8] quam maxime *Schaefer*
[9] disdidi *cod.² ut vid.*: disdi *cod.¹*   [10] vides in *Haines*
[11] res *cod.²*: re *cod.¹*   [12] ubi *Haupt*

182

is entitled "on his own luxury," in which he speaks as follows: "I ordered the notebook to be produced where my
speech had been written down about that matter, that I
had made a judicial wager with M. Cornelius [F 203]. The
tablets were produced; the good deeds of the ancestors
were read out; then what I had done on behalf of the *res
publica* was read. When both of those had been read out,
then it had been written in the speech: 'Never have I given
away money freely, neither mine nor that of allies, in the
course of electioneering.' Ah, do not, do not write that, I
say: they do not wish to hear it. Then he recited: 'Never
have <I> imposed prefects across the towns of your allies,
who would seize their property and children.' That too
delete: they do not wish to hear it. Recite further. 'Never
have I divided up among just a small number of my friends
booty, neither what was captured from the enemy nor the
general's share, so as to snatch it away from those who had
captured it.' That too delete: they wish nothing to be said
less than that; there is no need to recite it. 'Never have I
made it a practice to give orders authorizing travel by state
transport, so that my friends should obtain a lot of money
by official permits.' Go on to delete that, too, as much as
anything. 'Never have I dealt out silver instead of the wine
given as a gratuity among my attendants and friends and
made them rich to the disadvantage of the state.' Well, that
too delete right up to the wood [i.e., remove the writing
and the wax on the tablet to reveal the wooden base].
Look, see in what position the *res publica* is, so that, what
I had done well for the *res publica*, whence I was accustomed to obtain appreciation, now I do not dare to recall

bam, nunc idem illud memorare non audeo, ne invidiae
siet. ita inductum est male facere inpoene, bene facere
non inpoene licere." haec forma παραλείψεως nova nec
ab ullo alio, quod ego sciam, usurpata est. iubet enim legi
tabulas et quod lectum sit iubet praeteriri.

F 174 Gell. *NA* 13.24.1–2

Verba M. Catonis, egere se multis rebus et nihil tamen
cupere dicentis.—[1] M. Cato consularis et censorius
publicis iam privatisque opulentis rebus villas suas inex-
cultas et rudes ne tectorio quidem praelitas fuisse dicit
ad annum usque aetatis suae septuagesimum. atque ibi
postea his verbis utitur: "neque mihi" inquit "aedificatio
neque vasum neque vestimentum ullum est manupretio-
sum, neque pretiosus servus neque ancilla. si quid est"
inquit "quod utar utor; si non est egeo. suum[1] cuique per
me uti atque frui licet." tum deinde addit: "vitio vertunt,
quia multa egeo; at ego illis, quia nequeunt egere." [2]
haec mera veritas Tusculani hominis egere se multis rebus
et nihil tamen cupere dicentis plus hercle promovet ad ex-
hortandam parsimoniam sustinendamque inopiam quam
Graecorum istorum[2] praestigiae philosophari sese dicen-
tium umbrasque verborum inanes fingentium, qui se nihil
habere et nihil tamen egere ac nihil cupere dicunt, cum et
habendo[3] et egendo et cupiendo ardeant.

[1] egeo. suum *Stephanus*: ego sum *codd.*   [2] Graecorum
Hertz: Graecae *codd.*: Graeculorum {istorum} *Boot* | istorum
codd.: sophistarum *Heraeus*   [3] habeant *Eussner*

that very same material, so that it might not be a cause for envy. To such an extent has it been established to behave badly without punishment, to behave well not without punishment." This novel form of *paraleipsis* was not used by anyone else, as far as I know. For he orders the tablets to be read and orders what was read to be passed over.

F 174 Gellius, *Attic Nights*

Words of M. Cato, saying that he lacks many things and still desires nothing.—[1] M. Cato, ex-consul and ex-censor, says that, when public and private affairs were already abounding in wealth, his country houses were un-adorned and plain, not even whitewashed with plaster [cf. F 175], up to the seventieth year of his age. And there he later uses these words on the subject: "I have no building," he says, "no crockery, no garment of costly workmanship, no costly slave, no maidservant. If there is anything that I would use," he says, "I use it; if there is not, I do without. So far as I am concerned, everyone may use and enjoy their own possessions." Then he adds: "They find fault because I lack many things; but I [find fault] with them because they cannot do without them." [2] This simple truth of a person from Tusculum, saying that he lacks many things and still desires nothing, by Hercules, accomplishes more toward encouraging frugality and coping with poverty than the sophistries of those Greeks who profess to be philosophers and invent vain shadows of words, who say that they have nothing and yet lack nothing and desire nothing, while they are passionate about having, lacking, and desiring.

CATO

F 175 Plut. *Cat. Mai.* 4.4–6

ἐσθῆτα μὲν γὰρ οὐδέποτέ φησι φορέσαι πολυτελε-
στέραν ἑκατὸν δραχμῶν, πιεῖν δὲ καὶ στρατηγῶν καὶ
ὑπατεύων τὸν αὐτὸν οἶνον τοῖς ἐργάταις, ὄψον δὲ
παρασκευάζεσθαι πρὸς τὸ δεῖπνον ἐξ ἀγορᾶς ἀσσα-
ρίων τριάκοντα, καὶ τοῦτο διὰ τὴν πόλιν, ὅπως ἰσχύοι
τὸ σῶμα πρὸς τὰς στρατείας, [5] ἐπίβλημα δὲ τῶν
ποικίλων Βαβυλώνιον ἐκ κληρονομίας κτησάμενος
εὐθὺς ἀποδόσθαι, τῶν δ᾽ ἐπαύλεων αὐτοῦ μηδεμίαν
εἶναι κεκονιαμένην, οὐδένα δὲ πώποτε πρίασθαι δοῦλον ὑπὲρ τὰς χιλίας δραχμὰς καὶ πεντακοσίας, ὡς ἂν
οὐ τρυφερῶν οὐδ᾽ ὡραίων, ἐργατικῶν δὲ καὶ στερεῶν
οἷον ἱπποκόμων καὶ βοηλατῶν, δεόμενος· καὶ τούτους
δὲ πρεσβυτέρους γενομένους ᾤετο δεῖν ἀποδίδοσθαι
καὶ μὴ βόσκειν ἀχρήστους. [6] ὅλως δὲ μηδὲν εὔωνον
εἶναι τῶν περιττῶν, ἀλλ᾽ οὗ τις οὐ δεῖται, κἂν ἀσ-
σαρίου πιπράσκηται, πολλοῦ νομίζειν· κτᾶσθαι δὲ τὰ
σπειρόμενα καὶ νεμόμενα μᾶλλον ἢ τὰ ῥαινόμενα καὶ
σαιρόμενα.

ON HIS OWN BEHALF AGAINST
C. CASSIUS (F 176)

*Cato apparently delivered a speech in his defense in re-
sponse to accusations by C. Cassius. This C. Cassius may
be C. Cassius Longinus (cos. 171 BC; MRR 1:416), who
was censor with M. Valerius Messalla in 154 BC (MRR*

F 175 Plutarch, *Life of Cato the Elder*

He [Cato] says that he never wore a garment worth more than a hundred drachmas, that, even when he was praetor and consul, he drank the same wine as the workmen [cf. F 53]; that he would procure supplements for dinner worth thirty asses from the market, and even this for the state's sake, so that his body would be strong for military service, [5] that he once received an embroidered Babylonian coverlet through inheritance, but gave it away at once, that not a single one of his country houses had plastered walls [cf. F 174; Plut. *Cat. Mai.* 31(4).4–5], that he never bought any slave for more than one thousand and five hundred drachmas, since he needed not any who were delicate and youthful, but sturdy workers, such as grooms and herdsmen, and these he thought it his duty to give away when they had become older and not to feed when they were useless; [6] that, in general, he thought nothing that was superfluous was cheap, but that what one does not need, even if bought for an as [i.e., a penny or cent], was dear [cf. *Op. cet.* F 3]; also that he bought lands that were sown and pastured [i.e., farmland] in preference to those that were sprinkled and swept [cf. *Op. cet.* F 6].

ON HIS OWN BEHALF AGAINST
C. CASSIUS (F 176)

1:449), but other identifications are also possible (Scullard 1973, 232–33, 270; Astin 1978, 108–9n15). The fragment includes the first attested address of the Roman People as Quirites *in a speech.*

F 176 Gell. *NA* 10.14.1–4

"iniuria mihi factum itur" quali verborum ordine ‹M.›
Cato dixerit.—[1] audio "illi iniuriam factum iri," audio
"contumeliam dictum iri" vulgo quoque ita dici, et[1] istam
esse verborum figuram iam in medio loquendi usu,[2] idcir-
coque exemplis supersedeo. [2] sed "contumelia illi" vel
"iniuria factum itur" paulo est remotius, exemplum igitur
ponemus. [3] M. Cato pro se contra C. Cassium:[3] "atque
evenit ita, Quirites, uti in hac contumelia quae mihi per
huiusce petulantiam factum itur rei quoque publicae medius fidius[4] miserear, Quirites." [4] sicut autem "contumeliam factum iri"[5] significat iri ad contumeliam faciendam,
id est operam dari quo fiat contumelia, ita ‹"contumelia›[6]
mihi factum itur" casu tantum inmutato idem dicit.

[1] et *unus cod., florilegium:* ‹vulgo› et *codd. rel.*   [2] usu
unus cod., florilegium: usus *codd. rel.*   [3] C. Cassium *vel* con-
casium *codd.*   [4] fidius *vel om. codd.*   [5] factum iri *vel*
facturi *codd.*   [6] *add. Lion*

ON PTOLEMY AGAINST THERMUS
(F 177–81)

*The opponent, named Thermus in the sources, could be L.
Minucius Thermus (cf. F 128–35), who was sent in 154 BC
with other Roman legates to negotiate in conflicts between
the Ptolemaic kings (MRR 1:451; Polyb. 33.11). Cato may
have felt that the legates had not carried out their task*

F 176 Gellius, *Attic Nights*

With which order of words ⟨M.⟩ Cato said *iniuria mihi factum itur.*—[1] I hear *illi iniuriam factum iri* ["that to him injury will be done"], I hear *contumeliam dictum iri* ["that insult will be offered"] commonly said thus too, and that this form of expression is now widely used in speaking; and therefore I refrain from citing examples. [2] But *contumelia illi* or *iniuria factum itur* ["injury or insult is going to be done to him"] is slightly more unusual; therefore, we shall give an example. [3] M. Cato, [in the speech] on his own behalf against C. Cassius, [says]: "And so it happens, Romans, that concerning this insult that is going to be put upon me [*quae mihi . . . factum itur*] through the insolence of this man, may I (so help me god) also pity the *res publica*, Romans." [4] But just as *contumeliam factum iri* means "to be going to have an injury done," that is, that an effort is being made that injury be done, just so ⟨*contumelia*⟩ *mihi factum itur* ["injury will be done to me"] expresses the same, merely with a change of case.

ON PTOLEMY AGAINST THERMUS
(F 177–81)

properly, that they had not supported the favored Ptolemy effectively, and that bribery had taken place (on the potential historical situation, see, e.g., Scullard 1973, 236–37, 271; Kienast 1979, 124–25).

F 177 Gell. *NA* 18.9.1–2

in libro vetere in quo erat oratio M. Catonis de Ptolemaeo
contra Thermum, sic scriptum fuit: "sed si omnia dolo
fecit, omnia avaritiae atque pecuniae causa fecit, eiusmodi
scelera nefaria ‹neque insecenda›,[1] quae neque fando[2]
neque legendo[3] audivimus, ‹fecit›, supplicium pro factis
dare oportet." [2] "insecenda" quid esset quaeri coeptum.

[1] ‹neque insecenda› . . . ‹fecit› *add. Holford-Strevens post F.
Skutsch* (‹atque insecenda fecit›)   [2] fando *Scioppius*: fanda
cod. deperd.   [3] legendo *Popma*: legenda *cod. deperd.*

F 178 Prisc., *GL* II, pp. 87.15–88.9

. . . ; vetustissimi tamen comparativis etiam huiuscemodi
sunt {est quando}[1] usi. . . . [*Orig.* F 152; *Orat.* F 19, 186]
. . . idem Cato de Ptolemaeo minore de Thermi quaes-
tione: "quantoque suam vitam superiorem atque ampli-
orem atque antiquiorem animum inducent esse quam in-
noxiiorem." . . . [*Orat.* F 161, 182].

[1] sunt *vel* sunt est quando *vel* est sunt quando *vel* est quando
vel ** est quando (st?) *codd.*

F 179 Gell. *NA* 20.11.5

sed quod apud sequestrem depositum erat, "sequestro
positum" per adverbium dicebant. Cato de Ptolemaeo
contra Thermum: "per deos immortales, nolite vos[1] atque * * *"

[1] nos *codd. pauci*

F 177 Gellius, *Attic Nights*

In an old book, in which there was M. Cato's speech on Ptolemy against Thermus, the following was written: "But if he did everything craftily, did everything for the sake of avarice and money, ⟨committed⟩ crimes of such a kind, abominable ⟨and not to be mentioned [*insecenda*]⟩, that we have never heard of in speaking or reading, he ought to suffer punishment for what has been done." [2] The question was raised what *insecenda* meant.[1]

  [1] Since the transmitted text of the fragment does not include the word *insecenda*, part of the quotation must have got lost or become confused. Accordingly, scholars have supplemented the text.

F 178 Priscian

. . . ; the very early [writers], though, used comparatives of this type too {it is when}. . . . [*Orig.* F 152; *Orat.* F 19, 186] . . . The same Cato [says in the speech] on the younger Ptolemy [of the brothers] about the inquiry concerning Thermus: "and by how much they will bring themselves to believe that their life is superior, and more magnificent, and more important, rather than more innocent." . . . [*Orat.* F 161, 182].

F 179 Gellius, *Attic Nights*

But that which had been deposited with the *sequester* ["agent, trustee"] they spoke of as *sequestro positum* ["placed in trust"], with an adverbial use. Cato [says in the speech] on Ptolemy against Thermus: "by the immortal gods, do not wish and . . ."[1]

  [1] The continuation of the quotation that must have included the phrase *sequestro positum* has been lost.

CATO

F 180 Prisc., *GL* II, pp. 91.21–92.2

"magnificentior" et "magnificentissimus" et "munificentior" et "munificentissimus" cum videantur a positivo
"magnificens" et "munificens" derivari, ut "eminens
eminentior eminentissimus," haec in usu non sunt, sed pro
his "magnificus" et "munificus," ex quibus comparativum
et superlativum ex his similibus secundum praedictam
regulam derivari invenio apud vetustissimos. M. Cato contra Thermum de Ptolemaeo: "rege optimo atque benefi-
cissimo."

F 181 Charis., *GL* I, p. 197.15–21 = pp. 256.23–57.2 B.

donicum pro donec. . . . sed et Cato: "tu otiosus ambulas,
qui apud regem fuisti, donicum ille tibi interdixit rem
capitalem."

FROM SPEECHES AGAINST THERMUS
(F 182–84)

*Because of the unspecific indication of the topic and the
object of this speech by the quoting authors, these fragments could belong to any of the speeches Cato is attested
to have delivered against a Thermus, who might be Q.*

F 180 Priscian

Although *magnificentior* and *magnificentissimus* and *munificentior* and *munificentissimus* seem to be derived from the positives *magnificens* and *munificens*, like *eminens*, *eminentior*, *eminentissimus* ["outstanding"], these [positives] are not in use, but instead of these *magnificus* ["magnificent"] and *munificus* ["generous"]; from those [and] from [words] similar to these I find a comparative and a superlative derived according to the stated rule among the very early [writers] [cf. F 92, 242]. M. Cato [says in the speech] against Thermus on Ptolemy: "with / under the best and most beneficent king [another, similar example: *beneficus* and *beneficissimus*]."

F 181 Charisius

donicum ["until"; alternative form of conjunction] instead of *donec*. . . . But also Cato: "You wander about at leisure, you who have been with the king, until that man banned you from a crime carrying capital punishment."[1]

[1] This fragment is generally attributed to this speech on the basis of the content, although the source does not identify the work of Cato from which it comes.

FROM SPEECHES AGAINST THERMUS
(F 182–84)

Minucius Thermus, or L. Minucius Thermus (cf. F 58, 59–63, 64–65, 128–35, 177–81), or another Thermus not mentioned elsewhere.

F 182 Prisc., *GL* II, pp. 87.15–88.12

. . . ; vetustissimi tamen comparativis etiam huiuscemodi
sunt {est quando} usi.[1] Cato [*Orig.* F 152; *Orat.* F 19, 186,
178, 161] . . . idem in Thermum: "sed a benefactis, ab
optimis artibus fugit maxima fugella perpetuissimo curri-
culo."

[1] sunt *vel* sunt est quando *vel* est sunt quando *vel* est quando
vel ** est quando (st?) *codd.*

F 183 Non., p. 64.22–23 M. = 88 L.

MOLETRINA, a molendo, quod pistrinum dicimus; ut furatrina[1] aut[2] fetutina. Cato in Thermum: "nervo, carcere,
moletrina."

[1] furatrina *Havet*: feratrina *codd.*: ferratrina *Mercerus*
[2] aut *vel* ut (*praec.* a) *codd.*

F 184 Prisc., *GL* II, pp. 545.26–46.2

praeterea notandum, quod "sepelio sepelivi" vel "sepelii"
"sepultum" in frequentiore usu est supinum, antiquissimi
etiam "sepelitum" dicebant; unde Cato in Thermum:
"mortuus est, sepelitus est."

F 182 Priscian

. . . ; the very early [writers], though, used comparatives of this type too {it is when}. Cato [*Orig.* F 152; *Orat.* F 19, 186, 178, 161] . . . The same [Cato] [in the speech] against Thermus: "but he fled from good deeds, from the best arts in the greatest flight and the most persistent running."

F 183 Nonius Marcellus

moletrina ["mill"; ante-class. word], from grinding in a mill [*molere*], which we call *pistrinum* ["mill"; more common word, from a different root]; like *furatrina* ["theft"] or *fetutina* ["cesspool"; same word formation]. Cato [says in the speech] against Thermus: "by shackles, by prison, by the mill [*moletrina*]."

F 184 Priscian

Moreover, it has to be noted that for *sepelio* ["I bury"], *sepelivi* or *sepelii* [different forms of perfect tense] *sepultum* is more frequently used as the supine and [that] the very early [writers] also said *sepelitum*. Hence Cato [says in the speech] against Thermus: "he is dead, he is buried [*sepelitus*]."

AGAINST MULTIPLE CONSULSHIPS
(F 185–86)

A *law preventing anyone from being consul more than
once* (Lex de consulatu non iterando: LPPR, pp. 290–91;
Elster 2003, 408–9; dated to ca. 151 BC), in existence by
134 BC (Liv. Epit. 56), could have been put forward in
connection with M. Claudius Marcellus becoming consul
for a third time without the necessary interval (cos. 166,

F 185 Fest., p. 282.4–9 L.

PAVIMENTA POENICA marmore Numidico constrata significat Cato, cum ait in ea, quam habuit, ne quis consul bis
fieret: "dicere possum, quibus villae atque aedes aedifica-
tae atque expolitae maximo opere citro atque ebore atque
pavimentis † Poeniciistent †."[1]

[1] Poenicis sient *Jordan*: Poenicis stent *Augustinus*: poenicis-
sant *Bruneau*

AGAINST MULTIPLE CONSULSHIPS
(F 185–86)

*155, 152 BC). In that context Cato might have spoken in
favor of such a regulation. Other comments made against
repeated tenure of offices (Op. cet. F 58.20, 63) could belong to the context of this speech or might have been made
on other occasions (Scullard 1973, 234, 270–71; Astin
1978, 120).*

F 185 Festus

Punic paved floors laid out with Numidian marble are
meant by Cato, when he says in that [speech] that he delivered, [arguing] that nobody should become consul
twice: "I can say: those for whom villas and houses have
been [?] erected and finished off by the greatest effort
with wood of the citron tree, and ivory, and Punic paved
floors [?]."[1]

[1] The translation tentatively reproduces Jordan's emendation
for the corrupt ending of the quotation. Bruneau's (1982) creative
conjecture ("they act in a Punic way") ingeniously explains the
corruption; yet then the quotation includes the lemma prompting
it allusively and not directly. Among other things, Bruneau (1982)
assumes that "Punic paved floors" did not exist in the full sense
of the term in Cato's time (rejected and their existence assumed
again by Gaggiotti 1988).

F 186 Prisc., *GL* II, pp. 87.15–88.4

. . . ; vetustissimi tamen comparativis etiam huiuscemodi
sunt {est quando} usi.[1] . . . [*Orig.* F 152; *Orat.* F 19] . . .
M. Cato in oratione, ne quis iterum consul fiat: "imperator
laudem capit, exercitum meliorem, industriiorem facit."
. . . [F 178, 161, 182].

  [1] sunt *vel* sunt est quando *vel* est sunt quando *vel* est quando
vel ** est quando (st?) *codd.*

ON THE ACHAEANS (F 187–89)

*After the defeat of Perseus, king of Macedonia, at the bat-
tle of Pydna in 168 BC, one thousand Greek men were
taken as hostages and then held in towns across Italy. In
150 BC the surviving individuals were eventually permitted to return to Greece. Over the course of their stay at*

F 187 Gell. *NA* 2.6.7

M. Catonis verba sunt ex oratione quam de Achaeis scripsit: "cumque Hannibal terram Italiam laceraret atque
vexaret"; "vexatam" Italiam dixit Cato ab Hannibale,
quando nullum calamitatis aut saevitiae aut immanitatis
genus reperiri queat quod in eo tempore Italia non per-
pessa sit.

Cf. Macrob. *Sat.* 6.7.10; Serv. auct. ad Verg. *E.* 6.76.

F 188 Plut. *Cat. Mai.* 1.7–8

Cf. T 55.

F 186 Priscian

. . . ; the very early [writers], though, used comparatives of this type too {it is when}. . . . [*Orig.* F 152; *Orat.* F 19] . . . M. Cato [says] in the speech [arguing] that nobody should become consul a second time: "a general wins praise; he makes the army better and more zealous." . . . [F 178, 161, 182].

ON THE ACHAEANS (F 187–89)

Rome, various attempts at their return were made. Cato contributed to discussions about their fate (F 189); a speech "on the Achaeans" (F 187) could describe an utterance in this context (Scullard 1973, 239, 271; Astin 1978, 124–25).

F 187 Gellius, *Attic Nights*

These are words from M. Cato's speech that he wrote on the Achaeans: "and when Hannibal was rending and harrying the land of Italy." Cato said that Italy was "harried" by Hannibal, when no kind of disaster, cruelty, or savagery could be found that Italy did not suffer at that time.

F 188 Plutarch, *Life of Cato the Elder*

Cf. T 55.[1]

[1] Because of the mention of Hannibal (cf. F 187), the statement could have been made in the same speech, but the autobiographical dimension equally enables other contexts.

CATO

F 189 Plut. *Cat. Mai.* 9.2–3

ὑπὲρ δὲ τῶν ἐξ Ἀχαΐας φυγάδων ἐντευχθεὶς διὰ Πολύβιον ὑπὸ Σκιπίωνος, ὡς πολὺς ἐν τῇ συγκλήτῳ λόγος ἐγίνετο, τῶν μὲν διδόντων κάθοδον αὐτοῖς, τῶν δ᾽
ἐνισταμένων, ἀναστὰς ὁ Κάτων "ὥσπερ οὐκ ἔχοντες"
εἶπεν "ὃ πράττωμεν, καθήμεθα τὴν ἡμέραν ὅλην περὶ
γεροντίων Γραικῶν ζητοῦντες, πότερον ὑπὸ τῶν παρ᾽
ἡμῖν ἢ τῶν ἐν Ἀχαΐᾳ νεκροφόρων ἐκκομισθῶσι." [3]
ψηφισθείσης δὲ τῆς καθόδου τοῖς ἀνδράσιν, ἡμέρας
ὀλίγας οἱ περὶ τὸν Πολύβιον διαλιπόντες, αὖθις ἐπεχείρουν εἰς τὴν σύγκλητον εἰσελθεῖν, ὅπως ἃς πρότερον εἶχον ἐν Ἀχαΐᾳ τιμὰς οἱ φυγάδες ἀναλάβοιεν, καὶ
τοῦ Κάτωνος ἀπεπειρῶντο τῆς γνώμης. ὁ δὲ μειδιάσας ἔφη τὸν Πολύβιον ὥσπερ τὸν Ὀδυσσέα βούλεσθαι πάλιν εἰς τὸ τοῦ Κύκλωπος σπήλαιον εἰσελθεῖν,
τὸ πιλίον ἐκεῖ καὶ τὴν ζώνην ἐπιλελησμένον.

Cf. Polyb. 35.6.

ON KING ATTALUS AND
DUES FROM ASIA (F 190)

*The praetor C. Licinius mentioned in the fragment could
be C. Licinius Crassus, involved in military preparations
for the war against Perseus, king of Macedonia (Liv.
42.27.3); such an identification would give a* terminus post
quem *of 172 BC (MRR 1:411) for the speech. The refer-*

200

F 189 Plutarch, *Life of Cato the Elder*

On behalf of the exiles from Achaea, his [Cato's] aid was solicited by Scipio [P. Cornelius Scipio Aemilianus Africanus minor (*ORF*⁴ 21)], at the instance of Polybius [Greek historian, one of the hostages]; after a long debate had taken place in the Senate, with some granting their return home and some opposing it, Cato rose and said [*Op. cet.* F 58.28]: "As if we had nothing to do, we are sitting around all day long, inquiring concerning some poor old Greeks, whether they should be buried by funerary men here or those in Achaea." [3] After the return for these men had been decreed, those around Polybius left an interval of a few days and then tried to get admission to that body again, with a proposal that the exiles resume the honors they had held previously in Greece, and asked Cato's opinion on the matter. He smiled and said that Polybius, like Odysseus [cf. Hom. *Od.* 9], wanted to go back into the cave of the Cyclops for the cap and the belt he had left behind there [*Op. cet.* F 64].[1]

---

[1] Only the first reported comment is said to have been made in the Senate; the second one is referred to a private conversation with the men around Polybius.

ON KING ATTALUS AND
DUES FROM ASIA (F 190)

ence to this praetorship would then be an allusion to earlier events, as the context for the speech described in the surrounding text might refer to the following situation: in the conflict between Attalus II Philadelphus, king of Pergamon (r. 159–138 BC), and Prusias II, king of Bithynia

*(r. ca. 182–149 BC), the Romans negotiated a treaty in 154
BC, requiring Prusias to make reparation payments. A few
years later (151/50 BC), Prusias had the Senate in Rome
asked to lighten the burden, while Attalus sent someone to
argue the opposite; Prusias was not successful (Polyb.
33.13; App. Mithr. 3.6–4.12). Cato would have spoken
against the request of a reduction, which amounts to a*

F 190 Fest., p. 266.23–29 L.

PORTISCULUS est, ut scribit Aelius Stilo, qui in portu modum dat classi. id autem est malleus, cuius meminit Cato
in dissuasione de rege Attalo et vectigalibus Asiae: "C.
Licinio praetore remiges scribti cives Romani{s}[1] sub por-
tisculum, sub flagrum conscribti veniere passim."

1 Romani{s} *edd.*: Romanis *cod.*

ON THE WAR WITH CARTHAGE
(F 191–95b)

*In the years leading up to the declaration of the Third
Punic War (149–146 BC), Cato delivered several speeches
arguing for war with Carthage (Liv. Epit. 48; 49 [T 34];
cf. also Op. cet. F 76), while the phrasing used on one occasion by Gellius (F 191) suggests that there was a single*

F 191 Gell. *NA* 9.14.9–10

sic autem "dies, dii" a veteribus declinatum est, ut "fames,
fami," "pernicies, pernicii," "progenies, progenii," "luxu-

dissuasio, *as the speech is characterized, whether in a debate in the Senate or in response to the proposal of a law (Fraccaro [1910c] 1956, 253–56; Scullard 1973, 238, 271; Astin 1978, 125, 271; Kienast 1979, 125; cf. a potential* Rogatio de rege Attalo et de vectigalibus Asiae: LPPR, *p 291; Elster 2003, 411–12).*

F 190 Festus

portisculus ["a kind of hammer used in beating time for rowers"] is, as Aelius Stilo [L. Aelius Stilo (F 30 *GRF*)] writes, [an instrument] that in the harbor gives a rhythm to the fleet. It is, however, a hammer, which Cato mentions in the dissuasive speech about king Attalus and dues from Asia: "In the praetorship of C. Licinius Roman citizens, enrolled as oarsmen under the hammer, enlisted under the whip, were sold indiscriminately."

ON THE WAR WITH CARTHAGE
(F 191–95b)

oration. Various fragments indicating utterances by Cato on Carthage could come from one or more of these interventions, which seem to include comments on the history of Carthage (Scullard 1973, 240–45, 271, 288).

F 191 Gellius, *Attic Nights*

But *dies, dii* ["day"; nom., gen.; unusual form of gen.] was declined by the ancients in the same way as *fames, fami* ["famine"; nom., gen.], *pernicies, pernicii* ["destruction"; nom., gen.], *progenies, progenii* ["offspring"; nom., gen.],

ries, luxurii," "acies, acii." [10] M. enim Cato in oratione, quam de bello Cartaginiensi composuit ita scripsit: "pueri atque mulieres extrudebantur fami causa."

F 192 Non., p. 89.24–25 M. = 128 L.

CALLISCERUNT prout calluerunt. Cato de bello Carthaginiensi: "aures nobis calliscerunt ad iniurias."

F 193 Gell. *NA* 3.14.19

item M. Cato de Carthaginiensibus ita scripsit: "homines defoderunt in terram dimidiatos ignemque circumposuerunt, ita interfecerunt."

F 194 Solin. 27.10

urbem istam, ut Cato in oratione senatoria autumat, cum rex Iapon rerum in Libya potiretur, Elissa mulier extruxit domo Phoenix et Carthadam dixit, quod Phoenicum ore exprimit civitatem novam. mox sermone verso in morem Punicum, et haec Elisa et illa Carthago dicta est: . . .

luxuries, *luxurii* ["luxury"; nom., gen.], *acies*, *acii* ["sharp edge"; nom., gen.]. [10] For M. Cato, in the speech that he composed on the war with Carthage, wrote as follows: "children and women were driven out because of famine [*fami*; gen.]."

F 192 Nonius Marcellus

calliscerunt ["they have grown insensitive"], like "they have grown hard." Cato [says in the piece] on the Carthaginian war: "our ears have grown insensitive to injuries."

F 193 Gellius, *Attic Nights*

Likewise, M. Cato wrote about the Carthaginians as follows: "They buried people halfway down in the ground and built a fire around them; in this way they killed them."[1]

1 Such a statement about customs of the Carthaginians could have been made in a number of contexts, including a speech on the war with Carthage.

F 194 Solinus

That city [Carthage], as Cato affirms in a senatorial speech,[1] was built, when king Iapon [i.e., Iarbas] reigned in Libya, by the woman Elissa [i.e., Dido], by origin a Phoenician, and was called Carthada, which means "new community" in the tongue of the Phoenicians. Soon, with the language changed to Punic conventions, she [the woman] was called Elisa and it [the city] Carthage [cf. Isid. *Orig.* 15.1.30]: . . .

1 The source does not indicate the topic of the senatorial speech to which this fragment belongs, but such a description of its history is likely to come from a speech about Carthage.

CATO

F 195 Iul. Vict., *Ars* 11, *RLM*, pp. 412.34–13.2 (=
p. 55.20–24 Giomini / Celentano)

sed enthymema gnomicon hoc a sententia differt, quod ibi
tantum simpliciter sententia pronuntiatur, hic autem simul et ratio sententiae redditur, quale est hoc: "Carthagini-
enses nobis iam hostes sunt; nam qui omnia parat contra
me, ut, quo tempore velit, bellum possit[1] inferre, hic iam
mihi hostis est, tametsi nondum armis agat."

[1] velit, bellum possit *Orelli*: possit bellum velit *cod.*

Cf. Dem. *Phil.* 3.8; 3.17.

F 195b *Rhet. Her.* 4.20

conplexio est quae utramque conplectitur exornationem,
ut et conversione et repetitione utamur, quam ante expo-
suimus, et ut repetatur idem verbum saepius et crebro ad
idem postremum revertamur, hoc modo: "qui sunt qui
foedera saepe ruperunt? Kartaginienses. qui sunt qui cru-
delissime bellum gesserunt? Kartaginienses. qui sunt qui
Italiam deformaverunt? Kartaginienses. qui sunt qui sibi
postulant ignosci? Kartaginienses. videte ergo quam con-
veniat eos impetrare."

Cf. Quint. *Inst.* 9.3.31.

---

[1] Some scholars assign this passage to a speech by Cato on the
war with Carthage (e.g., Nenci 1962; Malcovati 1975; 1978, 379–
80; added in *ORF⁴*); others do not believe that these are words of
Cato (e.g., Calboli 1978, 240–43; Sblendorio Cugusi 1982, 371–
72), as an author is not identified, and this could be a rhetorical
example (recurring in Quintilian) created in the rhetorical tradition (cf. F 195).

F 195 Iulius Victor

But an *enthymema gnomicon* [a kind of syllogism] differs in that respect from a *sententia* ["proposition"] that in the latter a *sententia* is only stated simply, but in the former at the same time a reasoning for the *sententia* is also given, such as this: "The Carthaginians are already our enemy; for those who prepare everything against me, so that they can start war at any time they wish, those are already my enemy, even if they are not yet using arms."[1]

---

[1] This statement about the Carthaginians is not attributed to any author or work. If it has not been made up by the rhetorician as an example (cf. F 195b), it could come from one of Cato's speeches, because of the strong opposition to Carthage implied (see Nenci 1962; Malcovati 1975; *contra* Sblendorio Cugusi 1982, 372). On the style of the passage, see Traglia 1985, 351–53.

F 195b *Rhetorica ad Herennium*

complexio [a stylistic figure involving effective repetition] is [the figure of speech] that encompasses both kinds of embellishment, so that we use both *conversio* [~ anaphora] and *repetitio* [~ epiphora / homoioteleuton], which we have set out above [*Rhet. Her.* 4.19], so that both the same word is repeated several times and we often return to the same at the end, in this way: "Who are they who have often broken treaties? The Carthaginians. Who are they who have waged war in the most cruel fashion? The Carthaginians. Who are they who have disfigured Italy? The Carthaginians. Who are they who ask for pardon for themselves? The Carthaginians. See then how appropriate it is for them to have their request granted."[1]

CATO

AGAINST SER. GALBA ABOUT
THE LUSITANIANS (F 196–99A)

*In 149 BC the Tribune of the People L. Scribonius Libo
(ORF⁴ 29) put forward a proposal for an inquiry, directed
against Ser. Sulpicius Galba (cos. 144 BC [ORF⁴ 19]; cf.
F 172), who had been a promagistrate in Further Iberia in
151 and 150 BC (MRR 1:455, 456–57), because Galba was
responsible for the fact that some Lusitanians (people in
the Iberian peninsula) had been killed and others sold into
slavery in violation of a treaty (TLRR 1; cf. Rogatio Scri-
bonia de Lusitanis: LPPR, p. 292; Elster 2003, 416–18).
Cato (T 34; for his support of people in Iberia, see T 3),
like L. Cornelius Cethegus, argued in favor of the bill (in
front of the People; CCMR, App. A: 173) or spoke as one*

F 196 Gell. *NA* 13.25.15

itidem Cato ex Originum VII [*Orig.* F 104] in oratione
quam contra Servium Galbam dixit conpluribus vocabulis
super eadem re usus est: "multa me dehortata sunt huc
prodire, anni aetas, vox vires {senectus};[1] verum enimvero,
cum tantam rem peragier[2] arbitrarer,[3] ⟨* * *⟩."[4]

[1] *del. Fraenkel (1968, 151)*   [2] peragier *vel* pagier *v.* p.
agier *vel* agier *codd.*   [3] arbitrarer *vel* arbitraret (-retur) *codd.*
[4] *lac. statuit Jordan*

AGAINST SER. GALBA ABOUT
THE LUSITANIANS (F 196–99A)

of Galba's prosecutors (different indications in the sources: F 198 vs. F 197). In his defense, Ser. Sulpicius Galba (ORF⁴ 19 F 12–14), supported by Q. Fulvius Nobilior (ORF⁴ 19A F 2), made an emotional plea and managed to get himself acquitted (on the oration and its testimonia, see Scivoletto 1961; Scullard 1973, 235–36, 271; Astin 1978, 111–13; Kienast 1979, 97–98). Cato's speech was given in the year of his death at the end of a long life and career. It may have been his last speech (T 14, 32b, 37, 82; Orat. F 198, 198B); it was written up and included in the Origines *(Orig. F 104–7; cf. Orat. F 198, 198A, 198B; T 14, 34; cf. Astin 1978, 155–56).*

F 196 Gellius, *Attic Nights*

In the same way [cf. F 59], from the seventh [book] of the *Origines* [*Orig.* F 104], in the speech that he delivered against Servius Galba, Cato used several words for the same thing: "many things have discouraged me from coming forward here, my years and my time of life, my voice and my strength{, my old age}; but nevertheless, since I believed that such an important matter was being dealt with, * * *."[1]

---

[1] The remainder of the quotation has been lost. A passage in a speech in Sallust's *The War with Iugurtha* (Sall. *Iug.* 31.1) might be inspired by this phrase of Cato's.

F 197 Gell. *NA* 1.12.17

M. Cato de Lusitanis, cum Ser.[1] Galbam accusavit: "tamen dicunt deficere voluisse. ego me nunc volo ius pontificium optime scire; iamne ea causa pontifex capiar? si volo augurium optime tenere, ecquis[2] me ob ⟨rem⟩[3] augurem capiat?"

[1] Ser. *de Buxis*: Sergium *codd.*   [2] ecquis *Gronovius*: et quis *vel* et quos *codd.*   [3] *add. de Buxis*: eam *vel* meam *codd.*

F 198 Cic. *Brut.* 89–90

[CICERO:] quae quidem vis tum[1] maxume cognitast, cum Lusitanis a Ser. Galba praetore contra interpositam, ut existumabatur, fidem interfectis L. Libone[2] tribuno plebis populum incitante et rogationem in Galbam privilegi similem ferente, summa senectute, ut ante dixi, M. Cato legem suadens in Galbam multa dixit; quam orationem in Origines suas rettulit, paucis ante quam mortuus est {an}[3] diebus an mensibus [*Orig.* F 107a; *FRHist* 5 T 13a]. [90] tum igitur ⟨nihil⟩[4] recusans Galba pro sese et populi Romani fidem implorans cum suos pueros tum C. Gali etiam filium flens commendabat, cuius orbitas et fletus mire miserabilis fuit propter recentem memoriam clarissimi patris; isque se tum eripuit flamma, propter pueros misericordia populi commota, sicut idem scriptum reliquit Cato.

[1] vis tum *edd.*: ut istum *codd.*
[2] L. Libone *Corradi (cf. Cic.* De or. *2.263)*: T. Libone *codd.*
[3] *del. Pareus*
[4] *add. Corradi*

F 197 Gellius, *Attic Nights*

M. Cato [said] about the Lusitanians, when he charged
Ser. Galba [cf. *Orig.* F 105]: "Yet they say that they wished
to defect [cf. F 166]. I myself now wish to know pontifical
law most accurately; for that reason should I already be
chosen as a pontiff? If I wish to understand augury most
accurately, should anyone for ⟨that reason⟩ choose me as
an augur?"

F 198 Cicero, *Brutus*

[CICERO:] This very power [i.e., appeal to the emotions]
was noticed particularly then when, after the Lusitanians
had been killed by Ser. Galba, the praetor, in violation (as
was believed) of the pledge given and thus L. Libo, a
Tribune of the People [L. Scribonius Libo (*ORF*[4] 29)],
stirred up the People and put forward a bill against Galba,
similar to a law directed at an individual, M. Cato, in extreme old age, as I have said before [Cic. *Brut.* 80: T 14],
arguing for the law, said many things against Galba; this
speech he incorporated into his *Origines*, a few days or
months before he died [*Orig.* F 107a; *FRHist* 5 T 13a].
[90] Then Galba, while asking ⟨nothing⟩ for himself and
appealing to the good faith of the Roman People, tearfully,
commended to their protection his own boys as well as
also the son of C. Galus [C. Sulpicius Galus, cos. 166
(*ORF*[4] 14)], whose orphaned state and weeping were particularly pitiful because of the recent memory of his most
illustrious father. And then that man [Galba] snatched
himself from the blaze, by arousing the People's pity because of the boys, as Cato has also recorded in writing.

CATO

F 198A Cic. *De or.* 1.227–28

[ANTONIUS:] idemque Servium Galbam, quem hominem
probe commeminisse se aiebat, pergraviter reprehendere
solebat, quod is, L. Scribonio quaestionem in eum ferente,
populi misericordiam concitasset, cum M. Cato, Galbae
gravis atque acer inimicus, aspere apud populum Romanum et vehementer esset locutus, quam orationem in Originibus suis exposuit ipse [*Orig.* F 107b; *FRHist* 5 T 13b].
[228] reprehendebat igitur Galbam Rutilius, quod is C.
Sulpici Gal{l}i[1] propinqui sui Q. pupillum filium ipse
paene in umeros suos extulisset, qui patris clarissimi re-
cordatione et memoria fletum populo moveret, et duos
filios suos parvos tutelae populi commendasset ac se tamquam in procinctu testamentum faceret sine libra atque
tabulis, populum R(omanum) tutorem instituere dixisset
illorum orbitati. itaque, cum et invidia et odio populi tum
Galba premeretur, hisce[2] eum tragoediis liberatum ferebat; quod item apud Catonem scriptum esse video: nisi
pueris et lacrimis usus esset, poenas eum daturum fuisse.
haec Rutilius valde vituperabat et huic humilitati dicebat
vel exsilium fuisse vel mortem anteponendam.

[1] Gal{l}i *Kumaniecki*: Galli *codd.*
[2] hisce *Heusinger*: isque *vel* iisque *vel* is quoque *vel* iss *codd.*

212

ORATIONS

F 198A Cicero, *On the Orator*

[ANTONIUS:] He [P. Rutilius Rufus, cos. 105 BC (*ORF*⁴ 44; *FRHist* 21)] also used to censure very severely Servius Galba, a man whom he claimed to remember well, for having worked upon the compassion of the People, when L. Scribonius was proposing a judicial inquiry against him, after M. Cato, a harsh and bitter foe to Galba, had spoken harshly and forcefully before the Roman People; this speech he [Cato] himself has set forth in his *Origines* [*Orig.* F 107b; *FRHist* 5 T 13b]. [228] Rutilius, then, used to find fault with Galba, for having almost lifted on to his shoulders his ward Quintus, the son of his near relative C. Sulpicius Galus [C. Sulpicius Galus, cos. 166 (*ORF*⁴ 14)], in order to move the People to tears, by recalling the memory of the most illustrious father, and for having committed his two small sons to the guardianship of the People, and for having proclaimed, like someone making their will on active military service, without scales or tablets, that he appointed the Roman People to be their guardians for their orphaned state. Accordingly, Galba, though at that time weighed down by ill will and hatred of the People, secured an acquittal by means of these histrionics; I also see this written in Cato, that, if he had not employed boys and tears, he would have paid the penalty. These methods Rutilius used to condemn strongly and to say that banishment or death was to be preferred to such abjectness.

F 198B Val. Max. 8.1.absol.2

acrem se tunc pudicitiae custodem populus Romanus,
postea plus iusto placidum iudicem praestitit. cum a Libone tribuno plebis Ser.[1] Galba pro rostris vehementer
increparetur, quod Lusitanorum magnam manum interposita fide praetor in Hispania interemisset, actionique
tribuniciae M. Cato ultimae senectutis oratione sua, quam
in Origines[2] rettulit [*Orig.* F 106c; *FRHist* 5 T 13c], sub-
scriberet, reus, pro se iam nihil recusans, parvulos liberos
suos et Gal{l}i[3] sanguine sibi coniunctum filium flens com-
mendare[4] coepit, eoque facto mitigata contione qui omnium consensu periturus erat paene nullum triste suffragium habuit. misericordia ergo illam quaestionem, non
aequitas rexit, quoniam quae innocentiae tribui nequierat
absolutio, respectui puerorum data est.

[1] Servius *codd.*: Sergius *epit. Iulii Paridis*   [2] Origines
codd. det.: Origine *codd.*   [3] Gal{l}i *Briscoe*: Galli *codd.*:
‹C.› Galli *Halm*   [4] con(m)endare *codd.*: populo commen-
dare *epit. Iulii Paridis*: populo *ante* parvolos *Kempf*

F 198C Quint. *Inst.* 2.15.8

Servium quidem Galbam miseratione sola, qua non suos
modo liberos parvolos in contione[1] produxerat, sed Galli
etiam Sulpici filium suis ipse manibus circumtulerat, elap-
sum esse cum aliorum monumentis, tum Catonis oratione
testatum est.

[1] contione *vel* contionem *codd.*

F 198B Valerius Maximus, *Memorable Doings and Sayings*

The Roman People showed itself on that occasion [in the case of M. Horatius' killing of his sister] a fierce guardian of chastity, but later an unduly lenient judge: when Ser. Galba was vehemently attacked from the speaker's platform by Libo, a Tribune of the People [L. Scribonius Libo (*ORF*[4] 29)], because, as praetor in the Iberian peninsula, he had killed a large body of Lusitanians, after giving a pledge, and M. Cato supported the Tribune's proceeding in a speech of his extreme old age, which he included into the *Origines* [*Orig.* F 106c; *FRHist* 5 T 13c], the accused, asking no longer anything for himself, began to commend with tears his little children and Galus' [C. Sulpicius Galus, cos. 166 (*ORF*[4] 14)] son, his blood relation. By this action he softened the hearts of the assembled People, and he, who had been about to perish by the consent of all, received hardly a single guilty vote. So it was pity, not justice, that governed that trial, since an acquittal that could not have been assigned because of innocence was granted out of compassion for the boys.

F 198C Quintilian, *The Orator's Education*

That Servius Galba escaped solely through the pity aroused by the fact that he had not only brought his own little children into the assembly, but had also himself embraced with his arms the son of Sulpicius Gallus [C. Sulpicius Galus, cos. 166 (*ORF*[4] 14)], is evidenced by the records of others and particularly by a speech of Cato's [cf. *Orig.* F 106b].

CATO

F 199 Fronto, *Ad M. Caes.* 3.21.4 (p. 52.1–4 van den Hout)

[Fronto:] Cato quid dicat de Galba absoluto, tu melius[1] scis: ego memini propter fratris filios eum absolutum. τὸ δὲ ἀκριβές ipse inspice. Cato igitur dissuadet neve suos neve alienos quis liberos ad misericordiam conciliandam producat neve uxores neve adfines vel ullas omnino feminas.

[1] ‹me› melius *Castiglioni*

F 199A Ps.-Asc. in Cic. *Div. Caec.* 66 (p. 203.24–25 Stangl)

Cf. F 154.

AGAINST LENTULUS BEFORE
THE CENSORS (F 200)

This Lentulus might be P. Cornelius Lentulus Caudinus (praet. 203 BC), but details about the context or the time of the speech (apart from its link to a censorial year) are

F 200 Gell. *NA* 5.13.1–4

seniorum hominum et Romae nobilium, atque in morum disciplinarumque veterum doctrina memoriaque praestantium, disceptatio quaedam fuit praesente et audiente me de gradu atque ordine officiorum, cum quaereretur quibus nos ea prioribus potioribusque facere oporteret, si necesse esset in opera danda faciendoque officio alios aliis

ORATIONS

F 199 Fronto, *Correspondence*

[FRONTO:] What Cato says about Galba having been acquitted, you know better; I remember that he was acquitted because of his brother's sons;[1] look into this in detail
yourself. Cato accordingly advises against anybody bringing into court their own or others' children to provoke pity,
nor wives, nor in-laws, nor any women at all [cf. *Orig.*
F 106a].

1 In fact, his own sons and the son of a relative (cf. F 198A),
not sons of a brother.

F 199A Ps.-Asconius on Cicero, *Divinatio in Caecilium*

Cf. F 154.

AGAINST LENTULUS BEFORE
THE CENSORS (F 200)

*not known (Scullard 1973, 272; Astin 1978, 109–10).
Speeches delivered against someone else before the censors
are rare.*

F 200 Gellius, *Attic Nights*

Among people of advanced age and high position at Rome,
who were also eminent for their learning and knowledge
of ancient practices and conduct, there was once a discussion, in my presence and hearing, of the rank and order of
obligations, when it was asked to whom we ought first and
foremost to discharge those, in case it should be necessary
to prefer some to others in giving assistance or doing a

anteferre. [2] conveniebat autem facile¹ constabatque ex
moribus populi Romani primum iuxta parentes locum
tenere pupillos debere fidei tutelaeque nostrae creditos;
secundum eos proximum locum clientes habere, qui sese
itidem in fidem patrociniumque nostrum dediderunt;
tunc in tertio loco esse hospites; postea esse cognatos adfi-
nesque. [3] huius moris observationisque multa sunt testimonia atque documenta in antiquitatibus perscripta, ex
quibus unum hoc interim de clientibus cognatisque, quod
prae manibus est, ponemus. [4] M. Cato in oratione quam
dixit apud censores in Lentulum ita scripsit: "quod maiores sanctius habuere defendi pupillos quam clientem non
fallere: adversus cognatos pro cliente testatur,² testimonium adversus clientem nemo dicit. patrem primum,
postea patronum proximum nomen hab⟨u⟩ere."³

¹ facile *de Buxis*: facere *codd.*
² testatur *codd.*: testamur *Gronovius*: testari, cum *Mommsen*
³ hab⟨u⟩ere *Maiansius*: habere *codd.*

AGAINST TI. SEMPRONIUS LONGUS
(F 201)

*Ti. Sempronius Longus (aed. 198, praet. 196, cos. 194 BC)
was among those standing as candidates for the censorship
in 184 BC, when Cato was elected (Liv. 39.40.2–3): Cato's*

service. [2] But it was readily agreed and accepted that, in accordance with the practices of the Roman People, the place next after parents should be held by wards consigned to our trust and tutelage; that the second place next to them should be had by clients, who had in the same way committed themselves to our trust and guardianship; that then in the third place there were guests; and after that there were relations by blood and by marriage. [3] Of this custom and practice there are numerous testimonies and proofs written in ancient records, of which, because it is at hand, we will put down only this single one for now, relating to clients and kindred. [4] M. Cato in the speech that he delivered before the censors against Lentulus wrote as follows: "because our forefathers held it to be a more sacred obligation that wards be defended than not to let down a client: one testifies on a client's behalf against one's relatives; testimony against a client is given by no one. They regarded 'father' as the first honorific title, after that 'patron' as a close second."[1]

[1] The fragment illustrates the value attached to the patron-client relationship in Cato's time (Neuhauser 1958, 87).

AGAINST TI. SEMPRONIUS LONGUS
(F 201)

speech against Longinus could belong to the context of this competition (Scullard 1973, 150, 259–60). Other contexts and identifications of the opponent are possible too.

F 201 Prisc., *GL* II, p. 279.15–18

. . . "supellex supellectilis"—vetustissimi tamen etiam "haec supellectilis" nominativum proferebant. Cato adversum Tiberium Sempronium Longum: "si posset auctio fieri de artibus tuis, quasi supellectilis[1] solet"—. . .

[1] ⟨in⟩ supellectili{s} *Fraenkel (1968, 152–53)*

AGAINST THE EXILE TIBERIUS
(F 202)

The identity of the opponent, called Tiberius exul *in the transmitted text, is uncertain: he might again be Ti. Sempronius Longus (F 201), though nothing is known about an exile of his, or another Tiberius who went into exile, or* exul *might be a cognomen. The single fragment (cf.* Dub. *F 11) does not provide information about the context*

F 202 Gell. *NA* 2.14.1–3

Quod M. Cato in libro qui inscriptus est contra Tiberium exulem "stitisses vadimonium" per "i" litteram dicit, non "stetisses"; eiusque verbi ratio reddita.—[1] in libro vetere M. Catonis, qui inscribitur contra Tiberium exulem,[1] scriptum[2] sic erat: "quid si vadimonium capite obvoluto

[1] exulem *codd. rec.*: exule *codd.*   [2] scriptum *codd. rec. nonnulli, Gronovius*: scriptum ⟨quid⟩ *vel* scriptum ⟨quidem⟩ *codd. rel.*

F 201 Priscian

. . . *supellex, supellectilis* ["furniture"; nom., gen. sg.]—
yet the very early [writers] also used the nominative (*haec*)
supellectilis. Cato [says in the speech] against Tiberius
Sempronius Longus: "if an auction could be held concerning your accomplishments, as it often occurs with furniture"[1]—. . .

[1] *supellectilis* in the quotation is most likely a genitive singular
(with *auctio*) and thus does not illustrate the ancient form of the
nominative of this word; the mismatch may be due to a misun-
derstanding of the construction.

AGAINST THE EXILE TIBERIUS
(F 202)

*(Scullard 1973, 260). If the question forming the fragment
is addressed to the opponent and he is envisaged to be
in exile, the direct address would be chosen for rhetorical effectiveness rather than being part of an actual ex-
change.*

F 202 Gellius, *Attic Nights*

That M. Cato, in the work that is entitled "against Tiberius
the exile" says *stitisses vadimonium* with the letter *i*, not
stetisses; and an explanation given for that word.—[1] In
an old work by M. Cato that is entitled "against Tiberius
the exile" it was written {something} as follows: "What if,
with veiled head, you had appeared in court on the ap-

CATO

stitisses?" [2] recte ille quidem "stitisses" scripsit; sed
† falsa et audax[3] emendatores[4] "e" scripto, et † per libros
"stetisses" fecerunt, tamquam "stitisses" vanum et nihili
verbum esset. [3] quin potius ipsi nequam et nihili sunt,
qui ignorant "stitisses" dictum a Catone quoniam "sisteretur" vadimonium, non "staretur."

[3] falsa et audax *vel* falsi et audaces *codd.*   [4] ‹emendatio
› emendatores *vel* ‹› emendatores *Hertz*: emendatorum
‹cohors *vel* manus *vel* natio *vel* grex› *Heraeus: alia alia*

ON A *SPONSIO* WITH M. CORNELIUS
(F 203)

*The identity of M. Cornelius is uncertain; the speech must
have been composed for the legal procedure of* sponsio, *a
kind of judicial wager or an engagement to pay a certain
sum of money to the successful party in a case (see Crook*

F 203 Fronto, *Ad M. Antoninum* 1.2.11–12 (pp. 90.15–
91.8 van den Hout)

Cf. F 173.

pointed day?" [2] Correctly indeed he wrote *stitisses*; but revisers have boldly and falsely [?] put *stetisses*, written with *e*, in all the editions, on the grounds that *stitisses* was a meaningless and worthless word. [3] Rather, they themselves are ignorant and worthless, as they do not know that *stitisses* was used by Cato because *sisteretur* is the word with "bail" [*vadimonium*], not *staretur*.[1]

[1] Gellius accepts only the perfect stem *stiti* for *sistere* (though *steti* is also found), and links *steti* with *stare*. Since *sistere* is the correct verb in the idiom discussed, the required form from the perfect stem in this example has to be *stitisses* in his view.

ON A *SPONSIO* WITH M. CORNELIUS
(F 203)

1976). Apart from the fact that Cato apparently kept a written copy of a version of this speech and drew on extracts from that oration on a later occasion (F 173), nothing is known about the context.

F 203 Fronto, *Correspondence*

Cf. F 173.

AGAINST CORNELIUS TO
THE PEOPLE (F 204)

*The context of this speech before the People and the iden-
tity of the opponent (and whether or not he might be the
same as M. Cornelius referred to in F 203) cannot be determined for sure (Scullard 1973, 268; Sblendorio Cugusi
1982, 394–95). Among other hypotheses, it has been suggested (see Scullard 1973, 268) that Cornelius could be M.*

F 204 Fest., p. 364.14–17 L.

REPULSIOR secunda conlatione dixit Cato in ea, quae est
contra Cornelium apud populum: "{ha}ecquis[1] incultior,
religiosior, desertior, publicis negoti<i>s[2] repulsior?"

1 {ha}ecquis *edd.*: haec quis *cod.*
2 negoti<i>s *Ursinus*: negotis *cod.*

AGAINST PANSA (F 205)

F 205 Non., p. 151.10–14 M. = 221 L.

PASCEOLUS, ex aluta sacculus. . . . Cato in Pansam: "pueris
in ludo stilos,[1] pasceolos furare."

1 ludo stilos *Roth*: ludos tellos *codd.*

AGAINST CORNELIUS TO
THE PEOPLE (F 204)

*Cornelius Scipio Maluginensis, a praetor in 176 BC, who
was assigned the province of Further Iberia (*MRR *1:400)
but did not go into the province for religious reasons and
was later removed from the Senate (Liv. 41.14.5, 41.15.5,
41.15.10, 41.27.2).*

F 204 Festus

repulsior ["more rejected"] in the comparative: Cato used
it in that [speech] that there is against Cornelius before
the People: "Is there anyone more uncouth, more super-
stitious, more left alone, more rejected from public business?"

AGAINST PANSA (F 205)

*Nothing is known about the context of this speech or the
identity of the addressee.*

F 205 Nonius Marcellus

pasceolus ["satchel"], a small bag made of leather. . . . Cato
[says in the speech] against Pansa: "from boys in schools
you [sg.] steal pens and small satchels."

CATO

ON BEHALF OF L. TURIUS AGAINST
CN. GELLIUS (F 206)

F 206 Gell. *NA* 14.2.21–26

[FAVORINUS:] ". . . [21] quod autem ad pecuniam pertinet
quam apud iudicem peti dixisti, suadeo hercle tibi utare
M. Catonis, prudentissimi viri, consilio, qui in oratione
quam pro L. Turio contra Cn. Gellium dixit ita esse a
maioribus[1] traditum observatumque ait, ut si quod inter
duos actum est neque tabulis neque testibus planum fieri
possit, tum apud iudicem qui de ea re cognosceret uter ex
his vir melior esset quaereretur, et si pares essent seu boni
pariter seu mali, tum illi unde petitur crederetur ac secundum eum iudicaretur. [22] . . ." . . . [26] verba ex oratione
M. Catonis cuius commeminit Favorinus haec sunt: "atque ego a maioribus memoria sic accepi: si quis quid alter
ab altero peteret,[2] si ambo pares essent, sive boni sive mali
essent, quod duo res gessissent, uti testes non interessent,
illi unde petitur, ei potius credendum esse. nunc si spon-
sionem fecissent[3] Gellius cum Turio, ni vir melior esset

---

[1] maioribus *Lion*: maioribus maiorum *vel* maioribus maioribus *codd.*: maioribus memoriae *codd. rec.*

[2] peteret *codd. rec. nonnulli*: peterent *codd. rel.*

[3] fecissent *vel* fecisset *codd.*

ON BEHALF OF L. TURIUS AGAINST
CN. GELLIUS (F 206)

*Cato spoke in a court case in which L. Turius and Cn.
Gellius were confronting each other; no further details can
be ascertained.*

F 206 Gellius, *Attic Nights*

[FAVORINUS:] ". . . [21] But as concerns the money that
you ['Gellius'] said was claimed before the judge, I advise
you, by Hercules, to follow the counsel of M. Cato, that
very sagacious man, who said in the speech that he delivered on behalf of L. Turius against Cn. Gellius that this
custom had been handed down and observed by the ancestors, that, if there was some dispute between two individuals and it [the outcome] could not be made clear either by documents or witnesses, then the question should
be raised before the judge who was trying the case as to
which of these two was the better man, and if they were
either equally good or equally bad, then the one upon
whom the claim was made should be believed and the
verdict should be given in his favor. [22] . . ." . . . [26] The
words from the speech of M. Cato that Favorinus mentioned are as follows: "And I have learned this from our
ancestors by tradition: if anyone claims anything from another, if both are equal, whether they are good or bad,
provided the two of them had transacted the business so
that there were no witnesses, the one from whom the
claim is made ought rather to be believed. Now, if Gellius
had made a judicial wager [cf. F 203] with Turius, provided Gellius were not a better man than Turius, nobody,

227

CATO

Gellius quam Turius, nemo, opinor, tam insanus esset qui
iudicaret meliorem esse Gellium quam Turium: si non
melior Gellius est Turio, potius oportet credi unde petitur."

ON BEHALF OF L. AUTRONIUS
(F 207)

*Cato defended a member of the gens Autronia, presumably
in connection with the committing of a crime. No further*

F 207 Prisc., *GL* II, p. 482.9–12

. . . ; vetustissimi tamen et "ausi" pro "ausus sum" et "gavisi" pro "gavisus sum" protulerunt. Cato Censorius in
oratione[1] pro Lucio Autronio: "venefici{i}[2] postridie ius-
sisti adesse in diem[3] ex die. non ausi[4] recusare."

[1] *om. unus cod.*   [2] venefici{i} *Mommsen*: beneficii *codd.*
[3] *Heinsius et Meyer hic distinguendi notam posuerunt: post*
die *Mommsen*: *codd. omnino non distinguunt*   [4] ausi⟨t⟩
Mazzarino (1978–79, 387 n. 2): ausi *def. Malcovati (1981, 466)*

ON BEHALF OF L. CAESETIUS
(F 208–9)

*The second fragment (F 209) has been attributed to the
same speech as the first (F 208) on the assumption of different errors in the transmission in the two places in which
it is preserved (concerning the author and the name of the
person supported). Then the first fragment (F 208) includes an address to soldiers (unusual in a judicial speech,
unless part of a vivid narrative), and the second one*

I think, would be so mad as to form the opinion that Gellius was better than Turius: if Gellius is not better than Turius, the one from whom the claim is made ought rather to be believed."

ON BEHALF OF L. AUTRONIUS
(F 207)

details of the context are known, and the defendant cannot be identified with certainty.

F 207 Priscian

. . . ; yet the very early [writers] also used *ausi* instead of *ausus sum* ["I dared"] and *gavisi* instead of *gavisus sum* ["I rejoiced"; active instead of deponent forms of perfect]. Cato, the ex-censor, [says] in the speech on behalf of Lucius Autronius: "Because of the poisoning you [sg.] have ordered presence [in court] on the following day, from one day to the next. I did not dare to refuse."[1]

[1] Text, punctuation, and interpretation of the fragment are uncertain and controversial (for discussion, see Malcovati 1981).

ON BEHALF OF L. CAESETIUS
(F 208–9)

(F 209) locates the oration among the People. Thus, soldiers may not be the main addressee, there may be more confusion in the transmission, or the pieces of information refer to different speeches (as posited by Meyer 1842, 136–37). Nothing further is known about the identity of the individual or the context of the speech (Scullard 1973, 270).

F 208 Fest., p. 388.7–14 L.

SULTIS, si voltis. . . . Cato pro L. Caesetio: "audite sultis, milites, si quis vestrum in[1] bello superfuerit, si quis non invenerit pecuniam, egebit."

[1] in *del. Jordan*

F 209a Diom., *GL* I, p. 376.2–5

ostendor ostentus, quoniam sit tendor tentus. nam ostentatus est frequens: P. Rutilius de vita sua "uni una ostentata est"; idem pro L. Cesutio[1] ad populum ex hoc derivavit participium, "quod ego me spero ostenturum."

[1] idem (*vel* item) pro l. cesutio *vel* idem . . . sutio (*lacuna trium fere litterarum relicta*) *vel* item pro l. caerutio *codd.*: item P. Lucius Cellius *edd. vet.*: pro Lucio Caerucio *Putschen*: ideo P. Lucius Celius *Busch*

F 209b Prisc., *GL* II, pp. 520.23–21.1

Cato pro Lucio Caesare ad populum: "quod ego me spero ostenturum."

ON BEHALF OF C . . . (F 210)

No further details can be established about this speech, as the text of the single source is lacunose. Even the name of the person supported is incomplete; thus, the fragment

ORATIONS

F 208 Festus

sultis ["if you please"], "if you wish." . . . Cato [says in the speech] on behalf of L. Caesetius: "Listen, if you please, soldiers, if any of you will have survived in the war, if any will not have found money, they will be in poverty."

F 209a Diomedes

ostendor, ostentus ["I am shown," "shown"], since there is *tendor, tentus* ["I am stretched," "stretched"]. For *ostentatus* ["shown"; past participle of *ostento*] is frequent: P. Rutilius [says in the work] on his own life [P. Rutilius Rufus (*FRHist* 21 F 9)]: "one [way / woman] has been shown [*ostentata*] to one person"; the same [Rutilius? Cato?],[1] [in the speech] on behalf of L. Cesutius before the People, derived a participle from that [*ostenturus* from *ostentus*; future participle]: "what I hope I will show."

[1] Here, a quotation might have dropped out, or there may be confusion as regards the names of authors; in F 209b the name of the defendant might be incorrect (replaced by a more familiar name).

F 209b Priscian

Cato [says in the speech] on behalf of Lucius Caesar before the People: "what I hope I will show."

ON BEHALF OF C . . . (F 210)

*might belong to any of the attested speeches Cato delivered on behalf of a client whose name (*praenomen *or* nomen*) starts with C or to another one otherwise unknown.*

231

CATO

F 210 Fest., pp. 464.33–66.2 L.

‹STIRICIDIUM q›uasi stillicidium, cum stil‹lae concretae frigore c›adunt.[1] Cato pro C . . . ". . . nihil[2] minus voluit semper . . . bus re praesenti cognosce‹re› . . . ere."[3]

  [1] *suppl. Epit.*   [2] nihil‹o› *Augustinus*
  [3] ‹atque statu›ere *Ursinus (fere)*

ABOUT HABITUS [?] (F 211)

As the single source is not very informative, details about this speech cannot be established; it is even unclear whether it concerns an individual called Habitus (de

F 211 Charis., *GL* I, p. 90.20–21 = p. 114.17–19 B.

sanguis masculino genere, et facit hunc sanguinem. sed Cato de habitu[1] ait: "sanguen[2] demittatur" . . .[3]

  [1] de Habito *Cauchii ex deperdito cod. excerpta*
  [2] sanguen *vel* sanguê *codd.*   [3] sed Cato de habitu, ut declinaretur ait, sanguen, sanguinis. sanguis, sanguis, sangui. id imitatur Lucretius *Putschen, Merula*

ON THE FLORIAN MATTER (F 212–14)

If res *in the description of the oration's topic* (de re Floria) *is understood in the sense of "property, wealth," the speech could refer to a private legal case about the property of a*

F 210 Festus

‹*stiricidium* ["fall of water in frozen drops"], l›ike *stilli-cidium* ["fall of liquid in successive drops"], when dro‹ps [*stillae*], hardened by cold, f›all. Cato [says in the speech] on behalf of C . . . ". . . he always wanted nothing less . . . on the spot to discove‹r› . . ."[1]

[1] The extract from Cato, which is mostly lost, must have included the word *stiricidium*, which the quotation is meant to illustrate.

ABOUT HABITUS [?] (F 211)

Habito), *or an issue concerning* habitus *("condition, bearing, constitution";* de habitu), *or whether the word is corrupt (Scullard 1973, 260).*

F 211 Charisius

sanguis ["blood"] in masculine gender, and it forms (*hunc*) *sanguinem* [acc. sg. masc.]. But Cato [says in the speech] about Habitus / *habitus*: "blood [neut.] might be shed / let" . . .

ON THE FLORIAN MATTER (F 212–14)

Florius (or Floria). If res *is taken to have a wider meaning ("thing, matter"), the context cannot be identified since the content of the fragments does not clearly denote a situation*

(cf. F 215). If the adjective is regarded as an alternative form for Floralis, *the term might indicate issues linked to the festival of* Floralia, *associated with licentiousness (for*

F 212 Gell. *NA* 9.12.7–8

ne quis autem de "suspicioso," quod supra posuimus, et de "formiduloso" in eam partem quae minus usitata est exemplum requirat, inveniet[1] de "suspicioso" aput M.[2] Catonem de re Floria ita scriptum: "sed nisi qui palam corpore pecuniam quaereret aut se lenoni locavisset, etsi famosus[3] et suspiciosus esset,[4] vim in corpus liberum non aecum censuere adferri." [8] "suspiciosum" enim {Cato}[5] hoc in loco suspectum significat, non suspicantem.

[1] inveniet *vel om. codd.*   [2] M. *vel om. codd.*   [3] famosus *Nonius Marcellus*: famulosus *codd.*   [4] esset *Nonius Marcellus*: fuisset *codd.*   [5] *del. de Buxis*

Cf. Non., p. 168.22–25 M. = 248 L.

F 213 Gell. *NA* 10.13.1–3

"partim hominum venerunt" plerumque dicitur, quod significat "pars hominum venit," id est quidam homines. nam "partim" hoc in loco adverbium est neque in casus inclinatur, sicuti "cum partim hominum" dici potest, id est cum quibusdam hominibus et quasi cum quadam parte hominum. [2] M. Cato in oratione de re Floria ita scripsit: "ibi pro scorto fuit, in cubiculum subreptitavit[1] e convivio, cum partim illorum iam saepe ad eundem modum erat."

[1] subreptitavit *"sunt qui legant" Ascensius*: subrectitavit (surre-) *codd.*

brief summaries of various suggestions, see Scullard 1973, 261; Sblendorio Cugusi 1982, 451–52).

F 212 Gellius, *Attic Nights*

Now, so that nobody should search for an example of *sus-piciosus* ["full of suspicion"], which we mentioned above [Gell. *NA* 9.12.1], and of *formidulosus* ["full of fear"], in so far as it is less used, they will find in M. Cato, [in the speech] on the Florian matter, the following written about *suspiciosus*: "But except in the case of one who was publicly earning money by prostitution or had hired themselves out to a procurer, even if [someone] should be ill-famed and suspected [*suspiciosus*], they were of the opinion that it was not fair for force to be applied against the person of a free man." [8] For in this passage he {Cato} uses *suspiciosus* in the sense of "suspected," not that of "suspecting."

F 213 Gellius, *Attic Nights*

partim hominum venerunt is a common expression, which means "part of the people came," that is, "some people." For *partim* ["partly, in part"] in this case is an adverb and is not declined by cases; thus, one can say *cum partim hominum*, that is "with some people" or, as it were, "with a certain part of the people." [2] M. Cato, in the speech on the Florian matter, wrote as follows: "there (s)he acted like a prostitute, (s)he went from the banquet secretly to the bedroom, and with part of them [*cum partim illorum*] (s)he often already conducted her/himself in the same

CATO

[3] imperitiores autem "cum parti" legunt, tamquam declinatum sit quasi vocabulum, non dictum quasi adverbium.

F 214 Cons. Fortun. 2.16, *RLM*, p. 111.16–21

concisa narratione tunc tantum utemur, quando quaedam adversa sunt nobis? immo et cum singulae res gestae maximam invidiam continent, adversariorum possumus narrationem concidere, ut propositis singulis rebus statim exaggeratione utamur. cur ita? ut indignationem iudicum non semel, sed saepius in rebus singulis excitemus, sicut fecit M. Cato de re Floriana.

ON THE MATTER CONCERNING
A. ATILIUS (F 215)

The attribution of this fragment to Cato is based on a generally accepted emendation of the name. Again (cf. F 212–14) it is unclear whether res in the description of the oration's topic is used in the sense of "property, wealth" or has a wider meaning ("thing, matter"). The identifica-

F 215 Fest., p. 464.28–33 L.

‹SONTICA› causa dicitur a morbo ‹sontico›... gerendum agere[1] ... is[2] Cato[3] de re A. Atili: "... tisse timidus ne ... ibi causam sonticam ..."[4]

---

[1] ‹sontico, propter quam quod est› gerendum agere ‹desistimus› *Ursinus (fere)*   [2] ‹M. Porci›us *Ursinus*   [3] Cato *Ursinus*: lato *cod.*   [4] de re ‹Floria›: "A. Atili, ‹quid dicam causae exti›tisse timidus ne ‹sis? an impedimento t›ibi causam sonticam ‹fuisse?›" *Ursinus*

manner." [3] The less educated, however, read *cum parti*, as if it [the word *partim*] was declined as a noun, not used as an adverb.

F 214 Consultus Fortunatianus

Shall we only use a cut-up narrative in circumstances where certain things are against us? On the contrary, also when individual deeds involve the greatest odium, we can cut up the narrative of the opponents, so that, when individual items are put forward, we immediately use intensification. Why so? So that we provoke the indignation of the judges not once, but frequently with respect to individual items, just as M. Cato did concerning the Florian matter.

ON THE MATTER CONCERNING
A. ATILIUS (F 215)

tion of Atilius with A. Atilius Serranus (praet. 192, 173, promag. 191, cos. 170 BC) is sometimes suggested (Scullard 1973, 259). The lacunose text of the fragment does not provide any indication.

F 215 Festus

⟨*sontica*⟩ *causa* ["a valid reason"] is derived from *morbus* ⟨*sonticus*⟩ ["serious disease, excusing a person from attendance at law court and other public duties"] . . . to do what needs to be carried out . . . Cato on the matter of A. Atilius: ". . . timid so that . . . there a valid reason . . ."

ON THE PROPERTY OF PULCHRA
(F 216)

The context shows that written copies of some of Cato's speeches were available in public libraries in the second century AD. Nothing further is known about the speech

F 216 Fronto, *Ad M. Caes.* 4.5.2–3 (p. 61.14–24 van den Hout)

[M. AURELIUS CAESAR:] legi[1] Catonis orationem de bonis Pulchrae[2] et aliam, qua tribuno diem dixit. "io,"[3] inquis puero tuo, "vade quantum potes,[4] de Apollonis[5] bibliotheca has mihi orationes adporta." frustra:[6] nam II[7] isti libri me secuti sunt. igitur Tiberianus bibliothecarius tibi subigitandus est; aliquid in eam rem insumendum, quod mihi ille, ut ad urbem venero, aequa divisione inpertiat. sed ego orationibus his perlectis paululum misere[8] scripsi, quod aut Lymphis aut Volcano dicarem: ἀληθῶς ἀτυχῶς σήμερον γέγραπταί μοι, venatoris plane aut vindemiatoris studiolum, qui[9] iubilis suis cubiculum meum perstrepunt, causidicali prosum[10] odio et taedio. quid hoc dixi? immo recte dixi, nam meus quidem magister orator est.

[1] legi *cod.²*: legit *cod.¹*   [2] pulchrae *cod.¹*: dulciae *aut* dulchae *cod.²*: Patulciae *Hübner*   [3] io *cod.²*: ioa *cod.¹*

[4] pote *Priebe*   [5] apollonis *cod.*: Ἀπόλλονος *Naber*: Apollinis *Haines*   [6] *post* frustra *add.* mittis *cod.²*: mittes *Naber*: *del. Mai*   [7] II *vel* it *cod.*: et *Mai*: duo *Kiessling*

[8] misere<re> *Mai*   [9] venatores plane ac vindemiatores quin *Cornelissen*   [10] prosecutus *Cornelissen*

---

[1] The emperor Augustus established a library in the Temple of Apollo at Rome. A further library was created by the emperor

ON THE PROPERTY OF PULCHRA
(F 216)

mentioned. The name of the person whose affairs are the topic of the speech is given as "Pulchra" in the uncorrected version of the manuscript.

F 216 Fronto, *Correspondence*

[M. AURELIUS CAESAR:] I have read Cato's speech on the property of Pulchra and another one, by which he called a Tribune to court [F 231]. "Go," you say to your boy, "as fast as you can, bring me these orations from Apollo's library." In vain: for those two books have followed me. Thus, you have to coax the librarian of Tiberius' library; on that matter something is to be expended, which that man shall share with me in equal distribution as soon as I have come to the city [of Rome].[1] But after having read these orations, I have written a little bit miserably, which I would dedicate to the Lymphae [deities of water] or Vulcan [god of fire]: today my writing has been truly unsuccessful, a short piece of composition clearly of the hunter or the grape picker, who make my bedroom resound with their wild shouts, with the boredom and weariness wholly of the law courts. Why have I said this? In fact, I have said [this] correctly; for, assuredly, my tutor is an orator.

Tiberius in a new Temple of Augustus. Since Marcus Aurelius has taken the edition of Cato's speeches from Apollo's library, Fronto will need to bribe the librarian of Tiberius' library to get a copy. As these are imperial libraries and the librarian thus works for the emperor, the writer ironically announces that he will ask for a share of the bribe once he has come to Rome.

CATO

ON THE AEDILES IMPROPERLY
ELECTED (F 217–18)

Nothing certain is known about the context of this speech.
Fraccaro ([1910a] 1956, 161), Ruebel (1972, 52–54), Astin
(1978, 18–19), and Kienast (1979, 39–42) suggest a link
with the events in 202 BC (Liv. 30.39.8), when the ple-

F 217 Gell. *NA* 13.18.1–3

Quid aput M. Catonem significent verba haec "inter os
atque offam."—[1] oratio est M. Catonis Censorii de aedi-
libus vitio creatis. ex ea oratione verba haec sunt: "nunc
ita aiunt in segetibus, in herbis bona frumenta esse. nolite
ibi nimiam spem habere. saepe audivi inter os atque offam
multa intervenire posse; verumvero inter offam atque her-
bam, ibi vero longum intervallum est." [2] Erucius Clarus,
qui praefectus urbi et bis consul fuit, vir morum et litterarum veterum studiosissimus, ad Sulpicium Apollinarem
scripsit, hominem memoriae nostrae doctissimum, quaerere sese et petere, uti sibi rescriberet quaenam esset
eorum verborum sententia. [3] tum Apollinaris nobis
praesentibus—nam id temporis ego adulescens Romae
sectabar eum discendi gratia—rescripsit Claro, ut viro
erudito brevissime, vetus esse proverbium "inter os et
offam," idem significans quod Graecus ille παροιμιώδης
versus: "πολλὰ μεταξὺ πέλει κύλικος καὶ χείλεος ἄκρου."

ON THE AEDILES IMPROPERLY
ELECTED (F 217–18)

*beian aediles (MRR 1:316) resigned (doubts in Scullard
1973, 256). The oration would then be one of the earliest
attested speeches by Cato.*

F 217 Gellius, *Attic Nights*

What in M. Cato these words "between mouth and morsel" mean.—[1] There is a speech by M. Cato, the ex-
censor, on the aediles improperly elected. From that oration are these words: "Now they say that in the fields of
standing corn, in the blade, there is good grain [i.e., to be
harvested]. On that account do not have too much hope.
I have often heard that many things may come between
mouth and morsel; but there certainly is a long distance
between a morsel and the blade." [2] Erucius Clarus, who
was prefect of the city and twice consul [Sex. Erucius
Clarus, cos. II AD 146], a man deeply devoted to studying
ancient customs and literature, wrote to Sulpicius Apollinaris, the most learned man in our time, begging and en-
treating that he would write back to him what the meaning
of those words was. [3] Then, in my presence—for at that
time I was a young man in Rome and in attendance upon
him for purposes of learning—Apollinaris wrote back to
Clarus, as to an educated man, very briefly that "between
mouth and morsel" was an old proverb, meaning the same
as that Greek adage in verse: "Between cup and lip there
is many a slip." [cf. Otto 1890, 259, s.v. *os* 2].

F 218 Fest., p. 158.10–13 L.

NEMINIS ⟨genetivo casu Cato usus est⟩:[1] . . . ⟨. . . idem de aedilibus⟩[2] vitio creatis: "neminisque . . .

[1] *suppl. Epit.*   [2] *suppl. Mueller*

Cf. Paul. *Fest.*, p. 159.4–5 L.: NEMINIS genetivo casu Cato usus est, cum dixit: "sunt multi corde quos non miseret neminis" [Enn. *Trag.* 50 *TrRF / FRL*].

ON THE SACROSANCTITY OF THE PLEBEIAN AEDILES (F 219)

In this speech Cato seems to have commented on the sacrosanct status of plebeian magistrates, which usually applied only to Tribunes of the People. Such officials were protected by a lex sacrata, *a commitment by the People to*

F 219 Fest., p. 422.17–24 L.

SACROSANCTUM dicitur, quod iure iurando interposito est institutum, si quis id violasset, ut morte poenas penderet. cuius generis sunt tribuni plebis aedilesque eiusdem ordinis; quod adfirmat M. Cato in ea, quam scripsit, aedilis plebis sacrosanctos esse.

F 218 Festus

neminis ["of nobody"] ⟨was used in the genitive case by
Cato⟩: . . . ⟨. . . the same [said in the speech] about the
aediles⟩ improperly elected: "and of nobody . . .[1]

[1] In the *Epitome* the quotation from Cato and the name of the
author of the next example must have got lost, as a passage by
Ennius is given as an example of Cato's usage. In Festus a sufficient amount of text remains to attribute the passage to this
speech of Cato.

ON THE SACROSANCTITY OF THE PLEBEIAN AEDILES (F 219)

*have every injury to these magistrates followed by punish-
ment of the culprit, who, by committing such a deed, became* sacer *("outlawed").*

F 219 Festus

sacrosanctum ["sacrosanct"] is the word used for what is
instituted by a sworn oath, so that, if anyone had violated
that [thing so instituted], they paid the penalty by death.
In this category are the Tribunes of the People and the
aediles of the same order; M. Cato confirms that in that
[speech] that he wrote, that the plebeian aediles are sacrosanct.

ON AUGURS (F 220)

F 220 Fest., p. 277.10–16 L.

PROBRUM virginis Vestalis ut capite puniretur, vir, qui eam
incestavisset, verberibus necaretur: lex fixa in atrio Libertatis cum multi<s> alis legibus incendio consumpta est, ut
ait M. Cato in ea oratione, quae de auguribus inscribitur.
adicit quoque virgines Vestales sacerdotio ex augurali . . .

ON DOWRY (F 221–22)

*This speech apparently concerned customs and laws refer-
ring to the rights and behavior of wives and husbands in
early Rome. The circumstances of the oration are unknown*

F 221–22 Gell. *NA* 10.23.1–5

Verba ex oratione M. Catonis de mulierum veterum victu
et moribus; atque inibi quod fuerit ius marito in adulterio
uxorem deprehensam necare.—[1] qui de victu atque
cultu populi Romani scripserunt, mulieres Romae atque
in Latio aetatem abstemias egisse, hoc est vino semper,

ORATIONS

ON AUGURS (F 220)

This speech seems to have discussed religious details, including laws about Vestal Virgins and items relating to augurs.

F 220 Festus

That a *probrum* ["offense"] of a Vestal virgin was punished with [taking away] her life [cf. e.g., Dion. Hal. *Ant. Rom.* 2.67.3–4; Plut. *Numa* 10.4–7; Liv. 22.57.1; Suet. *Dom.* 8.3] and that a man who had dishonored her was killed by flogging: the law [i.e., document with the text of the law], put up in the atrium of Libertas [building containing offices and records of the censors] with many other laws, was destroyed by fire, as M. Cato says in that speech that is entitled "on augurs." He adds also that the Vestal Virgins from the augural priesthood . . .

ON DOWRY (F 221–22)

(Scullard 1973, 269). A reference to a Lex Maenia *(de dote?) has sometimes been assumed (cf.* LPPR, *pp. 286–87; Elster 2003, 393–95).*

F 221–22 Gellius, *Attic Nights*

Words from a speech of M. Cato on the mode of life and manners of women of old; and in that context that it was lawful for a husband to kill his wife when she had been caught in adultery.—[1] Those who have written about the mode of life and civilization of the Roman People say that the women in Rome and in Latium lived their lives abste-

quod temetum prisca lingua appellabatur, abstinuisse dicunt, institutumque ut cognatis osculum ferrent deprehendendi[1] causa, ut odor indicium faceret si bibissent
[*Inc*. F 6]. [2] bibere autem solitas ferunt loream passum
murrinam et quae id genus sapiant potu dulcia. atque haec
quidem in his quibus dixi libris pervulgata sunt; [3] sed
Marcus Cato non solum † existimatas †,[2] set et multatas
quoque a iudice mulieres refert non minus si vinum in se
quam si probrum et adulterium admisissent. [4] verba
Marci Catonis adscripsi ex oratione quae inscribitur de
dote, in qua id quoque scriptum est, in adulterio uxores
deprehensas ius fuisse maritis necare: "vir" inquit "cum
divortium fecit, mulieri iudex pro censore est, imperium
quod videtur habet, si quid perverse taetreque factum est
a muliere; multatur, si vinum bibit; si cum alieno viro pro-
bri quid fecit, condemnatur." [5] de iure autem occidendi[3]
ita scriptum: "in adulterio uxorem tuam si prehendisses,
sine iudicio inpune necares; illa te, si adulterares sive tu
adulterarere,[4] digito non auderet contingere, neque ius
est."

[1] deprehendendi *florilegium, Lambecius*: deprehendi *vel* re-
prehendendi *vel* reprehendi *codd.*

[2] existimatas *vel* existimatus *vel* existimat *codd.*: *fort.* ⟨parvi⟩
aut ⟨nihili⟩ existimatas *Holford-Strevens in app.*: ⟨malas⟩ *Gustav*

[3] occidendi *de Buxis*: dicendi *codd.*

[4] adulterarere *Salmasius*: adulteriare *vel* adulterare *vel* adulterare ⟨velles⟩ *codd.*

miously, that is, that they always abstained from wine, which in the early language was called *temetum*, and that it was an established custom for them to kiss their kinsfolk for the purpose of detection, so that the odor would provide evidence if they had been drinking [*Inc.* F 6]. [2] But they report that the women were accustomed to drink wine made in the second brewing, raisin wine, liqueur wine, and such other drinks of that kind as are sweet tasting. And these things are indeed made generally known in those books that I have mentioned. [3] But Marcus Cato reports that women were not only badly thought of [?] but also punished by a judge no less severely if they had given themselves up to wine than if they had given themselves up to disgrace and adultery. [4] I have copied Marcus Cato's words from the oration that is entitled "on dowry," in which it is also written that it was lawful for husbands to kill wives caught in adultery: "When a husband divorces his wife," he says, "he is a judge in relation to the woman, like a censor, and he has the power that seems appropriate, if anything wrong or shameful has been done by the woman; she is fined if she has drunk wine; if she has done something indecent with another man, she is convicted." [5] Further, as to the right of putting her to death it [is] thus written: "If you had caught your wife in adultery, without a trial and with impunity you would put her to death; if you should commit adultery or made to commit adultery, she should not dare to lay a finger on you, nor is this lawful."

CATO

ON HOLDING POWER (F 223)

*This oration of Cato's seems to be a political speech con-
cerned with the transfer of power between magistrates and
their successors. Several potential contexts have been considered, but no details can be established; it is uncertain*

F 223   Gell. *NA* 20.2.1–3

Vocabulum "siticinum" in M. Catonis oratione quid significet.—[1] "siticines" scriptum est in oratione M. Catonis
quae ‹in›scribitur ne imperium sit veteri, ubi novus ve-
nerit: "siticines" inquit "et liticines et tubicines." [2] sed
Caesellius Vindex in commentariis lectionum antiquarum
scire quidem se ait liticines lituo cantare et tubicines tuba,
quid istuc autem sit quo{d}[1] siticines cantant, homo inge-
nuae veritatis scire sese negat. [3] nos autem in Capitonis
Atei coniectaneis invenimus "siticines" appellatos qui
apud sitos canere soliti essent, hoc est vita functos et se-
pultos, eosque habuisse proprium genus tubae qua ca-
nerent, a ceterorum tubicinum differens.

[1] quo{d} *Magius*: quod *codd.*

Cf. Non., p. 54.20–25 M. = 77 L.

ORATIONS

ON HOLDING POWER (F 223)

whether this speech might refer to a Senate decree or a bill on that issue (Lex de imperio veteris proconsulis [?]: LPPR, *pp. 280–81; Elster 2003, 359).*

F 223 Gellius, *Attic Nights*

What the word *siticinum*[1] means in M. Cato's oration.—
[1] *siticines* is written in M. Cato's speech that is entitled "let not the previous [official] retain power [*imperium*], when the successor has arrived": "*siticines*," he says, "and *liticines*, and *tubicines*." [2] But Caesellius Vindex [scholar of 2nd cent. AD (cf. Vitale 1977, 239–40)], in the notes on what is read in early texts, says that he knows that *liticines* played on the *lituus* ["clarion"] and *tubicines* on the *tuba* ["trumpet"]; but, being a man of conscientious honesty, he says that he does not know what it is that *siticines* play on. [3] But we have found in the miscellanies [F 7 Strzelecki] of Ateius Capito [C. Ateius Capito, Roman jurist, cos. suff. AD 5] that *siticines* was the name given to those who customarily played in the presence of those who were "laid away" [*siti*], that is, dead and buried, and that they had a special kind of trumpet on which they played, differing from those of other trumpeters.

[1] According to the report that follows, the word occurs in the speech in another form.

ON DIVIDING BOOTY AMONG
SOLDIERS (F 224–26)

*This seems to be another of Cato's speeches concerned with
the appropriate division of booty (cf. F 97, 98). Appar-*

F 224 Gell. *NA* 11.18.18

sed enim M. Cato in oratione quam de praeda militibus
dividenda scripsit vehementibus et inlustribus verbis de
inpunitate peculatus atque licentia conqueritur. ea verba
quoniam nobis inpense placuerant adscripsimus: "fures"
inquit "privatorum furtorum in nervo atque in compedi-
bus aetatem agunt, fures publici in auro atque in purpura."

F 225 Non., p. 475.13–14 M. = 762 L.

FITE, imperativo modo. Cato de praeda militum dividenda: "tu † dives fite."[1]

   [1] tum dites fite *Quicherat*: tu dives fito *Laurenberg*: *fort.* tu-
dites fite *Lindsay in app.*

F 226 Non., pp. 510.15–19 M. = 820–21 L.

AVARITER, pro avare. . . . Cato de praeda militum dividenda: "fraudulenter atque avariter."

ON DIVIDING BOOTY AMONG
SOLDIERS (F 224–26)

*ently, he argued for giving soldiers their share of the booty
rather than powerful individuals enriching themselves.*

F 224 Gellius, *Attic Nights*

But M. Cato in the speech that he wrote on dividing booty
among soldiers, complains in strong and lucid words about
the lack of punishment for embezzlement of public money
and about licentiousness. We have appended those words,
since they had pleased us greatly: "Thieves guilty of thefts
from private individuals," he says," pass their lives in con-
finement and fetters, thieves holding public office in pur-
ple and gold."

F 225 Nonius Marcellus

fite ["you (pl.) should become"], in imperative mode. Cato
[says in the speech] on dividing booty with respect to soldiers: "you [sg.] rich, you should become [pl.] [?]."[1]

1 The quotation is too corrupt for a proper translation.

F 226 Nonius Marcellus

avariter ["greedily"], instead of *avare* [more common
form of adverb]. . . . Cato [says in the speech] on dividing
booty with respect to soldiers: "fraudulently and greedily
[*avariter*]."

IN SUPPORT OF A LAW OF POPILIUS
(F 227)

F 227 Non., p. 87.13–15 M. = 124 L.

CONPLURIES, frequenter. Cato suasione in legem Popili:[1]
"quod conpluries usu venit omni tempore anteventum
e{sse} re{m} publica{m}[2] credimus."[3]

[1] Popili *Jordan*: populi *codd.*: M. Popili *Mommsen*: Petillii
Bolhuisius   [2] e{sse} re{m} publica{m} *Mueller post Keilium*:
esse rem publicam *codd.*   [3] credimus *Keil ap. Jordan*: red-
dimus *codd.*

IN SUPPORT OF *LEX MAEVIA* (F 228)

It is uncertain which Lex Maevia *(as the name of the law
is transmitted) was supported by this speech. It has been
suggested that it might be a* Lex Maevia (de provincia
Asia?) *of about 189 BC* (LPPR, *p. 274; Elster 2003, 327).
King Seleucus mentioned in the fragment could be Seleu-*

F 228 Prisc., *GL* II, p. 587.3–7

. . . ; itaque neutrum quoque eorum in e finitur: "nostrate,"
"vestrate," ex quo ostenditur illorum quoque nominativus

IN SUPPORT OF A LAW OF POPILIUS
(F 227)

The name of the proposer of the law supported by Cato is based on emendation (for "law of the People"), and nothing is known about the potential identity (Scullard 1973, 268).

F 227 Nonius Marcellus

conpluries ["several times"], "frequently." Cato [says] in the speech in support of a law of Popilius: "what occurs frequently, we believe, has been anticipated at all times in the interest of the *res publica*."

IN SUPPORT OF *LEX MAEVIA* (F 228)

cus IV Philopator (d. 175 BC), who participated in the war between his father (Antiochus III the Great) and the Romans in 190 BC, and who became co-regent with his father in 189 BC and king in 187 BC.

F 228 Priscian

. . . ; therefore, their neuter [i.e., of pronouns of this type] too ends in *-e*: *nostrate* ["produced in our country, resembling those made in our country"], *vestrate* ["produced in your country, resembling those made in your country"]; whence it is shown that their nominative too was expressed

in "tis" secundum analogiam a vetustissimis prolatus esse. . . . M. Cato in legis Maeviae[1] suasione: "rex Seleucus arma nostratia facit."

[1] maeviae *vel* meviae *vel* meae viae *codd.*: Maeniae *Popma*

ABOUT SERCIA [?] (F 229)

Various suggestions on how to read the word indicating the focus or the title of the work of Cato quoted have been proposed. Presumably, the transmitted word is the corruption of a personal name. If the reference is to a speech, in

F 229 Non., pp. 200.16–28 M. = 294–95 L.

COLLUS masculino . . . Cato in Sercia:[1] "accipe, si vultis, hoc onus in vestros collos."

[1] in Ser. Galbam *Wasse*: in Sergium *Scaliger MS*: Setia *Maiansius*

IN THE SENATE (F 230)

F 230 Prisc., *GL* II, p. 337.23–26

idem [Cato] in oratione, qua suasit in senatu, "Samnitis" dixit pro "Samnis": "accessit ager quem, privatim habent Gallicus, Samnitis, Apulus, Bruttius."

as ending in *-tis* according to analogy by the very early [writers] [e.g., *nostratis* for *nostras*]. . . . M. Cato [says] in the speech in support of *Lex Maevia*: "king Seleucus makes our kind of weapons."

ABOUT SERCIA [?] (F 229)

line with usual practice, an accusative form, indicating the opponent (in Serciam), would be most likely (unless the preposition preceding the name is corrupt).

F 229 Nonius Marcellus

collus ["neck"], in the masculine [usually neut.] . . . Cato [says] [in the speech?] about Sercia [?]: "accept, if you wish, this burden on your necks [acc. pl. masc.]."

IN THE SENATE (F 230)

This fragment comes from a speech by which Cato put forward a proposal in the Senate, but no further details are known about the issue or the occasion.

F 230 Priscian

The same [Cato], in the speech by which he made a recommendation in the Senate, said *Samnitis* instead of *Samnis* ["Samnite"; common nominative (cf. *Orig.* F 23)]: "there was added the Gallic, the Samnite, the Apulian and the Bruttian territory [areas in Italy], which they have severally."

AGAINST A TRIBUNE (F 231)

*No further details are known about the court case to which
this speech belongs. The suggestion that this Tribune might
be M. Caelius (cf. F 111–20) is an uncertain hypothesis,*

F 231 Fronto, *Ad M. Caes.* 4.5.2–3 (p. 61.14–24 van den
Hout)

Cf. F 216.

ON ABOLISHING LAWS (F 232)

*This speech comes from a discussion on abolishing laws
(*abrogare*). When this took place and which laws were*

F 232 Charis., *GL* I, p. 104.28–29 = p. 133.16–18 B.

bovile vetat dici Varro ad Ciceronem VIII et ipse semper
"bubile"[1] dixit; sed et[2] Cato de abrogandis legibus "bovile"
dixit.

> [1] bubile *Müller*: buuile *cod.*   [2] et *add. ex deperdito cod.*

TO THE PEOPLE (F 233)

*The single remaining fragment of this speech is corrupt; it
is even unclear where it starts. The oration is defined as a*
contio *("speech before the People"); and since a* contio *by
Cato among the population of Epirus has little plausibility,*

AGAINST A TRIBUNE (F 231)

*since this was not the only conflict of Cato's with a Tribune
(cf. Scullard 1973, 263).*

F 231 Fronto, *Correspondence*

Cf. F 216.

ON ABOLISHING LAWS (F 232)

*considered is not known. If the plural is correct, the issue
concerned several laws or a group of laws.*

F 232 Charisius

Varro forbids the use of the word *bovile* ["stall for cattle"]
in [Book] 8 [of his work] dedicated to Cicero [Varro, *Ling.*
8.54], and himself always said *bubile*; but even Cato said
bovile [in the speech] on abolishing laws.

TO THE PEOPLE (F 233)

*the reference to them is probably part of the fragment. The
comment might be an allusion to Roman wars involving
Epirus, which resulted in Rome gaining control and a
reorganization of the area in 167 BC.*

F 233 Schol. Veron. ad Verg. *Aen.* 2.670

⟨"numquam[1] omnes ho⟩die." sic in Bucolicis: "numquam
hodie effugies." . . . Cato in contione: "Apirensium bellum[2]
fecimus . . . tris missi adversus . . . quos . . . censorem
habuistis neque . . . upli pectore adsecutus."[3]

[1] numquam *edd.*   [2] Epirensium *coni. et hanc vocem loco
sequenti Catoniano coniungens Mai*: Apirensium: "bellum *Hagen,
Baschera*:   [3] ad⟨versus . . . quos . . . censorem habuistis ne-
que⟩ . . . upli pectore adsecutus *Mai, Keil*: ad⟨versus . . . quos
censorem habuistis neque . . . upli pectore adsecutus⟩ *Hagen*

AGAINST A LAW (F 234)

*This fragment comes from a speech by which Cato argued
against* (dissuadere) *the approval of a law. The name and*

F 234 Fest., p. 466.9–14 L.

⟨SIREMPS⟩ ponitur pro eadem, vel proinde ⟨ac ea, quasi
similis res ips⟩a.[1] Cato in dissuadendo leg⟨em⟩ . . . licta
est, et praeterea rogas . . . ea si populus condempnave⟨rit,
uti siremps lex⟩[2] siet, quasi adversus le[3] . . .

[1] *suppl. Mueller (post Ursinum)*   [2] *suppl. Scaliger*
[3] le⟨ges fecisset⟩ *Scaliger (fere)*

Cf. Paul. *Fest.*, p. 467.5–6 L.: SIREMPS dicitur quasi similis res
ipsa. habetur hic in libris Catonis.

F 233 Scholia Veronensia to Virgil, *Aeneid*

"‹never all to›day": thus in the *Eclogues* [Verg. *Ecl.* 3.49]:
"never will you escape today." . . . Cato in a speech to the
People: "we have waged war against the Apirenses [i.e.,
people from Epirus] . . . sent against . . . those who . . . you
had a censor nor . . . achieved with courage."[1]

[1] The phrase prompting the quotation (*numquam hodie*,
"never today") probably appeared in the corrupt and lacunose
phrase from Cato.

AGAINST A LAW (F 234)

*the nature of law cannot be determined on the basis of the
lacunose text.*

F 234 Festus

‹siremps› ["in precisely the same way"] is used for the
same [matter] or in the same manner ‹as that, as if the
matter itself [is] similar›. Cato [says in the speech] arguing
against a la‹w› . . . is, and moreover you ask . . . if the
People should have disappro‹ved so that the law› should
be ‹in precisely the same way› as if against . . .

Cf. Paul the Deacon, *Epitome of Festus*: ‹siremps› ["in precisely
the same way"] is used as if the matter itself [is] similar. It is found
in works of Cato.[1]

[1] As often, Paul's summary simplifies and generalizes. Thus,
the plural in this testimonium does not necessarily mean that
several instances of this word in Cato were known.

CATO

ON HIS INTEGRITY (F 234A–B)

*It is uncertain whether the comment in Gellius (F 234A)
denotes a separate speech or, if the attribution to Cato
(based on the restitution of the text) is correct, refers to one
of Cato's other known orations. Since only what seems to
be the chapter heading in Gellius survives, there is no
further contextual information. Some scholars have ar-*

F 234A Gell. *NA* 20.10(9)

‹Quid significet M. Cato in oratione quam in›scripsit de
innocentia sua, cum ita dictitat: "numquam vestimenta a
populo poposci."

F 234B Isid. *Orig.* 20.3.8

Cf. F 132.

FROM UNIDENTIFIED SPEECHES
(F 235–54)

*For some of these fragments the context indicates an ora-
torical situation; others are attributed to the genre of
speeches within Cato's works because they are addressed
to interlocutors or because of their content (while precise
details or a link to any attested speeches cannot be established). Some fragments (especially short or lacunose ones)*

ON HIS INTEGRITY (F 234A–B)

gued for a separate Catonian speech. Then, another fragment, transmitted with the same description (F 132 = 234B), has to be assigned to this speech (on these attributions, see Müller 1869; Sblendorio Cugusi 1982, 396–97; 1984; 1987, 46; Perini 1985, 131–37; 1986; Mazzarino 1986).

F 234A Gellius, *Attic Nights*

‹What M. Cato means in the speech that› he entitled "on his integrity," when he declares repeatedly as follows: "I have never asked the People for garments."

F 234B Isidore, *Origins*

Cf. F 132.

FROM UNIDENTIFIED SPEECHES
(F 235–54)

are typically listed in this category by editors; but, like some of the fragments assigned to particular speeches, they could also come from one of Cato's works in another literary genre (see *Introduction to* Incertorum operum reliquiae).

CATO

F 235 Charis., *GL* I, p. 206.9–10 = p. 267.16–17 B.

malitiose Cato senex: "malitiose istorum † iuratorque eo verto" ut Maximus[1]

[1] *suppl. ex Cauchii ex deperdito cod. excerptis, ubi exhibentur*: istorum iuratorque eo verto ut maximus: *ap. Bondam*: istorum iura. iuratorque eo verbo ut maximus, *unde con. Vulcanius*: utiturque eo verbo et Maximus (*"Keil certe erravit, si in cod. ita sibi legisse visus est*: iuratorem . . . verto ut . . . quod . . ." *Barwick*): istorum iura torque pro versute, ut Maximus *Stroux, Zetzel*: malitiose istorum iura torque (eo verto *superscr.*) ut Maximus *Mazzarino (1983)*: malitiose istorum iura torque eo verbo *Sblendorio Cugusi (1996a)*.

F 236–37 Quint. *Inst.* 9.2.20–21

a quo schemate non procul abest illa quae dicitur communicatio, cum aut ipsos adversarios consulimus, ut . . . , [21] aut cum iudicibus quasi deliberamus, quod est frequentissimum: "quid suadetis?" et "vos interrogo" et "quid tandem fieri oportuit?" ut Cato: "cedo, si vos in eo loco essetis, quid aliud fecissetis?" et alibi: "communem rem agi putatote ac vos huic rei praepositos esse."

Cf. Iul. Rufin., §10, *RLM*, p. 41.8–25: ἀνακοίνωσις communicatio est, cum aut ipsos adversarios consulimus aut cum iudicibus deliberamus. . . . Cato: "si vos in eo loco essetis, quid aliud faceretis?" et alibi: "communem rem putatote, ac vos huic praepositos."

F 235 Charisius

malitiose ["maliciously"]: Cato the Elder [says]: "maliciously distort the rights of those with that word" [?],[1] as Maximus [Statilius Maximus (F 4 Zetzel)]

[1] The translation of the corrupt text of the fragment tentatively reproduces the conjecture by Sblendorio Cugusi (1996a).

F 236–37 Quintilian, *The Orator's Education*

From this figure of speech the one that is called *communicatio* ["conversation"] is not very different: either when we consult our opponents themselves, as . . . , [21] or when we conduct a sort of discussion with the judges, which is very frequent: "What do you advise?" and "I ask you." and "What then ought to have been done?," as Cato [does]: "Come now, if you were in that situation, what else would you have done?," and elsewhere: "Imagine that a matter of common concern is being dealt with and you have been put in charge of this matter."

CATO

F 238 Cic. *Off.* 3.104

qui ius igitur iurandum violat, is Fidem violat, quam in
Capitolio vicinam Iovis Optimi Maximi, ut in Catonis oratione est, maiores nostri esse voluerunt.

F 239 Quint. *Inst.* 3.6.97

nothum qui non sit legitimus Graeci vocant, Latinum rei
nomen, ut Cato quoque in oratione quadam testatus est,
non habemus, ideoque utimur peregrino; . . .

F 240 Quint. *Inst.* 5.11.39

si causam veneficii dicat adultera,[1] non M. Catonis iudicio
damnanda videatur,[2] qui nullam adulteram non eandem
esse veneficam dixit?

[1] dicat adultera *vel* dicam adulteram (dicam in adulteram)
codd.   [2] damnanda videatur *vel* damnata videtur *codd.*

264

F 238 Cicero, *On Duties*

Whoever, therefore, violates an oath, violates Good Faith; and it was she, as is said in a speech of Cato's, that our forefathers wanted to be on the Capitol as a neighbor to Jupiter Supreme and Best [*Iupiter Optimus Maximus*].[1]

[1] Cicero's phrasing might be inspired by what was in Cato's speech, so that the words *vicinam Iovis Optimi Maximi* have been suggested as a literal quotation. The Temple of Fides on the Capitoline Hill (in Rome), close to the important temple of Iupiter Optimus Maximus or Iupiter Capitolinus, was inaugurated by A. Atilius Calatinus around 250 BC.

F 239 Quintilian, *The Orator's Education*

nothus[1] is what the Greeks call a child who is not legitimate; a Latin word for this matter, as Cato too has testified in one of his speeches, we do not have, and therefore we use the foreign one; . . .

[1] On the evolution of this term (first attested in Latin in Cato), see Sblendorio Cugusi 1996b, 220–32.

F 240 Quintilian, *The Orator's Education*

If an adulteress should be on trial for poisoning, would it not seem that she should be condemned by the judgment of M. Cato, who said that there was no adulteress who was not also a poisoner?[1]

[1] For this argument see also *Rhet. Her.* 4.23; Sen. *Controv.* 7.3.6.

F 241 Fest., p. 280.11–13 L.

‹PRAEMIOSAM pro pecuniosa Cato›[1] in oratione{m} quam scrib‹sit› . . . us inpudentiam praemio‹sam.

[1] *suppl. Mueller (post Ursinum)*

F 242a Fest., p. 142.12–16 L.

MUNIFICIOR[1] quoque . . . a munifice,[2] cum dicamus ‹nunc munificentior, quam›vis[3] munificens non sit ‹in usu› . . . in[4] ea, quam scripsit id . . . munificior q . . . s . . .

[1] munificior *ex Epit.*: magnificior *cod.*   [2] ‹idem deduxisse videtur› a munifice *Ursinus* | munifico *Epit.*
[3] *suppl. Epit.*   [4] ‹Cato› in *Ursinus*

F 242b Paul. *Fest.*, p. 143.4–6 L.

MUNIFICIOR a munifico identidem Cato dixit, cum nunc munificentior dicamus, quamvis munificens non sit in usu.

F 243 Fest., p. 280.5–8 L.

PELLICULATIO‹NEM Cato a pellicien›do,[1] quod est inducen‹do, dixit in ea oration›e{m},[2] quam scribsit de . . .

[1] *suppl. Epit.*   [2] *suppl. Epit.*

Cf. Paul. *Fest.*, p. 281.1 L.

F 241 Festus

⟨*praemiosa* ["well-rewarded, profitable"; fem.] instead of *pecuniosa* ["moneyed"]: Cato⟩ [uses it] in the oration that he wro⟨te⟩ . . . well-rewarded shamelessness [acc. sg. fem.].[1]

[1] As the cited expression appears in a list of quotations from Cato, it is often attributed to Cato and the text emended accordingly.

F 242a Festus

munificior ["more generous"] also . . . from *munifex*, while we ⟨now⟩ say ⟨*munificentio*r, a⟩lthough *munificens* is not ⟨in use⟩ [cf. F 92, 180] . . . in that [speech] that he wrote . . . more generous . . .

F 242b Paul the Deacon, *Epitome of Festus*

munificior ["more generous"], from *munificus*, was likewise said by Cato, while we now say *munificentior*, although *munificens* is not in use [cf. F 92, 180].

F 243 Festus

pelliculatio ["attraction"]: ⟨Cato used [that word], derived from *pellice*⟩*re* ["to attract"], which is "to induc⟨e," in that spee⟩ch, that he wrote about . . .

CATO

F 244 Isid. *Diff.* 1.118(220)

inter falsitatem et mendacium. negare quod verum[1] est, falsitas est;[2] fingere quod verum non[3] est, mendacium est. unde et[4] Cato: "tu, inquam,[5] si verum supprimis,[6] falsarius agnosceris; si falsa confingis, mendax esse videris."

[1] verum *vel* iterum *codd.*   [2] est *vel* dicitur *codd.*
[3] verum non *vel* verum *vel* falsum *codd.*
[4] et *vel om. codd.*   [5] tu inquam *vel* tumque *vel* tu inquit *codd.*   [6] supprimis *vel* suppremis *vel* comprimis *vel* nobis compremis *vel*: que primus *codd.*

F 245 Fest., p. 282.1–4 L.

PRODIDISSE non solum in illis dicitur, qui patriam hostibus prodiderunt, sed etiam tempus longius fecisse. ut Cato: "te, C. Caecili{i},[1] diem prodi‹di›sse militibus legionis III, cum proditionem non haberent."

[1] Caecilii *cod.*

F 246 Paul. *Fest.*, p. 519.11–13 L.

VECTICULARIA VITA dicitur eorum, qui vectibus parietes alienos perfodiunt furandi gratia. Cato: "vecticularium[1] vitam vivere, repente largiter habere, repente nihil."

[1] vectaculariam *Watt (1984, 248–49)*

F 244 Isidore, *On Differences between Words*

[The difference] between a falsehood and a lie. To reject what is true is a falsehood; to make up what is not true is a lie. Hence Cato also [says]: "You, I say, if you suppress the truth, will be recognized as a deceiver; if you make up false things, you will be seen to be a liar."

F 245 Festus

prodidisse ["to have betrayed / deferred"] is not only used of those who have betrayed their country to the enemy, but also for "to have made time longer." For instance, Cato: "that you, C. Caecilius, have deferred the appointed day for the soldiers of the third legion, when they did not have the right of deferral."[1]

[1] Agnew (1939) suggests that this fragment (providing the earliest evidence for legion numbering) may belong to the speech on military matters in Istria (F 147). The proper name would have to be read as C. Caelius (different versions of the name in different authors), and the third legion would be the one engaged in 178 BC in the Istrian expedition of consul A. Manlius Vulso (Liv. 41.1.6–7, 41.2.9, 41.3.5–6, 41.4.3).

F 246 Paul the Deacon, *Epitome of Festus*

vecticularia vita ["a life by means of a crowbar, i.e., a life by burglary"] is used of those who make holes in the walls of others with crowbars [*vectis*] in order to steal. Cato [says]: "to live a life by burglary, suddenly have a lot, suddenly nothing."

CATO

F 247 Charis., *GL* I, p. 240.1–2 = p. 313.1–3 B.

"vita deum immortalium" Cato senex; ubi Statilius Maximus "ἐκφώνησις" inquit "ἀρχαική, ὡς ὢ πόποι."

F 248 Charis., *GL* I, p. 221.8 = p. 285.22–23 B.

taetre Cato senex: "taetre aetatem exigit,"[1] ‹ut Maximus›.[2]

   [1] aetatem exigit *in cod. esse adnotat Lindemann*: aetatem exigit, ut Maximus *Cauchii ex deperdito cod. excerpta, Putschen*
   [2] *add. ex deperdito cod.*

F 249 Paul. *Fest.*, p. 44.13–14 L.

CULIGNA vas potorium. Cato: "culignam," inquit, "in feno Graeco ponit, ut bene oleat."

Cf. Osbern, *Derivationes* C 72.5 (p. 150 Bertini): . . . et hec culigna ne .i. quoddam vas rotundum, unde Cato "culignam," inquit "ponit in feno Greco ut bene oleat."; C 419 (p. 172 Bertini): culigna, quoddam vas rotundum. Cato "culignam ponit in feno Greco ut bene oleat."

F 250 Paul. *Fest.*, p. 52.2–3 L.

COEPIAM futurum tempus ab eo, quod est coepi. Cato: "coepiam seditiosa verba loqui."

F 251 Paul. *Fest.*, p. 52.15–16 L.

COMPLURIENS a compluribus significat saepe. Cato: "contumelias mihi dixisti compluriens."

F 247 Charisius

"the life of the immortal gods": Cato the Elder; there Statilius Maximus [Statilius Maximus (F 20 Zetzel)] says: "an archaic statement, like *o popoi* [Greek exclamation of surprise, anger, or pain]."

F 248 Charisius

taetre ["abominably"]: Cato the Elder [cf. *Orat.* F 221]: (s)he lives life abominably," ⟨just as Maximus⟩ [Statilius Maximus (F 19 Zetzel)].

F 249 Paul the Deacon, *Epitome of Festus*

culigna ["cup"], a vessel for drinking. Cato says: "(s)he puts the cup in fenugreek, so that it smells good."

F 250 Paul the Deacon, *Epitome of Festus*

coepiam ["I will begin"], future tense derived from *coepi* ["I have begun"]. Cato [says]: "I will begin to say seditious words."

F 251 Paul the Deacon, *Epitome of Festus*

compluriens ["several times"], derived from *complures* ["several"], means "frequently." Cato [says]: "you have uttered insults against me several times" [cf. *Orig.* F 81].

CATO

F 252   Fest., p. 408.31–36 L.

STRUERE, antiqui dicebant pro adicere, augere. unde industrios quoque. M. Cato: "iure, lege, libertate, republica communiter uti oportet: gloria atque honore, quomodo sibi quisque struxit"; . . .

F 253   Quint. *Inst.* 1.6.42

similis circa auctoritatem ratio. nam etiamsi potest videri nihil peccare qui utitur iis verbis quae summi auctores tradiderunt, multum tamen refert non solum quid dixerint, sed etiam quid persuaserint. neque enim "tuburchinabundum"[1] et "lurchinabundum"[2] iam in nobis quisquam ferat, licet Cato sit auctor, nec . . . . : quae nec ipsi iam dicerent.

[1] tuburchinabundum *vel* tuburchiabundum *codd.*: tuburcinabundum *Philander*   [2] lurchinabundum *vel* lurchiabundum *codd.*: lurcinabundum *Halm (cf. Philandrum)*

F 254   Plut. *Cat. Mai.* 8.1

μέλλων ποτὲ τὸν Ῥωμαίων δῆμον ὡρμημένον ἀκαίρως ἐπὶ σιτομετρίας καὶ διανομὰς ἀποτρέπειν, ἤρξατο τῶν λόγων οὕτως· "χαλεπὸν μέν ἐστιν, ὦ πολῖται, πρὸς γαστέρα λέγειν ὦτα οὐκ ἔχουσαν." [*Op. cet.* F 58.1, 63].

F 252 Festus

struere ["to build"]: the ancients used it for "to add," "to increase." Hence also industrious [*industrius*]. M. Cato [says]: "equity, law, liberty, public institutions one must hold in common, glory and honor in whatever way each individual has built them up / added them [*struxit*] for themselves"; . . .

F 253 Quintilian, *The Orator's Education*

A similar principle applies to authority. For though anyone who uses those words that the best authors have transmitted cannot be seen to make any mistake, it still matters a great deal not only what they said but what they made acceptable for use. For no one among us would now put up with *tuburchinabundus* ["eating greedily"] and *lurchinabundus* ["guzzling"], even though Cato is the authority for these, nor . . . : they would not use these [words] themselves nowadays.

F 254 Plutarch, *Life of Cato the Elder*

Once wishing to dissuade the Roman People from insisting unseasonably upon a distribution of grain rations, he [Cato] began his speech as follows: "It is hard, citizens, to talk to a belly as it does not have ears." [*Op. cet.* F 58.1, 63; cf. Plut. *Mor.* 131E (*De tuend. san. praec.* 18); *Mor.* 996D (*De esu carn.* 2.1); cf. Otto 1890, 374, s.v. *venter* 3].

CATO

F 254A Περὶ πολιτικῆς ἐπιστήμης (Cod. Vat. Gr. 1298, fol. 350v, ll. 21–28 = pp. 41.28–42.7 Mazzucchi)

[. . . κ]αλὸν γὰρ καὶ τοῦ Κάτωνος τοῦ πρεσβύτου. ὁρῶν γὰρ [το]ὺς Ῥωμαίοις περὶ τὰς μαντείας ἐπτοη-μέ‹νους› ἔλεγεν· "[τ]ί, ἄνδρες πολῖται, τί δήποτε ζη-τοῦμεν τὰ καθ᾽ ἡ[μ]ᾶς ἔξωθεν [ἡ]μων; ἰδοὺ γὰρ πολι-τεῦσαι ἄλλα καὶ δή περ ἄλλα ἐν ἡμῖν α[ὐ]τοῖς. δυοῖν οὖν πότερον ἂν βουλοίμεθ[α ἑλ]έσθαι; τοῦ[το δ᾽] ἐστὶ δικαιοσύνη καὶ ἀδικία. εἰ μὲν γὰρ δικαίως [π]ολιτευ-σαίμεθα πρός τε ἀλλήλους καὶ τοὺς ἔξωθ[εν, ε]ὖ βιω-σόμεθα, εἰ δὲ ἀδίκως, ἐνα〈ν〉τίως."

F 254A *On Political Science*

[. . .] For excellent is also this [statement] of Cato the
Elder. For, seeing the Romans scared with regard to
prophecies, he said: "Why, citizens, why then are we looking for the things concerning us outside of us? For, look,
we are making a number of political decisions among ourselves. Which of the two then would we like to select? This
is justice and injustice. For if we run political affairs justly
toward each other and those outside, we will live well, if
unjustly, in the contrary manner."[1]

[1] For highlighting this passage as a possible fragment of Cato's
speeches, see Fotiou 1981–1982; for considerations of potential
contexts, see Sblendorio Cugusi 1987, 46–47 (on the source text,
see Fiaccadori 1979; Mazzucchi 1982).

OPERA CETERA

LIBRI AD MARCUM FILIUM (F 1–15)

*Various sources show that Cato wrote a work addressed to
his son Marcus: the piece is identified as "to his son" in the
surrounding texts (Op. cet. F 4, 12, 13, 14), or addresses
to the son are included in fragments (Op. cet. F 1, 5).
Nonius Marcellus calls the work "precepts to his son" (Op.
cet. F 10): this does not have to be a title and could instead
refer to the didactic nature of the text (cf. Op. cet. F 8).
Priscian once refers to the work as "letter" (Op. cet. F 14;
attributed to Cato's* Epistulae *as F 8 by Cugusi; see also
Cugusi 1970a, 48–49), and Servius describes it as an "oration" or an "address" (Op. cet. F 11): these terms do not
need to be precise generic definitions and could rather
indicate a piece addressed to someone (on the same passage, Priscian [Op. cet. F 14] elsewhere just says "to his
son"). That Servius also uses the phrase (in the plural) "in
the books to his son" (Op. cet. F 12, 13) may indicate that
the work consisted of several sections or encompassed several themes; alternatively, the expression could reflect the
view of Servius or his sources or be a generic statement,
and it therefore does not necessarily indicate the piece's
original structure.*

The fragments clearly attributed to a work addressed

OTHER FRAGMENTS

LIBRI AD MARCUM FILIUM (F 1–15)

*to Cato's son indicate that it covered at least three topics
(also featuring in other writings by Cato): medicine (Op.
cet. F 4, 5, 14), agriculture (Op. cet. F 12, 13; perhaps F 6),
and oratory (Op. cet. F 1, 8; perhaps F 9, 15). Correspond-
ing subjects are identified occasionally in the references
(Op. cet. F 9: "on the orator" [doubtful]; F 13: "on agriculture"). While it used to be assumed that these themes
were treated in separate parts (thus altogether amounting
to an "encyclopedia," consisting of almost independent
sections), it is now believed that the work is an assemblage
of general precepts on a variety of matters, some of which
could be assigned to the areas identified by ancient and
modern readers. The text would then not be as much of a
generic novelty in Rome as an "encyclopedia" might be.
Nevertheless, it is noteworthy that such advice of a parent,
which may not have been entirely unusual in Rome, was
written down and entered general circulation; thus, the
piece could still be regarded as the seed for technical writing directed toward an addressee (for an overview of the
scholarly history and the main arguments of this discussion, see Astin 1978, 332–40; for earlier views see Della
Corte 1942; Barwick 1948).*

CATO

A number of references to comments by Cato on agri-cultural matters or what may be issues connected with agriculture have been assigned by Cugusi and Sblendorio Cugusi (2001, 432–34: Ad Marc. F 11–17) to the agricul-tural section of the work to the son, as they are not in-cluded in De agricultura. *Since such statements could also be made in other contexts, the passages are here given among the* Incertorum operum reliquiae *(Inc. F 2–5, 7–9). A section of* Op. cet. F 5 *(Plin.* HN 29.14) *is printed as an* Incertum *in the letter collection assumed by Cugusi in the edition of epistolary writers (1970, 69; see Introduction to* Epistula(e)*).*

The work addressed to the son was probably written for Cato's elder son, M. Porcius Cato Licinianus (T 7c, 61, 62,

F 1 Sen. *Controv.* 1, *praef.* 9–10

quis aequalium vestrorum quid[1] dicam satis ingeniosus, satis studiosus, immo quis satis vir est? emolliti enerves-que quod nati sunt inviti[2] manent, expugnatores alienae pudicitiae, neglegentes suae. in hos ne dii tantum mali ut cadat eloquentia; quam non mirarer, nisi animos, in quos se conferret, eligeret. erratis, optimi iuvenes, nisi illam vocem non M. Catonis sed oraculi creditis; quid enim est oraculum? nempe voluntas divina hominis ore enuntiata;

[1] quid *ed. Frob.*: quis *codd.*
[2] in vita *Sander*

79, 97), presumably with a didactic intent when the boy was still young (and might have later been passed on to Cato's second son, M. Porcius Cato Salonianus); such a collection of advice would complement what may have been a separate history written in large characters for the son's education (Inc. F 12; see also Introduction to Origines). With the production of a work of this type and the image that later authors created on its basis, Cato stands at the beginning of a Roman tradition of didactic pieces addressed by fathers to their sons, and his writings may provide some insight into educational practices in the second century BC (LeMoine 1991, 344–47). Whether Cato intended the work to be circulated more widely cannot be established.

F 1 Seneca the Elder, *Controversiae*

Which of your [Seneca the Elder's sons] contemporaries is, not to say sufficiently talented and sufficiently diligent, who is in fact sufficiently a man? As they are born feeble and spineless, they stay like that unwillingly, conquerors of the chastity of others, careless of their own. God forbid so much evil that eloquence falls to these; I would not be surprised if that [eloquence] did not choose the minds on whom it bestows itself. You are in error, my excellent young men, unless you credit this famous utterance not to M. Cato, but to an oracle. For what is an oracle? Surely the divine will pronounced through the mouth of a human

et quem tandem antistitem sanctiorem sibi invenire divi-
nitas potuit quam M. Catonem, per quem humano generi
non praeciperet sed convicium faceret? ille ergo vir quid
ait? "orator est, Marce fili, vir bonus dicendi peritus." [10]
ite nunc et in istis vulsis atque expolitis et nusquam nisi in
libidine viris quaerite oratores. merito talia habent exempla qualia ingenia.

Cf. Quint. *Inst.* 12.1.1; Plin. *Ep.* 4.7.5; Fronto, *Ad M. Caes.* 4.1.2
(pp. 53.23–54.2 van den Hout); *Ad Ver. Imp.* 2.24 (p. 132.9–11
van den Hout); Chir. Fortun. *Ars rhet.* 1, *RLM*, p. 81.5; Cassiod.
Inst.: Ars rhet., *RLM*, p. 495.5–6; Serv. ad Verg. *Aen.* 1.151; Isid.
Orig. 2.3.1.

F 2a Sen. *Ben.* 5.7.5

gentes facilius est barbaras inpatientesque arbitrii alieni
regere, quam animum suum continere et tradere sibi. Pla-
ton, inquit, agit Socrati gratias, quod ab illo didicit; quare
Socrates sibi non agat, quod ipse se docuit? M. Cato ait:
"quod tibi deerit, a te ipso mutuare"; quare donare mihi
non possim, si commodare possum?

being; and what high priest could the divinity ever have found for itself more holy than M. Cato, through whom it would not teach humankind, but scold it? What, then, did that great man say? "An orator, my son Marcus, is a good man skilled in speaking."[1] [10] Go now and look for orators among those men, who are plucked, and smooth-skinned, and nowhere [to be found] but in their lusts. Justly do they have models that match their intellects.

[1] Cato's statement became proverbial and is cited and adapted frequently in the rhetorical tradition, also without attribution (see references). The definition might reflect a traditional Roman view of an orator in Roman politics, for whom a good character and the ability to speak for specific purposes is sufficient while targeted rhetorical training is not yet regarded as necessary (Neuhauser 1958, 154–55).

F 2a Seneca the Younger, *On Benefits*

It is easier to rule nations savage and impatient of the authority of others than to restrain one's own spirit and submit to one's own control. Plato, they say, expressed gratitude to Socrates because he learned from him; why should not Socrates express gratitude to himself because he taught himself? M. Cato says: "Whatever you lack borrow from yourself"; why should I not be able to confer a gift on myself if I am able to lend [to myself]?

CATO

F 2b Sen. *Ep.* 119.2

paratum tibi creditorem dabo Catonianum illud: "a te
mutuum sumes."

F 3 Sen. *Ep.* 94.27

praeterea ipsa quae praecipiuntur per se multum habent
ponderis, utique si aut carmini intexta sunt aut prosa oratione in sententiam coartata, sicut illa Catoniana: "emas
non quod opus est, sed quod necesse est; quod non opus
est asse carum est," . . .

F 4 Plin. *HN* 7.171

et cum innumerabilia sint mortis signa, salutis securita-
tisque nulla sunt, quippe cum censorius Cato ad filium de
validis quoque observationem ut ex oraculo aliquo prodi-
derit, senilem iuventam praematurae mortis esse signum.

F 2b Seneca the Younger, *Epistles*

I will provide you with a ready creditor, Cato's famous
statement: "You shall take a loan from yourself."[1]

[1] Seneca the Younger twice refers to a statement of Cato of
the same basic content, but with different wording: as Seneca is
interested in the content and may be quoting from memory, both
references could go back to the same passage in Cato (cf. Otto
1890, 236–37, s.v. *mutuari, mutuus*). In neither case is the quotation assigned to a specific work; since it seems to give an instruction, it is usually attributed to the work addressed to Cato's son.

F 3 Seneca the Younger, *Epistles*

Moreover, precepts that are given are of great weight in
themselves, whether they be woven into the fabric of po-
etry or condensed into a saying in prose, like that famous
remark of Cato's [cf. *Orat.* F 175]: "Buy not what is
needed, but what is essential. What is not needed is dear
even at an as [i.e., a penny or cent],"[1] . . .

[1] Again, the framework for this statement of Cato is not identified. It sounds like an instruction deriving from a context similar
to that of the previous quotation (F 2); therefore, it is usually
attributed to the work addressed to Cato's son. For the expression, see Otto 1890, 39, s.v. *as* 1.

F 4 Pliny the Elder, *Natural History*

And whereas the signs of death are innumerable, there are
none of health and freedom from care, inasmuch as the
ex-censor Cato transmitted to his son an observation also
about healthy people, as if uttered by some oracle, namely
that characteristics of old age in youth are a sign of pre-
mature death.

F 5 Plin. *HN* 29.12–16, 27

etenim percensere insignia priscorum in his moribus con-
venit. Cassius Hemina ex antiquissimis auctor est primum
e medicis venisse Romam Peloponneso Archagathum Ly-
saniae filium L. Aemilio M. Livio cos. anno urbis DXXXV,
eique ius Quiritium datum et tabernam in compito Acilio
emptam ob id publice. [13] vulnerarium eum fuisse egregium,[1] mireque gratum adventum eius initio, mox a saevi-
tia secandi urendique transisse nomen in carnificem et in
taedium artem omnesque medicos, quod clarissime intellegi potest ex M. Catone, cuius auctoritati triumphus
atque censura minimum conferunt; tanto plus in ipso est.
quam ob rem verba eius ipsa ponemus: [14] "dicam de
istis Graecis suo loco, M. fili, quid Athenis exquisitum
habeam et quod bonum sit illorum litteras inspicere, non
perdiscere. vincam nequissimum et indocile genus illorum, et hoc puta vatem dixisse: quandoque ista gens suas
litteras dabit, omnia conrumpet, tum etiam magis, si medicos suos hoc mittet. iurarunt inter se barbaros necare
omnes medicina, sed[2] hoc ipsum mercede faciunt, ut fides
iis sit et facile disperdant. nos quoque dictitant barbaros

---

[1] egregium *(corruptum in* ecrecium) *Mayhoff*: credunt *vel*
cre- *codd.*: e re dictum *ed. Harduini cum Gronovio*: tradunt
edd.   [2] sed *vel* set *codd.*: et *ed. Harduini*

F 5 Pliny the Elder, *Natural History*

And indeed it is appropriate to review what is noteworthy among the ancients in these practices. Cassius Hemina [L. Cassius Hemina (*FRHist* 6 F 27)], one of the earliest [writers], is a witness that the first of the physicians to come to Rome was Archagathus, Lysanias' son, from the Peloponnese, in the consulship of L. Aemilius [Paulus] and M. Livius [Salinator], in the year of the city 535 [219 BC], and that citizen rights were given to him, and that a surgery at the Compitum Acili [crossroads with small sanctuary in Rome] was bought with public money for that purpose. [13] That he was an outstanding wound specialist, and that his arrival at first was wonderfully popular, but that soon, from his savage use of cutting and burning, his name changed to "executioner," and that his profession and all physicians became objects of loathing. This can be learned most plainly from M. Cato, to whose authority his triumph [194 BC] and censorship [184 BC] contribute very little; so much more is in the man itself. Therefore, we will put down his very words: [14] "I shall speak about those Greeks in their proper place, my son Marcus, as regards what I have found out in Athens [prob. 191 BC] and what benefit there is from dipping into their literature, not studying it closely. I will convincingly prove their nation to be extremely worthless and stubborn, and you should think that a prophet said this: whenever that nation will pass on its literature, it will corrupt all things, then even more if it sends hither its physicians. They have conspired together to kill all 'barbarians' with medicine, but this very thing they do for a fee, so that they gain credit and destroy people easily. They are also always calling us 'barbarians,'

et spurcius nos quam alios Ὀπικῶν³ appellatione foedant.
interdixi tibi de medicis." [15] atque hic Cato sescente-
simo quinto anno urbis nostrae obiit, octogensimo quinto
suo, ne quis illi defuisse publice tempora aut privatim vitae spatia ad experiendum arbitretur. quid ergo? damna-
tam ab eo rem utilissimam credimus? minime, Hercules.
subicit enim qua medicina se et coniugem usque ad lon-
gam senectam perduxerit, his ipsis scilicet, quae nunc nos
tractamus, profiteturque esse commentarium sibi, quo
medeatur filio, servis, familiaribus, quem nos per genera
usus sui digerimus. [16] non rem antiqui damnabant, sed
artem, maxime vero quaestum esse manipretio vitae recu-
sabant. ideo templum Aesculapii, etiam cum reciperetur
is deus, extra urbem fecisse iterumque in insula traduntur
nec,⁴ cum Graecos Italia pellerent, diu etiam post Catonem, excepisse medicos. [17] . . . [27] ita est profecto: lues

³ Ὀπικῶν *Urlichs cum Jahnio*: opicos *Hermolaus Barbarus*:
hoppicos (hippicos) *vel* hoppificos *vel* opificos *vel* hoppocos *codd.*
⁴ nec *Silligius*: et *codd.*

1 I.e., "Oscans," then "uncultured, barbarous." On the usage
of this term, see Otto 1890, 256–57, s.v. *Opicus (Oscus)*; on its
origin, meaning, and implications, see Dubuisson 1983.
2 Cato apparently wrote about medicine in at least three
places: in this work addressed to his son, in a private notebook
(cf. *Inc.* F 14), and in *De agricultura*, including veterinary medicine (*Agr.* 70–73, 126–27; cf. Plin. *HN* 25.4).   3 The temple
of Aesculapius / Asclepius in Rome was built on the Tiber island
at the end of the third century BC; this area was outside the city
boundary at the time.   4 Because of the context, the text is
usually emended to include a negation: that physicians were not
excepted suits the context and might be highlighted in contrast to

and they besmirch us more foully than others by the name of 'Opici.'[1] I have banned you from the physicians." [15] And this Cato died in the six hundred and fifth year of our city and the eighty-fifth of his life [149 BC], so that nobody can think that he lacked opportunities in public life or an extended period of private life, to gather experiences. What then? Do we believe that a very useful thing was condemned by him? Not in the least, by Hercules. For he adds the medical treatment by which he brought himself and his wife far into old age, by these very remedies in fact that we are now dealing with, and he claims to have a notebook,[2] according to which he treats his son, servants, and household; that material we rearrange by the types of their use. [16] The ancients did not condemn the substance, but the profession; in particular, in fact, they did not accept that profit was being made by taking payment for [a person's] life. For this reason, they are said to have built the temple of Aesculapius, even when he was received as a god, outside the city and, moreover, on an island,[3] and, when they banished Greeks from Italy, even a long time after Cato, not to have excepted physicians.[4] [17] . . . [27] It is indeed like this: the degeneracy of our

a measure of the emperor Augustus (Suet. *Aug.* 42.3), who banished all foreigners from Rome in times of a shortage of grain, excepting physicians, teachers, and some slaves. In the Republican period after Cato's time, a *Lex Iunia de peregrinis* of 126 BC and a *Lex Papia de peregrinis* of 65 BC removed foreigners without any special arrangements for physicians. Cato's stance might not signal opposition to Greek doctors as such and rather to the risk that they might undermine traditional structures of society by obtaining a wealthy and influential position (Wöhrle 1992).

morum, nec aliunde maior quam ex medicina, vatem prorsus cottidie facit Catonem et oraculum: satis esse ingenia
Graecorum inspicere, non perdiscere.

F 6 Plut. *Cat. Mai.* 4.4–6

Cf. *Orat.* F 175.

F 7 Plut. *Cat. Mai.* 21.3–4

ἐν ἀρχῇ μὲν οὖν ἔτι πένης ὢν καὶ στρατευόμενος
πρὸς οὐδὲν ἐδυσκόλαινε τῶν περὶ δίαιταν, ἀλλ᾽ αἴσχι-
στον ἀπέφαινε διὰ γαστέρα πρὸς οἰκέτην ζυγομαχεῖν.
[4] ὕστερον δὲ τῶν πραγμάτων ἐπιδιδόντων ποιού-
μενος ἑστιάσεις φίλων καὶ συναρχόντων, ἐκόλαζεν
εὐθὺς μετὰ τὸ δεῖπνον ἱμάντι τοὺς ἀμελέστερον ὑπ-
ουργήσαντας ὁτιοῦν ἢ σκευάσαντας.

morals, for no other reason more than because of medicine, daily reveals Cato as a prophet and an oracle in every respect: that it is enough to dip into the sophisticated works of the Greeks, not to study them closely [cf. *Inc.* F 14].

F 6 Plutarch, *Life of Cato the Elder*

Cf. *Orat.* F 175.[1]

[1] The statements reported are not attributed to a specific work of Cato. Since they exhort frugality, they might go with F 2 and F 3 of the piece addressed to his son. As they include advice for buying farmland, the fragment has been connected with this work's agricultural section.

F 7 Plutarch, *Life of Cato the Elder*

At the outset, when he [Cato] was still poor and in military service, he found no fault at all with any aspects of life's necessities; instead, he declared that it was shameful to quarrel with a household slave on account of the belly.[1] [4] Later, when his circumstances were improving, having arranged dinners for friends and colleagues, immediately after the meal he would punish with a whip those who had been remiss in any way in serving or preparing [cf. *Inc.* F 13].

[1] It is uncertain whether this remark comes from a written work of Cato and, if so, which one. A context of providing advice to his son on household matters has been envisaged.

F 8 Iul. Vict., *Ars* 1, *RLM*, p. 374.15–18 (= p. 3.8–10 Giomini / Celentano)

scire autem est rem, de qua dicturus sis, universam ante
pernoscere (in hanc rem constat etiam Catonis praecep-
tum paene divinum, qui ait: "rem tene, verba sequentur"),
et. . . .

F 9 Diom., *GL* I, p. 362.21–23 Keil

adnotabimus tamen veteres etiam sic declinasse, edo, edis,
edit: Cato ad filium vel de oratore[1] "lepus multum somni
adfert qui illum edit," . . .

   [1] de aratore *Lersch*

Cf. Plin. *HN* 28.260: somnos fieri lepore sumpto in cibis Cato
arbitrabatur, . . .

F 8 Iulius Victor

But one must know that you should be thoroughly acquainted in advance with the entire matter about which you are to speak (on this issue there exists also the almost divine precept of Cato, who says: "keep hold of the subject matter; the words will follow"),[1] and . . .

1 While a context for Cato's remark is not given, it is usually assumed that it comes from advice to his son on oratorical matters; on the reception of this maxim, see Sierra de Cózar 1991.

F 9 Diomedes

Yet we will note that the ancients conjugated also in this way: *edo, edis, edit* "[I eat," "you eat," "he/she/it eats"; variant forms for second and third person]: Cato [says in the work] to his son or on the orator:[1] "a hare brings much sleep [to someone] who eats it [*edit*]," . . .

Cf. Pliny the Elder, *Natural History*: Cato thought that sleep ensued when a hare had been taken as food, . . .

1 The fragment must come from Cato's work addressed to his son, though the context is unclear: the transmitted text of the quoting author Diomedes classifies the provenance of the phrase as "to his son or on the orator"; yet the quoted remark does not seem to be about oratory. The emendation "on the farmer" does not fully resolve the issue. On the basis of the content, a medical context within that work has been assumed (cf. *Inc.* F 14). Pliny the Elder probably alludes to the same passage, but refers to it from memory and does not quote it verbatim.

CATO

F 10 Non., p. 143.4–8 M. = 208 L.

MEDIASTRINOS, non balnearum, sed ministros et cura-
tores aedium legimus. . . . Cato in praeceptis ad filium: "illi
imperator tu, ille ceteris mediastrinus."[1]

[1] mediastrinus *Bentinus*: mediastrinum *codd.*: mediastrino
Mueller (qui ante illi *collocat)*

F 11 Serv. ad Verg. *G.* 1.46

"attritus splendescere vomer": . . . quod evenire frequenti
aratione novimus, ut et splendidior fiat et teratur: Cato in
oratione[1] ad filium: "vir bonus est, Marce fili, colendi peritus, cuius ferramenta splendent."

[1] de aratione *Iahn*

F 12 Serv. ad Verg. *G.* 2.95

"quo te carmine dicam / Raetica": hanc uvam Cato praecipue laudat in libris quos scripsit ad filium; contra Catullus eam vituperat et dicit nulli rei esse aptam, miraturque
cur eam laudaverit Cato.

Cf. Brevis expos. ad Verg. *G.* 2.96; Schol. Bern. ad Verg. *G.* 2.96.

F 10 Nonius Marcellus

mediastrini ["servants"]: we read of them not for baths, but as aides and supervisors for houses. . . . Cato [says] in the precepts to his son: "you [sg.] [are] a general to him, he [is] a servant to others."[1]

  [1] Text and precise meaning of the quoted phrase (lacking any verbs) are uncertain. The translation reproduces a widely accepted emendation.

F 11 Servius, *Commentary on Virgil*

"the plowshare, rubbed . . . to become shiny": . . . That this happens with frequent plowing we know, so that it becomes both more shiny and is worn. Cato [says] in an address[1] to his son: "a good man, my son Marcus, is someone skilled in agriculture, whose iron tools shine [from frequent use or through good care]."

  [1] This fragment presumably belongs to Cato's piece addressed to his son. When the work is identified as *in oratione* ["in an address"], *oratio* does not need to have the technical meaning of "speech," but may rather denote a formal utterance addressed to someone (see Introduction to *Libri ad Marcum filium*).

F 12 Servius, *Commentary on Virgil*

"with what song shall I praise you, Raetian [grapevine]": Cato praises this grape [from Raetia, Roman province in the Alpine region south of the river Danube] particularly in the books that he wrote addressed to his son; by contrast, Catullus [F 8 Lachmann] finds fault with it and says that it is of no use for anything, and he wonders why Cato praised it.

293

F 13 Serv. ad Verg. *G.* 2.412

"laudato ingentia rura / exiguum colito": hoc etiam Cato
ait in libris ad filium de agricultura.

F 14 Prisc., *GL* II, p. 268.16–20

excipitur "haec alvus huius alvi," quod veteres frequenter
masculino genere protulerunt. . . . Cato ad filium: "ex
dolore, ex febri, ex siti, ex medicamentis bibendis, ex cata-
plasmatis, ex alvo lavando."

Cf. Prisc., *GL* II, pp. 336.6–37.6: quae vero et in "im" et in "em,"
haec tam in i quam in e: . . . Cato in epistula ad filium: "ex dolore,
ex febri, ex siti, ex medicamentis bibendis."

F 15 *De adtributis personae et negotio*, *RLM*, p. 308.23–
26

ergo factum solum negotium est; propositio facti cum persona[1] vel quolibet[2] alio modo invidiam conparans aut ex-
tenuans summa dicetur. et haec est quam Cato in libro suo
appellat vires causae.

[1] cum persona *codd. Halmii*: cum persona eius qui arguitur
Orelli   [2] quolibet *vel* quodlibet *codd.*

F 13 Servius, *Commentary on Virgil*

"praise immense fields, farm a small one": Cato says this too in the books to his son on agriculture.

F 14 Priscian

An exception is *haec alvus, huius alvi* ["this belly"; nom., gen.; fem.], which the ancients frequently used in masculine gender. . . . Cato [says in the piece] to his son: "from grief, from fever, from thirst, from drinking medicine, from poultices, from washing out the bowels [*alvus*; masc.]."

Cf. Priscian: But what [ends] both in -*im* and in -*em* [acc. sg.], this [has endings] in -*i* as well as in -*e* [abl. sg.]: . . . Cato [says] in a letter to his son [see Introduction to *Libri ad Marcum filium*]: "from grief, from fever, from thirst, from drinking medicine."

F 15 Anonymous rhetorical work

Thus, the fact only is the issue; the statement of the fact, with the personality [i.e., of the individual concerned] or any other means creating or diminishing ill will, will be termed the main point. And this is what Cato in his book[1] calls the core of the case.

[1] The title of the book is not given, but the comment must belong to a discussion of oratory; as this topic was included in the piece addressed to Cato's son, the fragment could come from that work, though other contexts are also possible (cf. T 48 and General Introduction).

CATO

DE RE MILITARI LIBER (F 16–31)

Several sources mention a single-volume work "on military matters" (Op. cet. F 19, 20, 21, 22, 23, 24, 25, 26, 30, 31). Two passages have the version "on military discipline" (Op. cet. F 17, 29), which seems to be a variation focused on the content and not a verbatim quotation. While one of these refers to the work as "a volume" (Op. cet. F 17), the other mentions "books" (Op. cet. F 29); this is the only source suggesting a multi-volume work, and it might be inaccurate or generic. The quotation including a comment on reactions to one's writings (Op. cet. F 17) could come from an introduction and thus suggest publication; a sepa-

F 16 Varro, *Ling.* 7.58

adcensos ministratores Cato esse scribit. potest id ⟨ab censione, id est⟩ ab arbitrio;[1] nam adest[2] ad arbitrium eius cuius minister.

[1] ⟨ab censione id est⟩ *add. Goetz and Schoell in app.*
[2] adest *A. Spengel*: inde *cod.*

F 17 Plin. *HN praef.* 30–32

non queo mihi temperare quo minus ad hoc pertinentia ipsa censorii Catonis verba ponam, ut appareat etiam Catoni de militari disciplina commentanti, qui sub Afri-

DE RE MILITARI LIBER (F 16–31)

*rate proem would show that this item is an individual work
and not part of the piece addressed to Cato's son (as some
scholars have suggested). The themes covered can be inferred only from the securely attested extant fragments:
they suggest various aspects of running military campaigns. Thus, the work might have been a kind of hand-
book of practical information about Roman military practices and methods. The book was known, at least indirectly,
until late antiquity (Op. cet. F 27; on its use by later authors and potential further fragments to be recovered from
their works see Nap 1927).*

F 16 Varro, *On the Latin Language*

That *adcensi* are attendants Cato writes.[1] That [word]
could [be derived] ‹from *censio* ["judgment"], that is›
from *arbitrium* ["decision, mastery"]: for he [the *accen-
sus*] is there according to the mastery [*arbitrium*] of the
person whose attendant [he is].

[1] The work in which Cato made this comment is not identified. It could come from a description of military hierarchy,
though *adcensus* here seems to be understood as "attendant" and
not to refer to a supernumerary in the military (see, e.g., Varro,
Ling. 5.82).

F 17 Pliny the Elder, *Natural History*

I am unable to refrain from putting down the very words
of the ex-censor Cato applying to this [i.e., criticism of
publications], so that it becomes evident that even for
Cato, writing on military discipline, who had learned his
soldiering under Africanus [P. Cornelius Scipio Africanus

cano, immo vero et sub Hannibale didicisset militare et ne
Africanum quidem ferre potuisset, qui imperator trium-
phum reportasset, paratos fuisse istos, qui obtrectatione
alienae scientiae famam sibi aucupantur. quid enim ait in
eo volumine? "scio ego, quae scripta sunt si palam pro-
ferantur, multos fore qui vitilitigent,[1] sed ii potissimum
qui verae laudis expertes sunt. eorum ego orationes sivi[2]
praeterfluere."[3] [31] . . . [32] ergo securi etiam contra vitilitigatores, quos Cato eleganter ex vitiis et litigatoribus
composuit—quid enim illi aliud quam litigant aut litem
quaerunt?—, exequemur reliqua proposti.

[1] vitilitigent *Fabricius, Camers*: vitii lit- *vel* vitilegent *vel* ut
eligant (-gat) *vel* ita reprobent ut eligant *codd.*: inviti legant *edd.*

[2] sivi *Jordan, Detlefsen*: sibi *codd.*: sino *edd.*: ibi *Ianus*

[3] praeterfluere *vel* praetereo *vel* praeter *vel om. codd.*: prae-
terire *Rossbach*

F 18 Frontin. *Str.* 4.1.16

Cf. *Orig.* F 134.

F 19 Fest., p. 236.27–31 L.

PEREMERE . . . : at Cato in libro[1] qui est de re militari pro
vitiare[2] usus est, cum ait: "cum[3] magistratus nihil audent
imperare, ne quid consul auspici peremat."[4]

[1] libro *vel* li. *codd.*   [2] vitiare *edd.*: viciare *codd.*
[3] *del. Jordan*   [4] consularis auspici peremant *Mommsen*

maior, cos. 205, 194, censor 199 BC (*ORF*[4] 4)], or rather under Hannibal as well, and had been unable to endure even Africanus, who, when commander in chief, had won a triumph, there were those ready to hunt after glory for themselves by disparaging someone else's knowledge. For what does he say in that volume? "I know that, if any writings are published, there will be many who litigiously find faults [*vitilitigare*; verb], but mostly those who lack true distinction. For my part, I have let these people's utterances run their course." [31] . . . [32] Accordingly, being safeguarded even against litigious faultfinders [*vitilitigatores*; noun], a name that Cato neatly put together from "faults" [*vitia*] and "litigants" [*litigatores*]—for what else do these people do but litigate or seek litigious action?—, we will follow out the remainder of our intended plan.

F 18 Frontinus, *Stratagems*

Cf. *Orig.* F 134.[1]

[1] This statement about punishment of soldiers could come from this work or from the *Origines*.

F 19 Festus

peremere ["to destroy, annul"] . . . : but Cato in the book that is on military matters used it instead of *vitiare* ["to spoil, impair"], when he says: "when the magistrates do not dare to give any orders, so that the consul does not spoil / annul the auspices in any way."

CATO

F 20   Fest., pp. 298.36–300.3 L.

PROCUBITORES dicuntur † fere vetites †,[1] qui noctu custodiae causa ante castra excubant, cum castra hostium in propinquo sunt, ut M. Cato in eo, quem de re militari scripsit.

[1] fere velites *Ursinus*

F 21   Fest., p. 300.3–5 L.

PROPERAM pro celeri ac strenua dixisse antiquos testimonio est Cato, cum ait in libro de re militari: "tertia e castris eductio celeris properaque est."

F 22   Fest., p. 400.6–12 L.

SUB CORONA venire dicuntur, quia captivi coronati solent venire, ut ait Cato in eo, qui est de re militari: "ut populus {suus}[1] sua opera potius ob rem bene gestam coronatus supplicatum eat, quam re mala gesta coronatus veneat."[2]

[1] *del. Mueller*   [2] veneat *edd., codd. rec. Gelli*: veniat *cod.*

Cf. Paul. *Fest.*, p. 401.1–4; Gell. *NA* 6.4.4–5.

F 23   Fest., p. 466.28–32 L.

SERRA PROELIARI dicitur, cum assidue acceditur recediturque, neque ullo consistitur tempore. Cato de re militari: "sive[1] forte opus sit cuneo, aut globo, aut forcipe, aut turribus, aut serra, uti adoriare."

[1] sive *Augustinus*: sine *cod.*

F 20 Festus

procubitores are called . . . [?] those who, at night, for the purpose of keeping guard, maintain a watch in front of the camp, when the camp of the enemy is close by, as M. Cato [says] in that [work] that he wrote on military matters.

F 21 Festus

That the ancients used *propera* ["quick, speedy"; fem. sg.], instead of *celeris* ["fast"; fem. sg.] and *strenua* ["energetic"; fem. sg.], Cato bears testimony, when he says in the book on military matters: "the third movement of troops out of the camp is fast and quick [*celeris properaque*]."

F 22 Festus

They are said to be sold "under the wreath," because captives are customarily sold wearing wreaths, as Cato says in that [work] that is on military matters: "so that {their} the People by their own effort would rather go to make offerings in celebration wearing wreaths because of a matter gone well, than be sold wearing wreaths after a matter had gone badly."

F 23 Festus

serra proeliari ["to fight in saw-like battle formation"] is used, when one continuously advances and retreats, and does not stand still at any time. Cato [says in the work] on military matters: "or there may perhaps be need of a wedge-shaped formation of soldiers, or a closely packed throng, or a pincer formation, or assaulting towers, or a saw-like battle formation,[1] so that you can attack."

---

[1] On these words as technical terms for battle formations in military language, see Gell. *NA* 10.9.1–2.

CATO

F 24 Non., p. 204.26–33 M. = 301 L.

FRONTEM feminino genere Vergilius {ait}[1] [Verg. *Aen.* 7.417] . . . masculino . . . Cato de re militari: "una depugnatio est fronte longo, quadrato exercitu."

  [1] ait *om. cod. unus*

Cf. Veg. *Mil.* 3.20.1: una depugnatio est fronte longa quadro exercitu, sicut etiam nunc et prope semper solet proelium fieri.

F 25 Non., p. 463.3–4 M. = 741 L.

DISCIPLINOSUS etiam ⟨de⟩[1] pessima arte potest dici. Cato de re militari: "quam gladiator disciplinosus."

  [1] *add. Mueller*

F 26 Non., p. 554.23–26 M. = 890 L.

FERENTARII, levis armatura, qui cui[1] opus esset auxilio ferrent excursu levi, armis gravibus non impediti. Cato de re militari:[2] "inde partem equitatus atque ferentarios praedatum[3] misit."

  [1] qui cui *Mueller*: quicquid *codd.*: qui quod *Mercerus*: qui quibus *fort. Lindsay in app.*   [2] de re militari *edd.*: ad rem militarem *codd.*   [3] praedatum *ed. a. 1476*: praedatos *codd.*

Cf. Paul. *Fest.*, p. 506.26–28 L.: Cato eos ferentarios dixit, qui tela ac potiones militibus proeliantibus ministrabant.

F 27a Veg. *Mil.* 1.8.10–12

haec necessitas compulit evolutis auctoribus ea me in hoc opusculo fidelissime dicere quae Cato ille Censorius de disciplina militari scripsit, [11] quae Cornelius Celsus,

F 24 Nonius Marcellus

frons ["front"]: in feminine gender Virgil {says} [Verg. *Aen.* 7.417] . . . in masculine [cf. *Orig.* F 95; *Orat.* F 47] . . . Cato [in the work] on military matters: "one method of fighting a battle is with a long front [*frons*; masc.], the army formed into a square."

Cf. Vegetius: One method of fighting a battle is with a long front [*frons*; here fem.], the army formed into a square, just as even now and almost always a battle tends to take place.

F 25 Nonius Marcellus

disciplinosus ["well-trained"] can also be used ‹with reference to› the worst art [cf. *Inc.* F 19]. Cato [says in the work] on military matters: "as / than a well-trained gladiator."

F 26 Nonius Marcellus

ferentarii ["light-armed soldiers"], light-armed troops, who could bring support to anyone who needed it with a light sortie, not hindered by heavy armor. Cato [says in the work] on military matters: "thence he sent part of the cavalry and the light-armed soldiers to acquire loot."

Cf. Paul the Deacon, *Epitome of Festus*: Cato calls those *ferentarii* ["light-armed soldiers"] who provided missile weapons and drinks to fighting soldiers.

F 27a Vegetius

This necessity forces me, after having gone through the authorities, to say in this little work most faithfully what that famous Cato, the ex-censor, wrote about military discipline, [11] what Cornelius Celsus [A. Cornelius Celsus],

quae Frontinus perstringenda duxerunt, quae Paternus, diligentissimus iuris militaris assertor, in libros redegit, quae Augusti et Traiani Adrianique constitutionibus cauta sunt. [12] nihil enim mihi auctoritatis assumo, sed horum quos supra rettuli quae dispersa sunt velut in ordinem epitomata conscribo.

F 27b Veg. *Mil.* 2.3.6–8

Cato ille Maior, cum et armis invictus esset et consul exercitus saepe duxisset, plus se rei publicae credidit profuturum si disciplinam militarem conferret in litteras. [7] nam unius aetatis sunt quae fortiter fiunt, quae vero pro utilitate rei publicae scribuntur aeterna sunt. idem fecerunt alii complures, sed praecipue Frontinus, divo Traiano ab eiusmodi comprobatus industria. [8] horum instituta, horum praecepta, in quantum valeo, strictim fideliterque signabo.

F 28 Veg. *Mil.* 1.13.6–8

deinde in aliis rebus, sicut ait Cato, si quid erratum est, potest postmodum corrigi: [7] proeliorum delicta emendationem non recipiunt, cum poena statim sequatur errorem; [8] nam aut confestim pereunt qui ignave imperiteque pugnaverint aut in fugam versi victoribus ultra pares esse non audent.

---

[1] The work in which Cato made this statement is not identified, but it clearly comes from a discussion of military matters; Vegetius identifies the book of Cato shortly afterward (*Op. cet.* F 29).

what Frontinus [Sex. Iulius Frontinus] considered it worthwhile to touch upon, what Paternus [P. Taruttienus Paternus], the most diligent champion of military law, brought together into books, and what is provided for in the legal decisions of Augustus, Trajan, and Hadrian. [12] For I do not claim any authority for myself; instead, I put together in writing, in order and in abbreviated form, as it were, the scattered remarks of these [writers] whom I have listed above.

F 27b Vegetius

That famous Cato the Elder, after he had been invincible in arms and had often led armies as consul [195 BC], believed that he would be more useful to the *res publica* if he were to bring together in writing [his knowledge of] military discipline. [7] For what is done bravely belongs to a single age; yet what is written down for the usefulness of the *res publica* is eternal. Several others have done the same, but particularly Frontinus [Sex. Iulius Frontinus], approved by the divine Trajan on account of the diligence in this respect. [8] Their instructions, their precepts, as far as I am able to, I will make known summarily and faithfully.

F 28 Vegetius

Then in other matters, as Cato says,[1] if any error has been made, it can be corrected later: [7] faults in battles are not receptive to emendation, since the punishment immediately follows the error; [8] for those who have fought in a cowardly and unskillful manner either perish without delay or, turned to flight, no longer dare to count themselves as equals with the victors.

F 29 Veg. *Mil.* 1.15.4

quantum utilitatis boni sagittarii in proeliis habeant et
Cato in libris de disciplina militari evidenter ostendit
et . . .

F 30 Prisc., *GL* II, p. 334.13–16

"hic" et "haec celer" vel "celeris" et "hoc celere," "ab hoc"
et "ab hac celeri" . . . M. Cato de re militari: "satis celeris
sis in tempore."

F 31 Serv. auct. / Philargyrius ad Verg. *G.* 2.417

"iam canit effectos extremus[1] vinitor antes": . . . et aliter:
Cato[2] de re militari: "pedites quattuor agminibus, equites
duobus antibus ducas." sunt autem extremae quadrarum
partes.

[1] effectos extremus *codd. Verg.*: effectus extremos *vel* extremos effectus *vel* effectos extremos *codd. Serv.*   [2] Cato *Ursinus*: coto *cod.*

CARMEN DE MORIBUS (F 32–34)

*Gellius (Op. cet. F 32–34) and Nonius Marcellus (Op. cet.
F 32) mention a separate* Carmen de moribus *("Poem on
morals / behavior") by Cato. The title* carmen *is interpreted by some as indicating a work originally in verse,
perhaps in Saturnians (Pighi 1966; Suerbaum 2002, 412),
while others regard it as a prose text, with* carmen *denoting a formal mode of expression, facilitating a sententious
style and learning by heart (Astin 1978, 185–86; Cu-*

F 29 Vegetius

Of how much use good archers are in battles, both Cato shows clearly in the books on military discipline and . . .

F 30 Priscian

hic and *haec celer* or *celeris* ["fast"; both forms used for nom. sg. masc. and fem.] and *hoc celere* [nom. sg. neut.], *ab hoc* and *ab hac celeri* [abl. sg. masc. / neut. and fem.] . . . M. Cato [says in the work] on military matters: "may you be fast [*celeris*; nom. sg. masc. or fem.] enough at the right time."

F 31 Servius Danielis / Philargyrius, *Commentary on Virgil*

"now the last vineyard worker sings of the finished rows [*antes*]": . . . and otherwise: Cato [says in the work] on military matters: "you should lead the infantry in four columns and the cavalry in two files [*antes*]." And indeed they are the uttermost parts of squares.

CARMEN DE MORIBUS (F 32–34)

gusi and Sblendorio Cugusi 2001, 2:442). The work seems to have included comments on morals and human behavior: it is often seen as a didactic piece on personal conduct, but could also be an antiquarian work on the customs of the ancient Romans (FRHist 1:193; on aspects of Roman views implied in these fragments see, e.g., Préaux 1966; Negri 1988).

F 32 Gell. *NA* 11.2.1–3

"elegans" homo non dicebatur cum laude, set id fere verbum ad aetatem M. Catonis vitii non laudis fuit. [2] est
namque hoc animadvertere, cum in quibusdam aliis, tum
in libro Catonis qui inscriptus est Carmen de moribus. ex
quo libro verba haec sunt: "avaritiam[1] omnia vitia habere[2]
putabant; sumptuosus, cupidus,[3] elegans, vinosus,[4] intercutitus[5] qui[6] habebatur, is laudabatur";[7] [3] ex quibus verbis apparet "elegantem" dictum antiquitus non ab ingenii
elegantia, sed qui nimis lecto amoenoque cultu victuque
esset.

[1] avaritiam *vel* avaritia *codd.*   [2] alere *Watt (1984, 249–50)*
[3] cuppes *Gronovius*   [4] vinosus *Meurs*: vitiosus *codd.,
Nonius Marcellus*   [5] intercutitus *Bergk*: inritus *codd.*: invi-
dus *cod. Scriverii ap. Gronovium*: incitus *Madvig*: in‹pro›vidus
Watt (1984, 250): nitidus *Lentano (1999, 19–20)*   [6] qui *vel*
que *codd.*   [7] is laudabatur *codd.*: is audiebat avarus *Baehrens*: ‹lautus› laudabatur *Lentano (1999)*

Cf. Non., pp. 465.10–17 M. = 744–45 L.: ELEGANTES non solum,
ut consuetudine, ab elegantia ingenii aut cultus electione et di-
lectu plerumque, dici potest; sed a veteribus etiam vitio datur. . . .
Cato carmine de moribus: "avaritiam omnia vitia habere putant;
sumtuosus, cupidus, elegans, vitiosus."

F 32 Gellius, *Attic Nights*

"Fastidious," of an individual, was not customarily used by way of praise; but, indeed, up to the time of M. Cato that word was generally a sign of reproach, not of praise. [2] And this in fact can be observed both in some other [works] and particularly in the book of Cato that is entitled *Carmen de moribus*. In that book there are the following words: "They believed that avarice included all vices; someone who was considered lavish, greedy, fastidious, intoxicated with wine, engaging in illicit sexual intercourse, was praised" [cf. Otto 1890, 51, s.v. *avarus*, *avaritia* 5].[1] [3] From these words it is evident that in the past someone was called "fastidious", not on the basis of their refinement of disposition, but whoever was of an excessively choice and extravagant attire and mode of life.

Cf. Nonius Marcellus: "Fastidious individuals" cannot only be called thus, as is common, on the basis of their refinement of disposition or of the general careful selection and choice of apparel; but by the ancients it [the description] was also given to a vice . . . Cato [says] in the *Carmen de moribus*: "They believe that avarice includes all the vices; lavish, greedy, fastidious, vicious."

[1] Apparently, Cato criticizes that some people regard avarice as a major vice and praise individuals with other characteristics indicating some sort of extravagance, which in Cato's view are equally vices. In Gellius' version the verbs are in the imperfect tense; thus, it is a statement about behavior in the past. The shortened version in Nonius Marcellus has the present tense, so that the description can have a wider application; but the quotation might be inaccurate. Since the argument is somewhat obscure, the transmission has been doubted, and suggestions for changing the text have been made (see Watt 1984, 249–50; Lentano 1999).

F 33 Gell. *NA* 11.2.5

praeterea ex eodem libro Catonis haec etiam sparsim et
intercise notavimus: "vestiri" inquit "in foro honeste mos
erat, domi quod satis erat. equos carius quam coquos eme-
bant. poeticae artis honos non erat. si quis in ea re stude-
bat aut sese ad convivia adplicabat, "grassator" vocabatur."

F 34 Gell. *NA* 11.2.6

illa quoque ex eodem libro praeclarae veritatis sententia
est: "nam vita" inquit "humana prope uti ferrum est. si
exerceas, conteritur; si non exerceas, tamen robigo inter-
ficit. item homines exercendo videmus conteri; si nihil
exerceas, inertia atque torpedo plus detrimenti facit quam
exercitio."

EPISTULA(E) (F 35–39)

*Three sources (Op. cet. F 35–37) mention a letter by Cato
to his son; one of these (Op. cet. F 37, with reconstructed
text) elsewhere refers to letters in the plural (Op. cet.
F 38), and yet another source reports what Cato said to
"Magnus" (Op. cet. F 39; see note). The text of the last two
passages has been questioned and emended. In addition,*

EPISTULA(E)

F 33 Gellius, *Attic Nights*

Moreover, from the same book of Cato [cf. *Op. cet.* F 32] we have also noted down these [remarks] in a scattered and discontinuous manner: "It was the custom," he says, "to dress becomingly in the Forum, at home as was sufficient. They purchased horses for more money than cooks [cf. Plin. *HN* 9.67]. There was no honor for the poetic art. If anyone devoted themselves to it or frequented banquets, they were called an 'idler.'"

F 34 Gellius, *Attic Nights*

This too, from the same book [cf. *Op. cet.* F 32], is a statement of splendid truthfulness [cf. Otto 1890, 134–35, s.v. *ferrum* 2]: "Indeed," he says, "human life is almost like iron. If you put it to use, it wears out; if you do not put it to use, rust nevertheless kills it. In the same way we see people worn out by putting it to use; if you do not put it to use in any way, sluggishness and torpor do more damage than use."

EPISTULA(E) (F 35–39)

there are testimonia showing that Cato sent letters in a military capacity (and was aware that those could be sent) to allies (Orat. F 34 = Epist. F 1 Cugusi), to opponents (T 82 = Epist. F 2 Cugusi), and as reports back to Rome (Liv. 34.42.1 = Epist. F 3 Cugusi). Cugusi and Sblendorio Cugusi (2001, 2:406) therefore assume a letter collection

*by Cato and add these passages to the epistolary frag-
ments; they posit a certain level of "publication" for at least
some of the letters by Cato himself (texts [no. LXVI] and
commentary also in Cugusi 1970, 1:65–70, 2:33–37; see
further Cugusi 1970a, 46–52).*

*What is certain is only that a letter from Cato to his son
Marcus was preserved and that its content and context
were known to later ancient authors (on Op. cet. F 14 =
Epist. F 8 Cugusi, see Introduction to Libri ad Marcum
filium). Over the course of his life Cato will have written
further private letters as well as official letters; there is no
evidence as to whether in his lifetime any of these letters
were in circulation or even intended to be. Thus, the assumption of a letter collection must remain a hypothesis.
Only references to specific letters, including a quotation or*

F 35 Cic. *Off.* 1.37

Marci quidem Catonis senis est epistula ad Marcum filium, in qua scribit se audisse eum missum factum esse
a consule cum in Macedonia bello Persico miles esset.
monet igitur ut caveat ne proelium ineat; negat enim ius
esse qui miles non sit cum hoste pugnare.

---

1 This passage is preceded by a section (Cic. *Off.* 1.36) narrat-
ing that Cato's son did military service under general Popillius
(M. Popillius Laenas [cos. 173 BC] or C. Popillius Laenas [cos.
172 BC]) in a province (referring to Liguria) and, when his legion
was dismissed, wrote to the commander to ask him to allow him
to remain in the army and renew his military oath. That section
is usually deleted, as suggested by Madvig (see Cugusi 1970a,

an indication of the content, are therefore assembled in this section.

Cato's letter to his son presumably was originally a private letter; although its content makes it suitable for wider circulation, it is not known whether publication was planned by Cato or realized in his lifetime (later, a text must have been available, from which the sources quote). This letter to the son, again the elder son, M. Porcius Licinianus (T 7c, 61, 62, 79, 97), takes the son's behavior in battle (different aspects highlighted in the various sources) as the starting point and then seems to talk about principles of military conduct. Thus, the piece is endowed with characteristics of a brief treatise and in some ways similar to the Libri ad Marcum filium (Schmidt 1972).

F 35 Cicero, *On Duties*

There is indeed a letter of Marcus Cato the Elder to his son Marcus, in which he writes that he has heard that he [the son] had been discharged by the consul [L. Aemilius Paullus, cos. 182, 168 BC (*ORF*[4] 12)], when he was serving as a soldier in Macedonia in the war with Perseus [171–168 BC]. Therefore, he [Cato] warns [the son] to be careful not to go into battle; for he says that it is not lawful for a man who is not a soldier to fight against the enemy.[1]

51–54), since it seems to duplicate some of the motifs in the subsequent passage while referring them to another military campaign (both sections quoted in: Io. Saresb. *Policraticus* 6.7 [*PL* 199, col. 599D–600A]).

CATO

Cf. Plut. *Mor.* 273E–F (*Quaest. Rom.* 39): διὰ τί τοῖς μὴ στρα-
τευομένοις μὲν ἐν στρατοπέδῳ δ᾽ ἄλλως ἀναστρεφομένοις
οὐκ ἐξῆν ἄνδρα βαλεῖν πολέμιον οὐδὲ τρῶσαι; καὶ τοῦτο
Κάτων ὁ πρεσβύτης ἐν ἐπιστολῇ τινι δεδήλωκε, γράφων
πρὸς τὸν υἱὸν καὶ κελεύων, εἰ παρεθείη τῆς στρατείας ἀπο-
πληρώσας τὸν χρόνον, ὑποστρέφειν, ἢ προσμένοντα λαβεῖν
παρὰ τοῦ στρατηγοῦ τὸ ἐξεῖναι τρῶσαι καὶ ἀνελεῖν πολέμιον.

F 36 Plut. *Cat. Mai.* 20.10–11

ὁ δέ, καίπερ οὕτως ἔχων ἀνὴρ ἀγαθὸς ἦν ἐν ταῖς
στρατείαις, καὶ τὴν πρὸς Περσέα μάχην ἠγωνίσατο
λαμπρῶς Παύλου στρατηγοῦντος. εἶτα μέντοι τοῦ ξίφους ἐκκρουσθέντος ὑπὸ πληγῆς ἢ δι᾽ ὑγρότητα τῆς
χειρὸς ἐξολισθόντος,[1] ἀχθεσθεὶς τρέπεται πρός τινας
τῶν συνήθων, καὶ παραλαβὼν ἐκείνους αὖθις εἰς τοὺς
πολεμίους ἐνέβαλε. [11] πολλῷ δ᾽ ἀγῶνι καὶ βίᾳ μεγάλῃ διαφωτίσας τὸν τόπον, ἀνεῦρε μόγις ἐν πολλοῖς
σάγμασιν ὅπλων καὶ σώμασι νεκρῶν ὁμοῦ φίλων τε
καὶ πολεμίων κατασεσωρευμένων. ἐφ᾽ ᾧ καὶ Παῦλος
ὁ στρατηγὸς ἠγάσθη τὸ μειράκιον, καὶ Κάτωνος αὐτοῦ φέρεταί τις ἐπιστολὴ πρὸς τὸν υἱόν, ὑπερφυῶς
ἐπαινοῦντος τὴν περὶ τὸ ξίφος φιλοτιμίαν αὐτοῦ καὶ
σπουδήν.

[1] ἐξολισθόντος Reiske: ἐξολισθέντος codd.

Cf. Plut. *Aem.* 21.1–5; Val. Max. 3.2.16; Iust. *Epit.* 33.2.1–4;
Frontin. *Str.* 4.5.17.

Cf. Plutarch, *Roman Questions*: Why was it not permitted to men not regularly enlisted, but merely being about in the camp, to throw missiles at the enemy or to wound them? And this Cato the Elder has made clear in some letter, writing to his son and urging him, if, after completing his term of service, he has been discharged, to return; or, if he should stay, to obtain permission from the general to wound or slay an enemy.

F 36 Plutarch, *Life of Cato the Elder*

He [Cato's son], although of such a kind [i.e., delicate], was a valiant man in military campaigns, and he fought brilliantly in the battle against Perseus [171–168 BC] when Paulus [L. Aemilius Paullus, cos. 182, 168 BC (*ORF*[4] 12)] was the general. Then indeed, when his sword was knocked out [of his hand] by a blow or slipped off because of the moistness of his hand, distressed, he turned to some of his companions and, taking them, threw himself again into the midst of the enemy. [11] After a long and forceful struggle, he cleared the place and found the sword at last among the many heaps of arms and bodies of the dead, friends and foes alike piled up. Because of this Paulus, the commander, was delighted with the young man, and there is extant a letter from Cato himself to his son, in which he praises him extravagantly for this love of honor and zeal concerning the sword [cf. T 61].

F 37 Fest., p. 140.36–37 L.

⟨MANSUES⟩ . . . m Cato in epistola ⟨ad filium⟩[1] . . . mansues ad . . .

    [1] *suppl. Mueller*: ad M. filium *Schmidt*

F 38 Fest., p. 280.23–24 L.

PRAEDONULOS Cato hypocoristicos dixit in epistularum:[1] "quia saepe utiles videntur praedonuli."

    [1] in epistula ⟨ad M. fil⟩ium *Schmidt*

Cf. Paul. *Fest.*, p. 281.9–10 L.: PRAEDONOLOS[1] hypocoristicos, id est deminutive, idem Cato posuit pro praedonibus.

    [1] praedonolos (pre-) *vel* prodonolos *codd.*

F 39 Diom., *GL* I, p. 366.7–13

tertia forma est qua a littera eximitur et iteratio syllabae fit, ut . . . ; et adiecta praepositione, ut est . . . praesto praestiti. apud antiquos hoc verbum pro melius est pone-

F 37 Festus

⟨*mansues* ["tame, mild"]⟩ . . . Cato in a letter ⟨to his son⟩
. . . mild toward . . .[1]

  1 The attribution of this piece to Cato's letter to his son relies
on a conjectural supplement to the transmitted text. Beyond the
fact that Cato used the word *mansues* in this passage, nothing can
be said about its content because of the corruption and gaps in
the Latin text. Thus, the fragment itself cannot contribute to
identifying its provenance.

F 38 Festus

praedonuli ["little brigands"]: Cato used it diminutively in
[a piece] of his letters: "because little brigands often seem
useful."

Cf. Paul the Deacon, *Epitome of Festus*: *praedonoli* ["little brigands"] diminutively, that is as a diminutive [Latin word]: the same
Cato used it instead of *praedones* ["brigands"].

F 39 Diomedes

The third pattern [of forming the perfect tense] is where
the letter *a* is removed and duplication of a syllable occurs,
as . . . ; and with a preposition added, as is . . . *praesto*,
praestiti ["I surpass / offer," "I have surpassed / offered"].
Among the ancients this word was used for "it is better,"

batur aut pro antecedit aut superat. nam in dandi significatione praebeo potius dicebant, nisi quod . . . ; et Cato ad Magnum[1] ait: "interempto[2] praestari" . . .

[1] Magnum *vel* magnam *codd.*: ad Magnium *edd. vet.*: *fort.* ad M. filium *Jordan, prob. Cugusi*   [2] *fort.* interemptum *Keil*

COMMENTARII IURIS CIVILIS (F 40)

Several sources note that Cato was an expert in law (T 4, 8, 20b, 22, 26, 32b, 37, 51); Cicero implies that Cato engaged with legal issues in his writings (T 22), and the Digest seems to suggest that legal writings by Cato existed (T 97; for an overview of Cato's activity as a jurisconsult and as a potential writer on juridical matters, see Wieacker 1988, 538–39). Festus (Op. cet. F 40) attests a work on civil law by a Cato. Since Cato's elder son was a well-known jurist who left legal writings (T 79, 97), the refer-

F 40 Fest., p. 144.14–21 L.

MUNDUS . . . : qui quid ita dicatur sic refert Cato in commentariis iuris civilis: "mundo nomen inpositum est ab eo

or for "it surpasses," or "it is superior." For as regards the sense of giving they rather used *praebeo* ["I offer"], unless . . .; and Cato says [in a work addressed] to Magnus:[1] "with someone killed [?] to be surpassed" . . .

[1] This (patchy) quotation can be assigned to Cato's letters if "to Magnus" indicates an addressee rather than a dedicatee of a piece in another genre or an interlocutor. Since in all other references to letter(s) mentioning an addressee (*Op. cet.* F 35–37), the addressee is Cato's son Marcus, changing "to Magnus" (a person of uncertain identity) to "to the son Marcus" has been suggested.

COMMENTARII IURIS CIVILIS (F 40)

ence in Festus might be to him rather than to his father (also Cic. De or. *2.142; references in the* Digest *other than T 97 are also likely to refer to the son: cf. Cugusi and Sblendorio Cugusi 2001, 2:460–63). Therefore, this fragment (and thus this work as a separate piece) is generally listed among the works of Cato, but often cautiously and marked as one of those whose authorship is doubtful. The single reference does not provide information on the nature or scope of these "commentaries on civil law."*

F 40 Festus

mundus ["subterranean vault," located in the Comitium in Rome, thought to lead to the underworld] . . . : why this is

mundo, qui supra nos est: forma enim eius est, ut[1] ex his
qui intravere cognoscere[2] potui, adsimilis illae": . . .

[1] ut *Ursinus*: est *cod.* [2] cognosci *Gothofredus*

DICTA MEMORABILIA (F 41–85)

Dicta memorabilia *is not an attested title of a specific work
by Cato, but rather a generic description for "memorable
utterances." Cato was well known for numerous pithy sayings (Op. cet. F 60, 64; T 56). Yet whether he ever assembled a collection of them is uncertain. Cicero was aware of
a collection put together by Cato of statements called* apophthegmata *(Op. cet. F 51; cf. F 44): it listed utterances
by others, and there is no evidence as to whether it also
included some of Cato's own. Plutarch reproduces (in
Greek) a range of utterances by Cato in the biography of
Cato and in the list of memorable sayings by famous individuals (Op. cet. F 58–78; T 58), presumably taken from
some collection. While these are probably two different
collections, sometimes given separately in editions, the relevant texts are combined here (as in Cugusi and Sblendorio
Cugusi 2001) since these passages illustrate Cato's engagement with forceful maxims and characterize his style of
speaking incorporating such statements.*

*In most cases it is unclear whether statements attributed
to Cato may have been made individually, for instance in
a conversation, or might ultimately derive from one of
Cato's written works of a particular literary genre. If these
sayings are not transmitted for a specific work of Cato and*

called thus, Cato reports in the commentaries on civil law as follows: "*mundus* has been given its name from that *mundus* that is above us ['sky, universe']: for its form, as I could learn from those who went in, [is] similar to that [form]": . . .

DICTA MEMORABILIA (F 41–85)

no proposals for assignment have been made, they are collected here; other phrases have been attributed more or less tentatively to particular works (e.g., Orig. F 129, 131, 135, 151; Orat. F 55, 79, 120, 145, 146, 151, 188, 189, 254). It is even possible that not all of the statements are authentic; they could rather have been ascribed to Cato because they came from his collection or could have been developed in the later tradition (especially those that are similarly also attributed to other figures and indicate a general philosophical, mainly Stoic, background); such a process would show how a particular impression of Cato emerged, as such sayings were important for shaping the standard portrayal of Cato (for an overview of proverbial sayings from all of Cato's works and a list of parallels, see Roos 1984, 27–40; for brief discussions of those transmitted by Plutarch, see Pastorino 1951, 32–42; Della Corte 1953, viii–x).

Cato's memorable sayings are sometimes referred to as Dicta Catonis *("Sayings of Cato"); they should not be confused with* Disticha Catonis *("Distichs of Cato"), a later collection of maxims of unknown origin, popular in late antiquity and the Middle Ages and also translated into Greek.*

F 41 Cic. *Verr.* 2.2.5

Cf. *Orig.* F 129.

F 42 Cic. *Flacc.* 71–72

in hisce agris tu praedia habere voluisti. omnino mallem,
et magis erat tuum, si iam te crassi agri delectabant, hic
alicubi in Crustumino aut in Capenati paravisses. [72] verum esto; Catonis est dictum, pedibus compensari pecuniam. longe omnino a Tiberi ad Caicum, quo in loco etiam
Agamemnon cum exercitu errasset, nisi ducem Telephum
invenisset.

Cf. Iul. Rufin., §23, *RLM*, p. 44.16–21.

F 43 Cic. *De or.* 2.256

Cf. *Orat.* F 151.

F 44 Cic. *De or.* 2.271

[CAESAR STRABO:] nam sicut,[1] quod apud Catonem est,
qui multa rettulit, ex quibus a me exempli causa complura[2]
ponuntur, per mihi scitum videtur, C. Publicium solitum
esse dicere P. Mummium[3] cuiusvis[4] temporis[5] hominem

---

[1] sicut *Bake*: sunt *vel om. codd.*   [2] complura *vel* multa
codd.: nonnulla *Orelli*: compluscula *Klotz*   [3] Mummium *vel*
Marium *codd.*   [4] cuiusvis *Lambinus*: quoiusvis *Friedrich*:
quidvis *vel* cuivis *codd.*   [5] temporis *vel* tempori *codd.*

F 41 Cicero, *Verrine Orations*

Cf. *Orig.* F 129.

F 42 Cicero, *Pro Flacco*

In this district [in Asia Minor] you [C. Appuleius Decianus, prosecutor] wanted to have an estate. Doubtless I would prefer it, and it would be more like you, if fertile lands now pleased you, that you should have acquired an estate somewhere here in the area of Crustumerium or of Capena [towns in Latium and Etruria]. [72] So be it; there is a saying of Cato that money [spent] is offset by feet [i.e., by traveling a long distance (cf. Otto 1890, 276, s.v. *pes* 14)]. It certainly is a long way from the Tiber to the Caicus [river in Mysia in Asia Minor], a place where even Agamemnon would have lost his way with his army, had he not found Telephus as a guide [toward Troy].

F 43 Cicero, *On the Orator*

Cf. *Orat.* F 151.

F 44 Cicero, *On the Orator*

[CAESAR STRABO:] For instance, what is found in Cato—who has recorded many [utterances], of which a fair number are put forward by me by way of example—seems to me very shrewd, namely that C. Publicius was accustomed to say that P. Mummius was a man for any occasion what-

esse: sic profecto res se habet, nullum ut sit vitae tempus, in quo non deceat leporem humanitatemque versari.

F 45 Cic. *De or.* 2.279

[CAESAR STRABO:] huic generi quasi contrarium est ridiculi genus patientis ac lenti, ut, cum Cato percussus esset ab eo qui arcam ferebat, cum ille diceret "cave," rogavit, num quid aliud ferret praeter arcam.

F 46 Cic. *Rep.* 2.1–3

Cf. *Orig.* F 131.

F 47 Cic. *Div.* 2.51–52

["CICERO":] vetus autem illud Catonis admodum scitum est, qui mirari se aiebat, quod non rideret haruspex, haruspicem cum vidisset. [52] quota enim quaque res evenit praedicta ab istis? aut, si evenit quippiam, quid adferri potest, cur non casu id evenerit?

Cf. Cic. *Nat. D.* 1.71.

F 48 Cic. *Sen.* 62

["CATO":] sed in omni oratione mementote eam me senectutem laudare, quae fundamentis adulescentiae constituta sit. ex quo efficitur id, quod ego magno quondam cum adsensu omnium dixi, miseram esse senectutem quae se

soever:[1] this is indeed the case that there is no occasion in life on which it is not fitting for wit and refined language to have their place.

[1] It is unclear which individuals of these names are referred to and what the context for the remark might be.

F 45 Cicero, *On the Orator*

[CAESAR STRABO:] Virtually the opposite of this kind is the kind of jest that is tolerant and calm, as, for example: when Cato had been jostled by a man who was carrying a box, and when that man said "look out," he [Cato] asked whether he was carrying anything else besides the box.

F 46 Cicero, *On the Republic*

Cf. *Orig.* F 131.

F 47 Cicero, *On Divination*

["CICERO":] But that ancient remark of Cato's is rather clever [cf. Otto 1890, 160, s.v. *haruspex*]: he said that he wondered that a soothsayer did not laugh when he had seen another soothsayer. [52] For how many things out of those predicted by them come true? Or, if anything does come true, then what can be advanced was the reason why that did not happen by chance?

F 48 Cicero, *On Old Age*

["CATO":] But bear in mind that in the entire discussion I am praising that old age that is built on foundations laid in youth. Hence that follows, which I once said with great approval of all, that this old age is wretched that defends

325

oratione defenderet; non cani nec rugae repente auctoritatem adripere possunt, sed honeste acta superior aetas
fructus capit auctoritatis extremos.

F 49 Cic. *Amic.* 76

["LAELIUS":] erumpunt saepe vitia amicorum, tum in ipsos amicos, tum in alienos, quorum tamen ad amicos re-
dundet infamia. tales igitur amicitiae sunt remissione usus
eluendae, et ut Catonem dicere audivi, dissuendae magis
quam discindendae, nisi quaedam admodum intolerabilis
iniuria exarserit, ut neque rectum neque honestum sit nec
fieri possit ut non statim alienatio disiunctioque facienda
sit.

Cf. Cic. *Amic.* 78; *Off.* 1.120.

F 50 Cic. *Amic.* 90

["LAELIUS":] scitum est enim illud Catonis, ut multa:
melius de quibusdam acerbos inimicos mereri quam eos
amicos qui dulces videantur; illos verum saepe dicere, hos
numquam.

Cf. August. ap. Hieron. *Ep.* 110.4.

F 51 Cic. *Off.* 1.104

duplex omnino est iocandi genus, unum inliberale petu-
lans flagitiosum obscenum, alterum elegans urbanum in-
geniosum facetum, quo genere non modo Plautus noster
et Atticorum antiqua comoedia, sed etiam philosophorum
Socraticorum libri referti sunt, multaque multorum facete
dicta, ut ea quae a sene Catone conlecta sunt, quae vocant
apophthegmata.

itself with words. Nor can gray hair and wrinkles suddenly seize influence; but the earlier part of a life spent nobly reaps the fruits of influence at the end.

F 49 Cicero, *On Friendship*

["LAELIUS":] Vices of friends often break out, sometimes in relation to their very friends, sometimes to strangers, yet so that the infamy of the vices overflows onto their friends. Therefore, such friendships should be washed off by a relaxation of intimacy, and, as I have heard Cato say, should be unraveled rather than rent apart, unless some utterly unbearable wrongdoing has burst into flame, so that it would be neither right nor honorable nor could not be the case that immediate estrangement and separation are not to be effected.

F 50 Cicero, *On Friendship*

["LAELIUS":] For that saying of Cato's is shrewd, like many: that sharp-tongued enemies do a better service to some people than those friends who seem sweet; the former often tell the truth, the latter never [cf. Otto 1890, 168, s.v. *hostis* 2].

F 51 Cicero, *On Duties*

There are, in general, two kinds of jest: the one, coarse, rude, vicious, indecent; the other, refined, polite, clever, witty. Of that latter kind not only our Plautus and the Old Comedy of the people of Attica, but also the books of Socratic philosophers are full; and there are many witty sayings of many people, like those that have been collected by Cato of old, which they call *apophthegmata*.

CATO

F 52 Cic. *Off.* 2.89

ex quo genere comparationis illud est Catonis senis; a quo
cum quaereretur quid maxime in re familiari expediret,
respondit: "bene pascere," quid secundum: "satis bene
pascere," quid tertium: "male pascere," quid quartum:
"arare." et cum ille qui quaesierat dixisset "quid faene-
rari?," tum Cato "quid hominem" inquit "occidere?"

Cf. Columella, *Rust.* 6, *praef.* 4–5; Plin. *HN* 18.29, 18.174; Serv.
ad Verg. *Aen.* 7.539.

F 53 Hor. *Sat.* 1.2.31–35

quidam notus homo cum exiret fornice, "macte / virtute
esto" inquit sententia dia Catonis. / "nam simul ac venas
inflavit tecta[1] libido, / huc iuvenes aequum est descendere,
non alienas / [35] permolere uxores."

1 tecta *vel* t(a)etra *codd.*

Cf. Porph. Comm. ad Hor. *Sat.* 1.2.31; Ps.-Acr. Comm. ad Hor.
Sat. 1.2.31–32 ("quidam notus homo"): Cato, cum vidisset ex lupanari adulescentem exeuntem, laudavit eum et ait "macte nova
virtute, puer." Catone transeunte quidam exit de fornice; quem,
cum fugeret, revocavit et laudavit. postea cum frequentius eum
exeuntem de eodem lupanari vidisset, dixisse fertur: adulescens,
ego te laudavi, tamquam huc intervenires, non tamquam hic habi-
tares., 1.2.32; Comm. Cruq. ad Hor. *Sat.* 1.2.31.

F 52 Cicero, *On Duties*

To that class of comparisons [of different external advantages] belongs that famous [saying] of Cato of old; when he was asked what was most profitable for one's fortune, he replied: "Raising cattle successfully." What second? "Raising cattle with fair success." What third? "Raising cattle with slight success." What fourth? "Raising crops." And when the person who had asked had said: "How about moneylending?," then Cato replied: "How about killing a human being?"

F 53 Horace, *Satires*

When some man known to him was emerging from a brothel, "be blessed for your virtue," says Cato's godlike utterance; "for as soon as hidden passion has swelled the veins, it is right that young men go down hither, rather than [35] grind other men's wives."

Cf. Ps.-Acro, *Commentary on Horace*: When Cato had seen a young man emerging from a brothel, he praised him and said: "Be blessed for your new virtue, boy." When Cato was passing by, someone emerged from a brothel; when he avoided him, he [Cato] called him back and praised him. Later, when he [Cato] had seen him emerge more frequently from the same brothel, he is said to have commented: "Young man, I have praised you, as someone dropping in here, not as someone living here."[1]

[1] The commentator gives a different version of Cato's comments on men frequenting brothels.

F 54 Liv. 34.9.11–13

paucos ibi moratus dies Cato, dum exploraret ubi et quan-
tae hostium copiae essent, ut ne mora quidem segnis esset,
omne id tempus exercendis militibus consumpsit. [12] id
erat forte tempus anni ut frumentum in areis Hispani
haberent; itaque redemptoribus vetitis frumentum parare
ac Romam dimissis, "bellum" inquit "se ipsum alet." [13]
profectus ab Emporiis agros hostium urit vastatque, omnia fuga et terrore complet.

F 55 Sen. *Ep.* 122.3

sunt quidam in eadem urbe antipodes, qui, ut M. Cato ait,
nec orientem umquam solem viderunt nec occidentem.
hos tu existimas scire quemadmodum vivendum sit, qui
nesciunt quando?

Cf. Cic. *Fin.* 2.23; Columella, *Rust.* 1, *praef.* 16; Plin. *HN* 14.141.

F 56 Plin. *HN* 19.24

deinde et sine ludis Marcellus Octavia Augusti sorore
genitus in aedilitate sua, avunculi xi consulatu,[1] a kal. Aug.
velis forum inumbravit, ut salubrius litigantes consiste-
rent, quantum mutati a[2] moribus Catonis censorii, qui
sternendum quoque forum muricibus censuerat!

[1] consulatu *Mayhoff*: cos. *codd.*: consule *edd.*
[2] mutati a *Mayhoff*: mutati *vel* mutatis *codd.*: mutatis *edd.*

F 54 Livy, *History of Rome*

While Cato was waiting there [at Emporiae, town in mod. Spain] for a few days until he could gather intelligence on where and how large the enemy forces were, so as not to be idle even in a period of enforced delay, he spent that whole time drilling the soldiers. [12] It happened to be the time of year when the Iberians had their wheat on the threshing floor; therefore, he forbade the contractors to procure grain, sent them back to Rome, and said: "The war will feed itself." [13] After having set off from Emporiae, he burned and razed the fields of the enemy, and filled everything with flight and panic.

F 55 Seneca, *Epistles*

There are some Antipodes [i.e., people living on the opposite side of the earth] in this same city, who, as M. Cato says, have never seen the sun either rise or set [cf. Otto 1890, 326, s.v. *sol* 2]. Do you think that these people know how one should live when they do not know when?

F 56 Pliny the Elder, *Natural History*

Next, even when there were no games, Marcellus, the son of Octavia, Augustus' sister, during his aedileship, in the eleventh consulship of his uncle [23 BC], from the Kalends of August, provided shade to the Forum by awnings of sailcloth, so that those engaged in lawsuits might take their places under healthier conditions: what a change from the habits of Cato the ex-censor, who had expressed the view that the Forum ought even to be paved with sharp-pointed stones!

CATO

F 57 Quint. *Inst.* 6.3.105

cur autem brevem esse eam voluerit, nescio, cum idem atque[1] in eodem libro dicat fuisse et in multis narrandi urbanitatem. paulo post ita finit, Catonis, ut ait, opinionem secutus: "urbanus homo {non}[2] erit cuius multa bene dicta responsaque erunt, et qui in sermonibus circulis conviviis, item in contionibus, omni denique loco ridicule commodeque dicet. risus erit quicumque haec faciet orator.[3]

[1] atque *Radermacher*: ad quem *cod.*   [2] *del. unus cod.* *suppletus corr.*   [3] risus . . . orator *dubium est et fort. delendum Winterbottom*: orator *del. Hendrickson*

F 58 Plut. *Mor.* 198D–99E (*Apophth. reg. et imp.*, *Cato the Elder* 1–29)

1. Κάτων ὁ πρεσβύτερος ἐν τῷ δήμῳ τῆς ἀσωτίας καὶ πολυτελείας καθαπτόμενος εἶπεν ὡς χαλεπόν ἐστι λέγειν πρὸς γαστέρα ὦτα μὴ ἔχουσαν [*Op. cet.* F 63; *Orat.* F 254].

2. θαυμάζειν δὲ πῶς σῴζεται πόλις, ἐν ᾗ πωλεῖται πλείονος ἰχθὺς ἢ βοῦς [*Op. cet.* F 63; *Orat.* F 145].

3. λοιδορῶν δέ ποτε τὴν ἐπιπολάζουσαν γυναικοκρατίαν, "πάντες" εἶπεν "ἄνθρωποι τῶν γυναικῶν ἄρχουσιν, ἡμεῖς δὲ πάντων ἀνθρώπων, ἡμῶν δὲ αἱ γυναῖκες" [*Op. cet.* F 63].

4. ἔφη δὲ βούλεσθαι μᾶλλον εὐεργετήσας μὴ κομίσασθαι χάριν ἢ μὴ ὑποσχεῖν κόλασιν ἀδικήσας, καὶ

F 57 Quintilian, *The Orator's Education*

But why he [Domitius Marsus, Augustan writer and author of *De urbanitate*] wishes it [urbanity] to be brief, I do not know, because he says as well, and in the same book, that in many [authors] there was also urbanity in the narrative. A little later he defines it in this way, following, as he says, Cato's[1] opinion: "A person will {not} be urbane of whom there will be many good sayings and replies, and who will speak amusingly and appropriately in conversations, at social gatherings, and dinners, and also in public meetings, in a word: on every occasion. There will be ridicule of any orator who will do this.

[1] The identity of the Cato referred to is uncertain. The text at the end of the passage is doubtful.

F 58 Plutarch, *Moralia (Sayings)*

1. Cato the Elder, assailing the prodigality and extravagance among the People, said that it was hard to talk to a belly as it did not have ears [*Op. cet.* F 63; *Orat.* F 254; cf. Stob. 3.6.61].

2. That he wondered how a city could be saved in which a fish sold for more than an ox [*Op. cet.* F 63; *Orat.* F 145; Plut. *Mor.* 668C–D (*Quaest. conv.* 4.4); Polyb. 31.24 (ap. Ath. 6, p. 274f)].

3. Criticizing once the prevailing domination of women, he said: "All men rule the women; yet, while we rule all men, the women rule us" [*Op. cet.* F 63].

4. He said that he preferred not to receive thanks when he had done a favor than not to suffer punishment when he

πᾶσιν ἀεὶ τοῖς ἁμαρτάνουσι χωρὶς ἑαυτοῦ διδόναι
συγγνώμην [Op. cet. F 63].

5. παρορμῶν δὲ τοὺς ἄρχοντας ἐπιτιμᾶν τοῖς ἁμαρτά-
νουσιν ἔλεγε τοὺς δυναμένους κωλύειν τοὺς κακῶς
ποιοῦντας, ἐὰν μὴ κωλύωσι, κελεύειν.

6. τῶν δὲ νέων ἔφη χαίρειν τοῖς ἐρυθριῶσι μᾶλλον ἢ
τοῖς ὠχριῶσι [Op. cet. F 64].

7. στρατιώτην δὲ μισεῖν, ὃς ἐν τῷ περιπατεῖν τὰς
χεῖρας, ἐν δὲ τῷ μάχεσθαι τοὺς πόδας κινεῖ, ῥέγχει
δὲ μεῖζον ἢ ἀλαλάζει [Op. cet. F 64].

8. κάκιστον δ' ἔλεγεν ἄρχοντα εἶναι τὸν ἄρχειν ἑαυτοῦ
μὴ δυνάμενον.

9. μάλιστα δ' ἐνόμιζε δεῖν ἕκαστον ἑαυτὸν αἰδεῖσθαι·
μηδένα γὰρ ἑαυτοῦ μηδέποτε χωρὶς εἶναι.

10. πολλῶν δ' ὁρῶν ἀνισταμένους ἀνδριάντας, "περὶ
ἐμοῦ" δ' ἔφη, "βούλομαι ἐρωτᾶν μᾶλλον τοὺς ἀνθρώ-
πους, διὰ τί ἀνδριὰς οὐ κεῖται {Κάτωνος}[1] ἢ διὰ τί
κεῖται" [Op. cet. F 71].

11. φείδεσθαι δὲ τῆς ἐξουσίας παρεκάλει τοὺς δυναμένους, ὅπως ἀεὶ παραμείνῃ τὸ ἐξεῖναι.

12. τοὺς δὲ τῆς ἀρετῆς τὴν τιμὴν ἀφαιροῦντας ἔλεγε
τὴν ἀρετὴν ἀφαιρεῖν τῆς νεότητος.

13. τὸν δ' ἄρχοντα ἢ κριτὴν ἔλεγε δεῖν μήτε ὑπὲρ τῶν
δικαίων λιπαρεῖσθαι μήτε ὑπὲρ τῶν ἀδίκων ἐκλιπα-
ρεῖσθαι.

[1] del. Cobet

had done a wrong, and that he always granted pardon to all who erred except to himself [*Op. cet.* F 63].

5. Urging the magistrates to rebuke those doing wrong, he said that those having the power to discourage evildoers encouraged them if they did not discourage them.

6. He said that he was more delighted at those young people who blushed than those who turned pale [*Op. cet.* F 64; Plut. *Mor.* 29E (*Quomodo adul. poet. aud. deb.* 10); 528F (*De vit. pud.* 1)].

7. That he hated a soldier who in walking moved his hands, but in fighting [moved] his feet, and who snored louder than he sounded the war cry [*Op. cet.* F 64].

8. He said that the worst ruler is one who could not rule himself [cf. Cic. *Parad.* 5.33].

9. He thought it especially necessary for everyone to respect themselves, since no one was ever without themselves.

10. Seeing that statues were being set up in honor of many, he said: "As for myself, I had rather that people asked why there is not a statue {of Cato} than why there is" [*Op. cet.* F 71].

11. He urged the powerful to be sparing in the exercise of their power, so that there would always remain the possibility of its exercise.

12. Those who rob virtue of honor, he said, rob youth of virtue.

13. A magistrate or a judge, he said, should neither be subjected to entreaty on behalf of those who are just, nor should they yield to entreaty on behalf of those who are unjust.

CATO

14. τὴν δὲ ἀδικίαν ἔλεγε τοῖς ἀδικοῦσιν ἂν² μὴ φέρῃ κίνδυνον, ἅπασι φέρειν.

15. τῷ δὲ γήρᾳ πολλῶν αἰσχρῶν παρόντων ἠξίου μὴ προστιθέναι τὴν ἀπὸ τῆς κακίας αἰσχύνην [Op. cet. F 64].

16. τὸν δὲ ὀργιζόμενον ἐνόμιζε τοῦ μαινομένου χρόνῳ διαφέρειν.

17. ἥκιστα δὲ φθονεῖσθαι τοὺς τῇ τύχῃ χρωμένους ἐπιεικῶς καὶ μετρίως· οὐ γὰρ ἡμῖν ἀλλὰ τοῖς περὶ ἡμᾶς φθονοῦσι.

18. τοὺς δὲ σπουδάζοντας ἐν τοῖς γελοίοις ἔλεγεν ἐν τοῖς σπουδαίοις ἔσεσθαι καταγελάστους.

19. τὰς δὲ καλὰς πράξεις ἔλεγε δεῖν καταλαμβάνειν πράξεσι καλαῖς, ἵνα μὴ τῆς δόξης ἀπορρέωσιν.

20. ἐπετίμα δὲ τοῖς πολίταις ἀεὶ τοὺς αὐτοὺς αἱρουμένοις ἄρχοντας· "δόξετε γάρ" εἶπεν "ἢ μὴ πολλοῦ τὸ ἄρχειν ἄξιον ἢ μὴ πολλοὺς τοῦ ἄρχειν ἀξίους ἡγεῖσθαι" [Op. cet. F 63].

21. τὸν δὲ τοὺς παραλίους ἀγροὺς πεπρακότα προσεποιεῖτο θαυμάζειν ὡς ἰσχυρότερον τῆς θαλάσσης· "ἃ γὰρ ἐκείνη μόλις ἐπικλύζει, οὗτος ῥᾳδίως καταπέπωκε" [Op. cet. F 63].

22. τιμητείαν δὲ μετιὼν καὶ τοὺς ἄλλους ὁρῶν δεομένους τῶν πολλῶν καὶ κολακεύοντας, αὐτὸς ἐβόα τὸν δῆμον ἀποτόμου χρείαν ἔχειν ἰατροῦ καὶ μεγάλου καθαρμοῦ· δεῖν οὖν μὴ τὸν ἥδιστον, ἀλλὰ τὸν ἀπα-

---

² ἀδικοῦσιν ἂν Hercher: ἀδικοῦσι(ν) κἂν codd.

14. Wrongdoing, he said, even if it does not bring danger to those who do wrong, brings it to everyone.

15. Since there are so many sources of shame for old age, he thought it fit not to add the shame resulting from badness [*Op. cet.* F 64].

16. He believed that someone who had lost their temper differed from someone who had lost their mind only in duration of time [cf. *Orig.* F 151; Cic. *Tusc.* 4.52; Hor. *Epist.* 1.2.62; Sen. *Ira* 1.1.2; Macrob. *Sat.* 4.2.9; cf. Otto 1890, 177, s.v. *ira*].

17. That those who use their good fortune reasonably and moderately are least envied; for people envy not us but our surroundings.

18. Those who are serious in ridiculous matters, he said, would be ridiculous in serious matters.

19. As for good deeds, he said, it is necessary to catch them with good deeds, so that they may not fall off in their repute.

20. He censured the citizens for always choosing the same men for high office: "For it will be thought then," he said, "that either you do not judge the holding of office to be of much worth or you do not judge many to be worthy of holding office" [*Op. cet.* F 63].

21. He pretended to admire a man who had sold his lands bordering on the sea as being himself stronger than the sea: "For what it [the sea] hardly sweeps away, that man has easily drunk up" [*Op. cet.* F 63].

22. When he was seeking the censorship [for 184 BC] and saw the others soliciting the populace and flattering them, he on his part shouted that the People had need of a stern physician and a thorough purging; therefore, they must choose not the most agreeable, but the most inexorable

CATO

ραίτητον αἱρεῖσθαι. καὶ ταῦτα λέγων ᾑρέθη πρὸ πάντων [Op. cet. F 69].

23. διδάσκων δὲ τοὺς νέους εὐθαρσῶς μάχεσθαι, πολλάκις ἔλεγε τοῦ ξίφους τὸν λόγον μᾶλλον καὶ τὴν
φωνὴν τῆς χειρὸς τρέπειν καὶ καταπλήττειν τοὺς πολεμίους [Op. cet. F 59].

24. ἐπεὶ δὲ πολεμῶν τοῖς περὶ τὸν Βαῖτιν ποταμὸν
οἰκοῦσιν εἰς κίνδυνον ὑπὸ πλήθους τῶν πολεμίων
κατέστη, τῶν μὲν Κελτιβήρων ἐπὶ διακοσίοις ταλάντοις βουλομένων βοηθεῖν, τῶν δὲ Ῥωμαίων οὐκ ἐών-
των ὁμολογεῖν μισθὸν ἀνθρώποις βαρβάροις, ἁμαρ-
τάνειν ἔφησεν αὐτούς· νικῶντας μὲν γὰρ ἀποδώσειν
οὐ παρ' αὐτῶν ἀλλὰ παρὰ τῶν πολεμίων, ἡττωμένων
δέ, μήτε τοὺς ἀπαιτουμένους μήτε τοὺς ἀπαιτοῦντας
ἔσεσθαι [Op. cet. F 65; Orat. F 55].

25. πλείονας δὲ πόλεις ἑλών, ὥς φησι, τῶν ἡμερῶν ἃς
διέτριψεν ἐν τοῖς πολεμίοις οὐδὲν αὐτὸς πλέον ἔλαβεν
ὧν ἔπιε καὶ ἔφαγεν ἐκ τῆς πολεμίας [Op. cet. F 65;
Orig. F 135; Orat. F 55].

26. τῶν δὲ στρατιωτῶν ἑκάστῳ λίτραν ἀργύρου δια-
νείμας φησὶ βέλτιον εἶναι πολλοὺς ἔχοντας ἀργύριον
ἢ ὀλίγους χρυσίον ἀπὸ τῆς στρατείας ἐπανελθεῖν·
τῶν γὰρ ἀρχόντων οὐδὲν ἄλλο δεῖν ἐν ταῖς ἐπαρχίαις
ἢ τὴν δόξαν αὐξάνεσθαι [Op. cet. F 65; Orig. F 135;
Orat. F 55].

27. πέντε δ' οἰκέτας εἶχεν ἐπὶ τῆς στρατείας [Orat.
F 51]. ὧν εἷς αἰχμάλωτα τρία σώματα πριάμενος, ὡς

person. And saying that, he was elected before all [*Op. cet.* F 69].

23. In instructing the young men to fight boldly, he said that often words are better than the sword and the voice is better than the hand to rout and bewilder the enemy [*Op. cet.* F 59].

24. When he was waging war [in 195 BC] against the peoples living by the river Baetis [mod. Guadalquivir], he was put in peril by the great number of the enemy. When the Celtiberians [peoples in the Iberian peninsula] were willing to help for two hundred talents, the Romans refused to agree to payment to individuals who were "barbarians." He said they [the Romans] were in error; for, when they were victorious, they would make the payment not from their own [resources], but from [those of] the enemy; and when they were vanquished, neither those being asked to pay nor those requesting payment would be there [*Op. cet.* F 65; *Orat.* F 55].

25. After he had captured cities more in number, as he says, than the days that he spent among the enemy, he himself took nothing from the enemy's country beyond what he ate and drank [*Op. cet.* F 65; *Orig.* F 135; *Orat.* F 55].

26. Distributing to each of the soldiers a pound of silver, he says that it is better that many return from the campaign with silver than a few with gold; for the officials should, in the government of their provinces, look for no other increase than one in their reputation [*Op. cet.* F 65; *Orig.* F 135; *Orat.* F 55].

27. He had five servants on the campaign [*Orat.* F 51]. One of them bought three captives; when this did not

CATO

οὐκ ἔλαθε τὸν Κάτωνα, πρὶν εἰς ὄψιν ἐλθεῖν, ἀπήγξατο [*Op. cet.* F 65; *Orat.* F 55].
28. παρακληθεὶς δ' ὑπὸ Σκιπίωνος Ἀφρικανοῦ τοῖς
Ἀχαιῶν συλλαβέσθαι φυγάσιν, ὅπως εἰς τὰς πατρί-
δας κατέλθωσιν, προσεποιεῖτο μηδὲν αὐτῷ μέλειν τοῦ
πράγματος· ἐν δὲ τῇ συγκλήτῳ πολλῶν γινομένων
λόγων ἀναστάς, "ὥσπερ οὐκ ἔχοντες" εἶπεν "ὃ πράττωμεν, καθήμεθα περὶ Γραικῶν γεροντίων ζητοῦντες
πότερον ὑπὸ τῶν παρ' ἡμῖν ἢ ὑπὸ τῶν ἐκεῖ νεκροφόρων ἐξενεχθῶσι" [*Orat.* F 189; cf. *Op. cet.* F 64].
29. Ποστουμίου δ' Ἀλβίνου γράψαντος ἱστορίας Ἑλληνιστὶ καὶ συγγνώμην παρὰ τῶν ἀκροωμένων αἰτοῦντος, εἰρωνευόμενος ὁ Κάτων ἔφη δοτέον εἶναι
συγγνώμην, εἰ τῶν Ἀμφικτυόνων ψηφισαμένων ἀναγκασθεὶς ἔγραψεν [*Op. cet.* F 67].

F 59 Plut. *Cat. Mai.* 1.2, 8

. . . αὐτὸς ἔλεγε καινὸς εἶναι πρὸς ἀρχὴν καὶ δόξαν, ἔργοις δὲ προγόνων καὶ ἀρεταῖς παμπάλαιος
[*T* 55]. . . . [*Orat.* F 188] . . . [8] . . . παρεῖχε δ' αὑτὸν
ἐν ταῖς μάχαις τῇ μὲν χειρὶ πλήκτην, τῷ δὲ ποδὶ
μόνιμον καὶ βέβαιον, γαῦρον δὲ τῷ προσώπῳ· λόγου
δ' ἀπειλῇ καὶ τραχύτητι φωνῆς πρὸς τοὺς πολεμίους
ἐχρῆτο, ὀρθῶς καὶ διανοούμενος καὶ διδάσκων ὅτι
πολλάκις τὰ τοιαῦτα τοῦ ξίφους μᾶλλον καταπλήττε-
ται τὸν ἐναντίον[1] [*Op. cet.* F 58.23].

[1] τὸν ἐναντίον vel τοὺς ἐναντίους codd.

Cf. Plut. *Coriol.* 8.3.

escape Cato's notice, before he came into his sight, he hanged himself [*Op. cet.* F 65; *Orat.* F 55].

28. Being urged by Scipio Africanus [P. Cornelius Scipio Aemilianus Africanus minor, cos. 147, 134, censor 142 BC (*ORF*[4] 21)] to assist the exiled Achaeans, so that they could return to their native places, he pretended that the matter did not concern him; in the Senate, however, when many speeches had been made, he arose and said: "As if we had nothing to do, we sit here, inquiring about some old Greeks whether they should be carried out to their burial by the funerary men among us or by the ones there" [*Orat.* F 189; cf. *Op. cet.* F 64].

29. When Postumius Albinus [A. Postumius Albinus (*FRHist* 4 T 3c)] had written a history in the Greek language and asked for indulgence from the recipients, Cato said sarcastically that he ought to be granted indulgence if he had written under duress by a decree of the Amphictyonic League [association of Greek peoples] [*Op. cet.* F 67].

F 59 Plutarch, *Life of Cato the Elder*

. . . , he himself [Cato] said that he was new as regards office and distinction, but with respect to deeds and valor of one's ancestors very old [T 55]. . . . [*Orat.* F 188] . . . [8] . . . In battles he showed himself violent with his hand, steady and stable on his feet, and haughty in his countenance. He employed threatening speech and a harsh tone of voice toward the enemy, for he rightly thought and demonstrated that often such things terrify the opponent more than the sword [*Op. cet.* F 58.23].

CATO

F 60 Plut. *Cat. Mai.* 3.2

. . . ἄλλην τε πολλὴν ἐπιείκειαν αὐτοῦ καὶ μετριότητα καί τινας καὶ λόγους ἀποφθεγματικοὺς διαμνημονευόντων, ἐκέλευσε κληθῆναι πρὸς τὸ δεῖπνον.

F 61 Plut. *Cat. Mai.* 3.5–6

διὸ καὶ Σκηπίωνι τῷ μεγάλῳ, νέῳ μὲν ὄντι τότε, πρὸς δὲ τὴν Φαβίου δύναμιν ἀνταίροντι καὶ φθονεῖσθαι δοκοῦντι, παρ' οὐδὲν ἐποιήσατο γενέσθαι διάφορος, ἀλλὰ καὶ ταμίας αὐτῷ πρὸς τὸν ἐν Λιβύῃ συνεκπεμφθεὶς πόλεμον, ὡς ἑώρα τῇ συνήθει πολυτελείᾳ χρώμενον τὸν ἄνδρα καὶ καταχορηγοῦντα τοῖς στρατεύμασιν ἀφειδῶς τῶν χρημάτων, ἐπαρρησιάζετο πρὸς αὐτόν, οὐ τὸ τῆς δαπάνης μέγιστον εἶναι φάσκων,[1] ἀλλ' ὅτι διαφθείρει[2] τὴν πάτριον εὐτέλειαν τῶν στρατιωτῶν, εἰς ἡδονὰς καὶ τρυφὰς τῷ περιόντι τῆς χρείας τρεπομένων. [6] εἰπόντος δὲ τοῦ Σκηπίωνος ὡς οὐδὲν δέοιτο ταμίου λίαν ἀκριβοῦς πλησίστιος ἐπὶ τὸν πόλεμον φερόμενος, πράξεων γάρ, οὐ χρημάτων, τῇ πόλει λόγον ὀφείλειν, ἀπῆλθεν ὁ Κάτων ἐκ Σικελίας, καὶ μετὰ τοῦ Φαβίου καταβοῶν ἐν τῷ συνεδρίῳ φθοράν τε χρημάτων ἀμυθήτων ὑπὸ τοῦ Σκηπίωνος καὶ διατριβὰς αὐτοῦ μειρακιώδεις ἐν παλαίστραις καὶ θεάτροις, ὥσπερ οὐ στρατηγοῦντος, ἀλλὰ πανηγυρί-

---

[1] φάσκων *vel* τοὺς φάμενος *codd.*
[2] διαφθείρει *vel* διατρίβει *codd.*

F 60 Plutarch, *Life of Cato the Elder*

. . . , when they [Valerius' servants] mentioned many other
instances of his [Cato's] virtuousness and moderation, and
also some pithy sayings, he [L. Valerius Flaccus, cos. 195
BC] ordered him [Cato] to be invited to dinner.

F 61 Plutarch, *Life of Cato the Elder*

Therefore, he [Cato] deemed it of no account to enter into
disagreement with Scipio the Great [P. Cornelius Scipio
Africanus maior, cos. 205, 194, censor 199 BC (*ORF*[4] 4)],
who was then a young man, rising up against the power of
Fabius [Q. Fabius Maximus Verrucosus Cunctator, cos.
233, 228, 215, 214, 209 BC (*ORF*[4] 3)] and was thought to
be envious of him. And indeed, when he [Cato] was sent
out as a quaestor with him to the war in Africa [204 BC],
and saw that the man [Scipio] was indulging in his usual
extravagance and was handing out money lavishly to the
soldiery, he [Cato] spoke to him openly, saying that the
matter of expense was not the biggest issue, but the fact
that he was corrupting the hereditary frugality of the soldiers, who were being turned toward pleasures and luxuries with what was beyond their needs. [6] Scipio said that
he did not need an overly strict quaestor when he was
borne under full sail toward the war; he owed the city an
account of actions, not of moneys. Cato then left Sicily
and, with Fabius, he inveighed in the Senate against
Scipio's unspeakably great waste of money and his juvenile
passing of time in sports halls and theaters, as though he
were not commanding an army, but celebrating a festival;

CATO

ζοντος, ἐξειργάσατο πεμφθῆναι δημάρχους ἐπ᾽ αὐτὸν
ἄξοντας εἰς Ῥώμην, ἄνπερ ἀληθεῖς αἱ κατηγορίαι
φανῶσιν.

F 62 Plut. *Cat. Mai.* 7.1–3
Cf. T 58.

F 63 Plut. *Cat. Mai.* 8.1–17

μέλλων ποτὲ τὸν Ῥωμαίων δῆμον ὡρμημένον ἀκαίρως
ἐπὶ σιτομετρίας καὶ διανομὰς ἀποτρέπειν, ἤρξατο τῶν
λόγων οὕτως· "χαλεπὸν μέν ἐστιν, ὦ πολῖται, πρὸς
γαστέρα λέγειν ὦτα οὐκ ἔχουσαν" [*Op. cet.* F 58.1;
Orat. F 254]. [2] κατηγορῶν δὲ τῆς πολυτελείας ἔφη
χαλεπὸν εἶναι σωθῆναι πόλιν ἐν ᾗ πωλεῖται πλείονος
ἰχθὺς ἢ βοῦς [*Op. cet.* F 58.2; *Orat.* F 145]. [3] ἐοικέναι
δὲ προβάτοις ἔφη τοὺς Ῥωμαίους· ὡς γὰρ ἐκεῖνα καθ᾽
ἕκαστον μὲν οὐ πείθεται, σύμπαντα δ᾽ ἕπεται μετ᾽ ἀλ-
λήλων τοῖς ἄγουσιν, "οὕτω καὶ ὑμεῖς" εἶπεν "οἷς οὐκ
ἂν ἀξιώσαιτε συμβούλοις χρῆσθαι κατ᾽ ἰδίαν, ὑπὸ
τούτων εἰς ἓν συνελθόντες ἄγεσθε." [4] περὶ δὲ τῆς
γυναικοκρατίας διαλεγόμενος "πάντες" εἶπεν "ἄνθρωποι τῶν γυναικῶν ἄρχουσιν, ἡμεῖς δὲ πάντων ἀνθρώπων, ἡμῶν δὲ αἱ γυναῖκες" [*Op. cet.* F 58.3]. τοῦτο μὲν
οὖν ἐστιν ἐκ τῶν Θεμιστοκλέους μετενηνεγμένον ἀπο-
φθεγμάτων. [5] ἐκεῖνος γὰρ ἐπιτάττοντος αὐτῷ πολλὰ
τοῦ υἱοῦ διὰ τῆς μητρός, "ὦ γύναι" εἶπεν, "Ἀθηναῖοι
μὲν ἄρχουσι τῶν Ἑλλήνων, ἐγὼ δὲ Ἀθηναίων, ἐμοῦ
δὲ σύ, σοῦ δὲ ὁ υἱός, ὥστε φειδέσθω τῆς ἐξουσίας, δι᾽

he secured that tribunes were sent to him [Scipio], to bring him back to Rome, [to check] if the charges against him should turn out to be true.

F 62 Plutarch, *Life of Cato the Elder*

Cf. T 58.

F 63 Plutarch, *Life of Cato the Elder*

Once wishing to dissuade the Roman People from insisting unseasonably upon a distribution of grain rations, he [Cato] began the speech as follows: "It is hard, citizens, to talk to a belly that does not have ears" [*Op. cet.* F 58.1; *Orat.* F 254]. [2] Inveighing against the extravagance, he said that it was hard for a city to be saved in which a fish sold for more than an ox [*Op. cet.* F 58.2; *Orat.* F 145]. [3] He said that the Romans were like sheep; for as these are not persuaded individually, but all in a body follow the leaders, "so you too," he said, "when you have come together, are led by those whom you would not consent to have as counselors individually." [4] Discoursing on the power of women, he said: "All men rule the women; yet, while we rule all men, the women rule us" [*Op. cet.* F 58.3]. This, in fact, is translated from the sayings of Themistocles [Plut. *Them.* 18.7; *Mor.* 1C, 185D (*Apophth. reg. et imp.*, *Them.* 10)]. [5] For that man, when his son gave him many orders through his mother, said: "Wife, the Athenians rule the Greeks, I rule the Athenians, you rule me, and the son rules you. Therefore, let him make sparing use of that authority, by which he, though without full

ἦν ἀνόητος ὢν πλεῖστον Ἑλλήνων δύναται." [6] τὸν δὲ
δῆμον ὁ Κάτων ἔφη τῶν Ῥωμαίων οὐ μόνον ταῖς πορ-
φύραις, ἀλλὰ καὶ τοῖς ἐπιτηδεύμασι τὰς τιμὰς ἐπι-
γράφειν. "ὡς γὰρ οἱ βαφεῖς" ἔφη "ταύτην μάλιστα
βάπτουσιν ᾗ χαίροντας ὁρῶσιν, οὕτως οἱ νέοι ταῦτα
μανθάνουσι καὶ ζηλοῦσιν οἷς ἂν ὁ παρ' ὑμῶν ἔπαινος
ἔπηται." [7] παρεκάλει δ' αὐτούς, εἰ μὲν ἀρετῇ καὶ σω-
φροσύνῃ γεγόνασι μεγάλοι, μηδὲν μεταβάλλεσθαι
πρὸς τὸ χεῖρον, εἰ δ' ἀκρασίᾳ καὶ κακίᾳ, μεταβάλλεσθαι πρὸς τὸ βέλτιον· ἱκανῶς γὰρ ἤδη μεγάλους ἀπ'
ἐκείνων γεγονέναι. [8] τοὺς δὲ πολλάκις ἄρχειν σπουδάζοντας ἔφη καθάπερ ἀγνοοῦντας τὴν ὁδὸν ἀεὶ μετὰ
ῥαβδούχων ζητεῖν πορεύεσθαι, μὴ πλανηθῶσιν. ἐπετίμα δὲ τοῖς πολίταις τοὺς αὐτοὺς αἱρουμένοις πολλάκις ἄρχοντας. [9] "δόξετε γάρ" ἔφη "ἢ μὴ πολλοῦ
τὸ ἄρχειν ἄξιον ἢ μὴ πολλοὺς τοῦ ἄρχειν ἀξίους
ἡγεῖσθαι" [Op. cet. F 58.20]. [10] περὶ δὲ τῶν ἐχθρῶν
τινος αἰσχρῶς καὶ ἀδόξως βιοῦν δοκοῦντος "ἡ τούτου
μήτηρ" ἔφη "κατάραν, οὐκ εὐχήν, ἡγεῖται τὸ τοῦτον
ὑπὲρ γῆς ἀπολιπεῖν." [11] τὸν δὲ πεπρακότα τοὺς
πατρῴους ἀγροὺς παραλίους ὄντας ἐπιδεικνύμενος
προσεποιεῖτο θαυμάζειν ὡς ἰσχυρότερον τῆς θαλάτ-
της · "ἃ γὰρ ἐκείνη μόλις ἔκλυζεν, οὗτος" ἔφη "ῥᾳδίως
καταπέπωκεν" [Op. cet. F 58.21]. [12] ἐπεὶ δ' Εὐμενοῦς
τοῦ βασιλέως ἐπιδημήσαντος εἰς Ῥώμην ἥ τε σύγ-
κλητος ὑπερφυῶς ἀπεδέξατο καὶ τῶν πρώτων ἅμιλλα
καὶ σπουδὴ περὶ αὐτὸν ἐγίνετο, δῆλος ἦν ὁ Κάτων
ὑφορώμενος καὶ φυλαττόμενος αὐτόν. [13] εἰπόντος δέ

understanding, is the most powerful of the Greeks." [6] The Roman People, Cato said, set down a value not only for dyes, but also for ways of life. "For," he said, "as dyers mostly use that dye that they see pleases people, so the young learn and aim for whatever will be followed by praise from you." [7] And he exhorted them, if they had become great through virtue and moderation, not to make a change for the worse; but if it was through intemperance and vice, to change for the better; they had already become sufficiently great as a result of those [qualities]. [8] Of those who were eager to hold high office frequently he said that, like men who did not know the route, they sought to go along their way always in the company of lictors, lest they go astray. He censured the citizens for frequently choosing the same men for high office: [9] "For it will be thought then," he said, "that either you do not judge the holding of office to be of much worth or you do not judge many to be worthy of holding office" [*Op. cet.* F 58.20]. [10] Of one of his enemies appearing to live disgracefully and disreputably he said: "This man's mother regards as a curse, not a prayer, that he should survive her." [11] Pointing to a man who had sold his ancestral lands bordering on the sea, he pretended to admire him as stronger than the sea [*Op. cet.* F 58.21]: "What it [the sea] hardly sweeps away," he said, "that man has easily drunk up." [12] When king Eumenes [Eumenes II Soter, king of Pergamum] came to visit Rome [in 172 BC (cf. Liv. 42.11.1–5)], the Senate received him lavishly, and there was an eager contest among the chief men as regards him, while Cato evidently looked upon him suspiciously and

CATO

τινος "ἀλλὰ μὴν χρηστός ἐστι καὶ φιλορώμαιος,"
"ἔστω" εἶπεν, "ἀλλὰ φύσει τοῦτο τὸ ζῷον {ὁ βασι-
λεὺς}¹ σαρκοφάγον ἐστίν." [14] οὐδένα δὲ τῶν εὐδαι-
μονιζομένων ἔφη βασιλέων ἄξιον εἶναι παραβάλλειν
πρὸς Ἐπαμεινώνδαν ἢ Περικλέα ἢ Θεμιστοκλέα ἢ
Μάνιον Κούριον ἢ Ἀμίλκαν τὸν ἐπικληθέντα Βάρκαν.
[15] αὐτῷ δ᾽ ἔλεγε τοὺς ἐχθροὺς φθονεῖν, ὅτι καθ᾽
ἡμέραν ἐκ νυκτὸς ἀνίσταται καὶ τῶν ἰδίων ἀμελῶν
τοῖς δημοσίοις σχολάζει. [16] βούλεσθαι δ᾽ ἔλεγε
μᾶλλον εὖ πράξας ἀποστερηθῆναι χάριν ἢ κακῶς μὴ
τυχεῖν κολάσεως, [17] καὶ συγγνώμην ἔφη διδόναι
πᾶσι τοῖς ἁμαρτάνουσι πλὴν αὑτοῦ [Op. cet. F 58.4].

¹ del. Coraes

F 64 Plut. *Cat. Mai.* 9.1–12

τῶν δὲ Ῥωμαίων εἰς Βιθυνίαν τρεῖς ἑλομένων πρέ-
σβεις, ὧν ὁ μὲν ποδαγρικὸς ἦν, ὁ δὲ τὴν κεφαλὴν ἐξ
ἀνατρήσεως καὶ περικοπῆς κοίλην εἶχεν, ὁ δὲ τρίτος
ἐδόκει μωρὸς εἶναι, καταγελῶν ὁ Κάτων ἔλεγε πρε-
σβείαν ὑπὸ Ῥωμαίων ἀποστέλλεσθαι μήτε πόδας
μήτε κεφαλὴν μήτε καρδίαν ἔχουσαν. [2] . . . [*Orat.*
F 189] . . . [3] ψηφισθείσης δὲ τῆς καθόδου τοῖς ἀν-

watchfully. [13] When someone said: "Surely, he is a good man and a friend of Rome," he [Cato] said: "Granted, but such an animal {the king} is by nature carnivorous." [14] He said further that not one of the kings regarded as fortunate was worthy of being compared with Epaminondas, or Pericles, or Themistocles, or Manius Curius [M'. Curius Dentatus, cos. 290, 275, 274, censor 272, 270 BC], or Hamilcar called Barcas. [15] He said that his enemies bore him a grudge because he rose every day while it was still night and, neglecting his private matters, devoted his time to public affairs. [16] He also said that he preferred to be denied thanks, when he had done right, than not to receive punishment, when he had done ill; [17] and he said that he granted pardon to all who erred except to himself [*Op. cet.* F 58.4].

F 64 Plutarch, *Life of Cato the Elder*

When the Romans had chosen three ambassadors to Bithynia [in Asia Minor],[1] one of whom was gouty, the second of whom had a hollow head as a result of perforation and mutilation, and the third of whom was deemed to be a fool, Cato mockingly said that the Romans were sending out an embassy that had neither feet nor head nor heart. [2] . . . [*Orat.* F 189] . . . [3] After the men's return [of Greeks in Rome] had been authorized by decree, those

---

[1] To negotiate between Prusias II of Bithynia (r. ca. 182–149 BC) and his son, the future king Nicomedes II Epiphanes (r. ca. 149–128 BC). On the embassy (and Cato's reaction), see Liv. *Epit.* 50; Liv. *Epit. Ox.* 50; App. *Mithr.* 6.19–20; Polyb. 36.14; Diod. Sic. 32.20. On the expression, cf. Otto 1890, 74, s.v. *caput* 1.

CATO

δράσιν, ἡμέρας ὀλίγας οἱ περὶ τὸν Πολύβιον διαλιπόντες, αὖθις ἐπεχείρουν εἰς τὴν σύγκλητον εἰσελθεῖν, ὅπως ἃς πρότερον εἶχον ἐν Ἀχαΐᾳ τιμὰς οἱ
φυγάδες ἀναλάβοιεν, καὶ τοῦ Κάτωνος ἀπεπειρῶντο
τῆς γνώμης. ὁ δὲ μειδιάσας ἔφη τὸν Πολύβιον ὥσπερ
τὸν Ὀδυσσέα βούλεσθαι πάλιν εἰς τὸ τοῦ Κύκλωπος
σπήλαιον εἰσελθεῖν, τὸ πιλίον ἐκεῖ καὶ τὴν ζώνην ἐπιλελησμένον. [4] τοὺς δὲ φρονίμους ἔλεγε μᾶλλον ὑπὸ
τῶν ἀφρόνων ἢ τοὺς ἄφρονας ὑπὸ τῶν φρονίμων ὠφε-
λεῖσθαι· τούτους μὲν γὰρ φυλάττεσθαι τὰς ἐκείνων
ἁμαρτίας, ἐκείνους δὲ τὰς τούτων μὴ μιμεῖσθαι κατ-
ορθώσεις. [5] τῶν δὲ νέων ἔφη χαίρειν τοῖς ἐρυθριῶσι
μᾶλλον ἢ τοῖς ὠχριῶσι, στρατιώτου δὲ μὴ δεῖσθαι
τὰς μὲν χεῖρας ἐν τῷ βαδίζειν [*Op. cet.* F 58.6], τοὺς
δὲ πόδας ἐν τῷ μάχεσθαι κινοῦντος, μεῖζον δὲ ῥέγχον-
τος ἢ ἀλαλάζοντος [*Op. cet.* F 58.7]. [6] τὸν δὲ ὑπέρπαχυν κακίζων "ποῦ δ᾽ ἄν" ἔφη "τῇ πόλει σῶμα τοιοῦτον
γένοιτο χρήσιμον, οὗ τὸ μεταξὺ λαιμοῦ καὶ βουβώνων ἅπαν ὑπὸ τῆς γαστρὸς κατέχεται;" [7] τῶν δὲ
φιληδόνων τινὰ βουλόμενον αὐτῷ συνεῖναι παραιτού-
μενος, ἔφη μὴ δύνασθαι ζῆν μετ᾽ ἀνθρώπου τῆς καρδίας τὴν ὑπερῴαν εὐαισθητοτέραν ἔχοντος. [8] τοῦ δ᾽
ἐρῶντος ἔλεγε τὴν ψυχὴν ἐν ἀλλοτρίῳ σώματι ζῆν. [9]
μεταμεληθῆναι δ᾽ αὐτὸς ἐν παντὶ τῷ βίῳ τρεῖς μετα-
μελείας· μίαν μὲν ἐπὶ τῷ γυναικὶ πιστεῦσαι λόγον
ἀπόρρητον, ἑτέραν δὲ πλεύσας ὅπου δυνατὸν ἦν πε-
ζεῦσαι, τὴν δὲ τρίτην ὅτι μίαν ἡμέραν ἀδιάθετος
ἔμεινε. [10] πρὸς δὲ πρεσβύτην πονηρευόμενον "ἄν-

around Polybius left an interval of a few days and then tried to get admission to the Senate again, with a proposal that the exiles should resume the honors they had held previously in Greece, and asked for Cato's opinion. He smiled and said that Polybius, like Odysseus [cf. Hom. *Od.* 9], wanted to go back into the cave of the Cyclops for the cap and the belt he had left there. [4] Wise men, he said, profited more from fools than fools from wise men; for the latter avoided the mistakes of the former, but the former did not imitate the accomplishments of the latter. [5] He said that he was more delighted at those young people who blushed than those who turned pale [*Op. cet.* F 58.6], and that he had no use for a soldier who in walking moved his hands, but in fighting [moved] his feet, and who snored louder than he sounded the war cry [*Op. cet.* F 58.7]. [6] Railing at the very fat man, he said: "How can such a body be of service to the state, when every part of it between gullet and groins is in the power of the belly?" [cf. *Orat.* F 79] [7] Rejecting someone of those fond of pleasure who wished to be in his company, he said that he could not live with a man who had a palate more sensitive than his heart. [8] As for the lover, he said his soul dwelt in the body of another [cf. Plut. *Mor.* 759C (*Amat.* 16)]. [9] That he had experienced repentance on three occasions in his whole life: one, when he entrusted a secret word to his wife; another, when he had sailed where it was possible to walk; and the third, when he remained intestate for one day. [10] To an old man acting wickedly he said [*Op. cet.* F 58.15;

θρωπε" εἶπε [Op. cet. F 58.15], "πολλὰ ἔχοντι τῷ γήρᾳ
τὰ αἰσχρὰ μὴ προστίθει τὴν ἀπὸ τῆς κακίας αἰσχύνην." [11] πρὸς δὲ δήμαρχον ἐν διαβολῇ μὲν φαρμακείας γενόμενον, φαῦλον δὲ νόμον εἰσφέροντα καὶ
βιαζόμενον, "ὦ μειράκιον" εἶπεν, "οὐκ οἶδα, πότερον
χεῖρόν ἐστιν ὃ κίρνης πιεῖν ἢ ὃ γράφεις κυρῶσαι."
[12] βλασφημούμενος δ᾽ ὑπ᾽ ἀνθρώπου βεβιωκότος
ἀσελγῶς καὶ κακῶς, "ἄνισος" εἶπεν "ἡ πρὸς σέ μοι
μάχη ἐστί· καὶ γὰρ ἀκούεις τὰ κακὰ ῥᾳδίως καὶ λέ-
γεις εὐχερῶς, ἐμοὶ δὲ καὶ λέγειν ἀηδὲς καὶ ἀκούειν
{ἄηθες}."[1] τὸ μὲν οὖν τῶν ἀπομνημονευμάτων γένος
τοιοῦτόν ἐστιν.

[1] ἄηθες om. unus cod.: ἀηδέστερον Reiske: an ἄηθες pro
ἄηδες ponendum? Ziegler

F 65 Plut. Cat. Mai. 10.1–6

Cf. Orig. F 135; Orat. F 55.

F 66 Plut. Cat. Mai. 11.3–4

. . .· ἐφ᾽ οἷς σχετλιάζοντα τὸν Σκηπίωνα κατειρωνευ-
όμενος οὕτως ἔφη τὴν Ῥώμην ἔσεσθαι μεγίστην, τῶν
μὲν ἐνδόξων καὶ μεγάλων τὰ τῆς ἀρετῆς πρωτεῖα μὴ
μεθιέντων τοῖς ἀσημοτέροις, τῶν δ᾽ ὥσπερ αὐτός ἐστι
δημοτικῶν ἁμιλλωμένων ἀρετῇ πρὸς τοὺς τῷ γένει
καὶ τῇ δόξῃ προήκοντας. [4] οὐ μὴν ἀλλὰ τῆς συγκλήτου ψηφισαμένης μηδὲν ἀλλάττειν μηδὲ κινεῖν

Plut. Mor. 784A (*An seni r. p. ger. sit* 1); 829F (*De vitando aere alieno* 6)]: "Sir, to old age that has many sources of shame do not add the shame resulting from badness." [11] To a Tribune of the People, who had been accused of using poison and was putting forward and trying to force through a bad bill, he said: "Young man, I do not know which is worse, to drink what you mix or to ratify what you write" [cf. *Orat.* F 120]. [12] And when he was reviled by a man who had lived licentiously and badly, he said: "The battle with you is unequal for me: for you both listen to abuse calmly and utter it easily; for me it is unpleasant both to utter it and to hear it {unusual}." Such, then, is the nature of his sayings.

F 65 Plutarch, *Life of Cato the Elder*

Cf. *Orig.* F 135; *Orat.* F 55.

F 66 Plutarch, *Life of Cato the Elder*

. . . ; when Scipio [P. Cornelius Scipio Africanus maior, cos. 205, 194, censor 199 BC (*ORF*[4] 4)] was enraged at these proceedings [Cato's military activities in the Iberian peninsula], he [Cato], employing irony, spoke thus, that Rome would be immensely great when great individuals of high repute did not yield the palm of virtue to those of lower rank and when common people, as he himself was, contended in virtue with their superiors in birth and reputation. [4] Yet when the Senate voted not to change or to

CATO

τῶν διῳκημένων ὑπὸ Κάτωνος, ἡ μὲν ἀρχὴ τῷ Σκηπίωνι τῆς αὐτοῦ μᾶλλον ἢ τῆς Κάτωνος ἀφελοῦσα
δόξης ἐν ἀπραξίᾳ καὶ σχολῇ μάτην διῆλθεν, ὁ δὲ
Κάτων θριαμβεύσας . . .

F 67a Plut. *Cat. Mai.* 12.5–7

πλεῖστον δὲ χρόνον ἐν Ἀθήναις διέτριψε, καὶ λέγεται
μέν τις αὐτοῦ φέρεσθαι λόγος ὃν Ἑλληνιστὶ πρὸς τὸν
δῆμον εἶπεν, ὡς ζηλῶν τε τὴν ἀρετὴν τῶν παλαιῶν
Ἀθηναίων, τῆς τε πόλεως διὰ τὸ κάλλος καὶ τὸ μέγεθος ἡδέως γεγονὼς θεατής· τοῦτο δ' οὐκ ἀληθές ἐστιν,
ἀλλὰ δι' ἑρμηνέως ἐνέτυχε τοῖς Ἀθηναίοις, δυνηθεὶς
ἂν αὐτὸς εἰπεῖν, ἐμμένων δὲ τοῖς πατρίοις καὶ καταγελῶν τῶν τὰ Ἑλληνικὰ τεθαυμακότων. [6] Ποστού-
μιον γοῦν Ἀλβῖνον ἱστορίαν Ἑλληνιστὶ γράψαντα
καὶ συγγνώμην αἰτούμενον ἐπέσκωψεν, εἰπὼν δοτέον
εἶναι τὴν συγγνώμην, εἰ τῶν Ἀμφικτυόνων ψηφισαμένων ἀναγκασθεὶς ὑπέμεινε τὸ ἔργον [*Op. cet.*
F 58.29]. [7] θαυμάσαι δέ φησι τοὺς Ἀθηναίους τὸ
τάχος αὐτοῦ καὶ τὴν ὀξύτητα τῆς φράσεως· ἃ γὰρ
αὐτὸς ἐξέφερε βραχέως, τὸν ἑρμηνέα μακρῶς καὶ διὰ
πολλῶν ἀπαγγέλλειν· τὸ δ' ὅλον οἴεσθαι τὰ ῥήματα
τοῖς μὲν Ἕλλησιν ἀπὸ χειλῶν, τοῖς δὲ Ῥωμαίοις ἀπὸ
καρδίας φέρεσθαι.

move anything of what had been arranged by Cato, the tenure of Scipio [in the province] passed in inactivity and idleness without effect, detracting from his own rather than Cato's reputation. Cato, on the other hand, celebrated a triumph [194 BC] . . .

F 67a Plutarch, *Life of Cato the Elder*

He [Cato] also spent a great deal of time at Athens, and a speech of his is said to be available, which he delivered to the People in Greek, declaring that he admired the virtues of the ancient Athenians and was glad to see this city because of its beauty and size. This is not true; instead, he conversed with the Athenians through an interpreter; even though he could have spoken himself, he clung to the native ways and mocked those who admired anything Greek. [6] Thus, he made fun of Postumius Albinus [A. Postumius Albinus (*FRHist* 4 T 3b)], who had written a history in Greek and asked for pardon, saying that he ought to be granted pardon if he had taken on the work under duress by a decree of the Amphictyonic League [association of Greek peoples] [*Op. cet.* F 58.29]. [7] He also says that the Athenians were astonished at the speed and pungency of his discourse; for what he himself set forth succinctly, the interpreter explained at length and with many words; that on the whole he thought that the Greeks' words were brought forth from their lips and the Romans' from their hearts.

F 67b Gell. *NA* 11.8.1–5

Quid senserit dixeritque M. Cato de ‹A.› Albino, qui
homo Romanus Graeca oratione res Romanas venia sibi
ante eius imperitiae petita composuit.—[1] iuste ve-
nusteque admodum reprehendisse dicitur Aulum Albi-
num M. Cato. [2] Albinus, qui cum L. Lucullo consul fuit,
res Romanas oratione Graeca scriptitavit. [3] in eius his-
toriae principio scriptum est ad hanc sententiam: neminem suscensere sibi convenire, si quid in his libris parum
composite aut minus eleganter scriptum foret; "nam sum"
inquit "homo Romanus natus in Latio, Graeca oratio a
nobis alienissima est," ideoque veniam gratiamque malae
existimationis, si quid esset erratum, postulavit. [4] ea[1]
cum legisset M. Cato: "ne tu," inquit, "Aule, nimium nuga-
tor es, cum maluisti culpam deprecari quam culpa vacare.
nam petere veniam solemus aut cum inprudentes erravi-
mus aut cum compulsi peccavimus. † tibi †,"[2] inquit, "oro
te, quis perpulit ut id committeres, quod priusquam fac-
eres peteres ut ignosceretur?" [5] scriptum hoc est in libro
Cornelii Nepotis de Inlustribus viris XIII.

[1] ea *Macrobius*: eam *codd.*   [2] te *Gryphius*

Cf. Macrob. *Sat.* 1, *praef.* 12–15; Polyb. 39.12.

F 67b Gellius, *Attic Nights*

What M. Cato thought and said of ⟨A.⟩ Albinus, who, as
a Roman, wrote about Roman matters in the Greek language, having first asked indulgence for his lack of knowledge.—[1] M. Cato is said to have rebuked Aulus Albinus
[A. Postumius Albinus (*FRHist* 4 T 3d, F 1b)], with great
justice and neatness. [2] Albinus, who had been consul
[151 BC] with L. Lucullus [L. Licinius Lucullus], wrote
about Roman matters in the Greek language. [3] In the
introduction to his history it is written along the following
lines: that it was not appropriate for anyone to be angry
with him if anything in these books was written in a not
sufficiently well-ordered way or less elegantly; "for," he
says, "I am a Roman, born in Latium; the Greek language
is very foreign to me"; and, accordingly, he asked for indulgence and goodwill in relation to any negative opinion
in case any errors had been made. [4] When M. Cato had
read that, he said: "Surely, Aulus, you are a great trifler
when you prefer to apologize for a fault rather than be free
from a fault. For we usually ask pardon when we have
either erred inadvertently or done wrong under compul-
sion. But tell me [?], I entreat you," he said, "who prompted
you to do that for which you ask pardon before doing it?"[1]
[5] This is written in Book 13 of Cornelius Nepos' [work]
on famous men [Nep. *Vir. ill.* F 56 Marshall].

[1] Because of the style and the language, Sblendorio Cugusi
(1996b, 232–41) argues for accepting this passage as a literal re-
production of an utterance by Cato and regarding it as a fragment
from the speeches or, perhaps more likely, a *dictum*.

CATO

F 68 Plut. *Cat. Mai.* 15.3–4

Cf. T 60.

F 69 Plut. *Cat. Mai.* 16.5–8

διὸ συμφρονήσαντες καὶ παρασκευάσαντες ἑπτὰ κα-
τῆγον ἐπὶ τὴν παραγγελίαν ἀντιπάλους τῷ Κάτωνι,
θεραπεύοντας ἐλπίσι χρησταῖς τὸ πλῆθος, ὡς δὴ μα-
λακῶς καὶ πρὸς ἡδονὴν ἄρχεσθαι δεόμενον. [6] τοὐναντίον δ᾽ ὁ Κάτων οὐδεμίαν ἐνδιδοὺς ἐπιείκειαν, ἀλλ᾽
ἄντικρυς ἀπειλῶν τε τοῖς πονηροῖς ἀπὸ τοῦ βήματος
καὶ κεκραγὼς μεγάλου καθαρμοῦ χρῄζειν τὴν πόλιν,
ἠξίου τοὺς πολλοὺς εἰ σωφρονοῦσι μὴ τὸν ἥδιστον,
ἀλλὰ τὸν σφοδρότατον αἱρεῖσθαι τῶν ἰατρῶν [*Op. cet.*
F 58.22]· [7] τοῦτον δ᾽ αὐτὸν εἶναι καὶ τῶν πατρικίων
ἕνα Φλάκκον Οὐαλέριον· μετ᾽ ἐκείνου γὰρ οἴεσθαι
μόνου τὴν τρυφὴν καὶ τὴν μαλακίαν ὥσπερ ὕδραν
τέμνων καὶ ἀποκαίων προὖργου τι ποιήσειν, τῶν δ᾽
ἄλλων ὁρᾶν ἕκαστον ἄρξαι κακῶς βιαζόμενον, ὅτι
τοὺς καλῶς ἄρξοντας δέδοικεν. [8] οὕτω δ᾽ ἄρα μέγας
ἦν ὡς ἀληθῶς καὶ μεγάλων ἄξιος δημαγωγῶν ὁ Ῥωμαίων δῆμος, ὥστε[1] μὴ φοβηθῆναι τὴν ἀνάτασιν καὶ
τὸν ὄγκον τοῦ ἀνδρός, ἀλλὰ τοὺς ἡδεῖς ἐκείνους καὶ
πρὸς χάριν ἅπαντα ποιήσειν δοκοῦντας ἀπορρίψας
ἑλέσθαι μετὰ τοῦ Κάτωνος τὸν Φλάκκον, ὥσπερ οὐκ
αἰτοῦντος ἀρχήν, ἀλλ᾽ ἄρχοντος ἤδη καὶ προστάττον-
τος ἀκροώμενος.

---

[1] ὥστε *vel* ὃς ᾤετο codd.

F 68 Plutarch, *Life of Cato the Elder*

Cf. T 60.

F 69 Plutarch, *Life of Cato the Elder*

Therefore, after consultation and preparation, they [distinguished senators] put up in opposition to Cato seven candidates for the canvassing for the office, who sought the favor of the multitude with pleasant expectations, assuming that it wanted to be ruled in a lax way and for their own pleasure. [6] Cato, on the contrary, did not grant any leniency, but outright threatened wrongdoers from the speaker's platform and shouted that the city needed a great purification; he required the People, if they were wise, not to choose the most agreeable physician, but the most zealous [*Op. cet.* F 58.22]. [7] He himself, he said, was such a one and one person from the patricians, Valerius Flaccus [L. Valerius Flaccus, cos. 195 BC]; that with him alone he thought he could do something useful, cutting and searing the hydra-like luxuriousness and moral weakness; that, as for the others, he saw that each of them persisting in the claim that they would govern badly, since they feared those who would govern well. [8] And so truly great and worthy of great leaders was the Roman People, that they did not fear the man's steadfastness and pride, but rejected those agreeable individuals who seemed ready to do everything to please them and elected Flaccus to the office along with Cato, listening to him, not as to one soliciting office, but as to one already in office and in command [cf. Liv. 39.41.1–4].

CATO

F 70 Plut. *Cat. Mai.* 17.1–7

προ{σ}έγραψε¹ μὲν οὖν ὁ Κάτων τῆς συγκλήτου τὸν
συνάρχοντα καὶ φίλον Λεύκιον Οὐαλλέριον Φλάκκον,
ἐξέβαλε δὲ τῆς βουλῆς ἄλλους τε συχνοὺς καὶ
Λεύκιον Κοΐντιον, ὕπατον μὲν ἑπτὰ πρότερον ἐνιαυ-
τοῖς γεγενημένον, ὃ δ' ἦν αὐτῷ πρὸς δόξαν ὑπατείας
μεῖζον, ἀδελφὸν Τίτου Φλαμινίνου τοῦ καταπολεμή-
σαντος Φίλιππον. [2] αἰτίαν δὲ τῆς ἐκβολῆς ἔσχε
τοιαύτην. μειράκιον ἐκ τῆς παιδικῆς ὥρας ἑταιροῦν
ἀνειληφὼς ὁ Λεύκιος ἀεὶ περὶ αὐτὸν εἶχε, καὶ συνεπή-
γετο στρατηγῶν ἐπὶ τιμῆς καὶ δυνάμεως τοσαύτης,
ὅσην οὐδεὶς εἶχε τῶν πρώτων παρ' αὐτῷ φίλων καὶ
οἰκείων. [3] ἐτύγχανε μὲν οὖν ἡγούμενος ὑπατικῆς
ἐπαρχίας· ἐν δὲ συμποσίῳ τινὶ τὸ μειράκιον ὥσπερ
εἰώθει συγκατακείμενον ἄλλην τε κολακείαν ἐκίνει
πρὸς ἄνθρωπον ἐν οἴνῳ ῥᾳδίως ἀγόμενον, καὶ φιλεῖν
αὐτὸν οὕτως ἔλεγεν, "ὥστ'" ἔφη "θέας οὔσης οἴκοι
μονομάχων οὐ τεθεαμένος πρότερον ἐξώρμησα πρὸς
σέ, καίπερ ἐπιθυμῶν ἰδεῖν ἄνθρωπον σφαττόμενον."
[4] ὁ δὲ Λεύκιος ἀντιφιλοφρονούμενος, "ἀλλὰ τούτου
γε χάριν" εἶπε "μή μοι κατάκεισο λυπούμενος, ἐγὼ
γὰρ ἰάσομαι." καὶ κελεύσας ἕνα τῶν ἐπὶ θανάτῳ
κατακρίτων εἰς τὸ συμπόσιον ἀχθῆναι καὶ τὸν ὑπη-
ρέτην ἔχοντα πέλεκυν παραστῆναι, πάλιν ἠρώτησε
τὸν ἐρώμενον εἰ βούλεται τυπτόμενον θεάσασθαι. φή-

¹ προ{σ}έγραψε *ed. Iunt.*: προσέγραψε *codd.*

360

F 70 Plutarch, *Life of Cato the Elder*

Cato then made Lucius Valerius Flaccus [cos. 195 BC], the leader of the Senate and his friend, his colleague [in the censorship of 184 BC]; he expelled many others from the Senate and also Lucius Quintius [L. Quinctius Flamininus, cos. 192 BC (cf. T 82; Val. Max. 2.9.3)], who had been consul seven years earlier, and, what was more important for his reputation than the consulship, was brother of the Titus Flamininus [T. Quinctius Flamininus, cos. 198, censor 189 BC] who had defeated Philip [Philip V, king of Macedonia, at Battle of Cynoscephalae in 197 BC]. [2] He [Cato] had the following reason for the expulsion [cf. Sen. *Controv.* 9.2]. There was a youth whom, since his boyhood, Lucius had taken as his companion and kept always about him, and whom he took with him on his campaigns, leading to such great honor and power as no one of his closest friends and kinsmen had. [3] Then it happened that he was administering the affairs of a consular province [Gaul, in 192 BC]; at one banquet this youth was reclining at his side, as was his custom; he began to pay flatteries to a man who, amid the wine, was too easily led, and said that he loved him so much "that," he said, "once, when there was a gladiatorial show at home and I had not seen it before, I rushed away to you, although I was keen to see a man slaughtered." [4] Lucius, receiving it kindly in turn, said: "Well, because of this, do not lie there feeling vexed, for I will remedy it." And he commanded that one of those condemned to death be brought to the banquet and that a lictor with an ax stand by his side; then he asked his beloved again whether he wished to see

CATO

σαντος δὲ βούλεσθαι, προσέταξεν ἀποκόψαι τοῦ ἀνθρώπου τὸν τράχηλον. [5] οἱ μὲν οὖν πλεῖστοι ταῦθ᾽ ἱστοροῦσι, καὶ ὅ γε Κικέρων αὐτὸν τὸν Κάτωνα διηγούμενον ἐν τῷ Περὶ γήρως διαλόγῳ πεποίηκεν· ὁ δὲ Λίβιος αὐτόμολον εἶναί φησι Γαλάτην τὸν ἀναιρεθέντα, τὸν δὲ Λεύκιον οὐ δι᾽ ὑπηρέτου κτεῖναι τὸν ἄνθρωπον, ἀλλ᾽ αὐτὸν ἰδίᾳ χειρί, καὶ ταῦτ᾽ ἐν λόγῳ γεγράφθαι Κάτωνος. ἐκβληθέντος οὖν τοῦ Λευκίου τῆς βουλῆς ὑπὸ τοῦ Κάτωνος, ὁ ἀδελφὸς αὐτοῦ βαρέως φέρων ἐπὶ τὸν δῆμον κατέφυγε καὶ τὴν αἰτίαν ἐκέλευσεν εἰπεῖν τὸν Κάτωνα τῆς ἐκβολῆς. [6] εἰπόντος δὲ καὶ διηγησαμένου τὸ συμπόσιον, ἐπεχείρει μὲν ὁ Λεύκιος ἀρνεῖσθαι, προκαλουμένου δὲ τοῦ Κάτωνος εἰς ὁρισμὸν ἀνεδύετο. καὶ τότε μὲν ἄξια παθεῖν κατεγνώσθη· θέας δ᾽ οὔσης ἐν θεάτρῳ, τὴν ὑπατικὴν χώραν παρελθὼν καὶ πορρωτάτω που καθεσθεὶς οἶκτον ἔσχε παρὰ τῷ δήμῳ, καὶ βοῶντες ἠνάγκασαν αὐτὸν μετελθεῖν, ὡς ἦν δυνατὸν ἐπανορθούμενοι καὶ θεραπεύοντες τὸ γεγενημένον. [7] ἄλλον δὲ βουλῆς ἐξέβαλεν ὑπατεύσειν ἐπίδοξον ὄντα, Μανίλιον, ὅτι τὴν αὑτοῦ γυναῖκα μεθ᾽ ἡμέραν ὁρώσης τῆς θυγατρὸς κατεφίλησεν. αὐτῷ δ᾽ ἔφη τὴν γυναῖκα μηδέποτε πλὴν βροντῆς μεγάλης γενομένης περιπλακῆναι, καὶ μετὰ παιδιᾶς εἰπεῖν αὐτὸν ὡς μακάριός ἐστι τοῦ Διὸς βροντῶντος.

someone smitten. When he said that he did, he ordered him [the lictor] to cut the man's throat. [5] Most, then, report this, and Cicero has represented Cato himself telling the story in the dialogue *On old age* [Cic. *Sen.* 42; cf. Plut. *Flam.* 18]. Livy says the victim was a Gallic deserter, that Lucius did not kill the man by means of a lictor, but himself with his own hand, and that this is written in a speech of Cato's [cf. *Orat.* F 69]. Then, upon the expulsion of Lucius from the Senate by Cato, his brother, taking it badly, had recourse to the People and demanded that Cato state the reason for the expulsion. [6] When he spoke and told about the banquet, Lucius attempted to deny, but when Cato challenged him to a formal trial with a wager, he withdrew. And then the punishment was recognized as just. But once, when a spectacle was given in the theater, he [Lucius] passed by the senatorial area and sat down somewhere at the furthest point; then he found pity with the People, and they shouted and made him go elsewhere, thus rectifying, as far as was possible, and alleviating what had happened. [7] He [Cato] expelled another man from the Senate, likely to become consul, Manilius,[1] because he kissed his wife in broad daylight in sight of his daughter [cf. Plut. *Mor.* 139E (*Coni. praec.* 13); Amm. Marc. 28.4.9]. For his own part, he said, he never embraced his wife unless it thundered loudly, and he said in jest that he was happy when it thundered.

[1] The identity of this Manilius, or perhaps Manlius, is not certain; a number of suggestions have been proposed (Astin 1978, 80–81 with n. 7; cf. *MRR* 2:493).

CATO

F 71 Plut. *Cat. Mai.* 19.4–7

φαίνεται δὲ θαυμαστῶς ἀποδεξάμενος αὐτοῦ τὴν τιμητείαν ὁ δῆμος. ἀνδριάντα γοῦν ἀναθεὶς ἐν τῷ ναῷ
τῆς Ὑγιείας ἐπέγραψεν οὐ τὰς στρατηγίας οὐδὲ τὸν
θρίαμβον τοῦ Κάτωνος, ἀλλ᾽ ὡς ἄν τις μεταφράσειε
τὴν ἐπιγραφήν, "ὅτι τὴν Ῥωμαίων πολιτείαν ἐγκεκλι-
μένην καὶ ῥέπουσαν ἐπὶ τὸ χεῖρον τιμητὴς γενόμενος
χρησταῖς ἀγωγαῖς καὶ σώφροσιν ἐθισμοῖς καὶ διδα-
σκαλίαις εἰς ὀρθὸν αὖθις ἀποκατέστησε." [5] καίτοι
πρότερον αὐτὸς κατεγέλα τῶν ἀγαπώντων τὰ τοιαῦτα,
καὶ λανθάνειν αὐτοὺς ἔλεγεν ἐπὶ χαλκέων καὶ ζωγρά-
φων ἔργοις μέγα φρονοῦντας, αὐτοῦ δὲ καλλίστας
εἰκόνας ἐν ταῖς ψυχαῖς περιφέρειν τοὺς πολίτας· [6]
πρὸς δὲ τοὺς θαυμάζοντας, ὅτι πολλῶν ἀδόξων ἀνδριάντας ἐχόντων ἐκεῖνος οὐκ ἔχει [*Op. cet.* F 58.10], "μᾶλλον γάρ" ἔφη "βούλομαι ζητεῖσθαι, διὰ τί μου ἀνδριὰς οὐ κεῖται ἢ διὰ τί κεῖται." τὸ δ᾽ ὅλον οὐδ᾽
ἐπαινούμενον ἠξίου τὸν ἀγαθὸν πολίτην ὑπομένειν, εἰ
μὴ τοῦτο χρησίμως γίνοιτο τῷ κοινῷ. [7] καί⟨τοι⟩[1]
πλεῖστα πάντων ἑαυτὸν ἐγκεκωμίακεν, ὅς γε καὶ τοὺς
ἁμαρτάνοντάς τι περὶ τὸν βίον, εἶτ᾽ ἐλεγχομένους λέγειν φησίν, ὡς οὐκ ἄξιον ἐγκαλεῖν αὐτοῖς· οὐ γὰρ
Κάτωνές εἰσι· καὶ τοὺς ἔνια μιμεῖσθαι τῶν ὑπ᾽ αὐτοῦ
πραττομένων οὐκ ἐμμελῶς ἐπιχειροῦντας ἐπαριστέ-
ρους καλεῖσθαι Κάτωνας· ἀφορᾶν δὲ τὴν βουλὴν

[1] καί⟨τοι⟩ Blass: καὶ codd.

F 71 Plutarch, *Life of Cato the Elder*

The People seem to have received his [Cato's] censorship [184 BC] with surprising enthusiasm. At any rate, after erecting a statue in the Temple of Health [Temple of Salus], they commemorated in the inscription upon it, not the military commands nor the triumph [194 BC] of Cato, but, as one might translate the inscription: "that, when the state of the Romans was inclining and sinking toward the worse, he was made censor, and by helpful guidance, wise habits, and teachings restored it to a sound position again." [5] And yet earlier he himself laughed at those who delighted in such things and said that they themselves went unnoticed while they thought highly of the works of statuaries and painters, and that the most beautiful images of himself were borne about by his fellow citizens in their hearts. [6] And to those who were amazed that, whereas many undistinguished individuals had statues, he had none, he said [*Op. cet.* F 58.10]: "For I would much rather be asked why there is not a statue of me than why there is." In general, he believed that a good citizen should not even allow himself to be praised, unless it was beneficial for the community. [7] And ⟨yet⟩ of all men he has praised himself most, he who says that even men failing somehow in their lives, when rebuked, say that it is not right to charge them, for they are not Catos; also that those trying to imitate some of his deeds and not doing it properly are called "left-handed Catos"; and that the Senate looks to

CATO

πρὸς αὐτὸν ἐν τοῖς ἐπισφαλεστάτοις καιροῖς ὥσπερ
ἐν πλῷ πρὸς κυβερνήτην, καὶ πολλάκις μὴ παρόντος
ὑπερτίθεσθαι τὰ πλείστης ἄξια σπουδῆς.

Cf. Amm. Marc. 14.6.8; Plut. *Mor.* 191D (*Apophth. reg. et imp.*,
Ages. 12), 215A (*Apophth. Spart.*, *Ages.* 79), 820B (*Praec. ger. rei
publ.* 27); *Ages.* 2.4; Cic. *Fam.* 5.12.7.

F 72 Plut. *Cat. Mai.* 20.3

τὸν δὲ τύπτοντα γαμετὴν ἢ παῖδα τοῖς ἁγιωτάτοις
ἔλεγεν ἱεροῖς προσφέρειν τὰς χεῖρας. ἐν ἐπαίνῳ δὲ
μείζονι τίθεσθαι τὸ γαμέτην ἀγαθὸν ἢ τὸ μέγαν εἶναι
συγκλητικόν· ἐπεὶ καὶ Σωκράτους οὐδὲν ἄλλο θαυμάζειν τοῦ παλαιοῦ πλὴν ὅτι γυναικὶ χαλεπῇ καὶ παισὶν
ἀποπλήκτοις χρώμενος ἐπιεικῶς καὶ πρᾴως διετέλεσε.

F 73 Plut. *Cat. Mai.* 21.8

προτρέπων δὲ τὸν υἱὸν ἐπὶ ταῦτα, φησὶν οὐκ ἀνδρός,
ἀλλὰ χήρας γυναικὸς εἶναι τὸ μειῶσαί τι τῶν ὑπαρ-
χόντων. ἐκεῖνο δ᾽ ἤδη σφοδρότερον τοῦ Κάτωνος, ὅτι
θαυμαστὸν ἄνδρα καὶ θεῖον εἰπεῖν ἐτόλμησε πρὸς δόξαν, ὃς ἀπολείπει πλέον ἐν τοῖς λόγοις ὃ προσέθηκεν
οὗ παρέλαβεν.

him in the most dangerous crises as if to a helmsman on a sea voyage and often, if he is not present, postpones business requiring the most serious attention.

F 72 Plutarch, *Life of Cato the Elder*

He [Cato] said that the man striking his wife or child laid violent hands on the most sacred and holy things. Also that he regarded it as more praiseworthy to be a good husband than a great senator; for even for Socrates of old there was nothing else to admire except that he was throughout kind and gentle in the treatment of a shrewish wife and stupid sons [on Socrates see Xen. *Symp.* 2.10; Arist. *Rh.* 2.15.3, 1390b31].

F 73 Plutarch, *Life of Cato the Elder*

Trying also to turn his [elder] son to such activities [i.e., ways to make money], he [Cato] said that it was not the part of a man, but of a widow woman, to lessen one's substance.[1] That surely was a rather excessive statement of Cato's, that he dared to say that a man was to be admired and regarded like a god in his reputation if he left more in the accounts, which he had added, than he had received.

---

[1] This could be a self-contained piece of advice given to the son and does not need to be connected to the *Libri ad Marcum filium*, though this is sometimes suggested.

CATO

F 74 Plut. *Cat. Mai.* 22.4–7

ταῦτα τοῖς μὲν ἄλλοις ἤρεσκε Ῥωμαίοις γινόμενα,
καὶ τὰ μειράκια παιδείας Ἑλληνικῆς μεταλαμβά-
νοντα καὶ συνόντα θαυμαζομένοις ἀνδράσιν ἡδέως
ἑώρων· [5] ὁ δὲ Κάτων ἐξ ἀρχῆς τε τοῦ ζήλου τῶν
λόγων παραρρέοντος εἰς τὴν πόλιν ἤχθετο φοβούμε-
νος μὴ τὸ φιλότιμον ἐνταῦθα τρέψαντες οἱ νέοι τὴν
ἐπὶ τῷ λέγειν δόξαν ἀγαπήσωσι μᾶλλον τῆς ἀπὸ τῶν
ἔργων καὶ τῶν στρατειῶν· ἐπεὶ δὲ προὔβαινεν ἡ δόξα
τῶν φιλοσόφων ἐν τῇ πόλει καὶ τοὺς πρώτους λόγους
αὐτῶν πρὸς τὴν σύγκλητον ἀνὴρ ἐπιφανὴς σπουδά-
σας αὐτὸς καὶ δεηθεὶς ἡρμήνευσε, Γάϊος Ἀκίλιος,
ἔγνω μετ᾽ εὐπρεπείας ἀποδιοπομπήσασθαι τοὺς φιλο-
σόφους ἅπαντας ἐκ τῆς πόλεως [*Inc.* F 14], [6] καὶ παρελθὼν εἰς τὴν σύγκλητον ἐμέμψατο τοῖς ἄρχουσιν,
ὅτι πρεσβεία κάθηται πολὺν χρόνον ἄπρακτος ἀν-
δρῶν, οἳ περὶ παντὸς οὗ βούλοιντο ῥᾳδίως πείθειν
δύνανται· [7] δεῖν οὖν τὴν ταχίστην γνῶναί τι καὶ ψη-
φίσασθαι περὶ τῆς πρεσβείας, ὅπως οὗτοι μὲν ἐπὶ
τὰς σχολὰς τραπόμενοι διαλέγωνται παισὶν Ἑλλήνων, οἱ δὲ Ῥωμαίων νέοι τῶν νόμων καὶ τῶν ἀρχόντων ὡς πρότερον ἀκούωσι.

Cf. Plin. *HN* 7.112–13.

F 74 Plutarch, *Life of Cato the Elder*

These developments [young men listening to Greek philosophers at Rome] pleased the other Romans, and they
saw with delight the young men partaking in Greek learning and being around such admirable men. [5] But, from
the outset, with this zeal for debate pouring into the city
[of Rome], Cato was distressed, fearing lest the young
men, diverting their love of honor in that direction, should
come to appreciate a reputation based on speaking more
than one achieved by deeds and military campaigns. And
when the reputation of the philosophers became more
prominent in the city [in 155 BC (cf. T 50)], and their first
speeches before the Senate were translated, at his own
instance and by his own request, by a distinguished man,
Gaius Acilius [C. Acilius (*FRHist* 7; cf. Gell. *NA* 6.14.9)],
he [Cato] determined, on some pretext, to send all the
philosophers out of the city [*Inc.* F 14]. [6] And, coming
into the Senate, he censured the magistrates because an
embassy had been sitting there idly for a long time, composed of men who could easily persuade of anything they
wished; [7] that it was therefore necessary to make a decision and adopt a decree about the embassy as quickly as
possible, so that those people might return to their schools
and lecture to the sons of the Greeks, while the young men
of the Romans could listen to the laws and the magistrates
as before [cf. *Op. cet.* F 58.28; *Orat.* F 189].

CATO

F 75 Plut. *Cat. Mai.* 24.3–8

ὡς οὖν ἔγνω τὸ πρᾶγμα δυσχεραινόμενον ὑπ᾽ αὐτῶν,
οὐδὲν ἐγκαλέσας οὐδὲ μεμψάμενος, ἀλλὰ καταβαίνων
ὥσπερ εἰώθει μετὰ φίλων εἰς ἀγορὰν, Σαλώνιόν τινα
τῶν ὑπογεγραμματευκότων αὐτῷ παρόντα καὶ συμ-
προπέμποντα μεγάλῃ φωνῇ προσαγορεύσας ἠρώτη-
σεν, εἰ τὸ θυγάτριον συνήρμοκε νυμφίῳ. [4] τοῦ δ᾽
ἀνθρώπου φήσαντος, ὡς οὐδὲ μέλλει μὴ πρότερον
ἐκείνῳ κοινωσάμενος, "καὶ μὴν ἐγώ σοι" φησίν
"εὕρηκα κηδεστὴν ἐπιτήδειον, εἰ μὴ νὴ Δία τὰ τῆς
ἡλικίας δυσχεραίνοιτο· τἆλλα γὰρ οὐ μεμπτός ἐστι,
σφόδρα δὲ πρεσβύτης." [5] ὡς οὖν ὁ Σαλώνιος αὐτὸν
ἐκέλευε ταῦτα φροντίζειν καὶ διδόναι τὴν κόρην ᾧ
προαιρεῖται, πελάτιν τ᾽ οὖσαν αὐτοῦ καὶ δεομένην τῆς
ἐκείνου κηδεμονίας, οὐδεμίαν ὁ Κάτων ἀναβολὴν ποι-
ησάμενος αὐτὸς ἔφη τὴν παρθένον αἰτεῖν αὐτῷ. [6] καὶ
τὸ μὲν πρῶτον ὡς εἰκὸς ὁ λόγος ἐξέπληξε τὸν ἄνθρωπον, πόρρω μὲν γάμου τὸν Κάτωνα, πόρρω δ᾽ αὐτὸν
οἰκίας ὑπατικῆς καὶ θριαμβικῶν κηδευμάτων τιθέμε-
νον· σπουδῇ δὲ χρώμενον ὁρῶν τὸν Κάτωνα, ἄσμενος
ἐδέξατο, καὶ καταβάντες εὐθὺς εἰς ἀγορὰν ἐποιοῦντο
τὴν ἐγγύην. [7] πραττομένου δὲ τοῦ γάμου, παραλαβὼν τοὺς ἐπιτηδείους ὁ υἱὸς τοῦ Κάτωνος ἠρώτησε
τὸν πατέρα, μή τι μεμφόμενος ἢ λελυπημένος ὑπ᾽
αὐτοῦ μητρυιὰν ἐπάγεται. ὁ δὲ Κάτων ἀναβοήσας
"εὐφήμησον" εἶπεν "ὦ παῖ· πάντα γὰρ ἀγαστά μοι τὰ
παρὰ σοῦ καὶ μεμπτὸν οὐδέν· ἐπιθυμῶ δὲ πλείονας

F 75 Plutarch, *Life of Cato the Elder*

When he [Cato] perceived that the matter [his affair with a slave girl] was displeasing to them [Cato's elder son and his wife], he did not voice any criticism or blame, but, when he was going down to the Forum with his clients, as he was accustomed to, he called out with a loud voice to a certain Salonius, who was one of his former undersecretaries and was among those escorting him, and asked him whether he had joined his young daughter in marriage to a bridegroom. [4] When the man said he would not be likely without first consulting him, he [Cato] said: "Well then, I have found a suitable son-in-law for you, unless, by Zeus, his age should be displeasing; in other ways no fault can be found with him, but he is a very old man." [5] When Salonius asked him to take care of the matter and give the maid to the man he had selected, since she was a dependent of his and in need of his kind services, Cato, allowing no delay, said that he was asking for the maid for himself. [6] At first, as was natural, the proposal amazed the man, who counted Cato far past marriage, and himself far beneath alliance with a house of consular dignity and triumphal honors; but when he saw that Cato was in earnest, he gladly accepted, and, going down to the Forum straightaway, they made the betrothal [cf. T 62, 79]. [7] While the marriage was being arranged, Cato's son, taking his friends, asked his father whether, being critical of or disappointed at him in some way, he was foisting a stepmother upon him. Cato, calling out "Hush, my son," said: "All your conduct toward me has been admirable and nothing to be

CATO

ἐμαυτῷ τε παῖδας καὶ πολίτας τῇ πατρίδι τοιούτους
ἀπολιπεῖν." [8] ταύτην δὲ τὴν γνώμην πρότερον εἰπεῖν
φασι Πεισίστρατον τὸν Ἀθηναίων τύραννον, ἐπιγή-
μαντα τοῖς ἐνηλίκοις παισὶ τὴν Ἀργολίδα Τιμώνασ-
σαν, ἐξ ἧς Ἰοφῶντα καὶ Θεσσαλὸν αὐτῷ λέγουσι
γενέσθαι.

F 76 Plut. *Cat. Mai.* 26.1–27.7

ἔσχατον δὲ τῶν πολιτευμάτων αὐτοῦ τὴν Καρχηδόνος
ἀνάστασιν οἴονται γεγονέναι, τῷ μὲν ἔργῳ¹ τέλος ἐπι-
θέντος τοῦ νέου Σκηπίωνος, βουλῇ δὲ καὶ γνώμῃ
μάλιστα τῇ Κάτωνος ἀραμένων τὸν πόλεμον ἐξ αἰτίας
τοιᾶσδε. [2] Κάτων ἐπέμφθη πρὸς Καρχηδονίους καὶ
Μασσανάσσην τὸν Νομάδα πολεμοῦντας ἀλλήλοις,
ἐπισκεψόμενος τὰς προφάσεις τῆς διαφορᾶς. ὁ μὲν
γὰρ ἦν τοῦ δήμου φίλος ἀπ᾽ ἀρχῆς,² οἱ δ᾽ ἐγεγόνεισαν
ἔνσπονδοι μετὰ τὴν ὑπὸ Σκηπίωνος ἧτταν, ἀφαιρέσει
τε τῆς ἀρχῆς καὶ βαρεῖ δασμῷ χρημάτων κολουθέν-
τες. [3] εὑρὼν δὲ τὴν πόλιν οὐχ ὡς ᾤοντο Ῥωμαῖοι
κεκακωμένην καὶ ταπεινὰ πράττουσαν, ἀλλὰ πολλῇ
μὲν εὐανδροῦσαν ἡλικίᾳ, μεγάλων δὲ πλούτων γέμου-
σαν, ὅπλων δὲ παντοδαπῶν καὶ παρασκευῆς πολε-
μιστηρίου μεστὴν καὶ μικρὸν οὐδὲν ἐπὶ τούτοις
φρονοῦσαν, οὐ τὰ Νομάδων ᾤετο καὶ Μασσανάσσου

¹ τῷ μὲν ἔργῳ *vel* ἔργῳ τὸ codd.
² ἀπ᾽ ἀρχῆς *om. unus cod.*

372

faulted; I desire to leave more sons for myself and citizens like this for the country." [8] They say, however, that this remark was uttered earlier by Peisistratus, the Athenian tyrant [6th cent. BC], who gave his grown-up sons a step-mother, namely Timonassa of Argolis, by whom, they say, Iophon and Thessalus were born to him.

F 76 Plutarch, *Life of Cato the Elder*

The last of his [Cato's] public services is thought to have been the destruction of Carthage [146 BC]: in fact Scipio the Younger [P. Cornelius Scipio Aemilianus Africanus minor, cos. 147, 134, censor 142 BC (*ORF*[4] 21)] brought the task to completion, but mainly as a result of the advice and counsel of Cato they [the Romans] undertook the war, for the following reason. [2] Cato was sent on an embassy to the Carthaginians and Massinissa the Numidian, who were at war with each other, to inquire into the grounds of their quarrel [ca. 153/52 BC; cf. Liv. *Epit.* 47; App. *Pun.* 67.302–69.314; see Scullard 1973, 287–88]. For the latter had been a friend of the [Roman] People from the start; the former had become party to a treaty after the defeat caused by Scipio [P. Cornelius Scipio Africanus maior, cos. 205, 194, censor 199 BC (*ORF*[4] 4)], curtailed by the re-moval of their empire and a grievous tribute of money. [3] Finding the city not, as the Romans supposed, in a poor and lowly state, but rather abounding in many men of military age, full of great wealth, filled with arms of every sort and with military equipment, and not a little puffed up by all this, he thought it no time for the Romans to be ordering and arranging the affairs of the Numidians and

πράγματα Ῥωμαίους ὥραν ἔχειν τίθεσθαι καὶ διαιτᾶν, ἀλλ' εἰ μὴ καταλήψονται πόλιν ἄνωθεν ἐχθρὰν
καὶ βαρύθυμον ηὐξημένην ἀπίστως, πάλιν ἐν τοῖς
ἴσοις κινδύνοις ἔσεσθαι. [4] ταχέως οὖν ὑποστρέψας
ἐδίδασκε τὴν βουλήν, ὡς αἱ πρότερον ἧτται καὶ συμ-
φοραὶ Καρχηδονίων οὐ τοσοῦτον τῆς δυνάμεως ὅσον
τῆς ἀνοίας ἀπαρύσασαι, κινδυνεύουσιν αὐτοὺς οὐκ
ἀσθενεστέρους, ἐμπειροτέρους δὲ πολεμεῖν ἀπεργά-
σασθαι, ἤδη δὲ καὶ προανακινεῖσθαι τοῖς Νομαδικοῖς
τοὺς πρὸς Ῥωμαίους ἀγῶνας, εἰρήνην δὲ καὶ σπονδὰς
ὄνομα τοῦ πολέμου τῇ μελλήσει κεῖσθαι καιρὸν περι-
μένοντος.³ [27.1] πρὸς τούτοις φασὶ τὸν Κάτωνα καὶ
σῦκα τῶν Λιβυκῶν ἐπίτηδες ἐκβαλεῖν ἐν τῇ βουλῇ,
τὴν τήβεννον ἀναβαλόμενον,⁴ εἶτα θαυμασάντων τὸ
μέγεθος καὶ τὸ κάλλος, εἰπεῖν ὡς ἡ ταῦτα φέρουσα
χώρα τριῶν ἡμερῶν πλοῦν ἀπέχει τῆς Ῥώμης. [2]
ἐκεῖνο δ' ἤδη καὶ βιαιότερον, τὸ περὶ παντὸς οὗ δήποτε πράγματος γνώμην ἀποφαινόμενον προσεπιφω-
νεῖν οὕτως· "δοκεῖ δέ μοι καὶ Καρχηδόνα μὴ εἶναι."
τοὐναντίον δὲ Πόπλιος Σκιπίων ὁ Νασικᾶς ἐπικαλού-

---

³ περιμένοντος Reiske: περιμένοντας codd.
⁴ ἀναβαλόμενον Reiske: ἀναβαλλόμενον codd.

---

[1] Most scholars interpret the anecdote of the fig as an illustra-
tion of the closeness of a strong enemy. Reviewing readings proposed so far, Günther (2008) suggests that the fig is meant to
symbolize that Carthage will soon have reached its full power, the
Romans will have to act fast to forestall any consequences, and
the best solution will be complete removal. Meijer (1984) argues

Massinissa, but that, unless they should repress a city, hostile and entertaining ill will from the beginning, so incredibly grown, they would again be in the same dangers. [4] Accordingly, he returned speedily and advised the Senate that the previous calamitous defeats of the Carthaginians had diminished not so much their power as their foolhardiness, and were likely to render them in the end not weaker, but more expert in fighting wars; that the contest with Numidia was already a prelude to one with Rome, while peace and treaty served as names for the delay of war as it awaited the right occasion. [27.1] In addition, they say, Cato also deliberately dropped Libyan figs in the Senate, throwing back his toga, then, as they admired their size and beauty, said that the country that produced them was three days' sail from Rome.[1] [2] And that was even more forceful, that, after giving his opinion on any matter whatsoever, he also said these words: "In my opinion Carthage should no longer be."[2] By contrast, Publius Scipio

that Cato is unlikely to have shown fresh figs from Africa (as the sea voyage on average probably took longer than Cato claims, and figs do not stay fresh for long), but would rather have used some from his estate, while that ploy would still have served his purposes.   [2] The famous phrase *ceterum censeo Carthaginem esse delendam* in this wording is attested only from the nineteenth century onward (on the evidence and the potential sources, see Thürlemann 1974). Inexact translations into Latin of reports in Greek sources might have contributed to the development. For a consideration of the Roman attitude to Carthage and Cato's comments in a broader context, see Waldherr 2000; O'Gorman 2004. On Cato's attitude toward Carthage (and Greece), see Crouzet 2006; on P. Scipio Nasica's position, see Gelzer [1931] 1963.

μένος ἀεὶ διετέλει λέγων καὶ ἀποφαινόμενος· "δοκεῖ
μοι Καρχηδόνα εἶναι." [3] πολλὰ γὰρ ὡς ἔοικεν ἤδη
τὸν δῆμον ὁρῶν ὕβρει πλημμελοῦντα καὶ δι᾽ εὐτυχίαν
καὶ φρόνημα τῇ βουλῇ δυσκάθεκτον ὄντα, καὶ τὴν
πόλιν ὅλην ὑπὸ δυνάμεως ὅπῃ ῥέψειε ταῖς ὁρμαῖς βίᾳ
συνεφελκόμενον, ἐβούλετο τοῦτον γοῦν τὸν φόβον
ὥσπερ χαλινὸν ἐπικεῖσθαι σωφρονιστῆρα τῇ θρα-
σύτητι τῶν πολλῶν, ἔλαττον μὲν ἡγούμενος ἰσχύειν
Καρχηδονίους τοῦ περιγενέσθαι Ῥωμαίων, μεῖζον δὲ
τοῦ καταφρονεῖσθαι. [4] τῷ δὲ Κάτωνι τοῦτ᾽ αὐτὸ δεινὸν ἐφαίνετο, βακχεύοντι τῷ δήμῳ καὶ σφαλλομένῳ
τὰ πολλὰ δι᾽ ἐξουσίαν πόλιν ἀεὶ μεγάλην, νῦν δὲ καὶ
νήφουσαν ὑπὸ συμφορῶν καὶ κεκολασμένην, ἐπι-
κρέμασθαι, καὶ μὴ παντάπασι τοὺς ἔξωθεν ἀνελεῖν
τῆς ἡγεμονίας φόβους, ἀναφορὰς αὐτοῖς πρὸς τὰς
οἴκοθεν ἁμαρτίας ἀπολιπόντας. [5] οὕτω μὲν ἐξεργά-
σασθαι λέγεται τὸν τρίτον καὶ τελευταῖον ὁ Κάτων
ἐπὶ Καρχηδονίους πόλεμον, ἀρξαμένων δὲ πολεμεῖν
ἐτελεύτησεν, ἀποθεσπίσας περὶ τοῦ μέλλοντος ἐπιθή-
σειν τῷ πολέμῳ τέλος ἀνδρός, ὃς ἦν μὲν τότε νεανίας,
χιλίαρχος δὲ στρατευόμενος ἀπεδείκνυτο καὶ γνώμης
ἔργα καὶ τόλμης πρὸς τοὺς ἀγῶνας. [6] ἀπαγγελλο-
μένων δὲ τούτων εἰς Ῥώμην πυνθανόμενον τὸν Κά-
τωνά φασιν εἰπεῖν· "οἷος πέπνυται, τοὶ δὲ σκιαὶ ἀίσ-

Nasica [P. Cornelius Scipia Nasica Corculum, cos. 162 and 155 BC], when called upon, always ended his speech with the declaration: "In my opinion Carthage should be there." [3] For he [Scipio] saw, it seems, that the People, through their arrogance, were already going far astray, and, owing to prosperity and pride, were proving difficult for the Senate to manage, and, by their power, were dragging, in a headlong rush and by force, the whole state wherever they inclined; he therefore wished that this fear at any rate, like a horse's bit, should weigh, chastising, upon the boldness of the multitude, believing that the Carthaginians had too little strength to prevail over the Romans, yet too much to be despised. [4] For Cato this very situation seemed terrible, that there was hanging over the [Roman] People, inebriated and often made to stumble on account of its power, a city that had always been great and was now sobered and chastened by its misfortunes; and that they had not altogether removed such external threats to sovereignty, leaving to themselves means of repairing their domestic failings. [5] In this way Cato is said to have brought about the third and last war against the Carthaginians [149–146 BC]; when they had started to wage war, he died [149 BC], having prophesied of the man [Scipio minor] who would bring an end to the war: this person was then a young man; as tribune in the army [149 BC (*MRR* 1:459)], he was giving proofs of judgment and daring in military confrontations. [6] When these were reported to Rome [in 149 BC], Cato, they say, said on hearing them [cf. Hom. *Od.* 10.495]: "Only he has wits; the rest are flut-

CATO

σουσι." [7] ταύτην μὲν οὖν τὴν ἀπόφασιν ταχὺ δι᾿ ἔργων ἐβεβαίωσεν ὁ Σκιπίων.

Cf. Vell. Pat. 1.13.1; Liv. *Epit.* 48, 49 [T 34]; Plin. *HN* 15.74–75; [Aurel. Vict.] *Vir. ill.* 47.8 [T 82]; Flor. 1.31(2.15).4–5; App. *Pun.* 69.315; Diod. Sic. 34/35.33.3; Tert. *Ad nat.* 2.16.4; August. *De civ. D.* 1.30.

F 77 Plut. *Mor.* 825D (*Praec. ger. rei publ.* 32)

προσοχῇ γάρ, ὥς φησιν ὁ Κάτων, καὶ τὸ μέγα γίνε-ται μικρὸν καὶ τὸ μικρὸν εἰς τὸ μηθὲν ἄγεται.

F 78 Plut. *Pel.* 1.1

Κάτων ὁ πρεσβύτερος πρός τινας ἐπαινοῦντας ἄν-θρωπον ἀλογίστως παράβολον καὶ τολμηρὸν ἐν τοῖς πολεμικοῖς διαφέρειν ἔφη τοῦ πολλοῦ τινα τὴν ἀρετὴν ἀξίαν {καὶ} τὸ μὴ[1] πολλοῦ τὸ ζῆν ἄξιον[2] νομίζειν, ὀρ-θῶς ἀποφαινόμενος.

[1] τοῦ . . . τὸ μὴ *unus cod.*: τοῦ . . . καὶ τὸ μὴ *codd. rel.*: τὸ . . . καὶ τὸ μὴ *Stephanus*   [2] τὸ ζῆν ἄξιον *transp. Ziegler*: ἄξιον τὸ ζῆν *codd.*

F 79 Tzetz. *Comm. in Hesiodi op.* 344

δείκνυσι τοῦτο Πλούταρχος. Θεμιστοκλέα γάρ φησιν ἢ Κάτωνα πιπράσκωντα τὸν ἀγρὸν λέγειν ὅτι ἀγα-θὸν ἔχει γείτονα.

tering shadows." [7] This utterance Scipio speedily confirmed by his deeds [cf. Plut. *Mor.* 200A (*Apophth. reg. et
imp.*, *Scipio the Younger* 3), 805A (*Praec. ger. rei publ.* 10);
Diod. Sic. 32.9a].

F 77 Plutarch, *Moralia* (*Precepts of Statecraft*)

For by attention, as Cato says, both the great is made
small, and the small is reduced to nothing.

F 78 Plutarch, *Life of Pelopidas*

Cato the Elder, when some praised a person who was in-
considerately rash and daring in hostilities, said to them
that there was a difference whether someone set a high
value on valor or a low value on life; he pointed this out
rightly.

F 79 Ioannes Tzetzes, Commentary on Hesiod, *Works
and Days*

Plutarch demonstrates this. For he says that Themistocles
[cf. Plut. *Them.* 18.8; *Mor.* 185E (*Apophth. reg. et imp.*,
Them. 12)] or Cato, selling a field of theirs, said that it had
a good neighbor.

F 80 Amm. Marc. 15.12.4

Cf. *Orig.* F 151.

F 81 Amm. Marc. 16.5.2

Cf. *Orat.* F 146.

F 82 Hieron. *Ep.* 66.9.2

scitum est illud quoque Catonis: sat cito, si sat bene, quod nos quondam adulescentuli, cum a perfecto[1] oratore in praefatiuncula diceretur, risimus.

[1] perfecto *codd.*: praefecto *Hilberg (praefectus orator magistrum rhetorum scholae praepositum significat)*

F 83 August. *Doctr. Christ.* 2.20.31

unde illud eleganter dictum est Catonis, qui cum esset consultus a quodam, qui sibi a soricibus erosas caligas diceret, respondit non esse illud monstrum, sed vere monstrum habendum fuisse, si sorices a caligis roderentur.

F 84 Macrob. *Sat.* 2.2.4

FLAVIANUS subiecit: "sacrificium apud veteres fuit quod vocabatur 'propter viam.' in eo mos erat ut si quid ex epulis superfuisset, igne consumeretur. hinc Catonis iocus est. namque Albidium quendam, qui bona sua comedisset et

DICTA MEMORABILIA

F 80 Ammianus Marcellinus

Cf. *Orig.* F 151.

F 81 Ammianus Marcellinus

Cf. *Orat.* F 146.

F 82 Jerome, *Letters*

Shrewd is also that [maxim] of Cato's [cf. Otto 1890, 79, s.v. *celeriter*]: "fast enough if well enough"; while still young men, we once laughed at this when it was said by an accomplished orator in an exordium.

F 83 Augustine, *On Christian Doctrine*

Hence that is an elegant statement of Cato's: when he had been approached for advice by someone, who said that his boots had been gnawed off by shrew mice, he replied that this was not a miracle, but it would have to have been truly regarded as a miracle if shrew mice were gnawed at by boots.[1]

---

[1] For a similar witty remark (attributed to someone else), cf. Clem. Al. *Strom.* 7.4.24

F 84 Macrobius, *Saturnalia*

FLAVIANUS added: "There was a sacrifice among the ancients that was called 'on account of the journey.' As regards that it was the custom that, if anything had been left over from the feasts, it would be consumed by fire. Hence derives a joke of Cato's. For he said that a certain Albidius,

novissime domum quae ei reliqua erat incendio perdidis-
set, propter viam fecisse dicebat: quod comesse non po-
tuerit, id combussisse."

F 85 Ps.-August. *Sermo de assumptione beatae Mariae
virginis* 6 (p. 454 Mai)

denique, fratres mei, attendite, quod dixit magnus ille
Cato de feminis: si absque femina esset mundus, con-
versatio nostra absque diis non esset.

INCERTORUM OPERUM RELIQUIAE
(F 1–55)

*This section includes the fragments that have been trans-
mitted for Cato without indication of a specific work and
context and that have not tentatively been attributed to
one of his known works or a particular genre in previous
editions of Cato's fragments, on which parts of this edition
are based (see General Introduction: Organization of This
Edition).*

The majority of what FRHist *classifies as "Possible fragments" of the* Origines *(Orig. F 129–56) are assigned to*
Incertorum operum reliquiae *by one or more previous
editions: while these quotations are attributed to Cato in
the transmission, none of them are attested as coming from
the* Origines. *Although in view of their content they might
belong to the* Origines, *other contexts can also be envisaged for at least some. Similarly, a large number of the*

who had eaten up his estate and most recently lost his house, which was the only thing left to him, in a fire, had performed a sacrifice 'on account of the journey': that he had burned down what he could not eat up."

F 85 Pseudo-Augustine, *Sermon on the Ascension of the Blessed Virgin Mary*

Finally, my brothers, pay attention to what that great Cato said about women: if the world was without a woman, our interaction would not be away from the gods.

INCERTORUM OPERUM RELIQUIAE
(F 1–55)

fragments assigned to Origines *1, 2, and 3 according to* FRHist *(F 46–75) are not explicitly attested for the* Origines, *though again this attribution is likely in view of the content and the context of these quotations. Finally, items tentatively assigned to the* Orations *by* ORF[4] *(Orat. F 24, 54, 55, 126, 127, 175, 188, 195, 235–54) might come from speeches, but also other types of texts. Thus, all these passages should be considered as potential additional items to this section (indicated in individual notes where it is not obvious and particular options are being considered).*

Conversely, Inc. *F 2–5 and 7–9 in this edition are assigned to the* Libri ad Marcum filium *by Cugusi (see Introduction to* Libri ad Marcum filium*), but there is no clear evidence to support this attribution.*

F 1 Varro, *Ling.* 9.107

sed consuetudo alterum utrum cum satis haberet, in toto corpore potius utitur lavamur, in partibus lavamus, quod dicimus lavo manus, sic pedes et cetera. quare e balneis non recte dicunt lavi, lavi manus recte. sed quoniam in balneis lavor lautus sum, sequitur, ut contra, quoniam est soleo, oporte⟨a⟩t[1] dici "solui," ut Cato et Ennius scribit, non ut dicit volgus, solitus sum, debere dici.

[1] oporte⟨a⟩t *Müller*

F 2 Columella, *Rust.* 1.3.7

malo enim praeteritorum quam praesentium meminisse, ne vicinum meum nominem, qui nec arborem prolixiorem stare nostrae regionis nec inviolatum seminarium nec pedamenta ad nexum vineae nec etiam pecudes neglegentius pasci sinit. iure igitur, quantum mea fert opinio, M. Porcius talem pestem vitare censuit et in primis futurum agricolam praemonuit ne sua sponte ad eam perveniret.

F 3 Columella, *Rust.* 2.16.2

M. quidem Porcius et illa commemoravit, quod nec tempestatibus adfligeretur ut aliae partes ruris minimeque

F 1 Varro, *On the Latin Language*

But although common usage accepts each of the two equally, for the entire body it rather uses "we wash ourselves" [*lavamur*: middle-passive], for parts "we wash" [*lavamus*: active], because we say "I wash my hands," and so too of feet and the rest. Therefore, when coming out of baths, they do not say correctly "I have washed [*lavi*: active perfect form]," but correctly "I have washed my hands." But since as regards baths [it is] "I wash myself, I have washed myself [*lavor, lautus sum*: middle-passive present / perfect form]," it follows that, by contrast, since it is "I am accustomed [*soleo*: active present form]," one ought to say "I have been accustomed" [*solui*: active perfect form], as Cato and Ennius [Enn. *Inc.* F 15 *FRL*] write, not that, as people commonly say, "I have been accustomed" [*solitus sum*: middle-passive perfect form] should be said.

F 2 Columella, *On Agriculture*

For I prefer to mention people of the past rather than the present, so as not to call by name a neighbor of mine who does not let a tree with an extended canopy stand on our boundary line, or a seedbed go unhurt or stakes to support the vines, or even the cattle graze with fairly little concern. Rightly, then, as far as my opinion goes, did M. Porcius [Cato] advise to avoid such a nuisance and particularly warn the future farmer not to come near it of his own free will.

F 3 Columella, *On Agriculture*

M. Porcius [Cato], indeed, mentioned also the following: that it [*pratum*, "meadow"] is not damaged by storms like

sumptus egens per omnis annos praeberet reditum neque eum simplicem, cum etiam in pabulo non minus redderet quam in faeno.

F 4 Columella, *Rust.* 3.2.31

quare prudentis magistri est eiusmodi nomenclationis aucupio, quo potiri nequeant,[1] studiosos non demorari, sed illud in totum praecipere, quod et Celsus ait et ante eum Marcus Cato, nullum genus vitium conserendum esse nisi fama, nullum diutius conservandum nisi experimento probatum.

[1] nequeant *codd. rec.*: nequeat *codd.*

F 5 Columella, *Rust.* 11.1.4

quisquis autem destinabitur huic negotio, sit oportet idem scientissimus robustissimusque, ut et doceat subiectos et ipse commode faciat quae praecipit. siquidem nihil recte sine exemplo docetur aut discitur, praestatque vilicum magistrum esse operariorum, non discipulum, cum etiam de patre familiae prisci moris exemplum Cato dixerit: "male agitur cum domino quem vilicus docet."

Cf. Columella, *Rust.* 1.2.2: nam illud vetus est Catonis: agrum pessime mulcari cuius dominus quid in eo faciendum non docet sed audit vilicum.

other parts of the farm and that, needing minimal outlay, it yields a return year after year, and not just one, because it even returns no less in pasturage than in hay.

F 4 Columella, *On Agriculture*

Therefore, it is a mark of a wise teacher not to delay students with hunting after nomenclature of such a kind [for different types of vines] that they are not able to master, but to prescribe generally what both Celsus [A. Cornelius Celsus (*Agr.* F 12 Marx)] says and before him Marcus Cato, that no kind of vine should be planted unless approved by common report and that none should be kept for longer unless approved [as still suitable] by testing.

F 5 Columella, *On Agriculture*

But whoever will be destined for this business [i.e., serving as a farm overseer], this person must be both very learned and very strong, that they may both teach those under their orders and themselves adequately carry out what they prescribe. For indeed nothing can be taught or learned correctly without an example, and it is better that a farm overseer should be the master, not the pupil, of the laborers. Indeed, Cato, a model of old-time morals, even said about the head of a family: "Things go ill with the master when the farm overseer teaches him."[1]

[1] Despite the differences in nuance, Columella is likely to allude to the same passage from Cato both here and in the sentence adduced below.

Cf. Columella, *On Agriculture*: For that is an old [saying] of Cato's, that land is most badly maltreated when its master does not direct what is to be done there, but listens to the overseer.

F 6 Plin. *HN* 14.90

Fabius Pictor in annalibus suis scripsit matronam, quod
loculos in quibus erant claves cellae vinariae resignavisset,
a suis inedia mori coactam, Cato ideo propinquos feminis
osculum dare, ut scirent an temetum olerent. hoc tum
nomen vino erat, unde et temulentia appellata.

F 7 Plin. *HN* 18.26

principium autem a Catone sumemus: "fortissimi viri et
milites strenuissimi ex agricolis gignuntur minimeque
male cogitantes." "praedium ne cupide emas." in re rus-
tica "operae ne parcas, in agro emendo minime." "quod
male emptum est semper paenitet." agrum paraturos ante
omnia intueri oportet "aquam, viam, vicinum." singula
magnas interpretationes habent nec dubias. Cato . . .

F 8 Plin. *HN* 18.34

agri ipsius bonitas quibus argumentis iudicanda sit, quamquam de terrae genere optimo disserentes abunde dixisse
possumus videri, etiamnum tamen traditas notas sub-

F 6 Pliny the Elder, *Natural History*

Fabius Pictor has written in his *Annals* that a matron was
forced by her relatives to die by starving because she had
broken open the box that contained the keys of the wine
store [Q. Fabius Pictor (*FRHist* 1 F 25)]. Cato [has writ-
ten] that male relatives gave women a kiss for the reason
that they knew whether they smelled of "tipple" [*temetum*]: this was then the word for wine, whence also "tipsi-
ness" [*temulentia*] has been named [cf. *Orat.* F 221–22].

F 7 Pliny the Elder, *Natural History*

And we will take the beginning from Cato: "The bravest
men, the most gallant soldiers, and the people least plan-
ning evil designs are produced by farmers" [cf. *Agr. praef.*
4]. "In buying a farm do not be too eager" [cf. *Agr.* 1.1].
In rural affairs "do not be sparing of trouble, least of all in
buying land" [cf. *Agr.* 1.1]. "A bad purchase is always a
source of regret."[1] Those about to buy land should before
all things look at "the water supply, the road, and the
neighbor" [cf. *Agr.* 1.2–3]. Each of these rules offers important and unquestionable explanations. Cato . . .

[1] Placed within a string of references to Cato based on the
opening of *De agricultura*, this statement is not found in that
work and could therefore be an allusion to another piece by Cato.

F 8 Pliny the Elder, *Natural History*

As to proofs by which the quality of the land itself can be
judged, we could be thought to have spoken of these with
sufficient fullness when discussing the best kind of soil
[Plin. *HN* 17.25–41]; nevertheless, we will still now sup-

signabimus Catonis maxime verbis: "ebulum vel prunus
silvestris vel rubus, bulbus minutus, trifolium, herba pra-
tensis, quercus, silvestris pirus malusque frumentarii soli
notae, item nigra terra et cinerei coloris. omnis creta co-
quet, nisi permacra, sabulumque, nisi id etiam pertenue
est, et multo campestribus magis quam clivosis respondent
eadem."

F 9 Plin. *HN* 18.44

nihil sero faciendum in agricultura omnes censent, iterumque suo quaeque tempore facienda, et tertio prae-
cepto praetermissa frustra revocari. de terra cariosa exe-
cratio Catonis abunde indicata est, quamquam praedicere
non cessa⟨n⟩tis.[1] "quidquid per asellum fieri potest vilis-
sime constat."[2]

[1] cessa⟨n⟩tis *Mayhoff*: cessat is *codd.*
[2] constat *vel* constare *codd.*

F 10a Quint. *Inst.* 1.7.23

quid? non Cato Censorius "dicam" et "faciam" "dice" et
"facie"[1] scripsit, eundemque in ceteris quae similiter cadunt modum tenuit? quod et ex veteribus eius libris manifestum est et a Messala in libro de s littera positum.

[1] dice et face *vel* dicae et faciae *codd.*

plement the transmitted notes by words of Cato in particular: "Danewort, or wild plum [cf. Plin. *HN* 15.44,
15.46], or bramble, small-bulb, trefoil, meadow grass, oak,
wild pear and wild apple are indications of a soil fit for
corn, also black earth and of ashen color. All chalk land
will scorch [the crop], unless it is an extremely thin soil,
and so will sand, unless it is also extremely fine; and the
same [soils] give a much better yield for [areas] on level
ground than for those on a slope."

F 9 Pliny the Elder, *Natural History*

That in agriculture nothing must be done too late is agreed
by all, and, secondly, that each thing must be done at its
time, and, as a third rule, that lost opportunities are revived in vain. Cato's malediction against decayed land has
been pointed out at sufficient length [Plin. *HN* 17.34],
though he never stops proclaiming it. "Whatever can be
done by means of an ass costs the least money."[1]

[1] In the context, this sentence could be another utterance by
Cato.

F 10a Quintilian, *The Orator's Education*

What? Did not Cato the ex-censor write *dicam* ["I will
say"] and *faciam* ["I will do"] as *dice* and *facie* and follow
the same pattern in other [words] that end similarly?[1] This
is obvious both from old books of his and has been stated
by Messala in the book on the letter *s* [M. Valerius Messala
Corvinus (*ORF*⁴ 176; F 1 *GRF*)].

F 10b Quint. *Inst.* 9.4.37–39

ceterum consonantes quoque, earumque praecipue quae
sunt asperiores, in commissura verborum rixantur, ut[1] s
ultima cum x proxima, quarum tristior etiam si binae col-
lidantur stridor est, ut "ars[2] studiorum." [38] quae fuit
causa et Servio ⟨Sulpicio⟩[3] subtrahendae s litterae quotiens ultima esset aliaque consonante susciperetur, quod
reprehendit Luranius, Messala defendit. nam neque Luci-
lium putat[4] uti eadem ultima, cum dicit "Aeserninus[5] fuit"
et "dignus locoque," et Cicero in Oratore plures antiquo-
rum tradit sic locutos. [39] inde "belligerare,"[6] "pos meridiem"[7] et illa Censori Catonis "dice" "facie"que,[8] m littera
in e mollita. quae in veteribus libris reperta mutare impe-
riti solent, et dum librariorum insectari volunt inscien-
tiam, suam confitentur.

[1] ut *Rollin*: et *cod.*

[2] ut ars *Regius (ex Diom., GL I, p. 467.16:* ars studiorum*):* ua
cod.

[3] *add. Bergk*

[4] putat *m. 2:* putant *cod.*

[5] Aeserninus *Schmidt (ap. Halm):* serinus *cod.*

[6] belligerare *unus cod. suppletus:* pelligerere *cod.*

[7] pos meridiem *Ritschl:* promeridiem *cod.:* pomeridiem *Regius*

[8] dice facieque *codd. suppl.:* dieae haceque *cod.:* dicae faciae-
que *Gertz*

F 10b Quintilian, *The Orator's Education*

Further, consonants also [in addition to vowels], and especially the harsher of them, clash violently at a juncture of words, for example a final *s* with a following initial *x*; the hiss produced if two *s* collide is even more disagreeable than that, like *ars studiorum* ["art of studies"]. [38] This is why Servius ‹Sulpicius› [prob. Ser. Sulpicius Rufus, cos. 51 BC] too dropped the letter *s* whenever it was final and was followed by another consonant: Luranius [otherwise unknown] criticized this, Messala [M. Valerius Messalla Corvinus (*ORF*⁴ 176; F 2 *GRF*)] defended it. For he thinks that Lucilius [F 149–50 M. = 172–73 W.] does not use this very final letter when he says *Aeserninus fuit* ["Aeserninus has been"] and *dignus locoque* ["worthy of . . . and in place"], and Cicero in the *Orator* reports that many of the ancients spoke like this [Cic. *Orat.* 161]. [39] Hence *belligerare* [instead of *bellum gerere*, "to wage war"], *pos meridiem* [instead of *post meridiem*, "after midday"], and Cato the ex-censor's famous *dice* and *facie*, with the letter *m* being softened into *e*.¹ The unlearned tend to change these things when they find them in old books, and, while they wish to censure the ignorance of the scribes, they reveal their own.

¹ Quintilian presumably outlines that another version of the future tense (cf. F 37; Dub. F 1, 3, 6) ending in *-em* was spelled without the final letter (i.e., as *-e*) that was barely pronounced (Churchill 2000a). Alternatively, the spelling *-ae* has been preferred and Quintilian's explanation interpreted to indicate that the final *m* in *-am* was pronounced softly in reduced form (Burkard 2018; on the presence or absence of final *-m* and the potential inferences for pronunciation, see also Vestergaard 1999).

CATO

F 11 Plut. *Cat. Mai.* 1.1

Cf. T 55.

F 12 Plut. *Cat. Mai.* 20.5–7

ἐπεὶ δ᾽ ἤρξατο συνιέναι, παραλαβὼν αὐτὸς ἐδίδασκε
γράμματα. καίτοι χαρίεντα δοῦλον εἶχε γραμματι-
στὴν ὄνομα Χίλωνα, πολλοὺς διδάσκοντα παῖδας· [6]
οὐκ ἠξίου δὲ τὸν υἱόν, ὥς φησιν αὐτός, ὑπὸ δούλου
κακῶς ἀκούειν ἢ τοῦ ὠτὸς ἀνατείνεσθαι μανθάνοντα
βράδιον, οὐδέ γε μαθήματος τηλικούτου {τῷ}¹ δούλῳ
χάριν ὀφείλειν, ἀλλ᾽ αὐτὸς μὲν ἦν γραμματιστής,
αὐτὸς δὲ νομοδιδάκτης, αὐτὸς δὲ γυμναστής, οὐ μόνον ἀκοντίζειν οὐδ᾽ ὁπλομαχεῖν οὐδ᾽ ἱππεύειν διδάσκων τὸν υἱόν, ἀλλὰ καὶ τῇ χειρὶ πὺξ παίειν καὶ
καῦμα καὶ ψῦχος ἀνέχεσθαι καὶ τὰ δινώδη καὶ τρα-
χύνοντα τοῦ ποταμοῦ διανηχόμενον ἀποβιάζεσθαι.
[7] καὶ τὰς ἱστορίας δὲ συγγράψαι φησὶν αὐτὸς ἰδίᾳ
χειρὶ καὶ μεγάλοις γράμμασιν, ὅπως οἴκοθεν ὑπάρχοι
τῷ παιδὶ πρὸς ἐμπειρίαν τῶν παλαιῶν καὶ πατρίων
ὠφελεῖσθαι· τὰ δ᾽ αἰσχρὰ τῶν ῥημάτων οὐχ ἧττον
εὐλαβεῖσθαι τοῦ παιδὸς παρόντος ἢ τῶν ἱερῶν παρ-
θένων ἃς Ἑστιάδας καλοῦσι· συλλούσασθαι δὲ μηδέποτε.

¹ del. *Hercher:* τῷ δούλῳ *vel om. codd.*

F 11 Plutarch, *Life of Cato the Elder*

Cf. T 55.

F 12 Plutarch, *Life of Cato the Elder*

As soon as he [Cato's son] showed signs of understanding,
he [Cato] took him under his charge and himself taught
him to read. Yet he had an accomplished slave, a teacher
of reading and writing, Chilo by name, who was teaching
many children. [6] Still, he [Cato] did not think it appropriate, as he himself says, that his son should be scolded
by a slave or have his ears tweaked when he was slow to
learn, still less that he should be indebted to a slave for
learning of such value. Instead, he himself was his teacher
in reading and writing, also his tutor in law, and his athletic
trainer, and he taught his son not merely to hurl the jav-
elin, to fight in armor, and to ride a horse, but also to box
with his hands, to endure heat and cold, and to force his
way swimming through the eddies and billows of the river.
[7] He himself says [*FRHist* 5 T 6b] that he wrote histories
with his own hand and in large characters, so as to provide
for the child from his own home an opportunity of ac-
quaintance with what was ancient and ancestral; that he
was on his guard against indecencies of speech no less
when his son was present than when the holy maidens
whom they called Vestal Virgins were; and that he never
bathed with him.

CATO

F 13 Plut. *Cat. Mai.* 21.3–5

ἐν ἀρχῇ μὲν οὖν ἔτι πένης ὢν καὶ στρατευόμενος,
πρὸς οὐδὲν ἐδυσκόλαινε τῶν περὶ δίαιταν, ἀλλ' αἴσχι-
στον ἀπέφαινε διὰ γαστέρα πρὸς οἰκέτην ζυγομαχεῖν.
[4] ὕστερον δὲ τῶν πραγμάτων ἐπιδιδόντων ποιούμε-
νος ἑστιάσεις φίλων καὶ συναρχόντων, ἐκόλαζεν εὐθὺς μετὰ τὸ δεῖπνον ἱμάντι τοὺς ἀμελέστερον ὑπουρ-
γήσαντας ὁτιοῦν ἢ σκευάσαντας. . . . [5] ἁπτόμενος
δὲ συντονώτερον πορισμοῦ, τὴν μὲν γεωργίαν μᾶλλον
ἡγεῖτο διαγωγὴν ἢ πρόσοδον, εἰς δ' ἀσφαλῆ πράγματα καὶ βέβαια κατατιθέμενος τὰς ἀφορμάς, ἐκτᾶτο
λίμνας, ὕδατα θερμά, τόπους κναφεῦσιν ἀνειμένους,
ἔργα πίσσια,¹ χώραν ἔχουσαν αὐτοφυεῖς νομὰς καὶ
ὕλας, ἀφ' ὧν αὐτῷ χρήματα προσῄει πολλὰ μηδ' ὑπὸ
τοῦ Διός, ὥς φησιν αὐτός, βλαβῆναι δυναμένων.

¹ ἔργα πίσσια *vel* ἐργατησίαν *codd.*

F 14 Plut. *Cat. Mai.* 23.1–6

ταῦτα δ' οὐχ (ὡς ἔνιοι νομίζουσι) Καρνεάδῃ δυσχερά-
νας ἔπραξεν, ἀλλ' ὅλως φιλοσοφίᾳ προσκεκρουκώς,
καὶ πᾶσαν Ἑλληνικὴν μοῦσαν καὶ παιδείαν ὑπὸ φι-
λοτιμίας προπηλακίζων, ὅς γε καὶ Σωκράτη φησὶ
λάλον γενόμενον καὶ βίαιον ἐπιχειρεῖν, ᾧ τρόπῳ δυ-
νατὸς ἦν, τυραννεῖν τῆς πατρίδος, καταλύοντα τὰ ἔθη
καὶ πρὸς ἐναντίας τοῖς νόμοις δόξας ἕλκοντα καὶ μεθ-
ιστάντα τοὺς πολίτας. [2] τὴν δ' Ἰσοκράτους διατρι-
βὴν ἐπισκώπτων, γηρᾶν φησι παρ' αὐτῷ τοὺς μαθη-

F 13 Plutarch, *Life of Cato the Elder*

At the outset, when he [Cato] was still poor and in military service, he found no fault at all with any aspects of life's necessities; instead, he declared that it was shameful to quarrel with a household slave on account of the belly. [4] Later, when his circumstances were improving, having arranged dinners for friends and colleagues, immediately after the meal he would punish with a whip those who had been remiss in any way in serving or preparing [cf. *Op. cet.* F 7]. . . . [5] When he applied himself to money-getting more earnestly, he came to regard agriculture more as an amusement than as an income; investing his resources in matters safe and sure, he bought ponds, hot springs, districts given over to fullers, pitch factories, land with natural pasture and forest, all of which brought him large profits, as they could not, as he himself says, be ruined by Jupiter.

F 14 Plutarch, *Life of Cato the Elder*

This he [Cato] did [initiative to remove embassy of Greek philosophers from Rome in 155 BC], not (as some think) because he was annoyed with Carneades [Greek Academic philosopher], but because he was wholly averse to philosophy, and made mock of all Greek culture and education out of a love of honor [cf. *Op. cet.* F 74]. He says that even Socrates was a prattler and attempted forcibly, in the way he was able to, to be his country's tyrant, by abolishing its customs and by dragging and moving his fellow citizens to opinions contrary to the laws. [2] Making fun of the school of Isocrates [Greek rhetorician, early 4th century BC], he says that the pupils became old with him,

τάς, ὡς ἐν Ἅιδου παρὰ Μίνῳ χρησομένους ταῖς
τέχναις καὶ δίκας ἐροῦντας. τὸν δὲ παῖδα διαβάλλων
πρὸς τὰ Ἑλληνικά, φωνῇ κέχρηται θρασυτέρᾳ τοῦ
γήρως, οἷον ἀποθεσπίζων καὶ προμαντεύων ὡς ἀπο-
λοῦσι Ῥωμαῖοι τὰ πράγματα, γραμμάτων Ἑλληνι-
κῶν ἀναπλησθέντες. [3] ἀλλὰ ταύτην μὲν αὐτοῦ τὴν
δυσφημίαν ὁ χρόνος ἀποδείκνυσι κενήν, ἐν ᾧ τοῖς τε
πράγμασιν ἡ πόλις ἤρθη μεγίστη καὶ πρὸς Ἑλληνικὰ μαθήματα καὶ παιδείαν ἅπασαν ἔσχεν οἰκείως.
ὁ δ' οὐ μόνον ἀπηχθάνετο τοῖς φιλοσοφοῦσιν Ἑλλήνων, ἀλλὰ καὶ τοὺς ἰατρεύοντας ἐν Ῥώμῃ δι' ὑπο-
ψίας εἶχε, [4] καὶ τὸν Ἱπποκράτους λόγον ὡς ἔοικεν
ἀκηκοώς, ὃν εἶπε τοῦ μεγάλου βασιλέως καλοῦντος
αὐτὸν ἐπὶ πολλοῖς τισι ταλάντοις, οὐκ ἄν ποτε βαρβάροις Ἑλλήνων πολεμίοις ἑαυτὸν παρασχεῖν, ἔλεγε
κοινὸν ὅρκον εἶναι τοῦτον ἰατρῶν ἁπάντων, καὶ παρ-
εκελεύετο φυλάττεσθαι τῷ παιδὶ πάντας· [5] αὐτῷ δὲ
γεγραμμένον ὑπόμνημα εἶναι, καὶ πρὸς τοῦτο θερα-
πεύειν καὶ διαιτᾶν τοὺς νοσοῦντας οἴκοι, νῆστιν μὲν
οὐδέποτε διατηρῶν οὐδένα, τρέφων δὲ λαχάνοις ἢ
σαρκιδίοις νήσσης ἢ φαβὸς ἢ λαγώ·[1] [6] καὶ γὰρ
τοῦτον[2] κοῦφον εἶναι καὶ πρόσφορον ἀσθενοῦσι, πλὴν
ὅτι πολλὰ συμβαίνει τοῖς φαγοῦσιν ἐνυπνιάζεσθαι·
τοιαύτῃ δὲ θεραπείᾳ καὶ διαίτῃ χρώμενος ὑγιαίνειν
μὲν αὐτός, ὑγιαίνοντας δὲ τοὺς αὑτοῦ διαφυλάττειν.

[1] φοβοσηλάτω vel φάσσης ἢ λαγώ codd. rel.
[2] τοῦτον Hercher: τοῦτο codd.

as if they were to use these arts and plead their cases before Minos in Hades.[1] And seeking to prejudice his son
against Greek things, he employs an utterance all too rash
for his age, declaring, as if he was speaking as a prophet
or a seer, that the Romans would lose their power when
filled with Greek letters. [3] But time has proved this ill-
boding speech of his to be empty: over that period the city
was established as the greatest in its power and became
familiar with all Greek learning and culture. He not only
hated those who philosophized among the Greeks, but was
also suspicious of those who practiced medicine at Rome
[cf. *Op. cet.* F 5]. [4] And he had heard, it seems, of Hip-
pocrates' comment that he made when the Great King [of
Persia] consulted him, with the promise of many talents,
namely that he would never make himself available to
"barbarians" who were enemies of the Greeks. He [Cato]
said that this oath was the same for all doctors and urged
his son to beware of them all. [5] He had, he says, a notebook written by himself, and according to that he cared
for and treated those sick in his family, never maintaining
any fasting, but feeding them on greens or bits of duck,
pigeon, or hare [cf. Plut. *Mor.* 131E (*De tuend. san. praec.*
18)]. [6] For such a diet, he says, was light and good for
sick people, except that it often happens to those eating it
that they dream [cf. *Op. cet.* F 9]. By following such care
and way of life he said he had good health himself and kept
his family in good health.

[1] Grilli (1997) suggests that these comments might come
from an otherwise unknown speech against philosophers and
orators, perhaps dating to 161 BC and delivered in the Senate.

CATO

F 15 Plut. *Cat. Mai.* 24.9–10

Cf. T 62.

F 16 Plut. *Cat. Mai.* 25.1–4

Cf. T 63.

F 17 Plut. *Cat. Mai.* 32 (= *Comp. Arist. et Cat. Mai.* 5).3

ἐγὼ δ᾽ οὐ μέμφομαι μὲν Κάτωνος τὸ μεγαλύνειν ἀεὶ
καὶ πρῶτον ἁπάντων ἑαυτὸν τίθεσθαι· καίτοι φησὶν
ἔν τινι λόγῳ τὸ ἐπαινεῖν αὐτὸν ὥσπερ τὸ λοιδορεῖν
ἄτοπον εἶναι. τελειότερος δέ μοι δοκεῖ πρὸς ἀρετὴν
τοῦ πολλάκις ἑαυτὸν ἐγκωμιάζοντος ὁ μηδ᾽ ἑτέρων
τοῦτο ποιούντων δεόμενος.

F 18 Gell. *NA* 2.17.6–9

neque vero "con" particula tum solum producitur, cum ea
littera, de qua Cicero dixit, insequitur. [7] nam et Cato et
Sallustius: "faenoribus" inquiunt "copertus[1] est." [8] praeterea "coligatus"[2] et "conexus"[3] producte dicitur. [9] sed
tamen videri potest in his quae posui ob eam causam particula haec produci, quoniam eliditur ex ea "n" littera: nam
detrimentum litterae productione syllabae compensatur.

[1] copertus *Hertz*: coopertus *codd.*
[2] coligatus *Carrio*: colligatus *codd.*: coiugatus Lachmann
[3] conexus *vel* connexus *codd.*

F 15 Plutarch, *Life of Cato the Elder*

Cf. T 62.

F 16 Plutarch, *Life of Cato the Elder*

Cf. T 63.

F 17 Plutarch, *Comparison of Aristides and Cato*

For my part, I do not blame Cato for his constant boasting and for rating himself above everybody else; yet he says in some utterance[1] that self-praise like self-depreciation is out of place. And, in my view, more accomplished in excellence than the person who is often praising themselves is the one who does not even need others doing so.

[1] Whether *logos* refers to a speech or another type of spoken or written pronouncement is uncertain.

F 18 Gellius, *Attic Nights*

Nor, indeed, is the particle *con* lengthened only then when that letter [f] about which Cicero [Cic. *Orat*. 159] spoke follows. [7] For both Cato and Sallust [C. Sallustius Crispus (*ORF*[4] 152); Sall. *Hist*. 4.52 M. = 4.49 R.] say *faenoribus copertus est* ["he is overwhelmed by debts / loans carrying interest"]. [8] Moreover, *coligatus* ["gathered together"] and *conexus* ["joined together"] are pronounced long. [9] But after all one can see in these cases that I have cited that this particle is lengthened for the reason that the letter *n* is dropped from it; for the loss of a letter is compensated by the lengthening of the syllable.

CATO

F 19 Gell. *NA* 4.9.12–14

quod si, ut ait Nigidius, omnia istiusmodi inclinamenta
nimium ac praeter modum significant et idcirco in culpas
cadunt, ut "vinosus," "mulierosus," ‹"gratiosus,"›[1] "morosus," "verbosus," "famosus," cur "ingeniosus" et "formosus" et "officiosus" et "speciosus",[2] quae pariter ab ingenio
et forma et officio ‹et specie›[3] inclinata sunt, cur etiam
"disciplinosus," "consiliosus," "victoriosus," quae M. Cato
ita figuravit, cur item "facundiosa," quod Sempronius
Asellio XIII rerum gestarum ita scripsit: "facta sua spec-
tare oportere, non dicta, si minus facundiosa essent," cur,
inquam, ista omnia numquam in culpam, sed in laudem
dicuntur, quamquam haec quoque[4] incrementum sui nimium demonstrent? an propterea quia illis quidem quae
supra posui[5] adhibendus est modus quidam necessarius?
[13] nam et gratia, si nimia atque inmodica, et mores, si
multi atque varii, et verba, si perpetua atque infinita et
obtundentia, et fama, si magna et inquinata[6] et invidiosast,[7] neque laudabilia neque utilia sunt; [14] ingenium
autem et officium et forma et disciplina et consilium et
victoria et facundia, sicut ipsae virtutum amplitudines,

---

[1] *add. Holford-Strevens (cf. §13)*

[2] {et speciosus} *del. Damsté*

[3] *add. Hosius*

[4] haec quoque *cod. unus, de Buxis*: haec cum *codd. rel.*: haec
item *Hosius*: aecum *Hertz*: haud minus *Damsté*: *alii alia*

[5] posui *cod. unus*: posuit *codd. rel.*

[6] inquinata *Watt (1994, 279–80)*: inquieta *codd.*

[7] invidiosast *Madvig*: invidiosa sit *codd.*

F 19 Gellius, *Attic Nights*

But if, as Nigidius [P. Nigidius Figulus, late Republican scholar (F 4 *GRF*)] says, all derivatives of that kind [adjectives ending in *-osus*] indicate an excessive and immoderate degree, and therefore denote criticisms, like *vinosus* ["of much wine"], *mulierosus* ["of many women"], ‹*gratiosus* ["of much charm"],› *morosus* ["of much pernicketiness"], *verbosus* ["of many words"], and *famosus* ["of much fame"], why are *ingeniosus* ["of much talent"], *formosus* ["of much beauty"], *officiosus* ["of much duty"], and *speciosus* ["of much good outward appearance"], which are derived in the same way from *ingenium*, *forma*, *officium*, and ‹*species*›, why too are *disciplinosus* ["of much training"; cf. *Op. cet.* F 25], *consiliosus* ["of much wisdom"], and *victoriosus* ["of much victory"], which M. Cato formed in this way, why likewise *facundiosus* ["of much eloquence"], which Sempronius Asellio used in the thirteenth [book] of his *Histories* as follows [*FRHist* 20 F 10]: "that one should inspect their deeds, not their words if they are less full of eloquence," why, I say, are all those [words] used, never for criticism, but for praise, although they too indicate an excessive amount of their respective quality? Could it be for the reason that for those at any rate that I cited first a certain necessary limit has to be applied? [13] For charm, if it is excessive and without limit, and habits, if they are many and varied, and words, if they are unceasing, endless, and deafening, and fame, if it is great, stained, and begetting envy, are neither praiseworthy nor useful; [14] but talent, duty, beauty, training, wisdom, victory, and eloquence, as they are in themselves eminent examples of virtues, are confined within no limits,

nullis finibus cohibentur, sed quanto maiora auctioraque
sunt, multo[8] etiam tanto laudatiora sunt.

[8] multo *Gronovius*: mito *vel* m ito vel ivito *vel* inito *vel* merito
codd.

F 20 Gell. *NA* 10.21.1–2

non paucis verbis, quorum frequens usus est nunc et fuit
M. Ciceronem noluisse uti manifestum est quod ea non
probaret; velut est et "novissimus" et "novissime." [2] nam
cum et M. Cato et[1] Sallustius et alii quoque aetatis eiusdem verbo isto promisce usitati sint, multi etiam non in-
docti viri in libris id suis scripserint, abstinuisse eo tamen
tamquam non Latino videtur, quoniam, qui doctissimus
eorum temporum fuerat, L. Aelius Stilo ut novo et inprobo
verbo uti vitaverat.

[1] M. Cato et *del. Perini (1978–1979)*

but the greater and more extensive they are, so much more are they also deserving of praise.

F 20 Gellius, *Attic Nights*

M. Cicero, it is obvious, did not wish to use not a few words that are now and were in general use, because he did not approve of them; examples are both *novissimus* ["the newest"; adj.] and *novissime* [adv.]. [2] For although M. Cato, Sallust [C. Sallustius Crispus (*ORF*⁴ 152); e.g., Sall. *Cat.* 33.2; *Iug.* 10.2, 19.7], and others also of the same period[1] have habitually used that word in general practice, and, further, many men, not without learning, wrote it in their works, still, he seems to have abstained from it, on the ground that it did not seem to be good Latin, since he who was the most learned man of those times, L. Aelius Stilo [T 15 *GRF*], had avoided its use as that of a novel and improper word.

  [1] Perini (1978–1979) argues that "M. Cato" should be deleted as developed from a gloss *in cat.* ("in *Bellum Catilinae*") and that this passage should no longer be counted as an item about Cato. If, with the transmitted text kept, "others also of the same period" is seen as referring not only to Sallust and the phrase rather understood as denoting a group of contemporaries of whom M. Cato and Sallust are examples, the comment would refer to Cato the Younger (thus Holford-Strevens 2020, 382, in app.). Yet the phrase could also refer to Sallust only; and as both readings are possible, this passage can be retained as a potential piece of information on Cato the Elder.

F 21 Gell. *NA* 16.12.7–8

"'faenerator'" enim, sicuti M. Varro in libro tertio de sermone Latino scripsit, "a faenore est nominatus"; "faenus"
autem dictum ait "a fetu et quasi a fetura quadam pecuniae parientis atque increscentis." [8] idcirco et M. Catonem et ceteros aetatis eius "feneratorem" sine "a" littera
pronuntiasse tradit, sicuti "fetus" ipse et "fecunditas" appellata.

F 22 Gell. *NA* 18.7.3

[DOMITIUS:] ego enim grammaticus vitae iam atque morum disciplinas quaero, vos philosophi mera estis, ut M.
Cato ait, "mortualia";[1] glossaria namque[2] colligitis[3] et lexi-
dia, res taetras et inanes et frivolas tamquam mulierum
voces praeficarum.

   [1] mortualia *Dousa*: mortuaria *codd.*   [2] namque *Dousa*:
nam qui *codd.*   [3] colligitis *Carrio*: collegitis *vel* collegisti
codd.

F 23 Gell. *NA* 19.10.10

at enim FRONTO iam voce atque vultu intentiore "itane,"
inquit, "magister? dehonestum tibi deculpatumque hoc
verbum videtur, quo et M. Cato et M. Varro et pleraque
aetas superior ut necessario et Latino usi sunt?"

F 21 Gellius, *Attic Nights*

For *"faenerator* ['usurer']," as M. Varro has written in the third book on Latin diction [M. Terentius Varro, F 57 Goetz / Schoell = F 36 *GRF*], "is named from *faenus* ['interest']"; and *"faenus"* is derived, he says, "from *fetus* ['bearing of fruit'] and from some *fetura* ['giving birth'], as it were, of money producing and growing." [8] For that reason, he reports, both M. Cato and others of that time pronounced *fenerator* without the letter *a*, just as *fetus* itself and *fecunditas* ["fertility"] [were] pronounced.

F 22 Gellius, *Attic Nights*

[DOMITIUS:] For I, a grammarian, am already inquiring into the conduct of life and manners; you philosophers are mere *mortualia* ["funeral dirges"], as M. Cato says: for you collect glossaries and word lists, filthy, trifling, silly things, like the dirges of female hired mourners.

F 23 Gellius, *Attic Nights*

But FRONTO, now with a raised voice and a more earnest expression, says: "Well, master [a grammarian]? Does this word [*praeterpropter*, 'more or less'] seem to you degraded and utterly faulty, a word that M. Cato, and M. Varro [M. Terentius Varro], and most [of the writers] of the earlier period have used as one that is necessary and good Latin?"

F 24 Paul. *Fest.*, p. 25.1 L.

AUDACIAS[1] pluraliter Cato dixit.

[1] audacias *vel* audatias *codd.*

F 25 Paul. *Fest.*, p. 25.7 L.

ALIORSUM et illorsum sicut introrsum dixit Cato.

F 26 Paul. *Fest.*, p. 41.11–12 L.

CADUCEATORES legati[1] pacem petentes. Cato: "caduceatori," inquit, "nemo homo[2] nocet."[3]

[1] legata *unus cod.*[1]   [2] homo *om. unus cod.*
[3] nocet *vel* nosset *codd.*

F 27 Paul. *Fest.*, p. 73.23–26 L.

FORMA significat modo faciem cuiusque[1] rei, modo calidam,[2] cum exta, quae dantur, deforma appellantur. et Cato ait de quodam aedificio: "aestate frigido, hieme formido."[3]

[1] cuiusque *vel* cuique *codd.*   [2] calida *Corssen*: calidum *Jordan*   [3] frigidum hieme formidum *Jordan*

F 28 Paul. *Fest.*, p. 79.5–6 L.

FUTARE arguere est, unde et confutare. sed Cato hoc pro saepius fuisse[1] posuit.

[1] fudisse *Corssen*

F 29 Paul. *Fest.*, p. 81.22 L.

FEROCIT apud Catonem ferociter agit.

F 24 Paul the Deacon, *Epitome of Festus*

audaciae ["boldnesses"; usually sg.] Cato used in the plural.

F 25 Paul the Deacon, *Epitome of Festus*

aliorsum ["to another place"] et *illorsum* ["to that place"], just as *introrsum* ["to within"], was used by Cato.

F 26 Paul the Deacon, *Epitome of Festus*

caduceatores ["heralds bearing a staff"], ambassadors asking for peace. Cato says: "no one harms a herald bearing a staff."

F 27 Paul the Deacon, *Epitome of Festus*

forma sometimes denotes the shape of any item, sometimes hot, when the internal organs that are presented are called mis-shapen [*de-forma*]. And Cato says about some building: "in summer cold [dat. / abl. sg. masc. / neut.], in winter warm [*formidus*]."[1]

[1] The passage mentions similar-sounding words relating to both "shape" and "warmth."

F 28 Paul the Deacon, *Epitome of Festus*

futare is "to prove," whence also *confutare* ["to disprove, restrain"]. But Cato used it instead of "to have been rather frequently."

F 29 Paul the Deacon, *Epitome of Festus*

ferocit ["he acts in a fierce manner"] in Cato [means] "he acts fiercely."

CATO

F 30 Paul. *Fest.*, p. 81.24–25 L.

FRUNISCOR et FRUNITUM dixit Cato; nosque cum adhuc
dicimus infrunitum, certum est antiquos dixisse frunitum.

F 31 Paul. *Fest.*, p. 81.26–27 L.

FELICES arbores Cato dixit, quae fructum ferunt, infelices, quae non ferunt.

F 32 Paul. *Fest.*, p. 108.20 L.

LATITAVERUNT Cato posuit pro saepe tulerunt.

F 33 Fest., p. 140.32–36 L.

⟨M⟩IHIPTE pro mihi ⟨ipsi Cato posuit⟩[1] . . .[2] decuit talen-
. . . versia, atque . . . entia item a . . .

   [1] *suppl. Epit.*   [2] ⟨cum dixit⟩ *Ursinus*

Cf. Paul. *Fest.*, p. 141.9 L.: MIHIPTE[1] Cato pro mihi ipsi posuit.

   [1] mihipte *vel* mihiptae *codd.*

F 30 Paul the Deacon, *Epitome of Festus*

fruniscor ["I enjoy"] and *frunitum* ["enjoyed"] were used by Cato; and while we still say *infrunitum* ["stupid"; negated participle / adjective], it is certain that the ancients said *frunitum*.

F 31 Paul the Deacon, *Epitome of Festus*

Cato called productive [*felices*] the trees that bear fruit, unproductive [*infelices*] those that do not.

F 32 Paul the Deacon, *Epitome of Festus*

latitaverunt ["they have carried frequently"; from participle *latus* + frequentative] Cato used for "they have carried often."

F 33 Festus

‹m›*ihipte* ‹Cato used› for *mihi* ‹*ipsi*› ["for me myself" (cf. F 44) . . . it was fitting . . . [?][1]

[1] What is presumably a quotation from one of Cato's works is too lacunose to be translated properly.

Cf. Paul the Deacon, *Epitome of Festus*: *mihipte* Cato used for *mihi ipsi* ["for me myself"].

F 34 Fest., p. 142.1–4 L.

⟨MERITAVER⟩E,[1] saepe merue⟨re dixit Cato⟩[2] . . . ⟨Po⟩e-
norum IIII suf⟨fetes⟩ . . . nis cohortes, omnis . . . averunt.[3]

  [1] *suppl. Ursinus*   [2] *suppl. Ursinus (ex Epit.)*
  [3] ⟨evocaverunt statim om⟩nis cohortes omnis ⟨etiam qui stipendia merit⟩averunt *Ursinus (post Scaligerum)*

Cf. Paul. *Fest.*, p. 143.1 L.: MERITAVERE idem Cato pro meruere.

F 35 Fest., p. 148.35–36 L.

⟨MOSCILLIS Cato pro par⟩vis[1] qui moribus dixit . . .

  [1] *suppl. Epit.*

Cf. Paul. *Fest.*, p. 149.5 L.: MOSCILLIS Cato pro parvis moribus
dixit.

F 36 Fest., p. 280.8–10 L.

⟨PROPERI⟩EM[1] Cato saepe dicit, ut . . . ⟨ar⟩boses[2] loco r
dicebant. . . . ⟨properie⟩m[3] mari opus est.

  [1] em *vel* se (*vix* s) *cod. teste Loewio*   *suppl. Lindsay*
  [2] ⟨antiqui s litteram in robose et ar⟩boses *Mueller (fere)*
  [3] ⟨properie⟩m *Lindsay*

F 34 Festus

‹*meritaver*›*e* ["they earned money habitually"], "they often earned money," ‹Cato used it› . . . four chief magistr‹ates of the Car›thaginians . . . cohorts, all . . . they have . . .[1]

[1] The passage illustrating Cato's use of *meritavere* is corrupt; it seems to have concerned Carthaginian officials.

Cf. Paul the Deacon, *Epitome of Festus*: *meritavere* ["they earned money habitually"], the same Cato [used] for "they earned money."

F 35 Festus

‹*moscillis* ["with little habits"; diminutive] instead of "with litt›le habits" ‹Cato›, who said . . .[1]

[1] The quotation of the passage in which Cato used this expression has been lost.

Cf. Paul the Deacon, *Epitome of Festus*: *moscillis* ["with little habits"] Cato used instead of "with little habits."

F 36 Festus

‹*properi*›*em* ["speedily"] Cato often says,[1] as . . . ‹tr›ees [form *arboses* instead of standard *arbores*] in place of *r* they said. . . . ‹speedil›y seawater is needed.

[1] The passage shows that Cato used the word *properiem*, while it is unclear in what way the subsequent lacunose text might hide an example of his usage.

F 37 Fest., p. 364.9–10 L.

RECIPIE apud Catonem pro recipiam, ut alia eiusmodi
complura.

F 38 Fest., pp. 396.29–98.7 L.

SUPP⟨REMUM modo significat⟩[1] summum, ut . . . alias
extrem⟨um⟩ . . . Cato d[2] . . . lentis numquam cuiq[3] . . .
⟨sup⟩premam advoca⟨tionem. alias pr⟩o maximo . . .

[1] *suppl. Epit.*   [2] d⟨e⟩ *Ursinus*   [3] cuiquam *cod. teste
Ursino*: cuiq *cod. teste Keilio*

Cf. Paul. *Fest.*, p. 397.10–11 L.: SUPPREMUM modo significat
summum, modo extremum, modo maximum.

F 39 Paul. *Fest.*, p. 507.4–6 L.

VETERNOSUS dicitur, qui gravi premitur somno. Cato ve-
ternosum hydropicum intellegi voluit, cum ait: "veternosus quam plurimum bibit, tam maxime sitit."

F 40 Paul. *Fest.*, p. 507.9 L.

VETERINAM bestiam iumentum[1] Cato appellavit a ve-
hendo.

[1] iumentum *om. aliqui codd.*

F 37 Festus

recipie in Cato instead of *recipiam* ["I will receive"; different forms of future tense], like many other [words] of that kind [cf. F 10].

F 38 Festus

supp⟨remum [neut. sg.] sometimes means⟩ "highest," as . . . , elsewhere "l⟨ast⟩" . . . Cato . . . [?] never . . . "⟨la⟩st postpone⟨ment."[1] Elsewhere in⟩stead of "greatest" . . .

[1] The text is too lacunose to enable a restoration of what is attributed to Cato. It probably is a comment on a legal matter.

Cf. Paul the Deacon, *Epitome of Festus*: *suppremum* sometimes means "highest," sometimes "last," sometimes "greatest."

F 39 Paul the Deacon, *Epitome of Festus*

veternosus ["someone afflicted with morbid lassitude / lethargy"] is the term for a person who is afflicted by heavy sleep. Cato wanted *veternosus* to be understood as *hydropicus* ["suffering from dropsy"], when he says: "as a person suffering from dropsy drinks very much, so they are thirsty to the greatest degree."

F 40 Paul the Deacon, *Epitome of Festus*

Cato called a draft animal *veterina bestia* ["beast of burden"] from *vehere* ["to draw / bear / carry"].

F 41 Paul. *Fest.*, p. 519.18 L.

ULS Cato pro ultra posuit.

F 42 Paul. *Fest.*, p. 519.27 L.

UNGULATROS ungues magnos atque asperos Cato appellavit.

F 43 Paul. *Fest.*, p. 519.28–29 L.

VERBERITARE idem Cato frequentative ab eo, quod est verbero, dixit.

F 44 Paul. *Fest.*, p. 519.30 L.

VOPTE pro vos ipsi Cato posuit.

F 45 Charis., *GL* I, p. 134.4–8 = p. 170.26–32 B.

iugeris . . . sed et Cato his "iugeris," ut notat Plinius eodem libro VI. "iugeribus quidam grammatici" inquit Plinius[1] "ita dicendum putant, quasi sit hoc iuger tam quam hoc tuber, et ab hoc iugere tam quam ab hoc tubere, et ita ut tuberibus iugeribus, et tantum iugerum."

  [1] *transp. Keil*: quidam inquit grammatici plinius *cod*.

F 46 Charis., *GL* I, p. 202.11–12 = p. 262.21–22 B.

imperabiliter Cato senex, ubi Maximus: pro nimis imperiose, dure.

F 41 Paul the Deacon, *Epitome of Festus*

Cato put *uls* for *ultra* ["on the far side, beyond"].

F 42 Paul the Deacon, *Epitome of Festus*

ungulatri is what Cato called large and rough nails / claws [*ungues*].

F 43 Paul the Deacon, *Epitome of Festus*

The same Cato used *verberitare* as a frequentative derived from *verbero* ["I beat"].

F 44 Paul the Deacon, *Epitome of Festus*

Cato put *vopte* instead of *vos ipsi* ["you yourselves"; cf. F 33].

F 45 Charisius

iugeris ["for / by acres"; dat. / abl. pl.] . . . But also Cato [uses] *iugeris*, as Pliny [the Elder] notes in the same Book 6 [F 58: *GRF*, p. 281 Mazzarino]. "Some grammarians," Pliny says, "believe that *iugeribus* [different form of dat. / abl. pl.] has to be said thus, as if it was ⟨*hoc*⟩ *iuger* [nom., instead of *iugerum*] just like ⟨*hoc*⟩ *tuber* ['swelling'], and ⟨*ab hoc*⟩ *iugere* [abl. sg.] just as ⟨*ab hoc*⟩ *tubere*, and thus, like *tuberibus*, *iugeribus* [dat. / abl. pl.], and only *iugerum* [gen. pl.]."

F 46 Charisius

imperabiliter ["in an authoritative manner"] [was used] by Cato of old, where Maximus [Statilius Maximus (F 3 Zetzel)] [says]: instead of "too authoritatively," "harshly."

417

F 47 Charis., *GL* I, p. 217.8–9 = p. 280.24–25 B.

rare Cicero pro raro,[1] ubi[2] idem Maximus notat Catonem quoque ita locutum.

[1] rare Cicero pro raro *Putschen*: raro Cicero pro rare *cod.*: rare idem pro raro *excerpta cod. Paris.*   [2] ubi *Putschen*: ut *cod.*

F 48 Charis., *GL* I, p. 217.14 = p. 281.5–6 B.

rarenter Cato,[1] ut idem Maximus notat, pro raro.[2]

[1] Cato *Cauchii ex deperdito cod. excerpta*: cat *cod.*
[2] rarenter cato pro rariter *excerpta cod. Paris.*

F 49 Charis., *GL* I, p. 219.19 = p. 283.28–29 B.

seorsum Cato senex: "suapte[1] natio sua separate seorsum."

[1] suapte *cod.*: qua arte *Cauchii ex deperdito cod. excerpta, Putschen*

F 50 Charis., *GL* I, p. 220.16 = p. 284.27 B.

secunde Cato senex, ut Maximus notat.

F 51 Marius Victorinus, *Art. gramm.* 1.4, *GL* VI, p. 13.3–8

cum adverbium temporis antiqui quattuor litteris scribebant {in} his, quum; apud Catonem {quam} rursus per o,

F 47 Charisius

rare ["rarely"] [is used] by Cicero instead of *raro* [more common form of adverb],[1] where the same Maximus [Statilius Maximus (F 11 Zetzel)] notes that Cato also spoke like this.

 [1] *rare* does not appear in the manuscripts of Cicero's extant works, but this may be due to corruption in the transmission (Zetzel 1974, 113). *rarenter* (F 48) is attested for Cato (*Agr.* 103).

F 48 Charisius

rarenter ["rarely"] [is used] by Cato, as the same Maximus [Statilius Maximus (F 12 Zetzel)] notes, instead of *raro* [more common form of adverb].

F 49 Charisius

seorsum ["separately"]: Cato of old [uses it]: "its very own affairs a nation under its own control distinctively and separately."[1]

 [1] This excerpt may ultimately derive from a quotation by Maximus, as some others (Zetzel 1974, 115).

F 50 Charisius

secunde ["successfully"] [was used] by Cato of old [cf. *Orat.* F 163], as Maximus [Statilius Maximus (F 18 Zetzel)] notes.

F 51 Marius Victorinus

The ancients spelled the temporal adverb *cum* with these four letters, *quum* ["when"]; in Cato again with *o*, *quom*.

quom.[1] sed antiqui cum ita scriberent, pronuntiabant tamen perinde, ac si per c scriptum[2] esset, illa quidem scriptura confusa, quod u pro consonanti et o pro vocali correpta accipiebant, ⟨quae,⟩[3] sicut apud Graecos, trium valebat vice, ut esset o breve, item longum et, ut ante dixi, ov.

[1] in his cum apud Catonem quam (quum) rursus ea quo am *codd.*: in his, quum apud Catonem quam (quam *om. ed. princ.*) rursus quom *ed. princ., ed. Basileensis*: tam his quum apud Catonem, quam rursus quom *Putschen*   [2] per c scriptum *vel* per cum scriptum *codd.*: per cum scriptum *ed. princ., ed. Basileensis*   [3] accipiebant .i. sicut *vel* accipiebant sicut *codd.*: accipiebant sicut *ed. princ.*

F 52 Servius, *Comm. in Donatum, GL* IV, p. 442.23–25

nam et praepositionem praepositioni sic cohaerentem, ut pro una parte orationis habeantur, invenimus saepius apud Catonem, ut circumcirca, id est circa.

F 53 Serv. auct. ad Verg. *Aen.* 3.314

"turbatus": lugente scilicet Andromache. Cato ait verba tertiato et quartato quempiam dicere prae metu.

F 54 *De dubiis nominibus, GL* V, p. 574.11

corbes generis feminini, ut Cato "corbes messorias."

But while the ancients spelled it thus, they still pronounced it as if it was spelled with *c*, with that spelling
confused, because they accepted *u* in place of a consonant
and *o* in place of a short vowel, ⟨which,⟩ as with the
Greeks, has three values in turn, so that it can be a short
o, likewise a long one, and, as I have said before, *u* [*ou* in
Greek].

F 52 Servius, *Commentary on Donatus*

For also as regards a preposition so connected with another preposition that they can be regarded as a single part
of speech, we find that rather frequently in Cato, such as
circumcirca ["round about"], that is *circa* ["round"].

F 53 Servius Danielis, *Commentary on Virgil*

"agitated" [i.e., Aeneas]: Obviously, because Andromache
grieves. Cato says that anyone utters words at the third and
fourth attempt out of fear [since Aeneas, emotionally
moved, is not able to speak fluently].

F 54 Anonymous grammatical work

corbes ["baskets"; also masc.], of feminine gender, as Cato:
"reaper's baskets" [acc. pl. fem.].

F 55 *De dubiis nominibus, GL* V, p. 586.17

putei generis masculini, ut Cato et Varro.

FRAGMENTA DUBIAE AUCTORITATIS
(F 1–15)

These items consist of rhetorical exercises mentioning Cato's name or topics he is known to have spoken about; passages with corrupt text, where the restoration of Cato's name or of what he might have said or the attribution to Cato as author are uncertain; and records of words reported to be in use among "the ancients" without an indication of writers, but possibly including Cato. Since it cannot be proven whether any of these items are to be

F 1 Paul. *Fest.*, p. 24.20 L.

ATTINGE pro attingam posuere.

F 2 Paul. *Fest.*, p. 25.10 L.

ALETUDO corporis pinguedo.

F 3 Paul. *Fest.*, p. 63.18 L.

DICE pro dicam antiqui posuere.

FRAGMENTA DUBIAE AUCTORITATIS

F 55 Anonymous grammatical work

putei ["wells"; also neut.], of masculine gender, like Cato
and Varro [cf. Varro, *Rust.* 1.57.2, with specific meaning].

FRAGMENTA DUBIAE AUCTORITATIS
(F 1–15)

*associated with Cato, while they have been connected with
Cato in the history of scholarship and might provide information about his language and his reception, they are
included as a separate category. Some editors assign fragments tentatively attributed to the* Orations *here, on the
basis of* ORF[4] *(Orat. F 91, 107A, 195, 195b, 241, 244), to
this more doubtful category.*

F 1 Paul the Deacon, *Epitome of Festus*

They put *attinge* instead of *attingam* ["I will touch"; different forms of future tense (cf. *Inc.* F 10)].

F 2 Paul the Deacon, *Epitome of Festus*

aletudo ["fatness"], fullness of body.[1]

> [1] This explanation is given in between the discussion of words
> attributed to Cato; thus, this word might also be among those
> used by him.

F 3 Paul the Deacon, *Epitome of Festus*

The ancients put *dice* instead of *dicam* ["I will say"; different forms of future tense (cf. *Inc.* F 10)].

F 4 Paul. *Fest.*, p. 81.22–23 L.

FEROCIT apud Catonem ferociter agit [*Inc.* F 29].
FIVERE item[1] pro figere.[2]

> [1] idem *Lindemann*   [2] figere *vel* fugere *codd.*

F 5 Fest., p. 138.27–36 L.

MATRONI⟨S AURUM REDDITUM⟩ . . . to[1] ait, quod . . . fuisse
re[2] . . . et eam a . . . ⟨testi⟩monio in . . .⟨ma⟩tronae orna
. . . Apolloniqui[3] . . . quod contule . . . a Gallis Senoni⟨bus⟩
. . . tum est a pop⟨ulo Romano.[4] . . .⟩

> [1] ⟨Ca⟩to *Mueller*: ⟨Sinnius Capi⟩to *Ursinus*
> [2] re⟨stitutum aurum ex quo P. R. craterem fecerat⟩ *Ursinus*   [3] et eam A⟨pollini Delphos miserat, ut est testi⟩monio in⟨dex tabella; quod quidem aurum dederunt ma⟩tronae orna⟨tui demptum suo, ut votum solveretur⟩ Apolloni *Ursinus*
> [4] qui⟨dam dicunt de eo potius esse intellegendum⟩ quod contule⟨runt olim matronae ad Capitolium⟩ a G. Senoni⟨bus liberandum; id eis postea reddi⟩tum est a populo Romano *Ursinus*

F 6 Fest., p. 220.7–8 L.

OSTENDE, ostendam; ut permultis[1] aliis exemplis eius
generis[2] manifestum est.

> [1] permultis *vel* pro multis *codd.*: pro multis *ed. princ.*
> [2] eius generis *om. unus cod. (non ed. princ.)*

FRAGMENTA DUBIAE AUCTORITATIS

F 4 Paul the Deacon, *Epitome of Festus*

ferocit ["he acts in a fierce manner"] in Cato [means] "he acts fiercely" [*Inc.* F 29].
fivere likewise[1] instead of *figere* ["to fasten, fix"].

---

1 This linking word might suggest that this lemma also refers to Cato.

F 5 Festus

"⟨gold returned to the⟩ ladie⟨s of the households⟩" . . . ⟨Ca⟩to[1] [?] says that . . . to have been . . . and her . . . by ⟨testi⟩mony for . . . ⟨la⟩dies of the household adorned . . . to Apollo . . . that . . . from the Gallic Senon⟨es⟩ [people in the Seine valley] . . . then it is from the Roman People . . . [?]

---

1 The ending *-to* of the name of the author of the following quotation might point to Cato, but could also be a residue of other names (e.g., Sinnius Capito, also quoted by Festus). The quotation is very lacunose.

F 6 Festus

ostende: *ostendam* ["I will show"; different forms of future tense (cf. *Inc.* F 10)]; as is clear by very many other examples of that sort.

CATO

F 7 Fest., p. 294.9–12 L.

⟨POSIMI⟩RIUM[1] esse ait Antistius . . . ⟨ponti⟩ficalis[2] pome-
rium, id est l[3] . . . Cato.[4] olim quidem omn[5] . . .

[1] *suppl. Epit.*   [2] ⟨in commentario iuris ponti⟩ficalis *Scaliger*   ficalis *cod.*: ⟨ponti⟩ficale *Mommsen (ex Epit.)*
[3] l *vel* b *cod. teste Loewio*   [4] l⟨ocum pro muro, ut ait⟩
Cato *Mueller*   [5] omn⟨em urbem conprehendebat praeter
Aven⟩tinum nunc etiam intra aed⟨ificia finitur⟩ *Mueller*

F 8 *P.Oxy.* XVII 2088

] . ineo . . . [
]isi si quis · sent[
]to · in sua · centu[ria
no]men · ferre · posset n[e quis suffragii?

?iure p]rivar[etur] hae · et · ceterae · cent[uriae
quae] nunc · sunt · omnes · Servi · Tulli · [
qui pri]mus · omnino · centurias · fecit · [
] . ceres · Ser · Tullius · rex · belli · stip[end
] causa · exercitum · conscripsit · co[.] . . . [
] cum · finitumis · belligerabat · deinde · o[mnes?

] . u perdito · divisit · pagosque · in tribu[s distribuit?

?post]ea · in · oppido 'quo' qui[[.o]]sque · pago · civis ·
ha[bitabat

---

[1] Heichelheim (1957) notes that the content and wording of
this papyrus from the second century AD resemble a report of
these matters in Dionysius of Halicarnassus, where he mentions
Cato as one of his sources (Dion. Hal. *Ant. Rom.* 4.15.1: *Orig.*

F 7 Festus

Antistius [M. Antistius Labeo, lawyer in the Augustan pe-
riod] says that ⟨*posimi*⟩*rium* is . . . ⟨ponti⟩fical . . . a
boundary, that is . . . Cato. Once at least . . .[1]

[1] Since the reading of the name Cato seems certain, it is likely
that the passage included a comment on his usage of the word
under discussion, though details can no longer be recovered.

F 8 Oxyrhynchus papyrus[1]

   . . .
   . . . if anyone . . .
   . . . in their century . . .
   . . . could enter the name so ⟨that nobody of the
      voting (?)
(?) right ⟨was⟩ deprived, these and other centu⟨ries
   which⟩ are now all those of Servius Tullius . . .
who⟩ was the first at all to create centuries . . .
   . . . king Ser. Tullius military serv⟨ice
   . . . for the sake of . . . recruited an army . . .
   . . . when he was waging war with neighbors, then
      ⟨all (?)
   . . . having been lost, he divided into districts and
      ⟨distributed⟩ (?) into tribes
lat⟩er (?) in the town, in which district each citizen liv⟨ed

F 17); Heichelheim therefore suggests that the papyrus, which
does not identify the author or the title of the text, is a fragment
from Cato's *Origines* I. Other scholars have argued against this
hypothesis (e.g., Schröder 1971, 189; Chassignet 1986, xxxix–xl;
Suerbaum 2002, 538 [with further references]), and it is not generally accepted (see also the brief commentary in *P.Oxy.*).

] exque · pagis · milites · conquirebantu[r et tributum?

e] pagis · cogebatur · primoque · in pago [arx?

con]dita · est · eaque · Roma · muro [. . .] . [
]quis · at · Romam · quadrata · r[
c]aput · Romam quad[rat]am [

F 9 Q. Gargilius Martialis, *Medicinae ex holeribus et po-mis* 30 (*De cauliculo*)

Cato tradit populum Romanum sexcentis fere annis medi-cina brassicae usum. nondum enim in urbem commeave-rant medici, qui in artem redegerunt quemadmodum magno sanitas constaret[1] et peregrina pigmenta secum attulerunt ut illis inponerent pretia quae vellent. ceterum militares viri gloriosas cicatrices gratuito holere curabant, eodem horto usi ad salutem dum illos pascit et sanat. po-nam primo in loco medicamentum re vera ita appellan-dum Catonis antidotum, quod ille ex brassica componen-dum putavit dolori capitis, oculorum caligini, stomacho et praecordiis profuturum. crudam cum coliandro et ruta et menta et radiculis laseris, ex aceto et melle conteri iubet

---

[1] constaret *Maire*: constet *vel* constat *codd.*

... and from the districts soldiers were sought ⟨and
       payment (?)
from⟩ the districts was forced, and in the first district
       ⟨the citadel (?)
was ⟨found⟩ed, and that Rome with a wall ...
... who ... Rome by square ...
the capital, *Roma quadrata* ["square Rome"][2] ...

[2] The original meaning of "square Rome" is uncertain, and
the phrase was later interpreted in various ways. It seems to have
described initially the area of early Rome and then become a
toponym, applied to a particular place in Rome (on the term's
meaning and application, see Wiseman 2015, 114–20).

F 9 Gargilius Martialis, *Medicines from Vegetables and
Fruit* (*On Cabbage*)

Cato reports that the Roman People used cabbage as a
medicine for about six hundred years. For doctors had not
yet come into the city, who turned into an art how much
health was worth and brought foreign ingredients for oint-
ments with them, so that they could place on them which-
ever prices they wished. For the rest, soldiers treated
honorable scars with cabbage for free, using the same
garden for their health, while it feeds and heals them. I
will put in first place the drug that truly should be called
"Cato's antidote," since he believed that something to be
made out of cabbage would help a headache, blindness of
the eyes, the stomach, and the heart. He instructs that it
be ground while raw, with coriander, roots, mint, and little

ac mane ieiunis duorum acetabulorum mensura propinari. ceterum brassica hoc modo curat: vulneribus non solum recentibus verum etiam veteribus, canceratis quoque, si prius aqua calida fota sint, crudam contritam bis die imponi ‹iubet›. et impetigines[2] credit hoc modo tritam sine ulceratione sanare. podagrae atque articularibus morbis cum ruta et coliandro et hordei farina et salis mica utiliter admoveri putat, fistulas itemque luxata discutere, tumores[3] aut evocare aut spargere inpositam, insomnia ac vigilias compescere si decocta cum sale et oleo ieiunis in cibo detur, decoctae aquam in fomento nervis articulisque prodesse. eius qui brassicam ederit urinam servari iubet; quam calefactam nervis utilem asseverat. pueros etiam numquam debiles fieri si ex ea urina frequenter laventur. hactenus de Catone. nunc ad medicos transeamus; . . .

2 ‹iubet›. et impetigines *Rose*
3 tumores *vel* humores *codd.*

pieces of root of the *silphium* plant, based on vinegar and honey, and be given to drink to people, in a measure of two small cups, early in the morning, before food is taken. Further, he heals with cabbage in this way: ⟨he instructs⟩ that it be applied, raw and ground, to wounds, not only fresh ones, but also old ones, even cancerous ones, if they have previously been warmed with hot water, twice a day. And he thinks that, rubbed on in this way, it heals sores on the skin without ulceration. He believes that it can be usefully applied to gout and illnesses of the joints, with roots, and coriander, and barley flour, and morsels of salt, breaks down ulcers and likewise sprains, draws out or disperses swellings, when placed upon them, settles insomnia and wakefulness if, cooked with salt and oil, it is given with food to those who have been fasting, and, its cooking water, in a warm application, helps muscles and joints. He instructs that the urine of someone who has eaten cabbage is saved; he declares that, heated up, it is useful for the muscles. And also that children never become weak if they are frequently washed with that urine. So far from Cato. Now let's turn to doctors; . . .[1]

[1] For Cato's views on cabbage and its use, see also *Agr.* 156–57; Plin. *HN* 19.136, 20.78, 20.80–83. On the basis of an analysis of content and structure of this passage, Schönberger (1969) suggests that it includes material ultimately taken from Cato, though this has been questioned, for instance, by Stok (1993, esp. 225–27), who regards Pliny (who in turn mentions Cato) as the main source; on this author and his role in the history of Latin writings on medicine, see Stok 1993.

CATO

F 10 Porph. ad Hom. *Il.* 9.383

ὡς δὲ Κάτων¹ ἱστορεῖ, ἡ Διόσπολις ἡ μεγάλη πρὸ τοῦ ὑπὸ Περσῶν ἀφανισθῆναι κώμας μὲν εἶχε τρισμυρίας ,γλ', ἀνθρώπων δὲ μυριάδας ψ', ἑκατὸν δὲ πυλαῖς διεκοσμεῖτο.

¹ Κάτων *codd.*: Κάστωρ *Wyttenbach ap. Dindorf*

F 11 Non., p. 134.29–31 M. = 195 L.

LATROCINARI, militare mercede. Plautus Cornicula{ria}: ". . . latrocinatus¹ annos decem {mercedem} Demetrio."² qui aput regem in latrocinio fuisti, stipendium acceptitasti.

¹ qui regi latrocinatu's *codd. Varro, Ling.* 7.52   ² annos X mercedem in tiberio *codd.*: decem annos Demetrio *codd. Varr.*: annos decem regi Demetrio *Onions*: annos decem {mercedem}. Cato in Tiberium *Müller*

F 10 Porphyry, *Commentary on Homer, Iliad*

As Cato[1] reports, before being routed by the Persians, Diospolis Magna [i.e., Egyptian Thebes] had 33,030 villages, 7,000,000 people, and it was adorned by one hundred gates.

[1] The transmitted text assigns the comment to Cato. Because of the content of the statement, this attribution has been doubted, and the text is often emended and assigned to Castor of Rhodes (*FGrHist* 250 F 20; cf. also Hekataios, *BNJ* 264 F 19a).

F 11 Nonius Marcellus

latrocinari ["to perform military service for pay"], for military pay. Plautus [says] in *Cornicula* [F 61 Lindsay = 63 Monda]: ". . . having performed military service for ten years for Demetrius." You, who have been in military service with the king, have accepted military pay.[1]

[1] The above version of the text seems widely accepted, also because of the quotation of what appears to be the same Plautus fragment in Varro (*Ling.* 7.52). Müller (1868) argues that repeated (and usually deleted) *mercedem* hides the name of the author of the next quotation, that *in tiberio* should not be emended to *Demetrio*, but rather to *in Tiberium*, and that therefore the following words should be assigned to Cato's speech against the exile Tiberius (*Orat.* F 202).

CATO

F 12 Iul. Vict., *Ars* 27, *RLM*, p. 448.1–5 (p. 105.18–23 Giomini / Celentano)

in familiaribus litteris primo brevitas observanda: ipsarum quoque sententiarum ne diu circumferatur, quod Cato ait, ambitio, sed ita recidantur, ut numquam verbi aliquid deesse videatur: unum "te" scilicet, quod intellegentia suppleatur, in epistolis Tullianis ad Atticum et Axium frequentissimum est.

F 13 Diom., *GL* I, p. 310.2–20

chriarum exercitatio in casus sic variatur. nominativo casu numero singulari, Marcus Porcius Cato dixit litterarum radices amaras esse, fructus iocundiores; genetivo casu, Marci Porcii Catonis dictum fertur litterarum radices amaras esse, fructus iocundiores; dativo, Marco Porcio Catoni placuit dicere litterarum radices amaras esse, fructus iocundiores; accusativo, Marcum Porcium Catonem dixisse ferunt litterarum radices amaras esse, fructus iocundiores; vocativo, o tu Marce Porci Cato, ne tu egregie dixisti litterarum radices amaras esse, fructus dulciores; ablativo, a Marco Porcio Catone dictum accepimus litterarum radices amaras esse, fructus dulciores; nominativo plurali, Marci Porcii Catones dixerunt litterarum radices

F 12 Iulius Victor

In private letters, first of all, brevity has to be observed, so that "the period," as Cato says,[1] also of the sentences themselves is not drawn out lengthily, and instead they are cut back in such a way that some word should never seem to be missing: only as regards "you," obviously, which is supplied by comprehension, it is very frequent in the letters of Tullius [Cicero] to Atticus and Axius.

[1] The reference to Cato in connection with such a technical term suggests a theoretical discussion of principles of writing. As there is no evidence that Cato the Elder wrote a work of this kind, the attribution of this statement to Cato has been doubted.

F 13 Diomedes

The exercise concerning *chriae* ["topics of general application set for rhetorical study and exercise"] goes through variations as regards the cases like this [cf. Otto 1890, 195, s.v. *litterae* 1]. In the nominative singular case, Marcus Porcius Cato said that the roots of learning are bitter, the fruits more pleasant; in the genitive case, a statement of Marcus Porcius Cato is said to be that the roots of learning are bitter, the fruits more pleasant; in the dative, it pleased Marcus Porcius Cato to say that the roots of learning are bitter, the fruits more pleasant; in the accusative, they say that Marcus Porcius Cato said that the roots of learning are bitter, the fruits more pleasant; in the vocative, you, Marcus Porcius Cato, how excellently have you said that the roots of learning are bitter, the fruits sweeter; in the ablative, we learn that it was said by Marcus Porcius Cato that the roots of learning are bitter, the fruits sweeter; in the nominative plural, the Marci Porcii Catones said that

CATO

amaras esse, fructus dulciores; genetivo, Marcorum Porciorum Catonum dictum fertur litterarum radices amaras esse, fructus dulciores; dativo, Marcis Porciis Catonibus placuit dicere, id quoque; accusativo, Marcos Porcios Catones dixisse ferunt, id quoque; vocativo, o Marci Porcii Catones, ne vos egregie dixistis, id quoque; ablativo, a Marcis Porciis Catonibus dictum accepimus litterarum radices amaras esse, fructus dulciores. hoc quoque exemplo ceterae chriae declinationes subicientur. . . . item nominativo, Marcus Porcius Cato dixit leges nervos esse civitatium: . . .

F 14 Lydus, *Mens.* 2.2

. . . Ῥωμαῖοι δὲ τὸ μὲν πρῶτον ἴσα τοῖς Βαβυλωνίοις κατὰ τὸν φυσικὸν νόμον καὶ αὐτοὶ τὴν ἡμέραν μόνην ἀπὸ ἀνατολῶν ἡλίου μέχρι δυσμῶν ἡμέραν ὡρίζοντο, τὴν νύκτα μηδὲν λογιζόμενοι· ὕστερον δὲ ἀπὸ μέσης νυκτὸς ἤγουν τῆς ἀρχῆς τῆς ἑβδόμης ὥρας αὐτῆς καὶ ἕως μέσης πάλιν τῆς ἐπιούσης νυκτὸς ἐτύπωσαν τὴν ἡμέραν καὶ νομίζεσθαι καὶ ὀνομάζεσθαι<, ὡς ὁ Κάτων[1] φησὶ καὶ ὁ Λαβεών>.[2]

[1] Κα<πί>των *Cumont (cf. Ateius Capito, F 35 Strzelecki)*
[2] *suppl. Cumont ex Anastasio*

the roots of learning are bitter, the fruits sweeter; in the genitive, a statement of the Marci Porcii Catones is said to be that the roots of learning are bitter, the fruits sweeter; in the dative, it pleased the Marci Porcii Catones to say, this again; in the accusative, they say that the Marci Porcii Catones said, this again; in the vocative, you, Marci Porcii Catones, how excellently have you said, this again; in the ablative, we learn that it was said by the Marci Porcii Catones that the roots of learning are bitter, the fruits sweeter. And to this example other declinations of topics will be appended. . . . Equally in the nominative, Marcus Porcius Cato said that laws are the sinews of communities: . . .[1]

[1] Since in the context of the discussion on cases Diomedes also mentions examples clearly taken from the works of authors whose writings survive in complete form (e.g., Virgil), what is attributed to Cato here might go back to an actual utterance by him or could be a phrase made up for the purposes of the exercise.

F 14 Lydus, *On the Months*

. . . , and the Romans, at the beginning, like the Babylonians, in line with the law of nature, themselves too defined the day only from the rising of the sun until its setting, not accounting for the night in any way; later, they decided that the day should be considered and indicated from the middle of the night, that is the beginning of its seventh hour, until the middle again of the following night‹, as Cato says and [Cornelius] Labeo›.[1]

[1] This passage includes a reference to Cato (or Capito) if the text of Lydus is supplemented by material in a work (*Hexaemeron* 1.9.9) by Anastasius of Sinai (and potentially emended), as suggested by Cumont (1929, 31–32; 1930).

F 15 Oxford, Bodleian Library, MS. Arch. Selden. B. 16, fol. 7r

Hoc excerptum ex libris Catonis de originibus

Dardanus ex Iove et Electra filia Athlantis natus. ab Italia ex responsis locum mutans, Samotrachiam insulam delatus est. et hinc Phrygiam devenit, quam Dardaniam a suo nomine nominavit. ex quo Erichthonius natus est, qui iisdem locis regnavit. ex Erichthonio Trous, qui iustitia et pietate laudabilis fuit. isque ut memoriam nominis sui faceret eternam, Troiam apellari iussit. duos filios habuit, Ilum Assaracumque. Ilusque maior natu erat. regnavit et Ilium Troiam vocari iussit. Assaracus privatus decessit et genuit Capyn filium. ex quo Anchises natus est pater Aeneae. Ilo Laomedon fuit filius, pater Priami, sub quo Troia capta est a Graecis. sicut Dares scripsit. qui et meminit . . .

F 15 Medieval manuscript

This is an excerpt from Cato's books on the origins

Dardanus was born from Jupiter and Electra, the daughter of Atlas. Moving his abode from Italy as a result of oracles, he came to the island of Samothrace. And from there he went to Phrygia, which he called Dardania from his name. From him Erichthonius was born, who reigned in the same area. From Erichthonius Tros [was born], who was praiseworthy on account of his justice and dutifulness. And so that he set up an eternal memory of his name, he ordered that [the place] should be called Troy. He had two sons, Ilus and Assaracus. And Ilus was the elder. He reigned and ordered that Troy was to be called Ilium. Assaracus withdrew to private life and fathered the son Capys. From him Anchises was born, the father of Aeneas. For Ilus Laomedon was a son, the father of Priam, under whom Troy was captured by the Greeks. Thus Dares writes. He also mentions . . .[1]

[1] This passage is found in a manuscript attributed to the medieval writer William of Malmesbury (ca. 1100). The section to which it belongs consists of a compilation of sources (including also, e.g., Dares, Virgil, Solinus) on genealogical stories connected with Troy; what is assigned to Cato is followed by summaries of further details linked to other writers. (On this manuscript and an indication of its mention of Cato, see Munk Olsen 1982, 58.) The passage is transmitted in similar form also in other sources without any mention of Cato. It is unlikely that here any information has been taken directly from Cato, but since in this source the passage is attributed to Cato, it is included in this edition (with spelling and punctuation standardized).

FRAGMENTA CATONI FALSO ATTRIBUTA (F 1–7)

These passages have been linked with Cato the Elder by individual scholars, but it is now thought that the attribution is based on incorrect identifications of the Cato mentioned, errors in the transmission, or hypothetical recon-

F 1 Sen. *Vit. beat.* 21.3–4

M. Cato cum laudaret Curium et Coruncanium et illud saeculum in quo censorium crimen erat paucae argenti lamellae, possidebat ipse quadragies sestertium, minus sine dubio quam Crassus, plus quam Censorius Cato. maiore spatio, si comparentur, proavum vicerat quam a Crasso vinceretur, et, si maiores illi obvenissent opes, non sprevisset. [4] nec enim se sapiens indignum ullis muneribus fortuitis putat: non amat divitias sed mavult; non in animum illas sed in domum recipit, nec respuit possessas sed continet, et maiorem virtuti suae materiam subministrari vult.

FRAGMENTA CATONI FALSO
ATTRIBUTA (F 1–7)

structions of lacunose texts (as indicated in notes to each passage). To present all material associated with Cato, they are given as part of this edition, yet in a separate category.

F 1 Seneca, *On the Happy Life*

When M. Cato[1] [the Younger] was praising Curius [M'. Curius Dentatus, cos. 290, 275, 274, censor 272 BC], and Coruncanius [Ti. Coruncanius, cos. 280 BC], and that age in which it was a censorial offense to have a few small silver coins, he himself possessed four million sesterces, less without doubt than Crassus [M. Licinius Crassus Dives (*ORF*[4] 102)], but more than Cato the ex-censor. If they are compared, he had outstripped his great-grandfather by a greater distance than he was outstripped by Crassus, and, if greater wealth had fallen to his lot, he would not have scorned it. [4] For indeed the wise man does not deem himself undeserving of any of the gifts of fortune. He does not love riches, but he would rather have them; he does not admit them to his heart, but to his house; and he does not reject the riches he has, but he keeps them, and he wishes ampler resources to be made available for the exercise of his virtue.

[1] The passage was identified as a possible fragment from the works of Cato the Elder by Klussmann (1860), but the context makes it clear that the reported statement belongs to Cato the Younger.

F 2 Gell. *NA* 6.10.1–3

⟨Ut⟩ "ususcapio" copulate recto vocabuli casu dicitur, ita
"pignoriscapio" coniuncte eadem vocabuli forma dictum
esse.—[1] ut[1] haec "ususcapio" dicitur copulato vocabulo,
"a" littera in eo tractim pronuntiata, ita "pignoriscapio"
iuncte {sunt}[2] et producte dicebatur. [2] verba Catonis[3]
sunt ex primo epistolicarum quaestionum: "pignoriscapio
ob aes militare, quod aes a tribuno aerario miles accipere
debebat, vocabulum seorsum fit."[4] [3] per quod satis dilu-
cet, hanc "capionem" posse dici quasi hanc "captionem"
et in usu et in pignore.

[1] ut *vel* et *codd.*
[2] *del. Hertz*
[3] Catonis *codd.*: Varronis *Lipsius*
[4] fit *vel* sit *vel* sibi *codd.*

F 3 Fest., p. 162.11–13 L.

NEGIBUNDUM a⟨ntiqui pro negante dixerunt⟩[1] . . . ea,[2]
quam scripsit . . . negibundus . . .

[1] *suppl. ex Epit.*
[2] ⟨Cato in⟩ ea *Ursinus*

F 2 Gellius, *Attic Nights*

That, ⟨as⟩ *ususcapio* ["acquisition of ownership through uninterrupted possession"] is used as the nominative case of a noun in compound format, so *pignoriscapio* ["seizing of a pledge to enforce payment of money due"] has been used as the same form of a noun in joined-up format.—[1] As ⟨*haec*⟩ *ususcapio* is used as a compound noun, in which the letter *a* is pronounced long, so *pignoriscapio* was pronounced as one word {are} and with a long syllable. [2] These are the words of Cato from the first [book] of the *Epistolary questions*:[1] "*pignoriscapio*, in connection with military pay that a soldier used to be entitled to receive from the public paymaster, forms a word by itself." [3] From this it is sufficiently clear that one can use ⟨*haec*⟩ *capio* as if it were ⟨*haec*⟩ *captio* in connection with both *usus* and *pignus*.

[1] The passage gives Cato a work entitled *Epistolary questions*, not attested otherwise. The transmitted name is often changed to Varro (passage included as F 224 in *GRF*; accepted in Cugusi 1967, 81), since a work of that title is mentioned for Varro elsewhere (F 223–28 *GRF*), and in *De lingua Latina* (Varro, *Ling.* 5.181) Varro talks about words for military pay.

F 3 Festus

negibundus ["denying"] the ⟨ancients used for *negans* ["denying"; participle of *nego*] . . . in that [speech] that he wrote . . . denying . . .[1]

[1] The passage was included as a fragment from an unidentified speech of Cato in Meyer's edition (1842, 150: *Orat. Inc.* F 33), on the basis of Ursinus' supplement of the lacunose transmitted text.

CATO

F 4 Macrob. *Sat.* 3.6.5

meminit huius arae et Cato[1] de liberis educandis in haec
verba: "nutrix haec omnia faciebat in verbenis ac tubis sine
hostia ut Deli ad Apollinis Genetivi aram."

[1] Cato *codd.*: Varro Cato *Meurs (Logist. F 11 Bolisani)*

F 5 Isid. *Diff.* 1, *praef.*

plerique veterum sermonum differentias distinguere
studuerunt, subtilius inter verba et verba aliquid inda-
gantes. . . . de his apud Latinos Cato primus scripsit, ad
cuius exemplum ipse paucissimas partim edidi, partim ex
auctorum libris[1] deprompsi tibique, lector, pro delectatione[2] notavi.

[1] decerpsi quidque verba pro simili significatione posita inter
se discrepent adiuncta proprietatis differentia *post* libris *add.*
cod. unus   [2] legentium *post* delectatione *add. codd. duo*

F 6 *Disticha Catonis, Epistula* (p. 4 Boas)

cum animadverterem quam plurimos graviter in via morum errare, succurrendum opinioni eorum et consu-
lendum famae existimavi, maxime ut gloriose viverent et

F 4 Macrobius, *Saturnalia*

Cato too mentions this altar [of Apollo] in [the work] on raising children,[1] with these words: "The nurse used to perform all these among sacred boughs and trumpets, without a victim, just as at the altar of Apollo the Begetter on Delos."

[1] A work with this title is elsewhere attributed to Varro. Therefore, the transmission is probably incorrect; thus, *Cato* is often changed to *Varro*, or the name of *Varro* is added (with *Cato* then seen as part of the title), or a lacuna is assumed.

F 5 Isidore, *On Differences between Words*

Many have endeavored to mark differences between old expressions, striving rather subtly to find something between one word and another. . . . The first to write about these [i.e., differences between meanings of words] among the Latins was Cato;[1] following his example, here, partly, I myself have published a very small number [of such distinctions], partly I have extracted them from the books of authors and put them down for your delectation, reader.

[1] A separate work on this topic by Cato is not attested elsewhere; the reference might be to comments on the meaning of words in other contexts.

F 6 *Disticha Catonis* (prefatory epistle)

When I noticed the great number of people who go seriously astray in the path of their habits of behavior, I believed that I should aid their esteem and take care of their reputation, especially so that they might live with glory

honorem contingerent. nunc te, fili carissime, docebo quo
pacto morem animi tui componas. igitur praecepta mea ita
legito ut intellegas. legere enim et non intellegere negle-
gere est.

F 7 Iosephus Iustus Scaliger, *Coniectanea in M. Teren-
tium Varronem De lingua Latina* (1565), p. 17 (ad Varro,
Ling. 5.42: . . . *Saturniam terram, ut etiam Ennius appellat*)

apparet manifesto esse versiculum Ennii, "Saturnius
illi / nomen erat, de quo late Saturnia terra." in fragmentis
Originum quae exstant nomine Catonis, idem Ennii ἀκρο-
τελεύτιον legitur: "a quo Saturnia olim, ubi nunc Capito-
lium: & ab ea latè Saturnia terra." itaque illud Virgilii
desumptum est ex Ennio, "Ianiculum huic, illi fuerat Saturnia nomen."

and obtain honor. Now, dearest son, I will teach you in what way to arrange the habit of your mind. Therefore, read my precepts in such a way that you understand them. For to read and not to understand is to ignore.[1]

[1] The passage, the introductory piece in the collection of *Disticha Catonis* (for a detailed discussion of its transmission, authenticity, and reception, see Boas 1934), is attributed to "Ps.-Cato" as an item in the letter collection assumed by Cugusi (1970, 69–70). It could be inspired by the historical Cato's writings to his son, but probably dates to a later period.

F 7 Joseph Justus Scaliger, *Notes on Varro's On the Latin Language* (on ". . . Saturnian land, as also Ennius calls it")

This clearly seems to be a little verse of Ennius [Enn. *Ann.* 25 V.² = 21 Skutsch]: "Saturnius was its name [old name of the Capitoline Hill], from which broadly Saturnian land [i.e., Latium or Italy]." In the fragments of the *Origines* that are extant under the name of Cato, the same phrase-ending from Ennius can be read: "from this once Saturnia, where the Capitol now [is], and from there broadly Saturnian land."[1] Therefore that [line] of Virgil has been taken from Ennius [Verg. *Aen.* 8.358]: "this one [i.e., one of two citadels] once had the name Ianiculum, that one Saturnia."

[1] This passage ascribed to Cato is found only in the early modern work by Scaliger, which has raised doubts on its authenticity. Chassignet (1986, xxxv–xxxvi) does not accept it as a fragment of Cato's *Origines*.

CONCORDANCES

Testimonia (T 1–99)
LCL → FRHist—ORF⁴—Cugusi

LCL	FRHist	ORF⁴	Cugusi
1	—	p. 18	—
2	—	—	—
3	—	—	—
4	—	—	—
5	—	p. 16	—
6	5a	—	II, p. 284
7a	—	—	—
7b	—	—	—
7c	—	—	—
7d	—	—	—
8	14a	—	—
9	—	—	—
10	10	—	—
11	5b	—	—
12	—	—	—
13	3, 16a	1	I, p. 250; II, p. 284
14	—	—	—
15	17	2	—
16	—	—	—

CONCORDANCES

LCL	FRHist	ORF[4]	Cugusi
17	—	—	—
18	—	—	—
19	—	—	—
20a	—	p. 17	—
20b	4	8	I, p. 250; II, p. 286
21	—	—	—
22	6a	—	—
23	—	—	II, p. 8
24	—	—	—
25	—	—	II, p. 8
26	1	3	I, p. 250; II, p. 284
27	18a	—	—
28	5c	—	—
29	11a	—	II, p. 286
30	—	—	—
31	8	—	II, p. 284
32a	—	—	—
32b	cf. 4	4	I, p. 250
32c	—	—	—
33	—	—	—
34	13d	—	—
35	2a	—	—
36	—	—	—
37	—	—	—
38	—	—	II, p. 8
39	—	—	—
40	23	—	—
41a	—	—	—

450

LCL	FRHist	ORF⁴	Cugusi
41b	—	—	—
42	—	5	I, p. 250
43	20	—	*Orig.* F 93; II, p. 286
44	—	—	II, p. 8
45	—	—	—
46	—	p. 18	I, p. 252
47	—	p. 17	—
48	—	—	II, p. 422
49	22a	—	—
50	—	—	—
51	—	6	—
52	—	p. 17	I, p. 250
53	—	7	—
54	—	—	—
55	—	9	I, p. 252
56	19a	p. 17	II, p. 468
57	—	10	—
58	—	—	—
59	21b	—	—
60	—	11	*Orat.* F 133
61	—	—	—
62	—	—	—
63	2b	—	II, pp. 8, 286
64	—	—	—
65	22b	—	—
66	22c	—	—
67	—	—	—
68	—	—	I, p. 252
69	—	—	—

LCL	FRHist	ORF[4]	Cugusi
70a	—	12	I, p. 252
70b	—	—	I, p. 252
71	18b, 22d	—	—
72	—	—	II, p. 8
73	18c	13	I, p. 252
74	—	14	I, p. 252
75	—	p. 18	I, p. 252
76	11b	—	II, p. 286
77	19b	—	I, p. 252
78	—	p. 18	I, p. 252
79	—	—	—
80	7	—	II, p. 286
81	—	15	—
82	—	—	—
83	11c	—	—
84	—	—	—
85	16b	—	—
86	—	—	I, p. 254
87	—	—	I, p. 254
88	22e	—	—
89a	—	—	—
89b	—	—	—
90	2c	—	II, p. 286
91a	—	—	I, p. 252
91b	—	16	I, p. 252
91c	—	—	I, p. 252
92	11d	—	II, p. 286
93	11e	—	*Orig.* F 54; II, p. 286

CONCORDANCES

LCL	FRHist	ORF[4]	Cugusi
94	—	—	—
95	—	—	II, p. 422
96	9 (*Orig.* F 3 Peter)	—	—
97	—	—	II, p. 458
98	—	—	II, p. 8
99	—	—	—

Origines (F 1–156)

LCL = FRHist → Jordan—Peter—Cugusi

LCL	Jordan	Peter	Cugusi
1a–b	I 1	1	1
2a–b	I 2	2	2
3	I 19	19	22
4a–b	I 8	4	10
5	I 9	8	11
6a–e	I 10	9	12a
7a–b	I 11	10	13
8a–b	—	11	14
9	I 12	12	15
10	—	—	16b
11	—	—	12b
12	I 13	13	16a
13a–b	I 17	17	20
14	I 15	15	18
15	I 21	22	25
16	I 16	16	19
17	I 22	23	27
18a–b	I 23	24	28
18c	*Op. inc.* 60	24	—
19	I 29	26	30
20	I 27	28	31
21	I 28	29	32
22	I 30	27	26
23	I 26	30	33
24a	I 4	7	9
24b	—	—	9

LCL	Jordan	Peter	Cugusi
25	I 24	25	29
26	I 25	21	24
27	II 3	36	40
28	II 33	63	68
29	II 31	65	70
30	II 30	33	36
31	II 12	35	39
32	II 34	64	69
33	II 2	34	38
34a–b	II 1	31–32	35, 34
35	II 28	61	64
36a–b	II 21	58	62
37	II 29	66	71
38	II 32	67	72
39	II 18	53	57
40	II 25	57	61
41	III 8	73	78
42	III 5	72	77
43	III 6	74	79
44	III 7	75	80
45	III 1	71	76
46a–b	II 10	43	47
47	II 16	52	53
48	II 11	39	44
49a–b	I 3	6	8
50	I 6	50	58
51	I 7	51	59
52	III 2	69	73
53	II 15	47	51

CONCORDANCES

LCL	Jordan	Peter	Cugusi
54	III 4	68	74
55	II 19	49	56
56	II 8	44	48
57	II 4	40	37
58	II 9	42	46
59	II 5	41	45
60	II 6	37	41
61	II 24	56	60
62	II 7	38	42
63	I 5	5	6
64	III 3	70	75
65	II 26	54	55
66a–b	I 18	18	21
67	II 22	59	65
68	II 23	60	66
69	II 17	48	52
70	II 13	45	49
71	II 20	46	50
72	II 14	62	67
73	I 14	14	17
74	—	—	7
75	—	—	43
76	IV 7	83	88
77a–b	IV 10	84	89
78	IV 12	86	91
79	IV 12	87	92
80	IV 1	77	81
81	IV 3	79	83
82	IV 4	82	86

LCL	Jordan	Peter	Cugusi
83	IV 14	91	96
84a–b	IV 2	78	82
85	IV 5	81	85
86	IV 13	90	95
87	V 1	95a	100
88	V 2	95b	101
89	V 3	95c	102
90	V 4	95d	103
91	V 5	95e	104
92	V 6	95f	105
93	V 7	95g	106
94	V 8	96	109
95	V 13	99	114
96	V 14	100	115
97	V 11	101	113
98	V 17	102	116
99	V 9	97	110
100	V 16	103	117
101	V 15	104	112
102	V 10	98	111
103	VI 1	105	118
104	VII 1	108	120
105	VII 2	109	121
106a	VII 3b	107	123
106b	VII 3b	—	123
107a–b	VII 3a	106	119, 122
108	VII 7	111	127
109	VII 8	113	128

CONCORDANCES

LCL	Jordan	Peter	Cugusi
110	VII 15	117	125
111	VII 4	110	124
112	VII 14	116	126
113a–c	VII 12	118	4
114a–b	IV 8	—	—
115	IV 9	88	93
116	VII 5	93	98
117	I 20	20	23
118	*Inc.* 1	125	135
119a–b	VII 9	114	129
120	*Inc.* 6	121	131
121	*Inc.* 5	120	130
122	*Inc.* 2	122	132
123	I 1	1	1
124	*Inc.* 4	123	133
125	II 27	55	63
126	—	—	—
127	*Inc.* 3	124	134
128	VII 6	94	99
129	*Dicta* 72	—	*Op. inc.* 3
130a–b	*Op. inc.* 15	127	3
131	*Dicta* 64	—	5
132	*Op. inc.* 16	132	*Op. inc.* 12
133	V 12	92	97
134	*Mil.* 15	131	*Op. inc.* 39
135	*Op. inc.* 68, *Dicta* 31	129	*Orat.* 11
136	*Op. inc.* 70	130	*Op. inc.* 25
137	VII 11	112	*Op. inc.* 1

CONCORDANCES

LCL	Jordan	Peter	Cugusi
138	*Op. inc.* 31	126	*Op. inc.* 4
139	*Op. inc.* 35	—	*Op. inc.* 7
140	*Op. inc.* 6	133	*Op. inc.* 31
141	*Op. inc.* 17	—	*Op. inc.* 9
142	*Op. inc.* 7	134	136
143	*Op. inc.* 1	136	*Op. inc.* 5
144	VII 13	119	*Op. inc.* 11
145	VII 10	115	*Op. inc.* 2
146	III 10	89	94
147	*Op. inc.* 11	139	*Op. inc.* 6
148	IV 6	80	84
149	*Op. inc.* 12	140	*Op. inc.* 8
150	IV 11	85	90
151	*Dicta* 79	—	*Op. inc.* 84
152	*Op. inc.* 2	142	*Op. inc.* 10
153	*Op. inc.* 3	141	*Op. inc.* 32, 38
154	*Op. inc.* 9	143	*Op. inc.* 16
155	—	143A	*Op. inc.* 85
156	*Op. inc.* 18	—	*Op. inc.* 41

Orationes (F 17–254A)

LCL = *ORF*[4] → Jordan—Cugusi

LCL	Jordan	Cugusi
17A	—	—
17	V 1	1
18	V 2	2
18A	—	*Dicta* 57
18B	—	—
18C	—	—
18D	—	—
18E	—	—
18F	—	—
18G	—	—
18H	—	—
19	IV	3
20	VII	4
21	I 1	5
22	I 2	6
23	I 3	7
24	*Dub.* 2	8
25	I 4	9
26	I 28	10
27	I 7	14
28	I 6	15
29	I 8	17
30	I 9	18
31	I 10	21
32	I 20	23; *Epist.* F 1
33	I 14	22

CONCORDANCES

LCL	Jordan	Cugusi
34	I 21	24
35	I 13	25
36	I 16	27
37	I 15	26
38	I 17	28
39	I 29	33
40	I 19	29
41	I 18	30
42	I 11	31
43	I 12	12
44	I 22	34
45	I 23	35
46	I 24	36
47	I 25	37
48	I 5	32
49	I 26	39
50	I 27	13
51	III 1	16
52	III 2	19
53	—	20
54	*Op. inc.* 67	38
55	*Op. inc.* 68; *Dicta* 31	11
56	VI 1	40
57	VI 2	41
58	IX	42; p. 252
59	VIII 1	43; p. 252
60	VIII 2	44
61	VIII 3	45
62	VIII 4	46
63	VIII 5	47

CONCORDANCES

LCL	Jordan	Cugusi
64	VIII / IX 1	155
65	VIII / IX 2	156
66	XIII	48
66A	—	—
67	XV	49
68	XVI	50
69	XVII 1	54
70	XVII 2	56
71	XVII 3	55
72	XVIII 2	59
73	XVIII 1	60
74	XVIII 3	61
75	XVIII 8	62
76	XVIII 4	63
77	XVIII 7	64
78	XVIII 5	65
79	*Dicta* 21	*Op. inc.* 30
80	XVIII 6	66
81	XVIII 9	67
82	XVIII 10	205
83	XX 1	57
84	XX 2	58
85	LXIV 1	68
86	LXIV 2	69
87	XXII	70
88	LXXVI	175
89	p. 65	176
90	LXII 1	177
91	LXII 2; *Dub.* 3	211
92	LXII 3	212

CONCORDANCES

LCL	Jordan	Cugusi
93	XXI	51
94	LXXII	52
95	XXIVa 1	53
96	XLVIII	178
97	LXXIII	71
98	LXXI	72
99	XIX 3	73
100	XIX 4	74
101	XIX 2	75
102	XIX 1	76
103	XIX 5	77
104	XIX 6	78
105	XIX 7	79
106	XLVII	80
107	LXI	179
107A	*Dub.* 3	*Dub.* 7
108	XVIII 11	180
109	XLVI	160
110	L	181
111	XL 1	81
112	XL 2	82
113	XL 3	86
114	XL 4	84
115	XL 5	85
116	XL 6	83
117	XL 7	87
118	XL 8	88
119	XL 9	89
120	*Dicta* 26	*Dicta* 20
121	XXIII 2	91

LCL	Jordan	Cugusi
122	XXIII 1	90
123	XLV	164
124	XXIVa 2	92
125	*Inc.* 3	213
126	*Op. inc.* 22	*Op. inc.* 15
127	*Op. inc.* 9	*Op. inc.* 16
128	XI 1	93
129	XI 2	94
130	XI 3	95
131	XI 4	96
132	LVI	163
133	XII 1	97
134	XII 2	98
135	XXIV	99
136	XXVI	182
137	XXV 1	100
138	XXV 2	101
139	XXVII 1	128
140	XXVII 2	129
141	XXVII 3	130
142	XXVII 4	210
143	XXVII 5	*Op. inc.* 35
144	*Orig.* VII 13	*Op. inc.* 11
145	*Dicta* 2	*Op. inc.* 24
146	*Dicta* 78	131
147	XXVIII	102
148	XIV 1	103
149	XIV 2; *Orig.* VII 12	104
150	XXIX	105
151	*Dicta* 66–67	106

CONCORDANCES

LCL	Jordan	Cugusi
152	XXX 1	107
153	XXX 2	108
154	cf. XXXI	109
155	XXXI	111
156	—	—
157	—	112
158	XXXII 1	113
159	XXXII 2	114
160	XXXII 3	115
161	XXXIII 1	116
162	XXXIII 2	117
163	XXXIV; *Orig.* V 1	118; *Orig.* 100
164	XXXIV; *Orig.* V 2	119; *Orig.* 101
165	XXXIV; *Orig.* V 3	120; *Orig.* 102
166	XXXIV; *Orig.* V 4	121; *Orig.* 103
167	XXXIV; *Orig.* V 5	122; *Orig.* 104
168	XXXIV; *Orig.* V 6	123; *Orig.* 105
169	XXXIV; *Orig.* V 7	125, 124; *Orig.* 107, 106
169A	—	126a; *Orig.* 108
170	XXXIV	—
171	XXXIV	—
172	XXXIX	127
173	II	169
174	*Inc.* 10	218
175	*Op. inc.* 66	*Op. inc.* 49
176	LIV	171
177	X 1	134
178	X 2	135
179	X 3	136

CONCORDANCES

LCL	Jordan	Cugusi
180	X 4	137
181	X 5	138
182	XI / XII 1	157
183	XI / XII 2	158
184	XI / XII 3	159
185	XXXVI 1	139
186	XXXVI 2	140
187	XXXV	142
188	*Op. inc.* 65	143
189	*Dicta* 17	144
190	LXIII	145
191	XXXVII 1	146
192	XXXVII 2	148
193	XXXVII 3	147
194	XXXVII 4	149
195	p. LXXXVI	*Dub.* 11
195b	p. LXXXVI	*Dub.* 12
196	XXXVIII; *Orig.* VII 1	151; *Orig.* 120
197	XXXVIII; *Orig.* VII 2	153; *Orig.* 121
198	XXXVIII; *Orig.* VII 3a	151, 154; *Orig.* 122
198A	cf. *Orig.* VII 3	cf. F 154
198B	—	cf. F 154
198C	cf. *Orig.* VII 3	—
199	XXXVIII; *Orig.* VII 3b	*Orig.* 123
199A	cf. *Orig.* VII	—
200	XLI 1	183
201	XLII	161
202	XLIII	184
203	II	168
204	XLIV	162

CONCORDANCES

LCL	Jordan	Cugusi
205	XLIX	185
206	LI	186
207	LIII	166
208	LII 1	187
209	LII 2	188
210	LV	189
211	LX	190
212	LVII 1	191
213	LVII 2	192
214	LVII 3	193; I, p. 252
215	LVIII	194
216	LIX	195
217	LXV 1	196
218	LXV 2	197
219	LXVI	198
220	LXVII	199
221	LXVIII 1	200
222	LXVIII 2	201
223	LXIX	167
224	LXX 1	172
225	LXX 2	173
226	LXX 3	174
227	LXIV	203
228	LXXV	165
229	LXXVII	204
230	LXIV 3	206
231	—	207
232	LXXVIII	208
233	LXXIX	170
234	LXXX	209

CONCORDANCES

LCL	Jordan	Cugusi
234A	—	163 *bis*
234B	LVI	163
235	*Op. inc.* 10	*Op. inc.* 17
236	*Inc.* 1	219
237	*Inc.* 2	220
238	*Inc.* 4	214
239	*Inc.* 5	215
240	*Inc.* 6	*Op. inc.* 34
241	*Inc.* 7	*Dub.* 6
242	*Inc.* 8	216
243	*Inc.* 9	217
244	*Inc.* 11	*Dub.* 1
245	*Inc.* 12	*Op. inc.* 13
246	*Inc.* 13	224
247	*Inc.* 14	*Op. inc.* 33
248	*Inc.* 15	225
249	*Inc.* 16	*Op. inc.* 43
250	*Inc.* 17	221
251	*Inc.* 18	222
252	*Inc.* 19	223
253	*Op. inc.* 49	*Op. inc.* 60
254	*Dicta* 1	226
245A	—	227

Other Fragments

Libri ad Marcum filium (F 1–15)
LCL → Jordan—Cugusi

LCL	Jordan	Cugusi
1	14	18
2	13	*Op. inc.* 36
3	10	*Op. inc.* 37
4	5	6
5	1, 2	1, 2; *Comm. Med.* F 1
6	11	10; *Op. inc.* 49
7	12	—
8	15	19
9	3	5
10	7	22
11	6	7
12	8	8
13	9	9
14	4	*Epist.* F 8
15	16	20

De re militari liber (F 16–31)
LCL → Jordan—Cugusi

LCL	Jordan	Cugusi
16	8	5
17	1	1; *Op. inc.* 50

CONCORDANCES

LCL	Jordan	Cugusi
18	15	*Op. inc.* 39
19	4	4
20	5	6
21	12	7
22	2	2
23	11	8
24	10	10
25	14	11
26	6	13
27a–b	—	—
28	3	3
29	7	12
30	13	14
31	9	9

Carmen de moribus (F 32–34)
LCL → Jordan—Cugusi

LCL	Jordan	Cugusi
32	1	1
33	2	2
34	3	3

Epistula(e) (F 35–39)
LCL → Jordan—Cugusi

LCL	Jordan	Cugusi
35	4	6
36	3	7

LCL	Jordan	Cugusi
37	2	4
38	1	5
39	5	9

Commentarii iuris civilis (F 40)
LCL → Jordan—Cugusi

LCL	Jordan	Cugusi
40	1	1

Dicta memorabilia (F 41–85)
LCL → Jordan—Cugusi

LCL	Jordan	Cugusi
41	72	*Op. inc.* 3
42	73	49
43	66–67	50
44	*Apo.* 2	II, p. 466
45	68	51
46	64	*Orig.* 5
47	65	54
48	71	—
49	70	52
50	69	53
51	p. 83	II, p. 466
52	63	55
53	75	58
54	74	57
55	76	*Op. inc.* 51

CONCORDANCES

LCL	Jordan	Cugusi
56	77	59
57	*Apo.* 1	II, p. 468
58	49–59	36–46
59	28–29	22–23
60	—	—
61	30	*Op. inc.* 21
62	p. 97	II, p. 468
63	1–15	1–11
64	16–27	12–21; *Op. inc.* 30
65	31–32	24
66	33	*Op. inc.* 22
67a–b	34; *Op. inc.* 69	25; *Op. inc.* 19
68	35–36	26
69	37	27
70	38	*Op. inc.* 23
71	39–41	28–30
72	42	31
73	42^a	*Op. inc.* 46
74	43	*Op. inc.* 27
75	44–45	32
76	46–48	33–35
77	60	47
78	62	48
79	61	—
80	79	*Op. inc.* 84
81	78	*Orat.* 131
82	80	61
83	81	62
84	83	60
85	82	63

CONCORDANCES

Incertorum operum reliquiae (F 1–55)

LCL → Jordan—Cugusi

LCL	Jordan	Cugusi
1	54	52
2	—	*Ad Marc.* 11
3	—	*Ad Marc.* 12
4	—	*Ad Marc.* 14
5	—	*Ad Marc.* 15
6	14	*Orat.* F 202
7	—	*Ad Marc.* 16
8	—	*Ad Marc.* 13
9	—	*Ad Marc.* 17
10a	55	58
10b	61	58
11	64	18
12	71–72	*Comm. Hist.* F 1; *Op. inc.* 44, 45
13	73	*Dicta* 56
14	74	29
15	75	48
16	76	26
17	77	20
18	50	14
19	42	62
20	51	61
21	62	—
22	19	28
23	53	63
24	20	65
25	21	66

CONCORDANCES

LCL	Jordan	Cugusi
26	4	*Op. inc.* 47
27	23	67
28	24	55
29	25	53
30	26	54
31	27	*Op. inc.* 42
32	28	56
33	29–30	68
34	32	*Orig.* F 87
35	33	71
36	34	72
37	56	59
38	36	73
39	5	74
40	37	75
41	38	76
42	39	77
43	40	57
44	41	69
45	46	78
46	43	79
47	44	80
48	45	cf. *Agr.* 103
49	8	70
50	47	—
51	63	81
52	52	64
53	13	40
54	—	82
55	48	83

Fragmenta dubiae auctoritatis (F 1–15)

LCL → Jordan—Cugusi

LCL	Jordan	Cugusi
1	*Op. inc.* 58	*Dub.* 2
2	*Or.* XVIII 6 n.	*Dub.* 5
3	*Op. inc.* 59	—
4	*Op. inc.* 25	*Dub.* 4
5	—	*Dub.* 10
6	*Op. inc.* 57	*Dub.* 3
7	1	*Dub.* 9
8	—	*Dub.* 13
9	—	*Ad Marc.* 3
10	—	—
11	—	—
12	—	*Ad Marc.* 21
13	—	*Dub.* 14
14	—	*Dub.* 8
15	—	—

Fragmenta Catoni falso attributa (F 1–7)

LCL → Jordan—Cugusi

LCL	Jordan	Cugusi
1	—	p. 549
2	—	*Fals.* 15
3	—	p. 549
4	—	—
5	—	—
6	—	*Fals.* 16
7	—	—

INDEX OF NAMES

This index gives the proper nouns (referring to individuals, peoples, and places) and derived adjectives that appear in the fragments of Cato and the sources about Cato (introductory essays and notes have not been indexed).

References are to pages in volumes I and II. Roman individuals appear with the Latin version of their names under their *nomen gentile* when the full name is known, otherwise under the part of the name that is transmitted. Names for peoples and places are Anglicized where a common English form exists; otherwise the ancient forms are kept. Main nouns and derived adjectives (e.g., Carthage and Carthaginian) are normally combined into a single entry.

INDEX OF NAMES